American Ethnic History

Themes and Perspectives

JASON McDONALD

RUTGERS UNIVERSITY PRESS
New Brunswick, New Jersey

For
CLAUDIA

First published in the United States 2007
by Rutgers University Press, New Brunswick, New Jersey

First published in Great Britain 2007
by Edinburgh University Press Ltd
22 George Square, Edinburgh

Library of Congress Cataloging-in-Publication Data

McDonald, Jason. (Jason J.)
    American ethnic history : themes and perspectives / Jason McDonald.
        p. cm.
    Includes bibliographical references and index.
    ISBN-13: 978-0-8135-4227-0 (hardcover : alk. paper)
    ISBN-13: 978-0-8135-4228-7 (pbk. : alk. paper)
    1. United States–Ethnic relations. 2. Pluralism (Social sciences)–United States–History. 3. Ethnicity–United States–History. 4. Ethnology–United States–History. 5. Minorities–United States–History. 6. Minorities–United States–Social conditions. 7. United States–Social conditions. I. Title.
    E184.A1M348 2007
    305.800973–dc22

                                    2007012709

Typeset in Ehrhardt
by Iolaire Typesetting, Newtonmore, and
printed and bound in Great Britain by
Cromwell Press, Trowbridge, Wilts

Contents

Acknowledgments

As someone who cringes at the excessive length and sentimentality of acknowledgments in books nowadays, I must beg the reader's forgiveness for including a few words of gratitude myself. First of all, I would like to thank Nicola Ramsey at Edinburgh University Press for her guidance and patience. My thanks also go out to the academics who have read various portions of the book and offered their comments; in reading this they will know to whom my thanks are directed. It would be foolish of me to try to put into words the depth of my gratitude to my parents and siblings for the support and encouragement they have given me in bringing this project to fruition. They know how much I owe to them and I hope that they know how much I appreciate their love and generosity. This book has not had an easy birth and I thank my wife and children for sharing the pains of it with me. I hope they feel that the end product was worth the sacrifices.

Preface

I am not an American, neither through birth nor naturalization. Although I have resided in the United States for extended periods of time, I have always been there as a visitor, a sojourner. This book, therefore, offers an outsider's view of American ethnic history and what historians, mostly American ones, have written about that history. I do not believe that my position as an outsider will afford me either a better or a worse understanding of American ethnic history than is attainable by an insider, an American, but I do suspect that, like other outsiders who have earlier written on this topic, such as Maldwyn Jones, my interpretation is likely to be noticeably different to what either a native-born or naturalized American of my own generation might offer.

Until recently, my main purpose in learning about the United States was to communicate my findings to a non-American audience – British university students. I offered, therefore, an outsider's view of America to an audience of fellow outsiders. Despite the prominences of American culture and influence in the United Kingdom, prior to entering university British students are afforded few opportunities for formal study of the United States. Consequently, once they get to university, students opting for courses in American topics have to acquire virtually from scratch an understanding of US history, politics, society, and culture. It is my belief that in undertaking this formidable task these non-American newcomers to American Studies could do a lot worse than begin by examining the issues and debates surrounding American ethnic history. Ethnicity has been a salient issue in every era of the American past and in every region of the nation. The list of major historical events in which ethnicity figured prominently is virtually endless: the framing of the Constitution, territorial expansion, slavery, reform movements, the Civil War, urbanization, industrialization, and so on. Moreover, ethnicity and ethnic interaction has played a significant role in shaping the distinctive character of specific states and regions. American ethnic history is also particularly relevant to the debate over American Exceptionalism. The United States is not the only modern state to have a history of dispossessing indigenous peoples, achieving economic development through the use of slave labor, populating itself with European immigrants, and discriminating against its nonwhite inhabitants, but it is the nation that in the popular imagination is most commonly associated with such a past, despite the fact that this perception is equally applicable in whole or in part to Brazil, Australia, South Africa, and even Russia, as well as countless other countries. Moreover, ethnicity has a persistent topicality in the United States. Every election, every new piece of legislation has either an ethnic dimension to it or major ramifications for certain ethnic groups, and hardly a year goes by in which the biggest news issue is one that largely centered on ethnicity, be it the trial of Michael Jackson or the national strike by undocumented immigrant workers.

The newcomer to American ethnic history will find that numerous scholarly examinations of the topic are currently available. These can be grouped into four main categories: first, works which equate "ethnic" with "immigrant" and fail to incorporate the histories of groups, such as African Americans and Native Americans, which appear to fall outside of traditional definitions of the latter term; second, works which are more inclusive in their coverage of ethnic groups, but tend to view each group in isolation and rarely make direct comparisons of the different ethnic experiences; third, works which cover all ethnic groups and offer some comparison, but provide little or no historiographical discussion (the problem with such works is that they frequently have a built-in bias toward either the assimilationist or pluralist perspective that is not explained to the reader); and, fourth, works that provide adequate discussion of theoretical issues, but examine only a limited range of ethnic groups and offer few detailed comparisons. In light of the obvious deficiencies of the approaches outlined above, my purpose in writing this book has been to provide newcomers to the field of American ethnic history with a framework for comparing the varying historical experiences of the nation's diverse ethnic groups. Instead of presenting my own viewpoint to the reader, it has been my aim to organize and write the book in a way that permits the complete novice to actively engage with the issues and debates covered herein, even as they become progressively more complex. Part I explores the conflicting meanings assigned to the terms like ethnicity, race, and so on, which are commonly used by scholars working in the field of American ethnic history. Part II examines broad perspectives on the origins and nature of American ethnic diversity. In Chapter 2, the question of whether America's ethnic diversity originated in mostly hegemonic acts like conquest and forced migration rather than voluntary migration is addressed. The various metaphors used to describe the type of society produced by the ethnic diversity of the United States are outlined and evaluated in Chapter 3. In Part III, we turn to mainstream society's perceptions of and policies towards the nation's different ethnic groups. Chapter 4 considers whether the dominant society's attitudes towards and treatment of all ethnic groups has been consistent with the nation's professed egalitarian ideals, while Chapter 5 delves more deeply into this debate by examining the three case studies of residential patterns, educational provision, and economic opportunity. The focus shifts in Part IV to how ethnic groups have responded to life in the United States. Chapter 6 examines the debates over the frequency and origins of ethnic collective action, as well as the effectiveness of its four main forms. Finally, in Chapter 7 the roles that factors like language, religion, class, gender, and intermarriage play in either strengthening or weakening ethnic identity and group solidarity are assessed.

It is hoped that this book will be a spur to further discussion about what exactly constitute American ethnic history's key issues rather than a definitive statement on the matter. As will be seen, my attempt to sketch an overall framework for this field of inquiry has revealed numerous gaps in the scholarship, so I hope that this book will contribute in some small way to the future filling of those gaps. To help clarify debates, I have labeled the main schools of thought on the various issues examined in the book. In doing so, I have occasionally taken the liberty of locating individual scholars in theoretical camps which reflect not necessarily where those authors may view themselves as belonging but rather my interpretation of where specific statements place them. Moreover, in pursuance of the aim to explain the context rather than the content of present debates in the evolving and very dynamic field of American ethnic history, I have generally focused my discussion on research published prior to the year 2000.

PART I

Defining Ethnicity

ONE

The Origins and Nature of Ethnic Identity

INTRODUCTION

One of the most salient, as well as perplexing, features of scholarship on American ethnic history is the variety of meanings historians attach to the word "ethnicity". Indeed, newcomers to the subject could be excused for believing that no two historians are alike in what they mean by the term. This diversity can partly be explained by the fact that, as successive generations of scholars have expanded the body of accumulated learning and provided ever-more penetrating insights into the nature of ethnicity, the meanings attached to the concept itself have accordingly evolved over time. However, some of the greatest variations of terminology have existed not between one generation of historians and another, but amongst contemporaneous scholars who disagree over how to define "ethnicity" and other related concepts. From a historiographical point of view, this controversy has largely centered on differing interpretations of how and why "ethnic" groups come into being. There is also an on-going debate over the relationship between "ethnicity" and "race", the main point of contention being whether or not these categories are mutually exclusive. These terminological complexities are further compounded by the fact that it is still not general practice among historians writing about "ethnicity" to either provide precise definitions of what they mean by the term or explain how their interpretation differs from those of other scholars.

While there is clearly a need for eliminating many of the ambiguities apparent in historians' current beliefs about ethnicity, the purpose of this chapter is not to offer a definitive description of the concept and its properties. Nor is it to provide an all-encompassing list of the many ways in which ethnicity has been defined. Even if such objectives were attainable, which in all probability is doubtful, they are clearly beyond the scope of an introductory text such as this. Rather, the aim here is to outline the main divisions under which most of the varying definitions of "ethnicity" and "race" can grouped, and to provide a general insight into the rationale behind scholars' terminological preferences.

TERMINOLOGY: ETHNIC, ETHNICITY, ETHNY

Before discussing the historiographical debates over the nature of ethnicity, it is worth briefly examining the origins and meaning of the term itself. The words "ethnic", "ethnicity", and "ethny", are all derived from the ancient Greek word *ethnos*, which is variously translated as "tribe", "race", "people" and, most commonly, "nation". The concept of *ethnos* has generally been rendered into Modern English by combining the adjective "ethnic" with collective nouns like "group" and "community" to form "ethnic group" and "ethnic community", but since the early 1980s a growing number of scholars have discarded these rather cumbersome and problematical terms in favor of the neologism "ethny", the plural being "ethnies" (Peterson, 1980, pp. 234–5; van den Berghe, 1983, p. 222; Chapman, et al., 1989, pp. 11–17; Gordon, 1978, p. 107). As an abstract noun, the word ethnicity – which itself only appeared in the English language for the first time in the 1940s – refers to both the feeling of belonging to and the quality possessed by an ethny (Schlesinger, 1992, p. 42; Hutchinson and Smith, 1996, p. 4).

Scholarly definitions of ethny are far from uniform and generally range from those permitting a fairly broad application of the term to those containing a very narrow set of criteria. As with much of the terminology used within the field of American ethnic history, the definition of ethny most commonly adopted by historians is one borrowed from the social sciences and generally associated with the work of the sociologist Milton Gordon. Gordon defined ethnicity as a "sense of peoplehood" and "ethnic group" as "a group with a shared feeling of peoplehood" (1978, p. 107; 1964, pp. 24, 29). Although these definitions are sufficiently open-ended to allow their application to an almost limitless number of social groups, scholars have normally reserved the designation of "ethnic" for groups that either in socio-economic or demographic terms constitute a "minority". A good example of this practice among historians can be found in *Natives and Strangers*, a popular standard narrative, in which the authors portray an ethny as "a people with a shared or common culture or a sense of identity based on religion, race, or nationality" (Dinnerstein, et al., 1996, p. ix: see also Gordon, 1978, pp. 110–11). Implicit in such definitions is the belief that, while individual blacks (leaving aside the issue of race for the moment), Indians, and immigrants belong to an ethny, native-born Americans of Anglo-Saxon ancestry do not (see also Olson, 1994,

p. 3). Despite treating race as a separate category in its own right, Richard Polenberg's definition of ethnicity – which, along with "country of origin" and "religion", includes "language" as a key component – is broadly similar to Milton Gordon's in that members of the dominant society are not considered to be "ethnic" (1980, pp. 8–9). Some scholars, however, have used Gordon's ideas as the basis for much broader conceptions of ethnicity. According to Harold Abramson (1980, pp. 150, 151) and William Peterson (1980, p. 240), for instance, new ethnies are continually emerging in the United States and some of these groups, such as the Mormons and "Mountain People" of the Appalachians, were mostly spawned by the white Anglo-Saxon Protestant, or "WASP", population. Abramson and Peterson both use the term "ethnogenesis" to denote the process by which new ethnies are created. Similarly, Philip Gleason has argued that American national identity is "generically the same" as ethnic identity, because it is "a distinctive sense of peoplehood, not different in essence from the peoplehood-sense of ethnic groups". Although Gleason characterizes American nationality as "more inclusive than the peoplehood of ethnic groups" and rejects claims that it is simply "WASP ethnicity", his argument does not preclude the possibility of WASPs being just one among many ethnies present in the United States (1980, pp. 54–7).

The trend towards adopting ever more inclusive definitions of ethnicity has not been without it detractors. The main criticisms leveled against what Russell Kazal calls the "expansive conceptions of ethnicity" adopted by Abramson, Gleason, and others, is that they are too vague and place too much emphasis upon identities originating in the recent past. Kazal's preference, therefore, is for a "more restrictive" definition of ethny as meaning a group with "a shared sense of peoplehood tied, in some fashion, to specific Old World ancestries" (1995, p. 439). According to this definition, which is clearly framed with immigrants and their offspring in mind, African Americans might qualify as an ethny, but indigenous populations (like Native Americans), home grown religious minorities (such as the Mormons) and possibly even New World immigrants (like Mexican Americans) would not. A somewhat different approach is that adopted by scholars who would narrow down the concept of ethnicity by excluding the category of race. Audrey Smedley (1993), for example, views ethnicity, in contrast to race, as a signifier of purely cultural rather than perceived physiological differences. Nonetheless, while there is as we shall see below a case for arguing that race is different to ethnicity, it is doubtful whether any of America's "racial" groups would fail to also be covered by Smedley's own definition of ethnicity as referring to "all those traditions, customs, activities, beliefs, and practices that pertain to a particular group of people who see themselves and are seen by others as having distinct cultural features, a separate history, and a specific socio-cultural identity" (Smedley, 1993, pp. 30, 32). Whereas Smedley implies that race is not a component of ethnicity, other academics argue that the highly politicized term "ethnic" – linked as it is with access to government compensation for past discrimination – should apply exclusively to racial minorities (Barkan, 1995, p. 38).

A definitive description of what constitutes an ethny, regardless of whether a broad or narrow approach is adopted, will probably continue to elude scholars because, as William Peterson has observed, "none of the group characteristics . . . that are used to denote ethnicity generally set off any subpopulation sharply" (1980, p. 236). In other words, while language, for example, might act as a clear-cut indicator of ethnicity for one group, it may play little or no role in distinguishing other ethnies from the general population and the same is true of culture, nationality, region, race and any other criterion used. To a large extent, the criteria historians use to denote ethnicity are actually determined by how they account for the appearance of ethnies. For instance, scholars who believe ethnicity to be an inherent characteristic, passed on from one generation to the next, would place emphasis on a different set of ethnic indicators to those highlighted by historians who view ethnies as socially constructed. In order to arrive at a reliable working definition of what constitutes an ethny, therefore, it is necessary to explore the debate over the origins of ethnicity.

ETHNICITY: INHERITED OR INVENTED?

If the precise combination of elements required to comprise an ethny remains elusive, it is no more so than a definitive explanation of how ethnies come into existence in the first place. There are two main schools of thought on this issue: first, the "primordialist" view that ethnicity is inherent in human beings and, second, the "situational" view that ethnies are socially constructed entities emerging out of specific socio-economic and political conditions. Moreover, the situational perspective, as will be seen, also contains a range of interpretations on how the social construction of ethnicity takes place and what factors activate it.

The Primordialist View

Ethnic attachments, according to the primordialist view, are intrinsic, indefinable, and immutable human traits. Ethnicity, in other words, is depicted as an innate feature of the emotional make-up of human beings and something over which the individual exercises little or no control (Eller and Coughlan, 1993, p. 187; Olzak, 1992, p. 6). Theoretical expositions of the primordialist viewpoint, examples of which include Harold R. Isaacs's *Idols of the Tribe* (1975), Clifford Geertz's *The Interpretation of Cultures* (1973) and Michael Novak's *The Rise of the Unmeltable Ethnics* (1973), are generally associated with the disciplines of anthropology, sociology and psychology (Eller and Coughlan, 1993, pp. 187–8; Conzen, et al., 1992, p. 4). Nonetheless, Audrey Smedley rightly claims that examples of this train of thought have long been present in historical writing on the subjects of ethnicity and race (1993, p. 23). Smedley identified Thomas Gossett's *Race: The History of an Idea in America* (1965) and Carl Degler's *Neither Black Nor White* (1971), among other historical works, as displaying strong primordialist tendencies. Many prominent historians still display primordialist tendencies – John Higham, for example, recently described both race and ethnicity as "inescapably given traits" that are "personal", "internal" and "part of the very substance of who we are" (1993, pp. 195–6) – but since the 1950s a general aversion to this way of thinking has been apparent among scholars working in the field of American ethnic history (see, for example, Handlin, 1957, p. 191). The primordialist argument, moreover, has been discredited across numerous disciplines in recent years by research that has exposed fundamental flaws, not least of which is its inability to explain instances of individuals exchanging one ethnicity for another (Olzak, 1992, p. 6; Eller and Coughlan, 1993, pp. 199–201).

The Situational View

In contraposition to primordialism is the "situational" – sometimes referred to as "emergent" – view of ethnicity as a social construction. An emblematic statement of the situational perspective's position can be found in an article, co-authored by Kathleen Neils Conzen, David Gerber, Ewa Morawska, George Pozzetta and Rudolph Vecoli, entitled "The Invention of Ethnicity" (1992). Ethnicity, according to these historians, is "a process of construction or invention which incorporates, adapts, and amplifies preexisting communal solidarities, cultural attributes, and historical memories". In a categorical rejection of the primordialist view, they state that ethnicity is "grounded in real life context and social experience" (1992, pp. 4–5). In their article, Conzen and her co-authors acknowledged the influence of scholarship emanating from other academic disciplines, especially Werner Sollors's *The Invention of Ethnicity* (1989). An influential sociological work that attempted to "demystify ethnicity" by exposing its "historical and structural foundations" was Stephen Steinberg's *The Ethnic Myth* (1989, p. xiv). An ethny's sense of peoplehood, therefore, came to be seen as not the primal source of group solidarity but an end-product of the social process known as "ethnicization", a concept not dissimilar to the earlier theory of "ethnogenesis" (Vecoli, 1995, p. 78; Conzen, et al., 1992, p. 9; Morawska, 1990, p. 213). Paralleling the general shift to a situational interpretation of ethnicity, Edmund Morgan's (1975) influential study of slavery in colonial Virginia suggested that race, too, is socially constructed. Moreover, following Barbara Fields' assertion that "the notion of race, in its popular manifestation, is an ideological construct and thus, above all, a historical product" (1982, p. 150: see also Davis, 1991, p. 15; Lee, 1993, p. 90; Root, 1992a, pp. 3–4; Spickard, 1992, p. 13), an outpouring of historical works appeared providing extensive evidence to support such a view (Stuckey, 1987; Saxton, 1990; Roediger, 1991 and 1994; Smedley, 1993). Nonetheless, it would be misleading to suggest that primordialism has been completely routed by the situationalist challenge. Reed Ueda, for example, has utilized ideas from both perspectives in a way which implies that they may not necessarily be totally incompatible. "To be sure", remarks Ueda about the origins and content of ethnic identities, "there were inherited qualities but others were adapted *ad hoc* from social surroundings to suit individual needs, tastes, and self-interest" (1994, p. 86). Indeed, Ueda's synthesis may offer a solution to the contentiousness caused by the rigidity of the primordial–situational dichotomy; alternatively, it might be viewed as a potentially misguided exercise in self-contradiction.

Accepting, as many historians now do, that ethnicity is socially constructed, there still remains the problem of explaining where, how, and why ethnies come into existence. Are ethnic identities, for instance, imported fully-formed from Old World homelands or created in the United States? Similarly, if ethnies are products of the American environment, are their boundaries, characteristics and functions defined externally, by the dominant society, internally, by group members themselves, or by a combination of both external and internal stimuli? What role, moreover, does the individual play in all of this: is membership of an ethny ascribed or a matter of personal choice?

Imported Ethnicity

Early works on American ethnic history tended to portray ethnicity as a collection of allegiances, beliefs, and customs imported into the United States by immigrants from the Old World. This view permeated the work of one of the pioneers of US immigration history, Marcus Lee Hansen, and was expressed more explicitly in his theory about generational shifts in the levels of ethnic attachment among the offspring of immigrants. According to Hansen's Law, which famously stated that "what the son wishes to forget the grandson wishes to remember", the thing lost by the second generation and sought by the third was a ready-made ethnic identity that the first generation (that is the "grandfathers") had brought to the United States from their country of origin (1990 [1937], pp. 194–5). This view of ethnicity as something imported into the United States by immigrants has a number of drawbacks: first, it assumes that New World ethnies are formed entirely around Old World nationality, thereby overlooking the role played by other factors in ethnicization; second, it cannot be used to explain ethnic consciousness among indigenous groups, like Native Americans; and, third, it can be construed as vindicating the much defamed primordialist perspective. Consequently, modern scholars, as Rudolph Vecoli recently noted, rarely view ethnicity as "a fixed quantity brought over in immigrant trunks" (1995, p. 78: see also Conzen, et al., 1992, pp. 5, 9; Barkan, 1995, pp. 52–4; Sánchez, 1993, p. 11; Buenker and Ratner, 1992, pp. 3–4).

The Ascription of Ethnicity

If ethnicity, then, was not a foreign import but a home-made product, by whom was it produced? One answer to this question locates the origins of ethnicity in the attitudes and behavior of the dominant WASP population. According to this view, the category of ethnicity was invented by Americans in the early nineteenth century and thereafter applied, often arbitrarily, to the various groups who – despite the emergence of a US national identity – still remained culturally and socially distinctive (Conzen, et al., 1992, pp. 6–7: on the development of American nationalism and nativism during the antebellum era, see Billington, 1938; Gleason, 1980, pp. 34–8; Higham, 1963). Although there is a case for arguing its applicability to all ethnies, European immigrants included, the involuntary, ascriptive character of ethnicity thus depicted is best exemplified by the experience of racial groups (Davis, 1991; Bonacich, 1972, p. 548; Glazer, 1975, p. 29; Gordon, 1978, pp. 112–13; Waters, 1990, p. 18). Both Native Americans and African Americans had ethnic status and in some senses even their group identities imposed upon them. The ethnic designation "Indian", for example, was a white invention imposed upon an extremely diverse group of indigenous tribal populations who, as Robert Berkhofer notes, had never "called themselves by a single term nor understood themselves as a collectivity" (1979, p. 3: see also Deloria, 1992, pp. 31, 33–4). Berkhofer describes this situation as a "paradigm of polarity" that "assumes uniqueness" for the dominant group as "classifiers" and subordinate groups as "the classified" (1979, p. xvi). The most extreme version of this argument was put forward by Stanley Elkins (1959), who claimed that antebellum blacks were reduced under southern slavery to a state of total psychological dependence upon and identification with the slave owners. However, John Blassingame has shown that even under the harsh conditions of plantation slavery it was possible for African Americans to independently develop a "distinctive culture" and "strong sense of group solidarity" (1979, pp. xi, 105, 147: see also Lane, 1971). This evidence clearly raises doubts about the dominant society's ability to impose its own vision of ethnicity upon any particular group. Indeed, Blassingame's portrayal of a "communalism born of oppression" (1979, p. 148) clearly indicates that ethnicization is to some extent instrumental or reactive in character.

The Instrumentalist Version of Ethnicity

This "instrumentalist" interpretation of ethnicity perceives ethnies as interest groups which emerge in response to specific, usually oppressive, social conditions (Glazer and Moynihan, 1963, p. 17; Handlin, 1973, pp. 152–79). According to Michael Hechter, an influential exponent of this view: "The existence of ethnic solidarity in a given group should . . . be regarded as a special instance of the general phenomenon of political mobilization" (1975, p. 41). Hechter's argument is also a useful corrective to the standard assumption that ethnies are homogeneous groups and thus do not require an internal dynamic to bring them into existence. In reality, ethnies were originally forged out of diverse elements, which in the case of immigrant groups were "divided by varying combinations of regional origin, dialect, class, politics, and religion". Consequently, emergent ethnies needed to invent traditions "to provide symbols and slogans which could unify the group despite such differences" (Conzen, et al., 1992, p. 5). This process was not restricted solely to immigrant ethnies; both African Americans (Collier-Thomas and Turner, 1994, pp. 5–10, 15, 19–20) and American Indians (Hertzberg, 1971) faced and had to surmount the same internal obstacles to ethnicization.

The major advantage of the instrumentalist perspective is that it acknowledges the agency exercised by ethnies, revealing how their members consciously participate in the process of ethnicization (Conzen, et al., 1992, p. 5). Nonetheless, this is still a fairly one-dimensional view of ethnicity and its origins. Undeniably, members of ethnies can now be seen as actors and not merely acted upon, but logic would imply that they must at various times have been both. In short, while the ascriptive model is useful for identifying the external determinants of ethnicity, and the instrumental model the internal ones, neither approach on its own provides a completely satisfactory insight into how and why ethnies are created.

Multi-Dimensional Models of Ethnicity

Recognizing this shortcoming in the existing scholarship, historians began to experiment with more interactive and multi-dimensional models of ethnicization. Although it is difficult to pinpoint exactly when this historiographical shift began, the publication of John Bodnar's highly influential book, *The Transplanted* (1985), definitely represented a noticeable change of direction away from one-dimensional interpretations of ethnicity. By the early 1990s a new and fairly coherent "interactive" perspective on ethnicity was clearly discernible in works by numerous scholars. Summarizing the core elements of the new interpretation, a distinguished group of its main exponents claim that the "invention of ethnicity as a status category within American society occurred in a complex dialogue between American imposition of ethnic categories and immigrant rallying of ethnic identities" (Conzen, et al., 1992, pp. 9–10: for similar expositions of this view, see Morawska, 1990, p. 214; Miller, 1990, pp. 97–8; Sánchez, 1993, p. 11). Moreover, ethnicization is not viewed by these historians as simply a two-way "process of negotiation" between an ethny and the dominant society, but also one between the various ethnies (Conzen, et al., 1992, p. 5).

Compared with earlier interpretive models, the interactive perspective has unquestionably provided us with a more reliable framework for analyzing the origins and nature of ethnicity. However, amid the theorizing about the many group related aspects of ethnicity there is a tendency – sometimes unintentional, sometimes quite deliberate – for scholars to overlook and even negate the role of the individual. For instance, Conzen, Gerber, Morawska, Pozzetta, and Vecoli (1992, pp. 4, 31–2) argued that traditional studies of ethnic history placed too much emphasis upon individuals and individualism. Elliott Barkan took issue with the "decidedly group orientation" of the aforementioned authors' viewpoint and stressed that individuals were central to the ethnic experience (1995, pp. 42, 44–9). Moreover, even when individuals are the focus of investigation, they are often treated as passive rather than active entities. Harold Abramson, writing essentially from the pluralist position (see Chapter 3, pp. 55–61), identified "four social and cultural conditions of ethnicity for the individual": (1) the "presence and certainty of both ethnic symbols and relationships"; (2) the "certainty of ethnic structure but ambiguity of ethnic culture"; (3) "the memories and symbols of an ethnic culture exist, but there are no primary networks and structural attachments"; and (4) "a lack or ambiguity of both ethnic culture and ethnic structure". Individuals experiencing the second, third and fourth conditions were characterized as progressively more pathetic cases, from "odd-man-in", to "odd-man-out" and, finally, the unenviable "isolated individual" (1980, pp. 155–6). In sharp contrast to this rather rigid and pessimistic view of the ethnic choices available to individuals, John Higham (1993, pp. 155–6) contended that:

> . . . race and ethnicity do not always confer desirable identities, nor are these identities unalterable, uncontested, or monolithic. They are surprisingly fluid, at least in America. In changing circumstances,

individuals continually reinvent their ethnic identities. They negotiate the loyalties they must choose among, or alter the dimensions of a predominant identity that begins to pinch.

(This quotation, it is worth noting, seems to contradict Higham's fairly primordialist statement cited above, both of which appeared in the same article.) Higham's argument implies that ethnicity may not necessarily originate in or take shape at the level of inter-group relationships, but rather in the intimate dialogue between the individual and society. The individual's perception and experience of ethnicity, therefore, might not only vary significantly from one ethny to another, but also between different members of the same ethny. Some scholars, particularly those stressing the inevitability of assimilation (see Chapter 3, p. 50–2), have even suggested that ethnicity for many people has become "symbolic", "more or less a leisure-time activity" and "not something that influences their lives unless they *want* it to". "The option of identifying as ethnic", asserts Mary Waters, "exists for all white Americans, and further choice of *which* ethnicity to choose is available to some of them". Viewed in this light, ethnicization at the personal level almost assumes the character of a journey to the candy store pick-and-mix counter, in which individuals choose from the particular selection of ethnic heritages present in their family ancestries. Nonetheless, it is important not to exaggerate the degree of agency exercised by individuals, because, as Waters points out, very few "ethnic options" are available to members of "racial" groups, especially African Americans, who "are highly socially constrained to identify as blacks, . . . even when they believe or know that their forebears included many non-blacks" (1990, pp. 7, 18–19, 130–1, 142–3). Such observations, moreover, indicate the need for greater clarification of how the categories of race and ethnicity relate to each other.

RACE: VARIANT OF ETHNICITY OR INDEPENDENT CATEGORY?

The history of race as an idea, and how it came to possess special social significance for some population groups, has generated a body of literature too vast and complex to permit anything but a perfunctory review of it here (for useful surveys, see Handlin, 1957; Snyder, 1962; Gossett, 1965; Smedley, 1993). Nonetheless, it is possible to summarize some of the key features and findings of this scholarship. First, historians usually distinguish "race" from "ethnicity" by using the former term to refer to imputed physiological differences between human groups and the latter to cultural ones. Second, variation in skin color is the most commonly used rationale for sub-dividing the human species, which usually results in the identification of three racial categories – Caucasoid (that is "white", European), Negroid ("black", African), and Mongoloid ("yellow", Asian) – but is often extended to four with the inclusion of Amerindian ("red", applied to both Native Americans and many Latinos) as a separate race (Handlin, 1957, pp. 190–1; Snyder, 1962, pp. 10–18). As Louis Snyder noted, skin color is as unreliable as any other indicator of race. This is demonstrated, for instance, by the easily observable fact that many individuals who are socially defined as "white" actually have darker skin than some "blacks" (Spickard, 1992, pp. 16–17). Third, these decidedly arbitrary classifications, which first appeared in the early 1700s, were by the late nineteenth century widely regarded as absolute divisions within a naturally ordained hierarchy of "superior" and "inferior" races, with whites ranked at the top and blacks at the bottom. This development was greatly facilitated by the growth of the eugenics movement, which raised pseudo-scientific racism to the status of a respectable academic endeavor. Indeed, scientific discourse in general, as John Haller has observed, "provided a vocabulary and a set of concepts which rationalized and helped to justify the value system upon which the idea of racial inferiority rested in American thought" (1971, p. x: see also Pickens, 1968; Stanton, 1960; Handlin, 1957; Higham, 1963). Racial classifications were given official sanction by the US Bureau of the Census and their continued use is an anomalous reminder of beliefs – particularly the theory that race is a biological fact rather than a socially constructed category – long since discarded by most historians and other academics (Lee, 1993: on the discrediting of pseudo-scientific racism during the twentieth century, see Barkan, 1992; Daniel, 1992; Handlin, 1957; Smedley, 1993). The idea that race and even ethnicity are genetic rather than culturally transmitted phenomena, although rejected by all serious academics, is still a widely held view among the general public (Waters, 1990, pp. 18, 167: for examples of historians refuting the biological basis of race, see Jordan, 1968, pp. 583–5; Nash, 1982, p. 5). Fourth, folk conceptions of "race" – a term first used in English at the beginning of the sixteenth century (Ruchames, 1967, p. 255) – predated and in many ways provided a fertile setting for the rise of pseudo-scientific racism. This last point requires further examination, because it bears major implications for efforts to explain the origins of racial thought and the form that it assumed in the United States.

If it were not for the fact that American perceptions of race are so intrinsically linked to a long history of extreme victimization and exploitation experienced by nonwhites at the hands of whites, there would not be the same imperative for historians to explore the question of which came first – prejudice or discrimination. Did white mistreatment of nonwhites emanate from pre-existing animosities towards peoples different in physical appearance to themselves, or were racist theories merely corollaries of emergent or well-established patterns of white domination and nonwhite subordination?

The search for an answer to this question has often led scholars to examine the origins of southern slavery in order to determine whether it was a cause or effect of anti-black racism. Carl Degler (1959) and Winthrop Jordan (1968), for example, have both claimed that white prejudice preceded and provided the basis for black slavery. Jordan's psycho-historical study, focusing upon the traditionally negative connotations attached to blackness in English culture, suggested that the English, even before coming into contact with Africans, were already predisposed to discriminate against them on the basis of skin color (1968, pp. 4–11). Edmund Morgan, by contrast, argues that in colonial Virginia the earliest contacts between Englishmen and blacks in the New World were "untroubled by racial prejudice" and that rigid race distinctions appeared later as an outgrowth of slavery. For Morgan, racial thought appears to originate more in economic and political expediencies than in color prejudices (1975, pp. 13, 313–15, 328–37, 385–7). An interpretation which incorporates and blends these apparently incompatible perspectives is provided by Gary B. Nash (1982, p. 160):

The mass enslavement of Africans profoundly affected white racial prejudice. Once institutionalized, slavery cast Africans into such lowly roles that the initial bias against them could only be confirmed and vastly strengthened. Initially unfavorable impressions of Africans had coincided with labor needs to bring about their mass enslavement. But it required slavery itself to harden the negative racial feelings into a deep and almost unshakable prejudice that continued to grow for centuries.

As well as providing a useful synthesis, Nash draws attention to the fact that white attitudes to blacks were not static and continued to evolve both during and after the era of slavery (ibid., p. 161: on the history of white perceptions of African Americans from the Revolution up until World War I, see Greene, 1954; Fredrickson, 1987 [1972]).

After African Americans, Native Americans are the next group most associated with the development of racial thought in the United States. Mirroring the debate on the origins of anti-black prejudice, scholars place varying degrees of emphasis on the influence of psychological, cultural, social, economic, and political factors. While authors like Roy Pearce (1988, pp. xix, 239–52) and Bernard Sheehan (1980, pp. x, 1–3, 8), for instance, saw the dichotomy between savagism and civilization in English culture as the key determinant of racial attitudes towards Native Americans, Karen Kupperman (1980) emphasized the importance of class-based prejudices. Rejecting Sheehan's view that anti-Indian prejudices were chiefly fuelled by cultural chauvinism, Kupperman stated that early English colonists actually admired the Native Americans' technical ingenuity and shared with them a very superstitious, pre-Enlightenment view of the universe. Although Kupperman did not discuss race directly, her findings imply that the roots of racial differentiation are to be found in the English upper class's traditional view of the poor as people born to serve others, which was generally projected onto Native Americans – except for tribal leaders, who it was thought shared some of the supposedly innate nobility of their English counterparts. Moreover, according to Kupperman the general view among early colonists was that "the Indians do not represent a fundamentally different race of people" (ibid., pp. vii–viii, 107, 140), an opinion which, despite the differences in their inter- pretations, she shared with Pearce and Sheehan. "The native skin color", asserted Sheehan, in words reminiscent of Winthrop Jordan's views on anti- black prejudice, "was free of the negative connotations that the English attached to blackness" (ibid., pp. 48–9). In fact, the racialization of Native Americans, noted Pearce (1988), occurred gradually and can be separated into three main stages: (1) from early contact up until the late eighteenth century, Indians were viewed as the equals of whites; (2) from the mid-eighteenth to early nineteenth century they were perceived as "noble savages" – human, but uncivilized; (3) from the mid-1820s onward, white perceptions of the Indians' racial status plummeted and the latter were viewed as the "zero sum of humanity".

Similar historiographical divisions have characterized discussions of how groups other than African Americans and Native Americans came to be viewed as nonwhite races. Whereas Stuart Miller (1969), for example, depicted white cultural prejudices as instrumental in the late nineteenth- century racialization of Chinese immigrants, Alexander Saxton (1971) viewed class tensions – particularly white workers' fears of job competition from nonwhites – as more influential. Arnoldo De León, in an impressive study of white attitudes towards Mexicans in nineteenth-century Texas, made a commendable attempt at synthesizing some of these contending perspectives, but shrouded his findings in ambiguity somewhat by claiming that they were compatible "with recent scholarship which argues that racism originated either in the Western psyche, in capitalist social development, or in religion" (1983, p. xi). In his book *Iron Cages*, Ronald Takaki used the theory of cultural hegemony – or domination by consent – to show how white "culture- makers and policy-makers" utilized and developed concepts of race as a means of securing the white population's acquiescence to the development of capitalism and class stratification. Although, by concentrating on the nine- teenth century, Takaki did not explore the more remote origins of racial thought, his comparison of white attitudes towards blacks, Indians, Mexicans, and Asians, clearly demonstrated that "whites did not artificially view each group in a vacuum; rather, in their minds, they lumped the different groups together or counterpointed them against each other" (1990 [1979]), pp. v–vii).

Clearly, there are many common features to the way that whites perceived the different nonwhite groups, but, when applied to African Americans, the concept of race assumed unique and more maleficent properties. The singular status of blacks is derived from what is generally known as the "one-drop rule", according to which a person is legally and socially defined as black if they have any traceable African black ancestry or, in common parlance, a single drop of "black blood". Although this conception of race originated in the South as an outgrowth of antebellum slavery and postbellum Jim Crow segregation, it has since become the standard definition used by both whites and blacks across the United States. African Americans, however, are the only nonwhite group classified according to the one-drop rule. "Not only does the one-drop rule apply to no other group than American blacks", observes F. James Davis, "but apparently the rule is unique in that it is found only in the United States and not in any other nation in the world" (1991, pp. 5, 12–13). Audrey Smedley agrees that US practices are distinctive, noting that "the dichotomous race categories of black and white are set and inflexible" and that "no legal or social mechanism exists for changing one's race" (1993, p. 9). It is unlikely, moreover, that officially sanctioned and rigid race designations – including the invidious one-drop rule – are likely to disappear from American life in the foreseeable future.

Despite the durability of the word "race", its usage has varied from one period to another and the meaning attached to it has often, as is presently the case, been contested. By the end of the nineteenth century, race had displaced "nation" as the standard term for distinguishing the major divisions of humankind, so that it was common for nationality groups to be referred to as, for example, "the Irish race" or "the German race" (Berkhofer, 1979, pp. 55–6; Abramson, 1980, p. 151; Peterson, 1980, p. 236; Omi and Winant, 1986, p. 5). However, during the twentieth century, "race" has in turn been superseded by "ethnicity" as the all-inclusive category, especially since World War II and the discrediting of the former term through its association with Nazi ideology.

Numerous arguments have been put forward for race being subsumed by ethnicity. Edna Bonacich (1972, p. 548), who viewed both race and ethnicity as "inherited" and "ascribed", suggested that geographic criteria play an important role in distinguishing between the two categories:

The main difference between race and ethnicity lies in the size of the locale from which a group stems, races generally coming from continents, and ethnicities from national sub-sections of continents. In the past the term "race" has been used to refer to both levels, but

general usage today has reversed this practice . . . Ethnicity has
become the generic term.

While Bonacich claimed that the distinction between an ethny and a race is
determined by an inherent characteristic of the group itself (that is size of
ancestral place of origin), Susan Olzak implied that the difference lies more in
the eye of the beholder. Despite starting from the different premise that
"racial and ethnic boundaries are socially and politically constructed", Olzak
arrived at the same conclusion as Bonacich of viewing race as subordinate to
ethnicity: "Since ethnicity is an outcome of boundary creation and maintenance, there is no obstacle to treating race as a special case of an ethnic
boundary, one that is believed to be correlated with inherited biotic characteristics" (1992, pp. 7–8). However, to subsume race within ethnicity, as
Pierre van den Berghe has noted, is not to ignore "the greater rigidity and
invidiousness of racial, as distinct from cultural distinctions", nor to deny that
they produce "qualitatively different situations" (1983, p. 222). This view,
that race is either a component or sub-category of ethnicity, has predominated
in historical writing over the past fifty years (Davis, 1991, p. 15; Dinnerstein,
et al., 1996, p. ix; Glazer, 1975, pp. 3–32; Gordon, 1978, pp. 110–11; Handlin,
1957, p. 191; Root, 1992a, p. 4; Sowell, 1981); so much so that authors often
fail to provide satisfactory definitions of the two terms or distinguish between
them properly (see, for example, Fuchs, 1990).

In recent decades, numerous scholars have challenged the convention of
subsuming race within ethnicity and argued that the former term denotes an
entirely independent category. This revisionist perspective first gained prominence in the 1960s, when many black, Chicano and Asian-American
scholars adopted more radical and nationalist approaches to the study of
their respective groups' histories and argued that the "racial" experience of
these nonwhite minorities – especially with regards to the level and intensity
of discrimination they suffered at the hands of the dominant society – was
significantly different to that of white "ethnic" experiences (Sánchez, 1993,
pp. 6–7). "Race", according to Ronald Takaki, "has been a social construction
that has historically set apart racial minorities from European immigrant
groups". Rejecting the assumptions underlying traditional scholarship, Takaki asserted that "race in America has not been the same as ethnicity" (1993,
p. 10). Omi and Winant (1986, p. 5), Saxton (1990, pp. 8, 13–18) and Smedley
(1993, pp. 19, 32–3) also adhere to the revisionist interpretation of race as an
independent and durable social category. Ironically, unlike conventional
academic interpretations, the revisionist view of "race" as mainly referring
to nonwhite and "ethnic" to white groups is similar in many ways to popular
understanding and usage of the two terms. However, the American public still
generally conceives of race and ethnicity as being biologically determined,

whereas revisionist scholars regard them as social constructions (Peterson, 1980, p. 236; Abramson, 1980, p. 151; Carter, et al., 1996, pp. 136, 154).

Somewhat surprisingly, one of the most persuasive arguments for treating race as a category independent of ethnicity has come from scholars whose work has focused primarily upon the historical experiences of whites rather than nonwhites. In their studies of nineteenth-century class relations, labor historians like Alexander Saxton (1990) and David Roediger (1991) have portrayed the hardening of white racial attitudes – especially conceptions of what constituted "whiteness" – as a product of the on-going process of conflict and compromise between workers and employers that was generated by the growth of industrial capitalism in the United States. By examining racial and ethnic identity among whites, Roediger was able to demonstrate that the two are "distinct" and "often counterposed forms of consciousness". Indeed, the ethnic consciousness of some European immigrant groups often undermined the development of an all-inclusive white identity. This was particularly true of the so-called "not-yet-white-ethnics", such as the Irish and Italians, whose claim to whiteness was often disputed by the dominant society. According to Roediger:

> . . . the "white ethnic" developed historically and . . . he or she was certainly not white because of his or her ethnicity. Indeed at times of great identification with homeland and ethnicity, immigrants' identification with whiteness was often minimal (1994, pp. 182, 184–8).

If Roediger's work can be credited with lending strong support to the case for rejecting the subsumption of race within ethnicity, then Audrey Smedley deserves recognition for providing revisionists with definitions that unequivocally differentiate between the two terms. "Race", asserted Smedley, "signifies rigidity and permanence of position/status within a ranking order that is based on what is believed to be the unalterable reality of innate biological differences". Ethnicity, by contrast, is "conditional, temporal, even volitional, and not amenable to biology or biological processes" (1993, p. 32). Interestingly, Smedley's definitions are not dissimilar to those of van den Berghe, nor are they entirely incompatible with the view that race is just a special, more rigid kind of ethnicity.

The absence of coherent definitions of race and ethnicity, and especially of what distinguishes the two terms from each other, is a common flaw of revisionist works (see, for example, Omi and Winant, 1986; Polenberg, 1980, p. 9; Takaki, 1990 [1979] and 1993). The most extreme position within the revisionist perspective is occupied, according to their critics, by those proponents of "multiculturalism" who treat race and ethnicity as one and the same thing. For these scholars, ethnicity is a highly politicized term and they believe that only "people of color" – that is African Americans, Asian Americans, Latinos, and Native Americans – qualify as ethnic. The danger of this viewpoint, contended John Higham (1993, pp. 210, 218), is that if ethnicity is "equated with race", then "all whites are lumped together" and there is no longer a term for describing cultural and other variations within the white population that originate in differences of ancestry. In the American Southwest, for instance, the common Hispanic practice of labeling all whites as Anglos seems to denigrate the cultural heritages of traditionally English-speaking groups like the Scots and Irish, not to mention whites whose European ancestry is in no way linked with the British Isles (ibid.; Barkan, 1995, p. 38). Definitions which equate ethnicity with race, therefore, tend by their very nature to homogenize population groups in general and whites in particular.

A further insight into the nature of the relationship between race and ethnicity can be gained by examining two of their commonly used derivatives – racism and ethnocentrism. Both of these terms relate to forms of prejudice based upon assumptions of difference and superiority, as is demonstrated by George Fredrickson and Dale Knobel's (1980, p. 830) definition of ethnocentrism as "a basic feeling that 'we' are different from 'them' in ways that make 'us' better than 'they' are". Racism, suggested Fredrickson and Knobel, although it emanates from assumptions of innate differences between groups, is essentially a more "accentuated" form and, therefore, sub-category of ethnocentrism. Louis Ruchames's ambiguous use of the term "ethnocentrism" gave the impression that it is a synonym for "racism" (1967, pp. 251–3). The central weakness of this fairly conventional viewpoint is that it tends to blur the distinctions between racism and ethnocentrism, permitting the terms to be used almost interchangeably and, critics claim, inappropriately. To illustrate this, it is worth looking at the debate over when exactly racism first appeared in history. Thomas Gossett, for example, has argued that racism, "even though it had no science of biology or anthropology behind it", dates back to at least the third millennium BCE (1965, pp. 3–16). However, critics would argue that Gossett is mistaking ethnocentrism for racism. Ethnocentrism, Dante Puzzo has noted, is indeed very ancient, but racism is a modern conception that first appeared in the sixteenth century and arose out of specific historical conditions centered upon Europe; most notably, the exploration and colonization of lands and peoples in other parts of the globe, the growth of the secular nation state, and the rise to global dominance. "It is this unique set of circumstances", asserted Puzzo, "which serves not only to account for the rise of racism but to set it off from earlier ethnocentric notions and simple patriotism" (1964, pp. 579, 581, 583). This differentiation between ethnocentrism, as an age-old phenomenon rooted in cultural chauvinism, and racism, as a Western invention that is intrinsically linked to the rise of both capitalism and white imperialism, now appears in many revisionist works on American ethnic history (see, for example, Berkhofer, 1979, p. 55; De León, 1983, p. xi). Nonetheless, the dilemma over whether race is independent of or subsumed by ethnicity is still a moot point, because neither the modern origins of racism nor its distinctive emphasis upon physical differences between human groups preclude it from being classified as a manifestation, albeit in a more potent form, of ethnocentrism.

SUMMARY

Ethnicity, then, is defined in both broad and narrow terms by scholars. The broader definition of ethnicity as a sense of peoplehood permits a wide variety of group experiences to be classified as ethnic, but this interpretation is criticized for being too vague and so inclusive that the term ethnicity is rendered almost meaningless. In contrast, narrow definitions, based upon set and easily recognizable criteria, provide a more exact picture of what constitutes an ethny. However, greater precision also has its drawbacks and can result in rather exclusive and static conceptions of ethnicity which tend to deny, among other things, the existence of ethnic awareness among members of the dominant society and the possibility of ethnogenesis – the creation of new ethnies – being an on-going process. Moreover, the quest for a definitive description is hampered by the fact that no single signifier of ethnicity, be it culture, residence patterns, or historical experience, clearly sets any group apart from all others.

The debate over the nature of ethnicity becomes even more complex when interpretations of its origins are examined. The primordialist perspective, which depicts ethnic identification as an innate human impulse, offers a convenient explanation for the longevity and continuity of many ethnies, but it cannot account for such phenomena as individuals who exchange one ethnicity for another. Moreover, the charge that primordialism is too impressionistic and over-emphasizes the "natural", indefinable qualities of ethnicity seems to be well founded. Conversely, the aim of the situational perspective is to demystify ethnicity by revealing how it emerges out of identifiable real life contexts and historical experiences. Ethnicity, according to this view, is a social construction not a natural human trait. Although occasional efforts have been made to broach the differences between the primordialist and situationalist perspectives by acknowledging the fact that pre-existing loyalties and immediate social circumstances both play a role in the formation of new ethnies, these attempts at synthesis usually founder upon the realization that even apparently primal allegiances must at some point have been socially constructed.

In the light of the fact that primordialism is both widely discredited and generally viewed as incompatible with the situationalist view, the historical debate over the origins of ethnicity mainly takes place within the confines of the latter perspective. The main questions asked by historians are: where and by whom was ethnicity "constructed"? The traditional response to the first of these questions has been to contend that the strong correlation between the cultures of Old World nationalities and New World ethnies is proof that ethnicity was imported into the United States by immigrants. However, this interpretation has a number of weaknesses: first, it was largely formulated with European immigrants in mind and, as a device for explaining the existence of ethnicity, is not really applicable to either non-European whites or non-immigrant ethnies; second, it wrongly suggests that national rather local or regional allegiances were strongest among European immigrants; and, third, it tends to overlook the influence that American society has had upon the ethnicization process. In contrast, the view that ethnicity was principally a home-grown phenomenon not only takes account of American social influences upon ethnicization, but is by inference applicable to non-immigrant ethnies and can also be used to explain differences between the cultures of immigrant ethnies and their ancestral homelands.

If it is assumed that ethnicity is a product of American society and not an import, the question then arises of by whom was ethnicity constructed. Some historians argue that ethnicity is ascriptive; that ethnic status is imposed upon some groups by the dominant society. This interpretation does well at illuminating the nature and extent of nativist and racist influences in American history, and is particularly good at explaining the ethnic status of nonwhites. However, the ascriptive model is less successful at explaining the persistence of ethnicity among whites of European ancestry, because, unlike nonwhites, members of this group often found it easy to enter into and become indistinguishable from the dominant society. The inverse of the ascriptive model is the instrumentalist perspective, which emphasizes the agency exercised by ethnies in the formation and maintenance of group boundaries. According to this view, ethnicity is often "reactive" in the sense that it is a form of group solidarity and political mobilization initiated in response to discrimination at the hands of the dominant group. While this argument helps to explain why diverse elements can often be forged into fairly coherent ethnic groupings, it fails to account for the fact that oppression does not always promote ethnicization and has on occasion actually undermined the process. In practice, the ascriptive–reactive dichotomy is resolved relatively easily by opting to view ethnicity as situational and emerging out of an interaction between internal forces (that is within each ethny) and external ones (that is from the wider society). As well as acknowledging the influence that ethnies have had upon each other in the process of group formation and development, this more interactive model clearly provides a plausible synthesis of competing interpretations. Consequently, the focus of debate has generally shifted away from the origins and nature of ethnies towards the relationship between individuals and groups. The division of interpretations over this issue essentially corresponds to the two main sides of the pluralist-assimilationist dichotomy discussed in more detail in Chapter 3. While pluralists argue that group allegiances generally prevail over individualism, assimilationists contend that ethnic identification is largely a matter of personal choice. The assimilationist interpretation acts as a useful counterbalance to the pluralist tendency to homogenize ethnies that are often quite heterogeneous in composition, but the perception of ethnicity as something fluid and optional or symbolic does have its limitations, especially when confronted with the issue of race. Unlike ethnicity, race designations in the United States are rigid and from the individual's point of view almost always ascribed. Nonetheless, the ensuing argument that race and ethnicity must therefore be mutually exclusive categories is not a conclusion drawn by all scholars of American ethnic history, many of whom adhere to the conventional position of viewing the former classification as a variant of the latter. Hence, race is still largely perceived as a form of ethnicity which attaches greater social significance to physiological differences between humans and thus results in more rigid group boundaries. Clearly, historians attach a wide variety of meanings to the term ethnicity, but regardless of whether they adopt a broad or narrow definition, primordialist or situationalist view of its origins, or perceive it as ascribed or self-constructed, there is a general agreement among scholars that the United States is probably the most ethnically diverse nation state in the world; the debates over how this came to be, therefore, will be the subject of the next chapter.

PART II

Perspectives on American Ethnic Diversity

TWO

The Making of American Ethnic Diversity

INTRODUCTION

The reality of America's ethnic diversity is beyond doubt. No other nation in history has possessed a population composed of so many different ethnic elements. Popular conceptions of this truism were famously encapsulated in John F. Kennedy's description of the United States as "a nation of immigrants". However, as Donna Gabaccia (2002, p. 1) has pointed out, while Kennedy's view of the origins of American ethnic diversity included the full range of European nationalities represented among the ranks of immigrants arriving during the period 1820–1920, it excluded many more groups. Moreover, the emphasis on voluntary immigration – as common in standard history texts as it has been in popular thought – creates a very distorted picture of the making of American ethnic diversity, because its hegemonic origins, such as conquest and forced migration, are virtually glossed over. This chapter examines the ways in which modern scholars have attempted, with varying degrees of success, to broaden the scope of research on the peopling of the United States and challenge conventional notions about the process.

HEGEMONIC ORIGINS: CONQUEST

American ethnic diversity has traditionally been viewed through the prism of nineteenth- and twentieth-century voluntary immigration from Europe, a tendency which inexorably disregards and hence minimizes the hegemonic origins of the population's heterogeneity. In particular, two significant groups were generally given scant acknowledgment in standard accounts of the peopling of the United States: first, indigenous populations who were incorporated into the nation through conquest and not as a result of their own choosing; and second, involuntary migrants who were transported against their will from Old World homelands to the New World. As we will see, revisionist scholarship, by broadening the scope of research to include the experiences of ethnies that come under these two categories, has successfully dispelled the myth that American ethnic diversity was principally the product of voluntary immigration.

While few if any scholars would challenge the fact that between the onset of white settlement and the end of the nineteenth century the aboriginal population of the lands that make up the modern-day United States suffered a continuous decline in numbers, the scale and causes of the phenomenon are still hotly contested issues. Having re-examined and revised upwards the estimates of the size of the pre-Columbian indigenous population, modern research suggests that in the past the scale of Native-American population decline was grossly underestimated. During the first half of the twentieth century, scholars estimated the size of the aboriginal population residing in 1492 in what is now the conterminous United States to be about 900,000. Since the 1960s, a combination of new methodological approaches and changed political outlook among academics has given rise to far more liberal estimates. While some researchers, like Henry F. Dobyns (1973), for instance, have suggested that the pre-Columbian Native-American population of the conterminous United States was as high as 12 to 15 million, a more generally accepted figure is that of 6 to 7 million (see also Thornton, 1987, pp. 25–32; Edmunds, 1995, p. 727). In the light of these revisions, some scholars argue that it is now more appropriate to describe the depopulating of the American Indian tribes as a "holocaust". Russell Thornton, one of the first scholars to use this term, noted that after the arrival of Europeans in the Americas the aboriginal populations "underwent centuries of demographic collapse" and their total numbers "still are far fewer today than in 1492" (1987, p. 42: see also Stannard, 1992).

Even more contentious than the debate about the scale of Native-American population decline are the questions of how and why it came about. Did European settlers and their descendants deliberately set out to decimate the Native-American tribes, or was aboriginal population decline merely an unplanned consequence of the policies pursued by whites? Traditional histories tended to adopt the latter position, while the former viewpoint has become more popular among modern scholars (see Jennings, 1976, pp. v, 15–16). Epitomized by the work of nineteenth-century America's pre-eminent historian, Francis Parkman, conventional accounts of white colonization portrayed the New World as a wilderness or virgin land inhabited by savages and European settlers as the agents of civilization. Moreover, Native-American depopulation was presented as the inevitable consequence of tribal resistance to the advance of progress. According to Parkman, "the Indians melted away, not because civilization destroyed them, but because their own ferocity and intractable indolence made it impossible that they should exist in its presence" (ibid., p. 85). This "cant of conquest" dominated historical writing until well into the twentieth century and was not seriously challenged until the 1960s and 1970s. Francis Jennings's *The Invasion of America* stands as a classic and eloquent exposition of the revisionist critique of the "basic conquest myth":

> The American land was more like a widow than a virgin. Europeans
> did not find a wilderness here; rather, however involuntarily, they
> made one . . . The so-called settlement of America was a
> *re*settlement, a reoccupation of a land made waste by the diseases and
> demoralization introduced by the newcomers (ibid., pp. 15, 30).

Since the 1960s, scholars have also shown a greater willingness to confess that many of the "battles" referred to in conventional histories of relations between the United States and Native Americans were actually unprovoked massacres carried out by whites. As more and more examples of such incidents were unearthed, many revisionist historians argued that, along with disease, warfare, forced relocation, and the destruction of traditional living patterns, genocide needed to be added to the list of factors that accounted for the depopulation of America's aboriginal societies (Thornton, 1987, pp. 44–53). While acknowledging the role played by deliberate acts of extermination, revisionists generally still believed that the introduction of Eastern Hemisphere diseases was "the single most important factor in American Indian population decline" (ibid., p. 44: for examinations of the impact of disease on native populations, see also Crosby, 1971 and 1976; Dobyns, 1973; Wood, 1989). Even this interpretation, however, came under criticism during the 1990s from scholars like David Stannard, who adopted a more extreme revisionist position. In his book *American Holocaust*, which examines the entire Western Hemisphere and not just the United States, Stannard asserted:

> It is true, in a plainly quantitative sense of body counting, that the
> barrage of disease unleashed by the Europeans among the so-called
> "virgin soil" populations of the Americas caused more deaths than
> any other single force of destruction. However, by focusing almost
> entirely on disease, by displacing responsibility for the mass killing
> onto an army of invading microbes, contemporary authors
> increasingly have created the impression that the eradication of those

tens of millions of people was inadvertent – a sad, but both inevitable and "unintended consequence" of human migration and progress (1992, p. xii).

Claiming that "the near-total destruction" of aboriginal populations was "neither inadvertent nor inevitable", Stannard concluded that:

> Although at times operating independently, for most of the long centuries of devastation that followed 1492, disease and genocide were interdependent forces acting dynamically – whipsawing their victims between plague and violence, each one feeding upon the other, and together driving countless numbers of entire ancient societies to the brink – and often over the brink – of total extermination (ibid., p. xii).

While a corrective of the standard interpretation was definitely required, by placing ever greater emphasis on the word "genocide", revisionist scholars like Thornton and Stannard (see also Costo and Costo, 1987) open themselves up to the charge that their choice of terminology is rooted more in emotive rhetoric than objective scholarship. Indeed, it is misleading to equate the United States' treatment of Native Americans with, say, the Nazi's deliberate and organized attempt to exterminate Europe's Jewish and Romany popula-tions. Undeniably, United States policy – both in intent and outcome – towards certain tribes at certain times did amount to genocide, but this was never the federal government's plan for all Native Americans at any one time nor for any particular tribal group at all times. Nonetheless, it is now generally agreed that Native-American population decline was a product, either in part or in whole, of white policies, so a great deal of attention has been paid to uncovering and explaining the motivations behind those policies.

One extreme though widely-held view is that whites were driven by rapacity and self-interest, and that their pitiless disregard for the fate of the indigenous population was rooted in racism and ethnocentrism. This tradition of taking a generally sympathetic view of the Native-American experience and a more critical one of federal policy, which dates back to the work of Grant Foreman (1932, 1934 and 1946) and Angie Debo (1934, 1940 and 1941), came to full expression during the 1960s and 1970s. In accounting for the population decline experienced by eastern Native Americans forcibly relocated during the 1830s to the Indian Territory (in what is now Oklahoma), Foreman argued that "the appalling destruction of the immigrant Indian tribes has been largely due to disease and other natural causes, but, more than all others, to the introduction among them of intoxicants by predatory white men utterly devoid of conscience or principle, who for sordid gain made a business of preying on the weakness, ignorance, and folly of helpless Indians" (1946, pp. 351–2). Though sympathetic to the plight of Native Americans, Foreman's view of them clearly contains some elements of nineteenth-century paternalism. In *Facing West*, Richard Drinnon (1980) provided a more sophisticated and forceful exposition of the revisionist perspective, arguing that the racism and territorial greed which motivated United States policies towards Native Americans up until the end of the nineteenth century were directed toward the Pacific region and Asia during the twentieth century, eventually culminating in the tragedy of Vietnam. Other works drawing a parallel, either implicitly or explicitly, between European-American expansionism in North America and United States imperialism in and foreign policy towards Asia, included Dee Brown's *Bury My Heart at Wounded Knee* (1971) and Cecil Eby's *"That Disgraceful Affair": The Black Hawk War* (1973). Critics of this view, such as Francis Paul Prucha (1981), while acknowledging the existence of cynicism and bigotry among whites, argue that federal policy, although frequently misguided, was essentially driven by humanitarian impulses and a genuine concern for the plight of Native Americans. An entirely different perspective has been offered by Karen Kupperman (1980, p. 140), who argues that white policy towards Native Americans, especially the decision to expropriate tribal lands by force, was a product of English class consciousness more than ethnocentrism.

One thing that tends to get overlooked in discussions of the issue of conquest is the fact that Native Americans were themselves not immune to territorial expansionism. Historical accounts, traditional and revisionist alike, are replete with examples of powerful tribes ousting weaker ones from cherished lands (see Anderson, 1980; Ewers, 1975; White, 1978). Europeans, therefore, were the not only conquerors active in North America after 1600, or even 1783 for that matter.

Although Native Americans figure prominently in the story of conquest, recent scholarship has also drawn attention to the fact that they were not the only group to be incorporated into the American nation in this way. Since the 1960s, Chicano scholars, particularly those subscribing to the "internal-colony" or "internal-colonialism" theory, have been at pains to demonstrate the similarities between the Native-American and Mexican-American experiences. The earliest and most renowned example of the internal-colony model being applied to the history of Chicanos is Rodolfo Acuña's *Occupied America* (1972). Writing in a similar vein, Albert Camarillo asserted:

> The history of the Chicano people as an ethnic minority in the United States was forged primarily from a set of nineteenth-century experiences. This country's war of annexation against Mexico (and the Texas Revolution a decade earlier) led to American acquisition of a

vast territory and its Spanish-speaking population. Chicano history is, thus, part of that larger history of westward expansion by the United States and its subsequent domination of societies with different racial, cultural, socioeconomic, and political characteristics (1979, p. 2).

This analogy, however, can only be taken so far, because the vast majority of Mexican Americans are descended not from the inhabitants of the lands ceded to the United States in 1848 but from the Mexican immigrants who have entered the country since the early decades of the twentieth century; a fact that even Acuña alludes to in later versions of his work (1988, pp. 144–58). Moreover, although the influx of Anglos into the American Southwest during the late nineteenth century led to a decline in the relative size of the Mexican population (that is the percentage that it made up of the total population), it did not lead to the same kind of drastic depopulation experienced by Native Americans. In 1848, it is estimated there were around 80,000 Mexicans living in the territories acquired by the United States under the Treaty of Guadalupe Hidalgo and by 1900 this group had probably grown to about 170,000 (Corwin, 1978, pp. 31–4).

HEGEMONIC ORIGINS: INVOLUNTARY MIGRATION

Whereas the role that conquest played in the creation of American diversity has only attained due recognition in scholarship since the 1960s, historical investigation into the phenomenon of involuntary immigration dates back a long time. Indeed, because the legacies of the slave trade and slavery have so frequently taken center stage in the American saga, it has been impossible for historians to ignore the significance of involuntary immigration. As early as 1770, asserted W. E. B. Du Bois in his classic study of the Atlantic slave trade, it had "become an almost unquestioned axiom in British practical economics" that "the slave-trade was the very life of the colonies" (1970 [1896], p. 4). The full scale of the Atlantic slave trade was not studied in a rigorous way until the 1960s. Prior to then, most studies grossly exaggerated the volume of the trade, with even some conservative estimates suggesting that during the period 1620–1870 almost 3 million Africans were transported to the area that makes up the modern United States. Reliance upon these earlier inflated figures is still a feature of many otherwise useful examinations of the Atlantic slave trade (Mannix and Cowley, 1963; Davis, 1966; Pope-Hennessey, 1967; Davidson, 1970; Thomas, 1997). Although the revised calculation of about 400,000 slaves imported is much lower than traditional estimates, the contribution that the transplantation of Africans made to American multiethnicity became apparent in the nation's first census which showed that in 1790 almost 20 per cent of the total population was black (Curtin, 1969, pp. 3–13, 72–5, 87: see also Rawley, 1981; Lovejoy, 1982). From the 1660s onwards, the black population became increasingly concentrated in the South, where in some colonies African Americans comprised from one-third to two-fifths of the total population (Wells, 1975, pp. 260, 265; Menard, 1991, p. 64). The actual and relative size of the black population continued to grow in most southern states up until the end of Reconstruction and African Americans even constituted the ethnic majority for long stretches of time in South Carolina, Mississippi, and Louisiana (Hall, 1935, pp. 7, 15). Throughout the nineteenth century, nine-tenths of African Americans resided in the South and, as will be seen in later chapters, this concentration has had profound effects upon the history of both the region and the nation as a whole.

The debate over the motivations behind the slave trade also has long antecedents. Under the influence of Ulrich B. Phillips (1959 [1918], pp. 341–3), the early twentieth century's leading authority on the subject of American slavery, historians generally viewed the transportation of Africans to the United States as a humanitarian, charitable act, delivering blacks from even more severe conditions in their native continent. This interpretation was challenged by black scholars like W. E. B. Du Bois (1997 [1904]), but their view that the slave trade originated in the white colonists' economic self-interest and racism only began to gain wider support among white historians after World War II. Although long ignored by mainstream (that is "white") historians, during the first half of the twentieth century African-American writers regularly challenged traditional perspectives on the role of racism in American history. The *Journal of Negro History*, established by Carter G. Woodson in 1916, played a pivotal role in establishing this alternative body of knowledge (see Franklin, 1986). Richard Hofstadter (1944) was the first white scholar to draw attention to and criticize the racist assumptions that under-pinned Phillips's work, an attack which opened the way for a major reappraisal of the origins of slavery. Carl Degler (1959) argued that slavery was rooted in white prejudice towards Africans, a predisposition which Winthrop Jordan (1968) attributed to deep-seated tenets of English culture. However, an older tradition of viewing slavery as the cause and not the effect of racism was resurrected in the late 1960s. In *Capitalism and Slavery*, Eric Williams presented the classic exposition of this interpretation: "Slavery was not born of racism: rather, racism was the consequence of slavery. Unfree labor in the New World was brown, white, black and yellow; Catholic, Protestant and pagan" (1966 [1944], p. 7). Oscar and Mary Handlin (1950) subsequently put forward a similar argument, as did Edmund Morgan (1975) and George Fredrickson (1981), all of whom suggested that imported Africans were initially not treated any differently to white servants in colonial America. The debate over whether slavery was born of racism or racism born of slavery has shifted in favor of the latter position in recent years as more and more research points to the economic origins of the slave trade, thereby suggesting that racism was the subsequent justification for rather than preceding cause of the importation and exploitation of African slaves (see Fogel, 1989; Vaughan, 1989; Wood, 1997). Although these developments in scholarship generally lend support to the view that the hegemonic origins of American ethnic diversity have been underrated in the past, it is worth noting that modern research also shows that Africans were far more complicit in the Atlantic slave trade than previously believed. Du Bois asserted that the "development of the trade depended largely upon the [European] commercial nations, and, as they put more and more ruthless enterprise into the traffic, it grew and flourished" (1997 [1904], pp. 246–7). Du Bois also suggested that Europeans were largely responsible for the capture as well as the transportation of African slaves. Revisionist studies have overturned both of these assumptions. Daniel Mannix and Malcolm Cowley's *Black Cargoes*, the first thorough and truly scholarly examination of the workings of the Atlantic slave trade, demonstrated that "contrary to popular opinion, very few of the slaves – possibly one or two out of a hundred – were free Africans kidnapped by Europeans". "The slaving captains", it was found, "had, as a rule, no moral prejudice against man-stealing, but they usually refrained from it on the ground that it was a dangerous business practice" and they "thought it safer to purchase their cargoes from native merchants" (1963, p. xi). Similarly, having found that Europeans "possessed no means, either economic or military, to compel African leaders to sell slaves", John Thornton concluded: "we must accept that African participation in the slave trade was voluntary and under the control of African decision makers" (1992, p. 125).

Just as Native Americans were not the only ethny to be incorporated into the American nation through conquest, African Americans were not the only "unfree" migrants involved in the peopling of the United States. Abbot Emerson Smith noted that the transportation of convicts to the American colonies was "a regular and systematic pursuit throughout the seventeenth century as well as the eighteenth", even though the practice had only received the sanction of Parliament in 1718 (1934, p. 232: see also Smith, 1947). Despite having attracted the attention of historians as long ago as the 1930s, it is only during the last ten to fifteen years that new studies, utilizing improved methods of calculating colonial immigration, have prepared the way for a radical re-evaluation of the scale and diversity of the unfree element in this population movement (Menard, 1973; Galenson, 1981; Salinger, 1987). Aaron S. Fogelman summarized the findings of this new research as follows:

> For the first two centuries of the history of British North America, one word best characterizes the status of the vast majority of

immigrants – servitude. From the founding of Jamestown until the Revolution, nearly three-fourths of all immigrants to the thirteen colonies arrived in some condition of unfreedom. These migrations of slaves, convicts, and servants played a critical role in the demographic, economic, social, and cultural development of the colonies (1998, p. 43).

According to Fogelman's estimates, slaves made up 17 per cent, convicts and prisoners 1 per cent, and indentured servants 49 per cent of total immigration to the American colonies during the seventeenth century, and 47 per cent, 9 per cent, and 18 per cent, respectively, during the eighteenth century. For the period 1607–1775 as a whole, the total number of unfree immigrants included 311,600 slaves, 54,500 convicts and prisoners, and 200,200 indentured servants. Unfree immigration, therefore, made a vital contribution to the building of a "pluralistic world of peoples from Europe, Africa, and the Americas" in colonial America (ibid., p. 43). After the American Revolution, however, a number of factors, including the disruption of trade and the colonists' embracing of egalitarian ideology, "transformed an immigration primarily of slaves, convicts, and indentured servants into one of free subjects" (ibid., p. 45).

One group popularly, though wrongly, associated with involuntary immigration are Chinese Americans. As Alexander Saxton (1971, pp. 72–5) has shown, Chinese immigrants in the American West were stereotyped as belonging to the flow of press-ganged contract labor – generally referred to as the "coolie trade" – emanating from China in the nineteenth century. Misconceptions about Chinese immigration have been as slow to be dispelled among academics as they have among the general public. For instance, even a distinguished scholar like Moses Rischin, in, of all places, the foreword to a groundbreaking study of anti-Chinese attitudes, erroneously referred to the late nineteenth-century influx of Chinese immigrants as the "coolie migration" (Miller, 1969, p. vii). Modern historians have convincingly demonstrated that, although mid-nineteenth-century Chinese emigration to the United States was contemporaneous to the coolie phenomenon, the latter never intermingled with the former. Thousands, possibly tens of thousands of "coolies" were shipped to various parts of the New World, but never to the United States (Chan, 1990, pp. 42–4, 69; Yun and Laremont, 2001). In a recent article Edward Rhoads (2002, p. 6) neatly summarized the current consensus among scholars:

Strictly speaking, "coolies" were Chinese who were taken abroad by deception or force, generally as replacement workers for Africans following the general international renunciation of the African slave trade; they most commonly were sent to work on the sugar plantations of Cuba and Peru. While most Chinese who came to the United States – with the possible exception of women – did so voluntarily, their critics nevertheless often equated them with "coolies", particularly if . . . they had been hired as gangs of contract laborers.

The unfree element among migrants to Britain's American colonies and the United States, therefore, is generally perceived as being mostly composed of African slaves and British convicts and indentured servants.

Clearly, there was a hegemonic dimension to the creation of American multiethnicity. Nonetheless, while recent research has demonstrated how the scale of Native-American population decline was previously underestimated and provided revealing insights into the motivations behind European appropriation of Native-American lands, some of the more extreme assertions made by contemporary scholars about the causal relationship between these two phenomena are less convincing. In contrast, modern studies of involuntary immigration have not only provided more accurate pictures of the scale of the Atlantic slave trade and the motivations behind it, but have also demonstrated that involuntary immigration's nonwhite element was less diverse and white element more numerous than previously acknowledged.

OVERCOMING BIASES IN IMMIGRATION HISTORY

Despite the important role that they played in the creation of American ethnic diversity, conquest and involuntary immigration, either alone or combined, cannot compete in terms of the sheer numbers of people involved with the more than 60 million voluntary immigrants arriving in the United States during the nineteenth and twentieth centuries. In an effort to explain and better understand this mass movement of people, and one that is unsurpassed in human history, scholars have long deliberated over a number of fundamental questions. Who – in terms of nationality, class, age, gender, and so on – were the immigrants? Where did they come from? Why did they emigrate in the first place? Were they pushed out of their homelands by adverse or deteriorating conditions or were they pulled to the United States by the allure of the opportunities thought to exist there? Moreover, is it possible to fully comprehend such a vast and complex phenomenon as international migration by viewing it through the prism of either the push–pull or any other paradigm? The approaches historians have adopted to resolve these problems are the subject of the remainder of this chapter.

It is important to note that two ingrained biases in traditional scholarship on immigration history have had particular relevance for the debate over the origins and complexity of American multiethnicity. The first bias is an ethnic one. Until recently, immigration history has focused predominantly upon the experience of European migrants. The sizeable streams of migration originating in Africa, Asia, and Latin America, were viewed as essentially separate and insignificant phenomena and therefore either overlooked entirely or only acknowledged incidentally. To illustrate this point, it is worth looking at the three books that for many years were the standard texts on American immigration history. Marcus Lee Hansen, for example, made no reference to the slave trade in his classic work, *The Atlantic Migration 1607–1860* (1940), which focused entirely on European voluntary immigration. Similarly, Oscar Handlin's epic, *The Uprooted* (1951), is essentially a study of the European immigrant experience. Asian immigration is only examined in the two chapters dealing with nativism and immigration restriction, but even then the topic is not given the prominence it deserves. In *American Immigration* (1960), Maldwyn Jones provided far more extensive coverage of Asian immigration than did Handlin and duly acknowledged its importance to the development of US immigration policy. However, Jones completely ignored Mexican immigration, which had totally transformed the ethnic landscape of the Southwest during the first half of the twentieth century.

One of the reasons for what Russell Menard aptly refers to as "the profound Eurocentrism of immigration history as practiced in the United States", is the fact that scholars of American immigration have tended to focus their attention on the national period, particularly the years 1820–1920, the period of massive European emigration. The colonial era, in particular, has long been neglected by historians of American immigration, a tendency which has produced a very skewed picture of the general phenomenon, for "America was as much an extension of Africa as of Europe" during the eighteenth century, because "blacks came to dominate the migrant stream, outnumbering whites in most years from 1700 to 1760" (1991, p. 62). As Sucheng Chan has pointed out, a further reason why conventional studies of American immigration have "suffered from constricted angles of visions" is the "Euro-American tradition of viewing peoples of color as inferior beings". The two important immigration waves that this charge is most applicable to are those from Asia and Mexico. To be fair, scholars examining more recent immigration, noted Chan, "have begun to redress the balance by placing increased emphasis on the influx of people from Asia, Central America, and the Caribbean" (1990, p. 37). An early example of this trend is David Reimers broad-ranging study, *Still the Golden Door* (1985). However, Chan asserted that "attempts to analyze the coming of white and nonwhite immigrants – especially in the pre-1968 period – as an equally important phenomenon" are still hampered by the absence of "a conceptual framework inclusive enough to permit treating the experiences of white and nonwhite immigrant groups meaningfully together" (1990, p. 37).

The second bias in conventional scholarship is a regional one. The problem is described by George Sánchez:

> Currently, Los Angeles International Airport welcomes more immigrants than any other port of entry in American history. Public mythology, however, still reveres Ellis Island and the Statue of Liberty and looks toward Europe. Historical writing on immigration in the United States surely suffers from this severe regional imbalance: most studies still focus on the Northeast and selected cities of the Old Northwest. The fact that the American Southwest has been the locus of one of the most profound and complex interactions between variant cultures in American history is repeatedly overlooked (1993, pp. 13–14).

As Sánchez's observations suggest, the regional bias in immigration historiography is not unrelated to the ethnic one discussed above. In fact, the connection between these two tendencies is such that they are mutually reinforcing, the existence of each serving to perpetuate the influence of the other.

The prevalence of a circumscribed ethnic-regional slant in the study of immigration history contributed significantly to the appearance of theories which created what have since been shown to be artificial and spurious distinctions between immigrant ethnies. One such concept is the old immigrant–new immigrant dichotomy which exerted a considerable influence over historical writing in the first half of the twentieth century. According to this perspective, the "new" immigrants from southern and eastern Europe, who after the 1880s became an increasingly more prominent element among the yearly entrants to the United States, were fundamentally different to the "old" immigrants from northern and western Europe. The "old" immigrants were characterized as being people, largely arriving in family units, who wanted to settle permanently and were easily assimilated into American society. In contrast, the "new" immigrants were depicted as undesirables who either only planned to stay in the country as long as suited their short-term economic interests or, if they did decide to remain longer, were wholly resistant to assimilation. Although late nineteenth- and early twentieth-century historians generally differentiated between old and new stock immigrants, expressing a more favorable opinion of the former – from whom most professional historians at the time were descended – than the latter, the practice was not formalized until the publication of the Dillingham Commission's report on immigration in 1911 (Saveth, 1965 [1948], pp. 200–1). This viewpoint was not fully overturned until the publication of Maldwyn

Jones's classic study, *American Immigration*, in 1960. Jones argued that the old immigrant–new immigrant dichotomy rested upon nothing more than bigoted and unsound assumptions:

> There seem . . . to be no valid grounds for the distinction, invented by late nineteenth-century nativists and adopted by subsequent historians, between "old" and "new" immigrants. The "new" immigrants came later than the "old" and there were more of them; but that is hardly reason to differentiate sharply between groups which, however much they differed culturally, were very much alike in their reasons for coming, in the resources and skills they brought with them, and in their ability to adapt to American conditions (1960, p. 4).

As we will see, subsequent scholarship has confirmed the accuracy of Jones's assertions.

A more enduring, yet equally fallacious and invidious distinction is the one that posits white and nonwhite ethnies on opposite sides of the immigrant–sojourner divide. Once again, Asian and Mexican immigrants are united in being the two ethnies most commonly viewed through the prism of an artificial dichotomy. Gunther Barth's influential *Bitter Strength* (1964), for example, characterized Asian immigrants as voluntary sojourners. Of immigrants from Asia, Chan commented that "[w]ith the single word *sojourner*, some oft-quoted scholars have banished Asians completely from the realm of immigration history" (1990, p. 38). Sources emphasizing the sojourner nature of much Mexican immigration are too numerous to mention, but it is worth noting that the practice is still widespread, even among Chicano scholars. For instance, at the very beginning of their book *Mexican Americans/American Mexicans*, Matt Meier and Feliciano Ribera stated that many Mexicans "considered themselves sojourners rather than immigrants – that is, they thought of their move to the United States as expedient and temporary" (1993, p. 4). This observation may well be accurate, but it does not justify differentiating Mexican immigrants from those coming from Europe and other parts of the world, for whom, according to John Bodnar's summary of research on return migration, the following was true: "Because everyone did not or was unable to return should not obscure the fact that a return was usually every emigrant's goal" (1985, p. 53).

The use of the term "sojourner" has been problematical for two reasons. First, differences in migration patterns between whites and nonwhites have traditionally been attributed to the sojourner mentality of the latter, rather than to factors external to the immigrants. As Lawrence Fuchs has argued, nonwhites did not so much choose to be sojourners as were they constrained to remain as such by the dominant society:

Sojourner pluralism, a system designed by Euro-Americans for immigrants regarded as temporary residents, was applied principally to two groups of non-European immigrants in the West and Southwest. Established after the Civil War and in the decades that followed, this form of pluralism was intended to meet the labor needs of an expanding American economy without having to admit nonwhite immigrant laborers to the civic culture. Workers from the Far East, who were kept ineligible for citizenship, were expected to return home following their terms of labor. Workers from Mexico were permitted to come back and forth across the border, moving north as American employers sought their labor, then were encouraged or compelled to return south as the demand for their labor diminished (1990, p. 78).

Fuchs's view is supported by numerous studies which show that, whereas European return migration was almost always voluntary, a coercive dimension was frequently present in the repatriation of Asian (Chan, 1991; Hing, 1993; Salyer, 1995; Gyory, 1998; Lee, 2002) and, especially, Mexican immigrants (Hoffman, 1974; García, 1980; Guerin-Gonzales, 1994; Balderrama and Rodríguez, 1995). Second, use of the term "sojourner" suggests that return migration is higher among nonwhite than white immigrants. Recent research has shown this not to be the case. Just as the oft-used term "birds of passage" artificially differentiated the so-called "new" European immigrants from the "old", so did the label "sojourner" in the case of nonwhite and white migrants (Chan, 1990, pp. 38–9; Cinel, 1982, pp. 43–70; Fuchs, 1990, p. 120; Gould, 1980; Meier and Ribera, 1993, pp. 172–84, 194–7; Thistlethwaite, 1964, p. 78; Wyman, 1993, pp. 3–14). Such findings have proved instrumental in discrediting the old–new and white/immigrant–nonwhite/sojourner dichotomies whose influence for so long bound scholarship on immigration history to a very narrow trajectory. That said, the terms "birds of passage" and "sojourner" are still sometimes used without due attention being paid to the negative connotations attached to them and the myths that they help to perpetuate about ethnic patterns of return migration (see, for example, Ueda, 1994, p. 13).

CAUSES OF IMMIGRATION

The historical literature on the dynamics of migration is vast and complex. Too vast and too complex for a comprehensive and definitive analysis to be undertaken in a single, standard length volume, let alone in one section of one chapter of such a book. Scholars examining this topic have sought to address a multitude of questions. Why do people migrate – because they want to or because they have to? What roles are played by, on the one hand, impersonal forces, and on the other, human agency? Is migration an individualistic or collectivist phenomenon? Is the migrant's relocation temporary or permanent? Do the experiences of migrants conform to a uniform pattern or are they too multifarious to make generalizations about? Moreover, the different approaches adopted by observers of the migration process are almost as numerous as the questions they address. Although some broad schools of thought can be discerned, these are quite nebulous and frequently overlap with each other or contain internal divergencies. Indeed, the theoretical landscape of this subject has over time become increasingly more fragmented, so the purpose of this section is to explain how this came to be and also to give an indication of the conceptual challenges that scholars of migration need to surmount.

Historical discussion of the causes of immigration regularly includes reference to the so-called "push" and "pull" factors. These terms, it is important to note, are laden with connotations that go far beyond their technical meaning. Indeed, a strong link exists between the push–pull and old immigration–new immigration dichotomies that dates back at least as far as the time of the Dillingham report. As John Briggs has observed: "Interpretations that emphasize the 'push' forces tend to present those dislodged from their homes as desperate, demoralized members of the lower strata of society, the meanest sort, poorly prepared to make their way in another environment". In contrast, "[a]dvocates of the 'pull' thesis project a more favorable image of the immigrants. They are intelligent, motivated, and ambitious – welcome additions to the countries receiving them" (1978, p. 1).

The "Pull" Thesis

Early scholarship on transatlantic migration suggested that its ebb and flow was linked to the upturns and downturns of the American business cycle. The economist, Harry Jerome (1926), was the originator of this thesis, which a decade later was first applied to a major historical study of a European immigrant group by Dorothy Swaine Thomas (1935). According to this tradition, the United States exerted an irresistible centrifugal force. Marcus Lee Hansen, viewed by many as the father of immigration history, suggested that "America was a huge magnet of varying intensity, drawing the people of Europe from those regions where conditions made them mobile and from which transportation provided a path". Hansen, it is important to note, believed that "American conditions determined the duration and height of the waves, European [conditions], the particular source" (1940, p. 192). The same imagery is evoked in Philip Taylor's classic study, *The Distant Magnet*. The attractions of the United States, noted Taylor, were "the variety of its economic growth, the freedom built into its institutions, and the abundance of its commercial and intellectual links with Europe", all of which guaranteed that for prospective emigrants it "continued to possess advantages that no other overseas land could rival" (1971, p. 26). The orthodox view, therefore, maintained that it was the pull of America's economic opportunities, above all other factors, which generated immigration. It is worth noting that there is some disagreement over where Brinley Thomas's classic, *Migration and Economic Growth: A Study of Great Britain and the Atlantic Economy* (1973), stands with respect to the push–pull debate. Frank Thistlethwaite, for instance, concluded that Thomas's study inferred that "migration was impelled more by 'push' factors in Europe than 'pull' factors in the United States" (1964, p. 86), whereas John Bodnar maintained that "Thomas began the tradition of emphasizing the pull of American economic activity as the prime motive underlying immigration" (1985, p. 2).

The "Push" Thesis

During the 1960s and 1970s, new research raised doubts about various elements of the "pull" theory. In a seminal essay, Frank Thistlethwaite outlined the major weaknesses of traditional scholarship, which was distorted by its "American-centredness" (1964, p. 75). By focusing primarily upon immigration and the immigrant experience in the receiving country, and only one receiving country at that – according to some estimates one-fifth of nineteenth-century European emigrants settled in places other than the United States, which generally had both a lower rate of immigration in proportion to the size of the total population and a smaller percentage of foreign-born inhabitants than such countries as Argentina, Canada, Australia and New Zealand (ibid., pp. 75–6; Gould, 1979, pp. 604–5) – standard accounts tended to overlook the fact that migration was "an intra-European as well as a trans-oceanic phenomenon" (Thistlethwaite, 1964, p. 79). Europe was a continent whose people were on the move: from villages to cities, farms to factories and back again. Moreover, traditional scholarship, which usually emphasized the permanent nature of these resettlements, generally ignored the high rate of return-migration among American immigrants, which ranged between 25 and 60 per cent (ibid., pp. 76–8; Bodnar, 1985, pp. 53–4). Such findings, concluded Thistlethwaite, called for a major revision of historians' perceptions of the migration process:

> In short, trans-oceanic migration was only one aspect of a
> bewilderingly complex pattern of tidal currents which carried not
> merely Norwegian settlers to Minnesota homesteads and Irish

immigrants to New York tenements, but Polish peasants to *and from* East German estates, Appalachian coalmines and Silesian steelworks, Italian labourers to and from Chicago, Illinois, and Homécourt, France, Italian hotel workers to and from Lausanne, Nice and Rio de Janeiro, Scotsmen to and from London and Buenos Aires and Spaniards to and from Marseilles and Santos. We are a long way from a simple case of "America fever" (1964, pp. 79–80).

By the early 1980s, sufficient evidence existed to launch a full assault on the orthodox perspective. In a masterful synthesis of the new research, John Bodnar drew attention to the fundamental flaws of the "pull" theory:

The essential problem with the scholarship which has emphasized the attractiveness of the American economy to the less fortunate of the world . . . is that it badly obscures the complexity of social and economic forces which were affecting emigrants in their homeland. If immigration was caused largely by the lure of America, then we would expect that struggling people everywhere would come here in relatively equal numbers with common intentions and, for that matter, backgrounds. But historical reality suggests a different explanation to this process. Rates of emigration were not the same everywhere (1985, pp. 2–3).

"Economic changes in the immigrant homeland", asserted Bodnar, "rather than America[n] industrial growth accounted for the cycle of each immigrant stream" (ibid., p. 54). These streams, characterized by "a small beginning, a peak in the middle, and a decline at the end", were closely linked to the spread of commercial agriculture and industrialization (ibid., p. 3). "These two manifestations of capitalism", which, like the flow of immigrants from Europe, started in the west of the continent and successively moved eastward, "served as the agents which precipitated emigration from some regions and not others" (ibid., p. 55). Hence, Bodnar concluded that the "movement to America of millions of immigrants in the century after the 1820s was not simply a flight of impoverished peasants abandoning underdeveloped, backward regions for the riches and unlimited opportunities offered by the American economy", because the immigrants actually came from the most developed parts of Europe and, moreover, it was the forces of modernization which gave impetus to their movement (ibid., p. 54). Immigration, therefore, originated primarily in "push" and not "pull" factors.

The point of contention within the push–pull dichotomy, it should be noted, is not generally viewed by historians as a strict choice between the causes of migration being either all "pull" or all "push", but rather as a matter of deciding which factors played the predominant role. "Few scholars", noted Briggs, "adopt one approach to the total exclusion of the other, but most have given greater importance to one" (1978, p. 1). In other words, push and pull are not seen as separate processes but two parts of the same process, that process being the free flow of labor across national borders. Push and pull can in this sense be equated with the supply and demand dimensions, respectively, of the international capitalist economy (Jerome, 1926; Thomas, 1973; Williamson, 1974; Gould, 1980).

"Human Agency" Theory and its Critics

In recent years, however, the entire push–pull paradigm has come under attack from a number of directions. Some scholars, for example, have pointed out that it places too much emphasis on the influence of impersonal forces and thereby underrates the role of human agency. According to these proponents of what is known as "social capital" theory, it is the migrant's desire to migrate and determination to turn that aspiration into a reality that drives and sustains migration (see, for example, Bodnar, 1985, pp. 38–43, 45–54, 56; Hoerder, 1985; Hoerder, 1991, pp. 78–107; Reimers, 1992, p. 130). The main drawback of this approach is that, by focusing upon micro-level rather than macro-level activity, it fails to provide an alternative model to the push-pull one for explaining general patterns of migration. Indeed, rather than being an alternative to the push–pull paradigm, the social capital approach can more properly be viewed as a modified version of it, in which "individual decisions in generating and sustaining migrations are seen as important, but are placed within the context of structural forces from both the pull and push sides of the process" (Morawska, 1991, p. 279).

Alternative Structuralist Explanations of Migration: World-System, Empire

More viable alternatives to the classic push–pull model have been put forward by exponents of the various dependency theories. A central weakness of both the push–pull theory and many of its critiques, argue Gilbert González and Raul Fernandez, is that national economies are viewed as "interactive (often described as 'interdependent') but without domination exerted by either party; hence independently functioning push and/or pull" (2003, p. 47). Scholars influenced by Immanuel Wallenstein's world-system theory, which views capitalism as a global economic system composed of dominant core regions and dependent peripheries, were among the first to argue that the economic relationship between sending and receiving countries in the migration process was not one of equality (Kritz, et al., 1981; Hoerder, 1996;

Sassen-Knoob, 1998). Ewa Morawska observed that historians working in the field of migration studies were much slower than their social science counterparts to experiment with the global system approach:

> The massive flow to the United States of immigrants from Southern and Eastern Europe in the period 1880–1914 has traditionally been interpreted in American historiography within a conventional push-and-pull theoretical model that views the movement of people between two unequally developed economies as an aggregate outcome of individual decisions and actions. More recent historical studies of this immigration are conducted within a modified push-and-pull framework that acknowledges the impact of structural forces, from both the push and the pull side of the process, but does not fully articulate the multiple reciprocal links connecting the two into a single system of world economy (1989, pp. 237–8, 266).

According to Morawska, there were distinct advantages to abandoning the conventional approaches and adopting the global system model:

> In this conceptualization, the development of the core and the underdevelopment of the peripheral societies are seen not as two distinct phenomena, but as two aspects of the same process – the expanding capitalist world system, explained in terms of each other. Generated by the economic imbalances and social dislocations resulting from the incorporation of the peripheries into the orbit of the core, international labor migrations between the developing and industrialized regions are viewed as part of a global circulation of resources within a single system of world economy. This interpretation shifts the central emphasis from the individual (and his/her decisions) to the broad structural determinants of human migrations within a global economic system (ibid., p. 237).

Nonetheless, even the global system approach fails to undermine the "core premise of push–pull – the imbalance of independent conditions in sending and host countries", according to González and Fernandez, who claim that:

> . . . the Achilles heel of world systems theory, and its predecessor, dependency theory, can be traced to their definitions of capitalism and of capitalists. According to these theories, the essence of capitalism lies not in the social relations, property patterns, ideology, and political institutions of society rather than in the existence of commercial relations (2003, p. 48).

This definition, argue González and Fernandez, "ipso facto elevates the degree of 'agency' of Third World elites", according them "a higher degree of freedom and independence in their dealings with stronger nations", and consequently global system theory "obscures and obfuscates a history of imperial domination". While González and Fernandez argue persuasively that, in the case of Mexican immigration, a "real alternative to push–pull requires a reconceptualization of migration within the context of empire", it is difficult to see how this paradigm could be applied to, say, nineteenth-century immigration from Europe (2003, p. 48).

Micro-Level Perspectives on Migration

One laudable though problematic development in recent writing is the tendency to view the migration process "from the bottom up" (Hoerder, 1991, p. 79). The emphasis upon macro-level rather than micro-level issues in traditional scholarship created the need for this corrective viewpoint. "Too often", noted Alan Kraut, "historians fail adequately to acknowledge that it was the single individual who decided to go or stay" (1982, pp. 3–4). "The immigrant", added Kraut, "might not always have been the sole arbiter of his or her own fate, but neither was the immigrant primarily a passive soul, reactive and compliant before impersonal social forces" (ibid., pp. 3–4; 2001, p. 5). Maldwyn Jones proceeded from a similar premise to conclude that it is foolhardy to "attempt to explain mass immigration by means of an all-embracing formula" (1960, p. 94). However, this retreat from theorizing and growing aversion to generalization has led to the proliferation of imprecise and timid explanations of immigration. Historians are right to draw attention to the complexity of the migration process, but they have a duty to the reader to try to demystify rather than obfuscate. It is not helpful, therefore, to either the reputation of the historical profession or the understanding of the general reader for prominent scholars to make such self-contradictory and virtually meaningless statements as Dirk Hoerder's assertion that immigrants "were transplanted by economic forces yet decided to move of their own free will" (1991, p. 80). Such pronouncements only lead to confusion. Scholars should not use blandishments about the complexity and multifaceted nature of immigration as a cover for their unwillingness to state whether migration is primarily generated at either the macro- or the micro-level. It is now obvious that both impersonal forces and agency play a role, so it is the duty of historians to analyze the relationship between these two factors and make clear statements about their relative importance.

Migration: Solitary or Group Activity?

Another debate which causes as much confusion as it does understanding is the discussion over whether migration is an individualistic or collectivist phenomenon. Scholars influenced by social capital theories have demonstrated that individual migrants generally formed part of a chain of migration in which networks of families and friends influenced the volume and direction of migration flows. In the introduction to his ground-breaking study of three immigrant groups from south-eastern Europe, Josef Barton observed that "migration proceeds according to a regular sequence of stages":

> In the earliest stage, the pioneer emigrant, motivated largely by private aspirations for a better life, journeys alone to a new society in search of a new position. A successful pioneer may communicate with family and friends at home and persuade them to follow him. The second stage is the development of a minor stream of migrants from one particular place to another. If this intermediate stage establishes a settlement, then a mass migration follows as villagers are carried forward by a pervasive social momentum. This third stage typically produces large urban settlements where immigrants form ethnic groups by establishing societies, parishes, and newspapers (1975, p. 6).

Barton found that migration "flowed mainly within well-defined streams" and that three out of four immigrants in Cleveland "proceeded along well-traveled courses to specific destinations in the city" (ibid., p. 49). Such discoveries, however, do not completely overturn conventional wisdom about migration. Each chain, for example, had to have been established by a pioneer migrant from a particular sending region, so the role of the individual is still important. Moreover, for an understanding of what motivated these pioneers we are once again drawn to looking at the macro-level, push and pull, rather than the micro-level factors, which only become relevant as causal factors once a particular chain has been established. Likewise, while some scholars emphasizing the communal nature of migration like to think that their findings are proof of agency, by stressing the importance of groups and networks they actually deny or at least underrate the agency of the individual. To be fair, while Barton drew attention to the previously neglected communal dimension of migration, he set his findings within the context of broader macro-level factors and also displayed due consideration for the role of the individual.

Unfortunately, subsequent scholarship incorporating the theme of communalism has not always been so successful at striking the right balance between emphasis on macro- and micro-level influences. For instance, Ewa Morawska claimed that her global-system approach study of Polish migration harmonized "the competing macro- and micro-explanatory frameworks of international migrations, by presenting the mediating role of local conditions and sociocultural environment from which Polish migrant laborers ventured into the outside world" (1989, pp. 266–7). Borrowing Fernand Braudel's concept of "multi-storied historical structures", Morawska argued that

> [w]hile the configuration and pressure of forces at the upper
> structural layers set the limits of the possible and the impossible
> within which people moved, it was at the level of their close,
> immediate surroundings that individuals made decisions, defined
> purposes, and undertook actions (ibid., p. 255).

However, Morawska then goes on to present a picture of local conditions which appears to leave little room for individual agency. Migration, both regional and transatlantic, asserted Morawska, was "not an individual, but a collective movement" (ibid., pp. 260–1). By emphasizing the influence that village customs, local public opinion, and social networks had upon "decisions regarding where to go in search of wages" and identifying the existence of "an extended transatlantic system of social control and long-distance management of family and local public affairs" (ibid., pp. 259–60, 262), Morawska's study gives the impression that individual migrants were actually very constricted in their exercise of personal choice. Undeniably, the discovery of migration chains is an important development in scholarship, but its relevance lies in its ability to explain how and not why migration takes place. For the answer to the latter question we must examine the motivations of individuals, for whom the existence of chains and networks were factors which no doubt facilitated their migration but were not the ones which caused them to decide to migrate in the first place.

Bewildered by the plethora of theories and paradigms existing within the field of migration studies, the novice can easily be excused for finding it difficult at first, or even after some time, to see the wood from the trees. In such moments of perplexity, the student, inexperienced and seasoned alike, would do well to recall J. D. Gould's pithy and timeless observation: "In the simplest terms, if migration is to take place there must be people who want and are able to leave where they are; countries which they wish and are permitted to enter; and an acceptable means of conveying them" (1979, p. 615). Any interpretation which ignores one or more of these elements cannot provide more than a very incomplete picture of the migration process.

While recent research has revealed the limitations and over-simplistic nature of the classic push–pull paradigm, the latter has not, despite the claims of its critics, been rendered obsolete by the appearance of models (which themselves are frequently over-complex and self-contradictory) emphasizing collectivism over individualism, or stressing imbalance rather than equilibrium within the global economy. In short, an impartial overview of the literature would seem to suggest that migration is not a matter of push or pull, but push and pull factors, not a matter of micro- or macro-level causes, but micro- and macro-level causes, nor a matter of voluntary or involuntary impetuses, but voluntary and involuntary impetuses all playing a role.

SUMMARY

At the beginning of the twenty-first century, most historical accounts of the peopling of the United States are no longer as narrowly focused on the experience of European immigrants as they had been twenty or thirty years ago. Nonetheless, much of this bias still remains. It is a sad reflection upon the pace of progress in the field when many of the criticisms made in the early 1970s by a leading scholar of Asian immigration, Roger Daniels (1974), were still relevant over twenty years later. Pondering over the reasons behind the omission of the Asian experience from many contemporary studies of immigration, Daniels proffered an explanation that is equally applicable to African Americans, Mexican Americans, and numerous other nonwhite or non-European origin ethnies:

> . . . the entire historiographical tradition of American immigration –
> a tradition which is less then eighty years old – has, until very
> recently, concentrated almost exclusively on Europeans. The first two
> generations of immigration historians . . . generally excluded Asians
> from the immigrant canon. Most contemporary immigration
> historians explicitly reject both nativism and racism, but tend, almost
> reflexively, to assume that, for most of the American past, the terms
> "immigrant" and "European" were interchangeable . . .
>   In addition, many, perhaps most, of the historians of immigration
> wrote about their own ethnic groups, and, even today, all but a
> handful of historians of immigration are Euro-Americans with a
> propensity to identify the immigrant past with Europe (1997, p. 14).

As Daniels rightly implied, the main problem with much contemporary scholarship is its particularism. It is not for want of available primary and secondary sources that a truly inclusive treatment of the peopling of the United States has yet to appear, but a lack of will on the part of historians. Today, scholars are just as well informed about the hegemonic origins of

American ethnic diversity, through conquest and forced migration, as they are about voluntary immigration, and high-quality studies of many previously ignored migrant groups are no longer in short supply, but few attempts have been made to integrate these stories into a single conceptual framework. Until this happens, revisionists cannot claim to have successfully overcome the ethnic and regional biases in scholarship on immigration or challenged traditional perspectives on the origins of American multiethnicity. Indeed, the task of trying to provide an all-inclusive account of the diverse origins of American ethnic groups has generally only been taken up by the authors of general texts on American ethnic history. In most cases, though, this takes the form of a brief and fairly superficial overview of the different processes that have contributed to the peopling of the United States. However, only occasionally, as in Roger Daniels's *Coming to America: A History of Immigration and Ethnicity in American Life* (1991), does a scholar perform this task with both readiness and skill.

THREE

Ethnic Adaptation

INTRODUCTION

American ethnic diversity originated in conquest and both forced and voluntary migration, but what type of society emerged from these processes? Was it one in which ethnic divisions broke down, either rapidly or slowly, over time, or did they remain fixed and impermeable? Moreover, what roles did agency and coercion play in shaping ethnic configurations in the United States? These questions, which penetrate fundamental problems about the nature of American civilization, have intrigued professional academics for over a century and amateur social commentators since the time of the nation's founding. This chapter charts the unfolding of that debate and evaluates the contributions of the two main schools of thought, the assimilationists and the pluralists. Both of these perspectives contain an internal division between scholars who stress the role played by agency in the adaptive process and those who emphasize coercion, so these variations upon the themes of assimilation and pluralism will also be examined. Discussion of American ethnic configurations has regularly been enlivened by the use of evocative metaphors, the most famous – or infamous, depending upon your point of view – being the melting pot, the mosaic, and the kaleidoscope. The exponents of these various metaphors, it is worth noting, regularly offer not only their own interpretation of past and present ethnic configurations, but also their vision of what pattern the United States should conform to in the future. It is important, therefore, to pay close attention to the task of distinguishing between historical fact and ideological rhetoric when evaluating the contending theories on ethnic adaptation. One more caveat is necessary at this stage. Partly for the reasons noted above, the use of conceptual metaphors for depicting the adaptive process is itself a point of contention among scholars of ethnicity. In their book *Multiculturalism in the United States*, John Buenker and Lorman Ratner argued that "the use of such metaphors . . . clouds more than it clarifies our understanding" of adaptation (1992, p. 3):

> Attempting to define the complex process by which myriad ethnic groups have adapted to mainstream American culture over the past two centuries has proven to be a protean task that has resisted the combined efforts of historians, anthropologists, sociologists, linguists, folklorists, geographers, political scientists, psychologists, and scholars of literature, religion, music, art, architecture, and drama. Great has been the temptation to eschew detailed, comparative analysis and to take refuge in a plethora of metaphorical and rhetorical imagery, such as a melting pot, a salad bowl, a mosaic, or a kaleidoscope. So complex are the variables involved in the adaptive process that they inherently resist reduction to any formula, equation, or definition (p. 231).

As noted in Chapter 2 (p. 44), this aversion to making generalizations is a common trait of much recent scholarship on American ethnic history.

ASSIMILATION: MELTING POT OR ANGLO-CONFORMITY?

The central argument in assimilation theory is that ethnic differences are not permanent and will eventually disappear. Interpretations vary, however, over whether assimilation ought to be seen as an egalitarian or hegemonic process. These two viewpoints are represented by the melting-pot and Anglo-conformity models, respectively.

The Melting Pot

The melting-pot model depicts assimilation as a multidirectional blending of peoples and cultures, the end product being the creation of an entirely new people and culture. This egalitarian slant on the theme of assimilation has a long tradition in the United States, dating back to the late eighteenth century. "Here", wrote the Frenchman J. Hector St John Crèvecoeur in his 1782 book *Letters from an American Farmer*, "individuals of all nations are melted into a new race of men" (Gordon, 1964, p. 116). During the nineteenth century, the conception of America as a melting pot was heralded by such eminent writers as Herman Melville, Ralph Waldo Emerson, and Wendell Phillips (Nash, 1995, p. 955). However, this viewpoint was not popularized until the beginning of the twentieth century, when the English-born Jewish playwright, Israel Zangwill, penned a highly successful drama entitled *The*

Melting Pot. In Zangwill's play, one of the main characters declares that "America is God's crucible, the great Melting Pot where all the races of Europe are melting and re-forming!" (quoted in Gordon, 1964, p. 120). Occasionally, Zangwill also implied that it was not just Europeans who were entering the American melting pot, but also members of the "black and yellow" races (Fuchs, 1990, p. 275).

Variations on the melting-pot model predominated in sociological and historical scholarship until well into the twentieth century. In 1893, Frederick Jackson Turner framed his influential frontier thesis in unmistakably assimilationist terms: "In the crucible of the frontier the immigrants were Americanized, liberated, and fused into a mixed race, English in neither nationality nor characteristics" (Turner, 1962 [1920], p. 23). It is difficult to overestimate Turner's influence upon subsequent scholarship, because, as Rudolph Vecoli has pointed out, "[t]he historians who established immigration history as a field of study after World War I were almost to a man Turnerians" (1970, p. 75). In the works of pioneering scholars like Theodore Blegen, George Stephenson, and Carl Wittke, "their theme was that of the adaptation of Old World cultures to New World environments" (ibid., pp. 75–6). Similarly, Marcus Lee Hansen believed that it was "the ultimate fate of any national group to be amalgamated into the composite American race" (1952, p. 499). This historiographical trend mirrored developments in sociological thinking in the United States at the beginning of the twentieth century. Continuing in the tradition of Karl Marx, Max Weber, and Ferdinand Toennies, the leading lights of the emerging Chicago school of sociology presumed that the forces of modernization would obliterate ethnic differences and foster cultural homogenization. Such opinions underpinned William I. Thomas and Florian Znaniecki's pioneering study, *The Polish Peasant in Europe and America* (1927 [1918–20]), and in 1926 came to full expression in the "race relations cycle" formulated by Robert Ezra Park (see Matthews, 1977; Persons, 1987; Conzen, 1996). Park's model depicted a process which, composed of four stages – "contacts, competition, accommodation, and eventual assimilation" – was "apparently progressive and irreversible", even for nonwhite ethnies, such as Asian immigrants on the West Coast (1950, p. 150). The fusion of these parallel historiographical and sociological traditions was achieved in Oscar Handlin's Pulitzer-prizewinning epic, *The Uprooted.* Reflecting the influence of American sociological theory, Handlin asserted that, "seen from the perspective of the individual received rather than of the receiving society, the history of immigration is a history of alienation and its consequences" (1951, p. 4). Despite being couched in modern terminology, Handlin's message was an old one. Like Crèvecoeur, Handlin believed the New World transformed the European peasant into a "new man": "The customary modes of behavior were no longer adequate, for the problems of life were new and different. With old ties snapped, men faced the enormous compulsion of working out new relationships, new meanings to their lives". Like Zangwill, Handlin viewed the adaptive process in egalitarian terms: "The immigrants could not impose their own ways upon society; but neither were they constrained to conform to those already established. To a significant degree, the newest Americans had a wide realm of choice" (ibid., p. 5).

The appeal of the melting-pot concept lies in its compatibility with both the universalist principles on which the republic was founded and the task of forging a nation out of a composite people. Integration implies equality, acculturation implies unity, and amalgamation implies harmony. Moreover, the emphasis placed upon the transformative power of the American environment, whether rural or urban, rather than on any particular cultural heritage, endowed the melting-pot ideal with an appeal that transcended ethnic differences.

Challenging the Melting Pot

Criticisms of the melting-pot perspective mounted as the twentieth century progressed. Early exponents of the melting pot were frequently among the first to concede that their original formulations had underestimated the durability of ethnic allegiances, which had not disappeared in the way that it was formerly believed they would. When Frederick Jackson Turner turned his attention in 1901 to the topic of immigrant life in America's urbanized East, he did not draw the same optimistic conclusions about the efficacy of the melting pot as he had a decade earlier when writing about the frontier West:

> The immigrant of the preceding period was assimilated with comparative ease, and it can hardly be doubted that valuable contributions to American character have come from this infusion of non-English stock into the American people. But the free lands that made the process of absorption easy have gone. The immigration is becoming increasingly more difficult of assimilation (quoted in Saveth, 1965 [1948], p. 132).

In contrast to the recently settled frontier West, which Turner viewed as "the line of the most rapid and effective Americanization" (1962 [1920], pp. 3–4), the older, more urbanized East "was not a good mixing bowl" (1935, p. 55). Likewise, the sociologist Park grew more cautious over time about emphasizing the inexorable nature of the race relations cycle, which he claimed could overcome "every sort of normal human difference, except for the purely external ones, like the color of the skin" (1950, pp. 205–6).

Anglo-Conformity

From the 1960s onwards, the melting-pot theory faced withering assaults from a multitude of directions. New scholarship took issue with the egalitarian pretensions of the assimilationist perspective, arguing that the historical record showed that while assimilationists played lip service to the ideal of creating a new American culture derived from numerous sources, in reality they meant forcing ethnic minorities to adopt Anglo-American values. In the early 1950s, some commentators were already questioning the reality of the melting pot and suggesting that American society actually resembled "a 'transmuting pot' in which all ingredients have been transformed and assimilated to an idealized 'Anglo-Saxon' model" (Herberg, 1955, pp. 33–4). Indeed, it is now generally accepted that many of the theorists, such as Robert Park and his followers, who "ideologized" the adaptation process as a melting pot were really exponents, whether implicitly or explicitly, of Anglo-conformity (Morawska, 1994, p. 77). By the early 1960s, the melting pot "vision of America" had come to be viewed as "something of an illusion", a "generous and idealistic one", "but one which exhibited a considerable degree of sociological naïveté" (Gordon, 1964, p. 129). By the mid-1970s, "the melting pot was a subject of mockery" (Higham, 1984, p. xii). As we will see, some scholars, partly inspired by the ethnic revival of the late 1960s and 1970s, challenged the view that assimilation had taken place at all and argued that ethnic pluralism was the American norm.

The Anglo-conformity model of assimilation depicts the adaptive process as one in which the members of ethnic minorities achieve integration through abandoning their traditional culture and adopting that of the dominant Anglo-American group. As a current in mainstream thought, the Anglo-conformity version of assimilation, like the melting pot, has a long tradition in the United States. Its existence is most manifest during periods of widespread racism and nativism, the antebellum and Progressive eras being two notable examples (Bennett, 1988; Billington, 1938; Hartmann, 1948; Knobel, 1996; Lissak, 1988; Luebke, 1974; Meyer, 1980). Some revisionist scholars, while not condoning the intolerance and coercion associated with the model, have argued that ethnic adaptation in the United States has broadly taken the form of Anglo-conformity. Two early and highly influential expositions of this viewpoint were Will Herberg's *Protestant-Catholic-Jew* (1955) and Milton Gordon's *Assimilation in American Life* (1964). "Anglo-conformity", concluded Gordon, "has probably been the most prevalent ideology of assimilation in the American historical experience" (1964, p. 115):

Given the prior arrival time of the English colonists, the numerical dominance of the English stock, and the cultural dominance of

Anglo-Saxon institutions, the invitation extended to non-English immigrants to "melt" could only result, if thoroughly accepted, in the latter's loss of group identity, the transformation of their cultural survivals into Anglo-Saxon patterns, and the development of their descendants in the image of the Anglo-Saxon American (ibid., p. 129).

The Anglo-conformity model "fell into disrepute" not long after Gordon's treatise appeared (Morawska, 1994, p. 76). It is worth noting that there is some dispute over which theoretical perspective Gordon's influential book belongs to: assimilationism or pluralism. This confusion is mostly attributable to Gordon's depiction of the American ethnic pattern as "structural pluralism accompanied by an ever-decreasing degree of cultural pluralism" (1964, p. 262: see Kazal, 1995, p. 451). In the early 1990s, Ewa Morawska persuasively argued for the Anglo-conformity model's resurrection in a modified, more "*historicized*" (that is "time-and-place specific and embedded in multidimensional contexts") form, not as "a universally applicable proposition", but as "one of a number of possible explanatory frameworks in which the immigrants' adaptation to the host (American) society can be accounted for" (1994, pp. 76, 85). The principal advantage of the Anglo-conformity model as a theoretical tool is that, compared to the melting-pot model, it provides a less romanticized picture of ethnic adaptation in the United States. The Anglo-conformity model draws attention to harsh historical realities and portrays assimilation as a frequently abrasive and contentious process.

Since the 1960s, despite recent attempts to resurrect certain elements of it, the Anglo-conformity model has, like all versions of the assimilationist paradigm, fallen out of favor with scholars working in the field of American ethnic history (Higham, 1982; Kazal, 1995; Morawska, 1990; Zunz, 1985). Indeed, closer inspection of the Anglo-conformity model reveals that it is based upon assumptions that make it even more problematical than the melting-pot theory. First, it assumes that ethnic adaptation is a unidirectional process in which the members of ethnies are passive, or at best compliant, participants. "Assimilationism", contended John Higham, is "unrealistic" because it "falsely assumes that ethnic ties dissolve fairly easily":

Many people resist for generation after generation the assault of technology and modern education on their sense of ethnic selfhood. No ethnic group, once established in the United States, has ever entirely disappeared; none seems about to do so. People are not as pliant as assimilationists have supposed (1984, pp. 235–6).

Second, the nation's essentially Anglo core culture is presumed to be unchanging and impervious to external influences. Implicit in these assumptions is a serious underestimation of both the complexity of the adaptive process and ethnies' capacity to exercise agency. At a more philosophical level, the Anglo-conformity model has been criticized by some scholars for being incompatible with the universalistic principles of the American republic (Fuchs, 1990, pp. 5, 61–7, 69–75).

PLURALIST MODELS

In contradiction to assimilationist viewpoints, the central argument of pluralist theories is that ethnic boundaries are extremely resilient and that as a result the enduring characteristic of the American ethnic landscape is diversity. Consequently, pluralists use metaphors like "salad bowl'', "patchwork", and, increasingly in recent years, "mosaic" to describe ethnic configurations in the United States. However, as with the assimilation perspective, pluralist interpretations vary over whether American ethnic patterns should be viewed as the product of egalitarian or hegemonic relationships. Similarly, like assimilationism, the pluralistic perspective cuts across traditional ideological divides, making it possible for both the Marxian-influenced historian Ronald Takaki (1993, p. 6) and free-market economist Thomas Sowell (1981, p. 4) to organize surveys of American ethnic history around the metaphor of the mosaic.

Although the lineage of the pluralist tradition can be traced back at least as far as the founding of the United States, it did not gain prominence in scholarly discussions until the beginning of the twentieth century and even then did not seriously challenge the position of the assimilation paradigm as the dominant school of thought in American ethnic history until the 1960s. That said, recent research indicates that the debate over the assimilation–pluralism dichotomy clearly took place within some ethnic communities long before it became a national issue (Conzen, et al., 1992, pp. 10–11). The pluralist perspective first emerged as a widely supported alternative to the assimilationist position during the Progressive era, largely in reaction to the Americanization movement that was then sweeping across the United States. As a counterpoise to the coercive overtones of Americanization ideology, early pluralist thinkers put forward a more voluntaristic vision of American society in which ethnic diversity was celebrated rather than deplored. Horace Kallen, a vehement opponent of the early twentieth-century Americanization movement, set forth a pluralistic vision of American society in his notable essay "Democracy versus the Melting Pot" (1915). Believing that, instead of a melting pot, the United States should aspire to be a "democracy of nationalities", Kallen perceived Americanization, that is forced assimilation, as being essentially undemocratic and argued that "democracy involves not the elimination of differences but the preservation and conservation of differences". By providing "the foundation and background for the realization of the distinctive individuality of each *natio* that composes it and the pooling of these in a harmony above them all", American civilization, asserted Kallen, could attain perfection through becoming "a multiplicity in a unity, an orchestration of mankind" (ibid., pp. 218–20). Ironically, despite being the undisputed founder of modern cultural pluralism, contemporary pluralist and multiculturalist scholars only reluctantly acknowledge the intellectual debt they owe to Kallen. For instance, out of the seven survey texts on American ethnic history that are predominantly pluralistic in outlook, only one (Gabaccia, 2002, pp. 177–8) makes any reference to Kallen's theories on pluralism (see also Barkan, 1996; Dinnerstein, et al., 1996; Kraut, 2001; Olson, 1994; Sowell, 1981; Takaki, 1993). The reason for Kallen's present almost pariah status is the fact that his theories were based upon Eurocentric and racialist assumptions. He appears to have believed biological and cultural inheritance were intrinsically linked. Moreover, the "democratic commonwealth" that he envisioned was composed only of Europeans and nonwhites were implicitly – and in the case of African Americans, explicitly – excluded from his formulations (Kallen, 1915, pp. 218–20, and 1924, p. 226). Therefore, much to the embarrassment of contemporary multiculturalists, "the pluralist thesis from the outset was encapsulated in white ethnocentrism" (Higham, 1984, p. 208). Admittedly, the writings of one of Kallen's contemporaries, Randolph S. Bourne, constituted a more inclusive version of the pluralist model. "America is coming to be", asserted Bourne in 1916, "not a nationality but a trans-nationality, a weaving back and forth, with the other lands, of many threads of all sizes and colors" (Bourne in Resek, 1964, p. 121). Like Kallen, Bourne anticipated the triumph of pluralism, or "cosmopolitanism" as he called it, with optimism:

> The failure of the melting-pot, far from closing the great American
> democratic experiment, means that it has only just begun. Whatever
> American nationalism turns out to be, we see already that it will have
> a color richer and more exciting than our ideal has hitherto
> encompassed. In a world which has dreamed of internationalism, we
> find that we have all unawares been building up the first
> international nation (ibid., p. 117).

While the influence of Kallen's theories upon academic discussion variously waxed and waned over succeeding decades, Bourne's ideas remained fairly obscure until the 1960s and 1970s (Higham, 1984, pp. 198–232; Kallen, 1956; Vaughn, 1991).

While early twentieth-century exponents of pluralism laid the intellectual foundations for a new school of thought, historical writing on American ethnicity remained largely unaffected by this until the 1960s. When a more irrepressible assault on conventional thought finally did take place, it was led, as has so often been the case in the field of American ethnicity, by scholars from the social sciences. The publication of Nathan Glazer and Daniel Patrick Moynihan's seminal work, *Beyond the Melting Pot*, which examined ethnic diversity in New York City, signified the birth of the modern pluralist school of thought. "The point about the melting pot", stated Glazer and Moynihan in unequivocal terms, "is that it did not happen" (1963, p. 290). The next year, Rudolph Vecoli's withering critique of the central text of the assimilationist canon, Handlin's *The Uprooted*, appeared in the *Journal of American History*. Basing his findings on a case study of south Italian immigrants in Chicago, Vecoli (1964, p. 417) challenged the main tenets of Handlin's viewpoint:

> Because it overemphasizes the power of environment and underestimates the toughness of cultural heritage, Handlin's thesis does not comprehend the experience of the immigrants from southern Italy. The basic error of this thesis is that it subordinates historical complexity to the symmetrical pattern of a sociological theory. Rather than constructing ideal types of "the peasant" or "the immigrant", the historian of immigration must study the distinctive cultural character of each ethnic group and the manner in which this influenced its adjustments in the New World.

"To speak of alienation as the essence of the immigrant experience", asserted Vecoli, "is to ignore the persistence of traditional forms of group life" (ibid., pp. 409–10). Vecoli's article has since become as much a classic as the book that it lambasted.

The social climate of the 1960s, it is important to note, played a major role in facilitating the pluralist perspective's rise in popularity among academics; a development closely linked to the emergence of the New Social History tradition of scholarship, which placed emphasis upon the agency exercised by marginalized groups (Kessler-Harris, 1990; Gardner and Adams, 1983). First, the African-American civil rights movement inadvertently triggered a so-called "ethnic revival" in which numerous ethnies, including many white groups, sought public recognition of their own particular minority experience. Michael Novak – whose book *The Rise of the Unmeltable Ethnics* was as much a clarion call for the ethnic revival among European-ancestry groups as it was an analysis of the phenomenon – claimed that the United States resembled not a melting pot but a "Nordic jungle" (1973, p. 85). This resurgence of ethnic particularism, which grew in strength during the 1970s, not only called into question the efficacy of assimilation, but also posed a challenge to the black–white (that is African American–European American) dichotomy that for so long had dominated historical research on American ethnic relations. Writing in the wake of the Kerner Commission report on urban rioting, which characterized the United States as "two societies, one black, one white", Rudolph Vecoli warned that the

> current concern with Afro-American history should not be allowed to obscure the larger whole of which it is a part . . . The historian of ethnicity has the responsibility of insisting upon a pluralistic rather than a dichotomized view of the past (1970, p. 84).

The first historian to take up this challenge was Ronald Takaki, whose book, *Iron Cages*, offered a "comparative analysis of racial domination" by examining the evolution of the dominant society's attitudes toward not only blacks, but also Native Americans, Mexicans, and Asians (1990 [1979], p. v).

Second, the civil rights movement spawned a number of theorists and concepts which laid the basis for a new version of the pluralist paradigm. In the 1960s and 1970s, many pluralist thinkers, unlike their early twentieth-century counterparts, stressed the involuntary, hegemonic nature of ethnic pluralism in the United States. The appearance of the internal-colony and related models has contributed to a fragmentation of the pluralist approach. Some scholars held true to the old belief in the voluntary basis of American pluralism. "In the United States", wrote Nathan Glazer, "one is required neither to put on ethnicity nor to take it off" (1975, p. 29). This practice, argued Glazer, had been a distinctive feature of the "American ethnic pattern" emerging over the previous 200 years:

> Undoubtedly, if this nation had chosen – as others had – either one of the two conflicting ideals that have been placed before us at different times, the "melting pot" or "cultural pluralism", the ambiguities of ethnic identity in the United States and the tensions it creates would be less . . . We have not set either course, neither the one eliminating all signs of ethnic identity – through force or through the attractions of assimilation – nor the other of providing the facilities for the maintenance of ethnic identity (ibid., pp. 29–30).

"Ethnicity in the United States", asserted Glazer, was merely "part of the burden of freedom" of all individuals living in modern societies "who must choose what they are to be" (ibid., p. 29).

Another group of scholars argued that the long history of legalized discrimination against and segregation of certain ethnies proved that pluralism took a hegemonic form in the United States. Writing in the late 1960s, Stokely

Carmichael and Charles Hamilton used the expression "internal colonialism" to describe the system that had long oppressed the African-American population, which they believed constituted a "colony" because its members were traditionally excluded from and exploited by mainstream society (1967, pp. 2–7). Carmichael, Hamilton, and other early exponents of internal-colony theory, such as Robert Allen (1970), Robert Blauner (1972), and Mario Barrera (1979), were greatly influenced in their theorizing by the black (and later Chicano) protest movement and spiraling urban rioting that they witnessed and in some cases even participated in during the 1960s and 1970s. As well as shattering the "optimistic projections" of the assimilation paradigm,

> the urban riots raised overwhelming doubts in the minds of these scholars that America's historical encounter with its racial minorities . . . could be subsumed under the same conceptual and theoretical model that applied to America's historical encounter with its white immigrant minorities (Ringer, 1983, p. 6).

This train of thought has led many pluralist scholars to differentiate between the "ethnic" experience of white immigrants and the "racial" one of nonwhite groups.

Adherents of voluntary pluralism respond to this by stating that, although coercive pluralism was the norm for many nonwhite groups at various periods in American history, during the twentieth century this path was finally abandoned by the United States. According to Nathan Glazer, scholars who argued that "racism defines our history" offered "a selective misreading of American history" (1975, pp. 6–7). While conceding that "[f]or fifty years, between the 1890s and the 1930s, exclusivism was dominant" and "affected many groups", Glazer maintained that since then the American pattern "has been to ever widen the circle of those eligible for inclusion" and that following the civil rights revolution the "circle now embraces . . . all humanity, without tests of race, color, national origin, or language" (ibid., pp. 17, 22). Despite its internal divisions, by the 1980s pluralism was firmly established as the dominant theoretical perspective in the field of American ethnic history.

The pluralist approach to American ethnic history has numerous advantages over the assimilationist one. First, it pays due attention to the efforts ethnies put into preserving their distinctive heritages. Pluralists portray ethnic groups as resilient entities which did not passively or easily succumb to assimilatory pressures. The view of ethnic adaptation emerging out of the 1960s was, therefore, the complete antithesis of conventional historical interpretations. This is graphically illustrated by the title chosen by John Bodnar for his impressive synthesis of the new scholarship. Signaling a rejection of Handlin's view in *The Uprooted* that the immigrants' Old World heritage was lost in the process of adaptation, Bodnar called his book *The Transplanted* and stressed immigrant resistance to Americanization (1985, pp. 184–205). Revisionism represented a moral as much as a historiographical shift. The new generation of social historians, Howard Rabinowitz has noted, "not only finds evidence of strong ethnic and racial identification, but usually celebrates it" and is inclined to "view such persistence quite favorably and treat it as something that should have happened" (1983, p. 28). Second, pluralist theorists, particularly those specializing in the experiences of non-white ethnies, have correctly pointed out that the traditional exclusion of various pariah groups from mainstream society has been a serious impediment to assimilation in the United States. As Blauner has noted, although immigrants from Europe "faced great hardships and even prejudice and discrimination on a scale that must have been disillusioning", they still "had the advantage of European ancestry and white skins" and so their participation in American society "involved a degree of choice and self-direction that was for the most part denied people of color". According to Blauner, this "element of choice" was "crucial in influencing the different careers and perspectives of immigrants and colonized in America" (1972, p. 56). This interpretation can be discerned in the works of such scholars as John Wunder (1994) on Native Americans, Mary Frances Berry and John Blassingame (1982) on African Americans, Ronald Takaki (1990) on Asian Americans, and Rodolfo Acuña (2004) on Mexican Americans.

While arguably it affords a less Anglo-centric and therefore more inclusive, comprehensive view of American ethnic history than assimilation theory, the pluralist perspective has itself increasingly attracted criticism in recent years. Under closer scrutiny many pluralist models appear to be based upon assumptions that are just as problematical as those of the assimilationists. First, pluralism tends to treat ethnic cultures and groupings as though they are static, unchangeable entities, thereby making the same mistake as the Anglo-conformity theorists do in their portrayal of the nation's core culture. The pluralist perspective, according to Higham, "assumes a rigidity of ethnic boundaries and a fixity of group commitment which American life does not permit". Ethnic boundaries, he claimed, "are more or less porous and elastic" (1984, p. 236). Similarly, Vecoli has suggested that neither the mainstream culture nor ethnic sub-cultures remain unchanged by the adaptation process: "This disorderly, rough, sometimes cruel society, we call America, has transformed all of us, Yankees, Africans, Japanese, Italians, and in the process we have transformed it" (Vecoli, 1995, p. 80). As Kathleen Neils Conzen recently pointed out, one of the reasons why contemporary pluralist research often exaggerates the extent of ethnic survival is that it "has tended to focus precisely on those kinds of places – areas of concentrated first-generation settlement – where the odds of finding evidence for ethnic maintenance are greatest" (1996, p. 21).

Second, the pluralist emphasis on the primacy of ethnic identification in American society does not match easily with evidence pointing towards the importance of other forms of allegiance, such as along class and gender lines. Research showing that class formation regularly promotes cultural homogenization poses a serious challenge to the pluralist perspective. Labor historians like Gary Gerstle (1989), Lizabeth Cohen (1990), and James R. Barrett (1992), for example, have all suggested that the development of a strong working-class culture in the early twentieth century weakened ethnic divisions and strengthened ethnic workers' identification with America. Such findings probably explain why many pluralist scholars choose to skirt around the issue of class (Higham, 1993, pp. 202–3, 251–2).

Third, many pluralists erroneously assume that the legacy of ethnic exclusion in the United States disproves the assimilation theory. Although segregation and discrimination may impede assimilation, they are not incompatible with it, because, in theory, once the dominant society has abandoned its exclusivity the path is then opened for minorities to integrate. The best example of this is the phenomenal growth of the African-American middle class during the years since the civil rights revolution of the 1960s (Landry, 1987; Wilson, 1987).

Fourth, at a philosophical level, pluralism, with its concomitant emphasis on the claims of collectivities, has been criticized by traditionalists for being incompatible with America's universalistic principles, which give prominence to individual not group rights. While assimilationism, John Higham has observed, "expresses the universalism of the Enlightenment" and stresses the "equality of individuals" and the individual's "right to define himself [*sic*]", pluralism "rests on the diversitarian premises of romantic thought", champions "equality of groups" and consequently "would put the individual at the mercy of the [ethnic] group" (1984, pp. 234, 235, 238). In *The Disuniting of America*, Arthur M. Schlesinger, Jr, offered a more impassioned critique of the pluralist perspective. According to Schlesinger, pluralism portrayed the United States as "composed of groups more or less ineradicable in their ethnic character", rather than "a nation composed of individuals making their own unhampered choices" (1992, p. 16). Schlesinger claimed that because pluralist dogma "belittles *unum* and glorifies *pluribus*" it threatened to lead America away from "assimilation" and "integration" and toward "fragmentation" and "separatism" (ibid., pp. 16–17).

BEYOND THE ASSIMILATION–PLURALISM DICHOTOMY

A growing recognition that, while the assimilationist and pluralist perspectives both have their strengths and weaknesses, neither paradigm is flexible or comprehensive enough to provide on its own an adequate picture of ethnic configurations in the United States, has prompted many scholars to look for a conceptual framework that transcends the assimilation–pluralism dichotomy. To meet this need, historians have in recent decades increasingly turned to a model sometimes known as "pluralistic integration", a term coined by John Higham in the mid-1970s (1984, p. 242). The pluralistic-integration perspective views assimilation and pluralism as parallel or concurrent rather than opposing, mutually exclusive processes. Reflecting its more fluid nature, the pluralistic-integration paradigm uses the metaphor of the "kaleidoscope" to depict the American ethnic landscape (ibid., p. 248; Fuchs, 1990, pp. xiii–xiv, xvi–xvii).

The pluralistic-integration perspective has three main strengths. First, by being a more encompassing approach, the kaleidoscope viewpoint is able to incorporate evidence of both assimilation and ethnic resilience into its portrayal of the adaptive process (Morawska, 1990, p. 218). For instance, according to exponents of pluralistic integration, "ethnicization" – the process by which individuals acquire ethnic identification and diffuse, heterogeneous collectivities from into distinct ethnic groups (Sarna, 1978) – is not just a source of pluralism but also the first stage on the path of integration into American society, because ethnic groups are themselves vehicles of assimilation. Lawrence Fuchs described this stage as "ethnic-Americanization", a process "in which ancestral loyalties (religious, linguistic, and cultural) are changed (and in some ways strengthened) to American circumstances even as immigrants and their children embrace American political ideals and participate in American political institutions" (1990, p. 20). It was not just white immigrant groups that underwent the process of ethnicization, "reconfiguring their ancestral identity" in order to "establish a new identity as ethnic-Americans", but also nonwhite immigrants, African Americans, and Native Americans (ibid., pp. 22, 42–8, 61–7, 144–5, 218, 234–8, 342–9). At the same time as it brought the members of particular groups together, ethnicization also increased the various ethnies' involvement in American society:

> For all of them, the reconfiguration of identity became and still is a mechanism for bridging differences and enlarging common interests and habits. It was and is also a way of gaining protection against the surprises and dangers of the new environment, and of making claims within it (ibid., p. 22).

Second, the pluralistic-integration model, because it stresses the fluidity and multidirectional nature of ethnic interaction and cultural exchange, lacks the rigidity which is one of the main weaknesses of both the assimilation and pluralism models. In contrast to the melting-pot and mosaic metaphors, the kaleidoscope one conveys a more open-ended picture of ethnic adaptation, which is treated as an ongoing process in which collectivities and cultures are changeable not static. According to one group of eminent scholars, the origins of this "pluralistic social order" are located in the successive waves of immigrants entering the United States:

> Anglo Americans had to assimilate these distinctive groups into their conception of the history and future of "their" country, and to prescribe appropriate social and cultural arrangements. Inevitably all Americans, native born and immigrant, were involved in a continual renegotiation of identities . . . [A] process of syncretism occurred by which much of ethnic cultures was incorporated into changing definitions of what was American and what it meant to be an American. Without corresponding to either the Anglo–conformity or Melting Pot models of assimilation, the interaction of mainstream ethnoculture and sidestream ethnoculture wrought major changes in both (Conzen, et al., 1992, p. 6).

Clearly, exponents of the pluralistic-integration model suggest that American national identity is very much and will continue to be a "work in progress". Nor do they apologize for this lack of precision. "Ambiguity about an American identity", asserted Higham, "has always been essential to the open and indeterminate character of American society" (1984, p. xi).

Third, the pluralistic-integration perspective provides an answer to the philosophical question of how to harmonize the apparently contradictory assimilationistic and pluralistic impulses that have long characterized the American ethnic scene. The kaleidoscope paradigm's solution to this problem lies in an all-encompassing civic culture which forms the basis of national unity through its acceptance of ethnic diversity. According to Fuchs, the Founding Fathers' affirmation of the principle that "individuals who comport themselves as good citizens . . . are free to differ from each other in religion and in other aspects of their private lives" had important ramifications for ethnic relations in the United States (1990, p. 5). The new nation's civic culture, "with its principles of separation of church and state and the right of free speech and assembly, facilitated and protected the expression of ancestral cultural values and sensibilities" and consequently formed the basis for what Fuchs claimed is an American innovation – "voluntary pluralism" (ibid., pp. 5, 23). Under voluntary pluralism, the individual members of ethnic groups are "free to maintain affection for and loyalty to their ancestral religions and cultures while at the same time claiming an American identity by embracing the founding myths and participating in the political life of the republic" (ibid., p. 5). The dilemma over whether to place individual rights above group rights, or vice versa, is resolved, therefore, by upholding the right of individual Americans to belong to ethnic groups if they so wish. As John Higham (1984, p. xiii) readily admitted, the essence of the pluralistic-integration paradigm is compromise:

> It is not by any means America's only tradition in ethnic relations. It will not appeal to the more militant champions of a particular ethnic heritage; nor will it satisfy those rationalists for whom all ethnic feelings are prejudices to expose or obstacles to overcome. But pluralistic integration is our best tradition. And the history of the twentieth century . . . gives us reason to believe that pluralistic integration will prevail.

Clearly, Higham indulged in a certain amount of advocacy here, but, to be fair, even critics of pluralistic integration agree that it is a sophisticated, formidable model and has numerous merits (Kazal, 1995, p. 464). Historical scholarship influenced by the kaleidoscope paradigm, Russell Kazal has observed, "tended to work against conceptions of Anglo-conformity and stress those of pluralism – but not the disconnected variety of the New Social History" (ibid.); Ewa Morawska has dubbed the latter the " 'ethnicity-for-ever' approach" (1990, p. 218). The advantage of the kaleidoscope school's model of pluralism, noted Kazal, was that it "had room for processes of homogenization above the ethnic-group level" (1995, p. 465).

As with the assimilationist and pluralist interpretations of the American ethnic pattern, the pluralist-integration model is not without its critics. Labor historians, among others, complain that the kaleidoscope perspective fails to tackle the issue of class. This is a valid point. For instance, the "integrated working-class culture" detected by Lizabeth Cohen (1990, p. 357) in her study of interwar-era Chicago and the evidence of "the gradual acculturation of immigrants and their socialization in working-class environments and contexts" found by James Barrett (1992, pp. 998) both suggest that the process of cultural homogenization had reached an advanced stage among the progeny of European immigrants as early as the 1930s. Moreover, discussions of class formation and identity are conspicuously absent from the major tomes of the pluralistic-integration perspective's canon; most notably, Fuchs's *American Kaleidoscope*, which fails to devote a single one of its over 600 pages to the issue of class (see also Vecoli, 1995, p. 77). However, the pluralistic-integration model of ethnic adaptation, through its capacity to deal with evidence of both assimilatory and pluralistic trends, is not incompatible with historical perspectives that emphasize the importance of class consciousness. Even critics of the model are prepared to concede this point. Gary Gerstle, in an essay challenging John Higham's advocacy of universalism over multiculturalism, acknowledged that America's universalist civic culture was not "necessarily hostile to talk of class inequality", adding that "Americans have repeatedly found in this language the words and symbols to advance egalitarian agendas" (1993, p. 233).

Another criticism of the pluralistic-integration approach is that it pays insufficient attention to the issue of race and particularly the recent trend towards the subsumption of ethnic groupings by broader racial ones. Once again, this is a valid point. For example, studies charting the emergence of pan-ethnic groupings in contemporary America show that while ethnic differences within the larger European-American (that is "white"), Native-American, African-American ("black"), Asian-American, and Latino/Hispanic groupings may be breaking down, the racial boundaries that separate these amalgamations from each other show little sign of doing so (Lopez and Espiritu, 1990; see also pp. 165–9, 175–6, 202–7 below). In contrast to the fluidity emphasized in the kaleidoscope metaphor, therefore, this research on the phenomenon of pan-ethnicity implies that the American ethnic pattern actually displays a stubborn rigidity. Likewise, recent investigation into the subject of "whiteness" and how it has historically been a prerequisite for entry into mainstream society, with even European immigrants having to prove their "white" status before being granted acceptance, suggests that the black–white divide in the United States may forever remain insurmountable (Roediger, 1991; Jacobson, 1998; see also Kolchin, 2002). However, this oversight on the part of pluralistic-integration scholars is also remediable, as long as racial groups are viewed as a special type of ethny rather than an entirely separate category (see discussion above, pp. 12–20). Moreover, Fuchs admitted that for a long time numerous "coercive pluralisms", which excluded various nonwhite ethnies from mainstream society, operated alongside "voluntary pluralism", but he argued that these oppressive systems were gradually abandoned over the course of the twentieth century (1990, pp. 77–9, 149–50).

Finally, it could be argued that the pluralistic-integration model is in fact simply a slowed-down version of the melting pot, a contention which pretty much takes the discussion in this chapter back to where it started. As flippant as they may appear, such criticisms of the pluralistic-integration paradigm nonetheless draw attention to the fact that it is easier to devise one-dimensional conceptual models portraying simply assimilation or pluralism, no matter how detached they might be from historical reality, than it is to construct one that incorporates both assimilation and pluralism into its interpretation of ethnic adaptation. The difficulty arises from the need to develop structures that "will uphold the validity of a common culture", "while sustaining the efforts of minorities to preserve and enhance their own integrity", two apparently contradictory ends. According to John Higham the solution to this problem lies in "distinguishing between boundaries and nucleus". "All boundaries", observed Higham, must be "understood to be permeable", while "ethnic nuclei" ought to be "respected as enduring centers of social action" (1984, p. 244). While this makes sense in theory, it has proved very difficult in practice for scholars to produce a sophisticated and historically accurate model that performs these two functions. When Elliott Barkan demonstrated how assimilation, which he described as a "two-way process", could take place amid "the nation's enduring pluralism" (1995, pp. 46, 65), his model was accused of portraying the core culture as essentially Anglo-American and assimilation to that core as "normal, expected, and uni-directional" (Zunz, 1995, p. 93; Vecoli, 1995, p. 79). This outcome is only to be expected if the observations of Stephen Steinberg are to be believed. According to Steinberg, a "flaw running through much of the recent literature on ethnicity is a failure to view contemporary patterns of ethnicity in the context of long-range historical trends" (1989, p. 72). With a growing number of American ethnic groups witnessing the dying out of the foreign-born generation, the demise of the ancestral language and many cultural practices, the maturing of an almost completely Americanized fourth generation, and rising rates of ethnic intermarriage, the United States may well be heading towards the kind of ever-increasing cultural homogenization that virtually every other nation in history has experienced (ibid., pp. 44–71). "History", Steinberg asserted, "seems to bear out the contention of the melting-pot theorists that amalgamation is an inevitable last step in the assimilation process" (ibid., p. 72). Displaying uncharacteristic long-sightedness for a sociologist, Steinberg implied that while a snapshot picture of the American ethnic pattern suggests pluralism, a more distended view makes it "difficult to avoid the conclusion that what we have been witnessing for several decades is the melting pot in the making" (ibid., p. 73).

SUMMARY

So, which metaphor best describes ethnic configurations, past and present, in the United States? Has the process of ethnic adaptation in America taken the shape of a melting pot, a mosaic, a kaleidoscope, or even some other metaphorical form? A trite, timid answer to these questions might be to say that "only time will tell". However, such a response is not entirely without merit. After all, the United States is by most standards still a young nation and American society is by all accounts still a very dynamic entity, so perhaps the beginning of the twenty-first century is still too early a point in the evolution of the American ethnic landscape to discern its historical pattern.

PART III

Mainstream Society's Perceptions and Policies

FOUR

Ethnicity and the American Creed

INTRODUCTION

As the discussion in the previous chapter has no doubt made apparent, the form of the American ethnic pattern – whether it be a melting pot, mosaic, or kaleidoscope – has to a great extent been determined by people's attitudes; those of the dominant ethny towards minorities and vice versa. Moreover, while the terms of ethnic adaptation in the United States were not entirely set by the mainstream culture, it generally exercised a deciding role in the matter. The resolution of the assimilation–pluralism dichotomy, therefore, is in part dependent upon the resolution of another dichotomy: the inclusion–exclusion one. The assimilationist position, for instance, rests upon the premise that the American Creed – which upholds the individual's right to the enjoyment of life, liberty and property – encompasses, in practice as well as in theory, all ethnic groups. However, if it can be shown that America's treatment of ethnic minorities has largely been characterized by a denial of these rights, then the assimilationist perspective becomes less tenable. Indeed, the assimilation model – whether in its voluntaristic, melting-pot or coercive, Anglo-conformity mode – requires the dominant society to display virtually a total commitment to the principle of ethnic inclusion, whereas pluralism can be a product of either inclusion, which facilitates voluntary pluralism, or exclusion, which creates involuntary pluralism.

The purpose of this chapter is to disaggregate the inclusion–exclusion dichotomy and analyze in turn each of its main components – namely, the issues of integration, equality, and freedom from persecution. While it is true that in scholarly assessments of the dominant society's attitudes and behavior towards ethnic minorities, the assimilationist perspective, on the one hand, tends to emphasize the themes of acceptance, equality and mild treatment, and the pluralist perspective, on the other hand, is inclined to stress the opposing themes of rejection, inequality and terrorization, it is important to note that the assimilation–pluralism and inclusion–exclusion dichotomies are not identical or even transposable. Indeed, both assimilationist and pluralist accounts generally depict the ethnic experience as characterized by a combination of the aforementioned contrasting themes. The beckoning question, therefore, is not whether American ethnic history has contained instances of either inclusion or exclusion, but rather which of these two recurring themes has been the dominant one.

A "WORLD-WIDE WELCOME"?

In its invocation of universalist and egalitarian principles as justification for the establishment of the United States on 4 July 1776, the Declaration of Independence pledged the new nation to a policy of indiscriminate treatment of all ethnies residing within its borders. According to Thomas Jefferson's famous document, the nation was founded upon the belief "that all men are created equal" and "endowed . . . with certain unalienable rights", such as "Life, Liberty, and the pursuit of Happiness". The commitment to inclusivism implicit in Jefferson's words was expressed more explicitly and its scope expanded considerably in subsequent expositions of the American Creed, a trend epitomized by Emma Lazarus's 1883 poem, "The New Colossus", which depicted the Statue of Liberty as a symbol of the "world-wide welcome" that greeted those who sought to enter America's "golden door". The historiography of this intellectual tradition is broadly divided into, on the one hand, orthodox scholarship, which accepts fairly uncritically the sincerity and actuality of the argument that American society is open to all and treats all alike, regardless of ethnicity, and on the other hand, revisionist interpretations, which assert either that the United States has failed to live up to its universalistic and egalitarian principles, or that its espousal of these was not genuine in the first place.

The Orthodox Emphasis on Ethnic Inclusivism

Up until the 1960s, most historical accounts of American ethnic relations adhered to the orthodox, essentially assimilationist, outlook, which characterized the dominant society's attitude toward ethnic minorities as being one of acceptance. Inclusivism appeared to most historians to be both compatible with and a natural consequence of the universalist and egalitarian principles upon which the United States was founded. However, the orthodox view did not rest solely upon a faith in the power of American idealism. From a practical point of view, it seemed as though it were only common sense for a fledgling republic inhabited by an ethnically diverse population to embrace integration as a means of creating unity and forging a new national identity. In contrast to organic states originating in a common sense of folk, the United States, according to Hans Kohn, developed a civic and rationalist form of nationality, which emphasized the common rights of its citizenry (1957, pp. 3–10). Ideology rather than ethnicity was the cement which held together the American people, who Kohn noted "do not claim common descent to form a nationality" (1965, p. 10). As Philip Gleason has pointed out, the conventional interpretation of the origins and nature of American nationality has major implications for the field of ethnicity. Membership of the American nation, according to this view, was not dependent upon the possession of "any particular national, linguistic, religious, or ethnic background", but only on a commitment to the nation's "political ideology centered on the abstract ideals of liberty, equality, and republicanism". In other words, "the universalist ideological character of American nationality meant that it was open to anyone who willed to become an American" (1980, p. 32). As Dale Knobel has observed:

> Historians disagree over the intentions that lay behind such a construction of American nationality – whether they were only the product of a desire to differentiate New World nationality from Old (especially English) and in so doing legitimize the revolt of the thirteen colonies, or whether they reflected an effort to sever Americans from ethnocultural obligation to England, or, on the contrary, were a palpable necessity to differentiate American from Englishman in order to create a nation out of a colonial population already substantially non-English (1986, p. 40).

Whatever the case, the assumption in conventional interpretations is that the founding generation of the republic believed that "the American was made, not born" (ibid., p. 41). Orthodox historians suggested that this belief was exemplified in the new nation's openness to immigration. "In the early nineteenth century", asserted Oscar Handlin, "those already established on this side of the [Atlantic] ocean regarded immigration as a positive good" and new arrivals were "accepted without question or condition" (1951, p. 264). According to Handlin, this "receptive attitude", which originated in both the idealism of the Revolution and the necessity of peopling the North American continent's vast interior, provided immigrants with a "sense of being welcome" (ibid., pp. 264–5).

For orthodox scholars, therefore, the American commitment to inclusivism was a product of both idealism and national self-interest. Such a view is not without its merits. It is undeniable that the United States has long been – particularly for immigrant groups, like European Jews, that were traditionally excluded and persecuted in their countries of origin – a far more open and tolerant society than most Old World countries (Cohen, 1984; Handlin, 1954; Karp, 1985; Rischin, 1962). There is also considerable evidence of integration being so extensive among some immigrant groups, the English, Scots, and Welsh being notable examples, that they rapidly ceased to exist as a distinct ethny (Berthoff, 1953; Erickson, 1990 [1972]; Fischer, 1989; Graham, 1956). Moreover, the failure of some ethnies to achieve full integration can often be explained by the group's own proclivity for self-segregation rather than a lack of acceptance from the dominant society. Groups that are often characterized as practicing self-segregation include not only small religious sects like the Amish (Hostetler, 1980) and Hasidic Jews (Levy, 1975; Poll, 1962), but also entire ethnies like the Chinese (Barth, 1964). Nonetheless, the orthodox perspective does suffer from one fatal flaw: it largely ignores the indisputable fact that American society has always been far more accepting of some ethnies – namely, white Protestants and especially those of Anglo-Saxon ancestry – than of others. Milton Gordon, for instance, acknowledged that, unlike most other groups, "white Protestant descendants of the 'Old' immigration" were permitted to "merge structurally" into mainstream society "with relative ease" (1964, p. 129: see also Barrett and Roediger, 1997).

The Revisionist Stress on Ethnic Exclusivism

Revisionist scholarship comes in many forms, not all of it anti-assimilationist in slant. Moreover, although the major scholarly assault upon the orthodox position only began in earnest during the 1960s, this was prefigured by a number of important historical works published in earlier decades; for example, two of the most influential studies of American nativism, Ray Allen Billington's *The Protestant Crusade* (1938) and John Higham's *Strangers in the Land* (1955). As the title of Billington's work suggests, he saw the rise of antebellum nativism, which took institutional form in the American "Know Nothing" Party, as originating in religious fanaticism. Billington, a staunch Turnerian, viewed the Know Nothings' virulent anti-Catholicism as an aberration in American history, a manifestation of the British cultural legacy that was rapidly losing ground to the more tolerant, democratic national ethos being forged on the frontier. In contrast, John Higham maintained that nativism, which he defined as "intense opposition to an internal minority on the ground of its foreign (i.e., 'un-American') connections", was not just the preserve of "crackpots" but a major characteristic of American public opinion (1955, pp. x, 4). According to this view, the "energizing force" behind nativism was not religious fanaticism but "modern nationalism" (ibid., p. 4). Moreover, Higham moved beyond equating American nativism with anti-Catholicism by demonstrating that it also drew upon a variety of other ideological traditions, including anti-radicalism and Anglo-Saxon racialism (ibid., pp. 5–11). However, the revisionist tradition dates back even earlier than the works of Billington and Higham and originated in a sub-field of American history long spurned by white academics – African-American history.

Around the turn of the twentieth century, a generation of black professional historians emerged who, led by the likes of W. E. B. Du Bois and Carter G. Woodson, produced over many decades a vast body of research that demonstrated beyond all doubt that the history of one of America's largest ethnic minorities, African Americans, verily did not conform to the orthodox picture of acceptance and inclusion (Franklin, 1986, pp. 14–16). The most influential work emanating from this historiographical tradition is Du Bois's *Black Reconstruction in America* (1935). However, it was not until the publication of a book entitled *The Strange Career of Jim Crow*, written by a white historian, C. Vann Woodward, that revisionism began to make a serious impression upon mainstream scholarship. Writing in the wake of the Supreme Court's famous decision to outlaw the "separate but equal" principle, Woodward's timely work highlighted the fact that African Americans, even after the abolition of slavery, were systematically subjected to a "racial ostracism" that resulted in their political and economic subordination, and under which they experienced "neither equality nor aspirations for equality in any department of life" (1955, pp. 7, 8). After *Strange Career*, the floodgates opened to release an outpouring of revisionist works that has continued to the present day.

This literature can be divided into two main types, which might be labeled liberal revisionism and radical revisionism. The former perspective is generally sympathetic to the nation's expressed principles but argues that it has not lived up to them in its dealings with ethnic minorities (see, for example, Higham, 1955; Woodward, 1955; Lipset, 1969), while the latter perspective, strongly influenced by internal-colony theory, questions both the authenticity and efficacy of the American Creed (Blauner, 1972; Bennett, 1988). Despite these differences between the liberal and radical versions of revisionism, they concur on certain fundamental points. First, revisionists maintain that the United States has a long history of ethnic prejudice and stereotyping (Appel and Appel, 1982; Berkhofer, 1979; De León, 1983; Fredrickson, 1987 [1972]; Jordan, 1968; Miller, 1969; Simon, 1985; Stedman, 1982; Takaki, 1990 [1979]). As Ruth Miller Elson demonstrated in *Guardians of Tradition* (1964), a study of nineteenth-century American schoolbooks, generations of American school children were exposed from an early age to a curriculum that preached the racial and cultural superiority of Anglo-Americans. Similarly, in recent decades, various studies have confirmed that while the persecution experienced by Jews in Europe was not replicated in the United States, the latter was not immune to anti-Semitism, which Leonard Dinnerstein asserted "has existed throughout American history" (1991, p. viii: see also Gerber, 1986; Mayo, 1988). Second, as we will see below, there is agreement among revisionists that this prejudice and stereotyping has regularly been accompanied by or acted as the prelude to ethnic exclusion in the form of both de facto and de jure segregation.

The themes of racism and nativism were not only emphasized by being given more prominence in both general and ethny-specific revisionist studies, but also by becoming the subject of investigation in their own right. For instance, building upon the foundations laid by Billington and Higham, a new generation of scholars turned their attention to the history of nativist movements in the United States. Donald Kinzer (1964) characterized the American Protective Association that flourished in the 1890s as more anti-Catholic than either anti-immigrant or anti-Semitic. In contrast, revisionist studies of the so-called "second" Ku Klux Klan, which emerged prior to World War I and flourished during the 1920s, depicted that movement as a veritable vortex of ethnic bigotry, encompassing racism, nativism, anti-Semitism and anti-Catholicism (Alexander, 1965; Chalmers, 1965; Jackson, 1967). "Following closely in the nativist tradition of the Know-Nothing party of the 1850s and the American Protective Association of the 1890s", noted Kenneth Jackson, ". . . the Ku Klux Klan presented itself as the defender of Americanism and the conservator of Christian ideals" (ibid., pp. xi–xii).

Critiques of Revisionism

Although the orthodox perspective has little to offer in the way of a refutation of the revisionist position, the latter, particularly in some of its more extreme forms, has increasingly been criticized for presenting an oversimplified picture of the issue of ethnic exclusion. For instance, historians specializing in the development of whiteness as a popular concept have demonstrated that the ethnic exclusion of white immigrant groups was not historically as proscriptive or insurmountable as that of nonwhite ethnies (Ignatiev, 1995; Roediger, 1991; Saxton, 1990). Moreover, it has been argued by some scholars – including exponents of both the assimilationist and pluralist-integrationist viewpoints, which are usually diametrically opposed to each other – that although the dominant society has in the past erected barriers to the inclusion of many ethnies, these exclusionary practices have lessened over time and, in recent decades, virtually disappeared. For example, Steinberg (1989 pp. 55–6) provides an assimilationist perspective on the decline of ethnic prejudice and discrimination, while Fuchs (1990, pp. 149–50) provides a pluralist-integration one. Similarly, recent research on the second Klan suggests that, despite its racist and nativist form, the movement was, both in its motivation and activities, more concerned with mainstream reform issues than those of race and ethnicity. Summarizing the new generation of studies to which his own work belongs, Leonard J. Moore suggested that it is more appropriate to view the second Klan as an essentially "populist" rather than "nativist" movement. "The Klan", stated Moore,

> appears to have acted as a kind of interest group for the average white
> Protestant who believed that his values should be dominant in

American society. Prohibition represented the great symbol of that desire, and support for Prohibition seemed to bond together the nation's Klansmen more tightly than any other single issue (1993, p. 34).

Research demonstrating links between the Progressive reform agenda of the 1900s and 1910s and issues upon which the 1920s Klan campaigned, such as improved government efficiency and accountability, even suggest that "the Klan became a means through which average citizens could resist elite political domination and attempt to make local and even state governments more responsive to popular interests" (ibid., p. 34: see also Jenkins, 1990; MacLean, 1994; Moore, 1991; Tucker, 1991).

"LAND OF THE FREE": EQUALITY OR INEQUALITY?

In the American ideological canon, the conceptualization of the United States as a welcoming society is intrinsically linked to the notion that it is also a country where all ethnies can expect to receive just and impartial treatment. Admittedly, inclusion may not in itself guarantee equality nor preclude inequality, but it is likely to make the former more attainable and the latter more difficult to sustain, just as exclusion is likely to do the opposite. The inclusion–exclusion and equality–inequality dichotomies, therefore, may not be absolutely identical, but they are almost inseparably intertwined. Moreover, in terms of historiography the orthodox and revisionist alignments on the two debates are virtually transposable.

The Orthodox Emphasis on Equality

For many decades, orthodox studies – using such documents as the Declaration of Independence and the Constitution as reference points – maintained that because American institutions were based upon universalist principles ethnies were legally invisible. Milton Gordon reflected a widely held view when he asserted that "the American political and legal system recognizes no distinction among its citizens on grounds of race, religion, or national origin" (1964, p. 4). In contrast to the Old World, it was argued, naturalization was a relatively quick and easy process in the United States and there are numerous examples of immigrant groups, such as the Irish, using citizenship as the route to a level of political involvement and representation generally denied them in their country of origin (Brown, 1966). Far from being excluded from membership of the body politic, claimed Oscar Handlin, "the newcomer was expected to become a citizen" and citizenship "made the foreigner an American, equal in rights with every other man" (1951, pp. 205–6). In tackling the anomalous cases of Native Americans and African Americans, two groups specifically referred to in both the Declaration of

Independence and the Constitution, orthodox scholars generally conceded that there had of course been exceptions to the rule of ethnic legal invisibility, but that is all that these cases are, exceptions. Gordon, for example, implied that the theory that American ethnies were "legally invisible" was not seriously compromised by the "special situation of the American Indian", or the "remaining Jim Crow laws of the South" and anti-miscegenation laws in many states which he correctly predicted were doomed to be declared unconstitutional by the Supreme Court (1964, p. 4).

The Revisionist Stress on Racial and Ethnic Inequality

From the late 1950s onwards, the orthodox position increasingly fell out of favor among historians and was criticized for being a very smug, complacent view of American ethnic history that inexcusably played down both the extent of inequality and its durability and long-term impact. The foundations for the revisionist critique had been laid in earlier decades. At the beginning of the twentieth century, Charles Beard's iconoclastic interpretation of the framing of the Constitution argued that the Founding Fathers were motivated more by their own class interests than a commitment to universalist principles (1914, pp. 1–18, 30, 151, 213). Although Beard's portrayal of the Constitution as an economic document has been roundly criticized, even his detractors acknowledged that both slaveholding states and those wishing to pursue aggressive policies against Native Americans perceived their interests to be best served by the establishment of the federal government (McDonald, 1958, pp. 129, 162, 369–74, 395).

An example of the traditional approach is Max Farrand's *The Framing of the Constitution of the United States* (1913). Farrand makes only one, very minor reference to Native Americans, while his most noteworthy comment relating to African Americans is the contention that "slavery was not the important question, . . . not the moral question that it became later" and consequently "there was comparatively little said on the subject in the convention" (p. 110). In contrast, Beard's work and the revisionist scholarship that it inspired revealed that Native Americans and African Americans, while barely receiving a mention in traditional accounts of the Philadelphia convention, were clearly on the minds of attending delegates. That said, the publication of Swedish social scientist Gunnar Myrdal's *An American Dilemma* (1944) probably constitutes a more plausible moment from which to date a recognizable shift in opinion away from the orthodox position. The dilemma Myrdal referred to was the nation's consistent failure to bring its treatment of ethnic minorities, specifically African Americans, into conformity with its expressed principles, or what he termed the "American Creed" that was based upon "the ideals of the essential dignity of the individual human being, of the fundamental equality of all men, and of certain inalienable rights to freedom, justice, and a fair opportunity" and was enshrined in such documents as the Declaration of Independence and the Constitution (1944, pp. xlvii, 4–5). By the late 1960s and early 1970s, the traditional depiction of the United States as the "land of the free" had been almost completely discredited by the findings of revisionist historians, who demonstrated irrefutably that there was a long history of ethnic-specific laws being enacted at both the state and federal levels. In *Red Man's Land/White Man's Law*, Wilcomb E. Washburn claimed that the framers of the Constitution treated Native Americans "not – with some exceptions – as individual citizens of the Union, but as members of distinct political communities with whom numerous treaty relationships, inherited by the United States from colonial days, existed" (1971, pp. 173, 242–3). This created a situation in which, as white domination of the American interior increased, individual Native Americans increasingly came under the control of the United States but could enjoy none of the rights of citizenship. A. Leon Higginbotham's book *In the Matter of Color* not only drew attention to the "failure of the nation's founders and their constitutional heirs to share the legacy of freedom with black Americans", but demonstrated that "judicial decisions and statutes" were among the primary "mechanisms of control" used to restrict African Americans' "activities and aspirations" (1978, pp. 6, 14). Like numerous revisionist scholars, Higginbotham revealed how many of white Americans' cherished achievements appeared differently when viewed from the position of the nation's ethnic minorities:

> From a black perspective, . . . the Constitution's references to justice, welfare, and liberty were mocked by the treatment meted out daily to blacks . . . through the courts, in legislative statutes, and in those provisions of the Constitution that sanctioned slavery for the majority of black Americans and allowed disparate treatment for those few blacks legally "free" (ibid., p. 6).

(On the legal discrimination, including disfranchisement and segregation, experienced by free blacks in the antebellum era, see Berlin, 1974; Curry, 1981; Litwack, 1961.)

With regards to the post-emancipation era, much has been written about the South's Jim Crow laws that segregated African Americans from the rest of the population and which served for many decades as "public symbols and constant reminders" of their inferior legal status (Woodward, 1955, p. 7). Revisionist studies revealed that this type of legislation was directed against a wide variety of ethnies, but particularly nonwhites, and invariably curtailed rather than expanded the constitutional rights of the groups concerned. Legalized discrimination, as modern studies of African Americans (Dittmer, 1977; McMillen, 1989; Rabinowitz, 1978), Asian Americans (Chan, 1991; Gyory,

1998; Konvitz, 1946; McClain, 1994; Salyer, 1995) and Mexican Americans (Carroll, 2003; González, 1990; Montejano, 1987) have shown, took numerous forms, including exclusion from citizenship, disenfranchisement, bars and limitations on immigration, economic sanctions, and bans on intermarriage.

Scholarship and the Historical Context: Civil Rights Era Origins of Revisionism

The scholarly assault on the orthodox perspective coincided with the African-American civil rights movement and the subsequent ethnic revival among white ethnies, both of which exerted a strong influence over the issues explored, groups examined and comparisons made in revisionist scholarship. Higginbotham, for instance, recalled how his historical research was inspired by his own involvement in a meeting convened on 5 April 1968 by President Lyndon Johnson to discuss responses to the wave of disturbances triggered by the assassination the day before of Martin Luther King, Jr:

> That morning, sitting in the White House, I knew there was an indisputable nexus between the dark shadow of repression under which, historically, most black Americans have lived and the rioting occurring within ten blocks of the White House. Why, I thought to myself, in the land of the free and the home of the brave, had even brave blacks so often failed to get free? Why had that very legal process that had been devised to protect the rights of individuals against the will of the government and the whim of the majority been often employed so malevolently against blacks? What were the options that ought to have been exercised years ago, even centuries ago, to narrow those disparities in meted-out justice that had periodically – and now once more – kindled black hatred and white fear? (1978, p. 4)

A wave of Chicano interpretations of Mexican-American history emerged at about the same time out of similar circumstances and concerns (De León, 1991; D. Gutiérrez, 1993). Rodolfo Acuña, whose *Occupied America: The Chicano's Struggle Toward Liberation* provided the first major revision of Mexican-American history since the appearance of Carey McWilliams's *North From Mexico* (1968 [1949]), later admitted that the first edition, published in 1972, "was angry, filled with moral outrage" and very much "influenced by the times" (1988, p. ix). At about the same time as white ethnics of various backgrounds, but particularly those of southern and eastern European ancestry, were beginning to complain vociferously that, like African Americans, they too had historically been denied equality of opportunity in the United States, revisionist scholars drew attention to the fact that conventional studies of the immigrant experience largely ignored the history of the so-called "new immigration" groups (Mann, 1979). Revisionists argued that because conventional histories usually chose the start of World War I – the event which heralded the end of mass immigration from Europe – as a cut-off point for their investigations into ethnic history, they failed to chart the countless episodes of ethnic discrimination experienced by southern and eastern European immigrants and their offspring in the years after 1914 (Vecoli, 1970, pp. 73, 80–1). "That the history of a society whose distinctive attribute has been its racial, cultural, linguistic, and religious pluralism", Rudolph Vecoli wryly noted, "should have been written for the most part from an Anglo-American monistic perspective is indeed a paradox" (ibid., pp. 73–4). This criticism of traditional accounts appears all the more damning when it is borne in mind that the 1920s witnessed a massive resurgence of nativist feeling, the effects of which – exemplified by draconian new immigration laws – were to last for many decades, of which facts scholars had long been aware (on the background to and impact of the restrictive immigration system established in the 1920s, see Higham, 1955; Divine, 1957).

The "New Ethnicity" Perspective: A Case of Jumping on the Bandwagon?

By drawing parallels between the previously overlooked white ethnics of southern and eastern European origin and more commonly acknowledged disadvantaged groups like African Americans, the "new ethnicity" perspective, as it came to be known, soon created cleavages within the ranks of revisionism. Specialists in the histories of African Americans, Mexican Americans, and Asian Americans, for instance, were at pains to rectify the misconception that the white "ethnic" experience was characterized by the same levels of exclusion and inequality as the nonwhite "racial" experience. Alexander Saxton was one of the first historians to differentiate between the experience of white ethnics and that of Asian Americans. The dominant society's treatment of Asian immigrants, observed Saxton, "while similar in many ways to what happened to other immigrants, is generally more like what happened to blacks, who were certainly not immigrants in the usual meaning of the term" (1971, p. 2). Later, Ronald Takaki expanded and clarified this conceptual distinction between white and nonwhite ethnies, asserting that race was the "social construction that has historically set apart racial minorities from European immigrant groups" and that "race in America has not been the same as ethnicity" (1993, p. 10). As already noted, this point was made most forcefully by exponents of the internal-colony model (Blauner, 1972, p. 56; Barrera, 1979, pp. 49–50). It also featured in early expositions of the split labor market theory, but these suggest that racial exclusion originated more in class conflict than the racism emphasized by internal-colony theorists (Bonacich, 1972, pp. 548, 552–3). These differences aside, the belief that the types of exclusion experienced by white "ethnic" groups and nonwhite "racial" ones are qualitatively different has since become the dominant opinion in revisionist circles (see, for example, Guglielmo and Lewis, 2003, p. 183).

Having exposed the long history of exclusion and inequality endured by America's nonwhite minorities in particular, revisionist scholars then turned to the task of explaining how these groups came to be racialized. Research revealed that numerous elements, including the state, organized labor, and even middle-class reformers, had played an important role in the process of racialization in the United States. In his pioneering study *The Indispensable Enemy*, Alexander Saxton revealed that trade union organizers, radical politicians, and Progressive reformers in late nineteenth- and early twentieth-century California all found that anti-Asian rhetoric consistently proved to be one of the most effective means of unifying the disparate elements from which their economic and political power were derived. To resolve the contradiction between the egalitarian ideals upon which the radical and reformist traditions were based and the rhetoric of exclusion frequently utilized by unionists, radicals, and reformers alike, the latter groups adopted a "racial definition of nationality", which provided justification for the "racial denial of citizenship". Moreover, Saxton persuasively argued that the Chinese experience in the American West was far from unique: not only had the attaching of a "racist addendum" to the American Creed long been practiced by eastern Democrats when dealing with the issue of black slavery, but "Chinese proscription" became a template for the treatment of other ethnies in other parts of the United States (1971, pp. 259, 261, 262–5, 268, 272, 279, 284). Michael Omi and Howard Winant (1986) called this process "racial formation" and claimed that the state played a central role in its development. Numerous studies have shown how lawmakers and judges consciously strove to bring legal interpretations of race into line with white assumptions about race and by doing so contributed to the hardening of racial demarcations within American society (Carter, et al., 1996; Fowler, 1987; Haney-Lopez, 1996; Pascoe, 1996). As F. James Davis has demonstrated, the most extreme example of this is the so-called "one-drop" rule by which "any person with any black ancestry" has traditionally been defined as black, regardless of how much non-black ancestry he or she might have (1991, p. 8). The fact that the dominant society fairly consciously promoted racialization as a means of excluding various ethnies is held up by revisionists as damning evidence of America's failure to adhere to its professed universalist ideals. Recently, a number of scholars working in the field of Native-American history have even gone so far as to challenge traditional views about the origins of America's universalist principles and institutions. Arguing that many of the ideas and mechanisms enshrined in the Constitution were actually borrowed from and are virtual replicas of Native-American practices, these historians suggest that the exclusion of the country's indigenous population from the body politic at the founding of the republic is steeped with irony (Grinde and Johansen, 1991; Lyons and Mohawk, 1992).

Revisionism, having begun in the 1950s as a sympathetic appeal to the nation to practice what it preached, had by the 1980s developed into a wholesale condemnation of American society's attitudes toward and treatment of ethnic minorities. Revisionism had become essentially pluralistic in outlook, depicting the United States as a country in which only white Anglo-Saxon Protestants, plus any white ethnics who were viewed as capable of and willing to embrace Anglo-conformity, could aspire to integration and equality of opportunity. In other words, a form of involuntary pluralism historically prevailed in the United States, which excluded and discriminated against all nonwhite and many white ethnies. This practice and the structures that supported it was often referred to as "institutional racism", an expression first used by Stokely Carmichael and Charles Hamilton in *Black Power* (1967, pp. 2–7). Probably the most sophisticated formulation of this viewpoint has come from Benjamin B. Ringer, in his 1983 opus *"We the People" and Others*. Ringer argued that ethnic relations in the United States have been characterized by a "Manichean dualism". The American duality arises from the existence of a "People's Domain" – established during the Revolution and defined by such documents as the Declaration of Independence and the Constitution – and the exclusion from this of nonwhites. "Within the Domain of the People", observed Ringer, "universalistic, egalitarian, achievement-oriented, and democratic norms and values were to be the ideals". However, American society's "normative environment", an inheritance of colonial times, "was still defined by a racial creed which stressed the separateness of the races and the inferiority of the nonwhite" (1983, p. 8). Consequently, nonwhites were excluded from the mainstream society and the rights that its members enjoyed. Ringer's study examines the cases of four nonwhite groups: Native Americans, African Americans, Asian Americans and Puerto Ricans. The experiences of nonwhites altered little during the transition from British colonial rule to American independence: Native Americans were still "overwhelmed by force of arms, deprived of their lands and resources, and treated as a conquered subject or inhuman enemy", while African Americans were still forced "to work as slaves and treated as dehumanized chattel property" (ibid., p. 8). Asian Americans "first got caught in this duality" after Chinese immigrants began arriving in the new state of California during the 1840s and 1850s (ibid., pp. 569, 578–9, 671–80). In the case of Puerto Rico, racial prejudice towards its predominantly nonwhite inhabitants motivated Congress to make the island "the first legally defined unincorporated territory without any promise of statehood or protection of the Constitution" (ibid., p. 947). After claiming that nonwhites, particularly African Americans, "continually challenged the legitimacy of the plural society that prevented them gaining access to the People's Domain" and called for an end to the duality, Ringer concluded that "America's historic treatment of its racial minorities has been both an expression and product of the dialectical tension and struggle between these two models" (ibid., p. 9).

Beyond the Equality–Inequality Dichotomy

During the 1980s and 1990s, this version of revisionism increasingly came under attack from scholars who argued that patterns of inclusion and exclusion, equality and inequality, were far more complex and variable than was credited by scholars subscribing to either the orthodox position or the extreme revisionist one. The emerging viewpoint represented a modification of revisionism that rested upon four sets of findings. Some scholars, while acknowledging the existence of institutionalized involuntary pluralism, noted that this was eventually phased out for all ethnies during the course of the twentieth century (Fuchs, 1990). Scholars investigating the history of whiteness conceded that integration and access to opportunity were dependent upon race, but showed that European immigrant ethnies were not immediately accepted into American society on terms of equality and had to earn their status as whites. Many newly-arrived European immigrants, James Barrett and David Roediger have noted, found themselves in an "inbetween" status:

> A whole range of evidence – laws; court cases; formal racial ideology; social conventions; popular culture in the form of slang, songs, films, cartoons, ethnic jokes, and popular theater – suggests that the native born and older immigrants often placed these newer immigrants not only *above* African and Asian Americans, for example, but also *below* "white" people (1997, p. 4).

Prior to World War II, it was unusual for a European ethny to be accepted as white without having first made a conscious effort to attain that status (ibid., pp. 28–34). According to Noel Ignatiev, the fact that immigrants from Ireland were eventually granted white status "was not the inevitable consequence of blind historic forces, still less of biology, but the result of choices made, by the Irish and others, from among available alternatives". "To enter the white race", stated Ignatiev, "was a strategy to secure an advantage in a competitive society" (1995, p. 2). Numerous studies also showed that the exclusion of nonwhite ethnies was not as complete as the radical revisionists had earlier suggested. For instance, Mexican Americans, and on occasions Asian Americans, appeared in some circumstances to occupy a half-way place between white and nonwhite status, a condition which even permitted some members of the minority group to gain relatively easy entry into mainstream society (Montejano, 1987, pp. 7, 84, 162,

180–1, 243–4; Kung, 1962, p. 216). Moreover, a growing body of research seemed to suggest that the concept of voluntary pluralism had become legitimized in American popular thought much earlier than previously believed. Many scholars now argue that, instead of being a scion of the Progressive Era that came to maturity in the 1960s, voluntary pluralism – and its accompanying commitment to equality of opportunity – was, for whites at least, the generally accepted ethnic pattern as early as the 1830s (Conzen, et al., 1992, pp. 10–11). Indeed, some interpretations pushed the date back even further. Lawrence Fuchs argued that voluntary pluralism originated in colonial Pennsylvania, which "sought immigrants who would be good citizens regardless of religious background" (1990, p. 8). According to Fuchs, the "Pennsylvania idea that European immigrants could become members of the polity on a basis of equal rights with native-born citizens regardless of the country they came from or the religion they believed in" triumphed over competing models that were either not pluralistic or not voluntaristic and became "the basis for US immigration and naturalization policy for white Europeans after the founding of the republic" (ibid., pp. 8, 33).

"SAFETY": ETHNIC VIOLENCE

It might be expected that of all the ideals exalted in the Declaration of Independence, "Life" and "Safety" would prove to be the easiest ones for the United States to live up to. After all, unlike other components of the American Creed, such as acceptance, freedom, and equality, the fulfillment of which involved acts of bestowal that were not without costs for the dominant society, particularly its elite members, the commitment to respect human life required only that the new nation refrained from depriving ethny members of something that they already possessed. If its worth is measured by the scarcity of scholarly research, then it would appear that this assumption is well founded, because the subject of dominant society violence against ethnic minorities has long been one of the most neglected in the field of American ethnic history.

The Orthodox Emphasis on Ethnic Harmony

An examination of the orthodox perspective on the intimidation of ethnic minorities quickly reveals why there has been a dearth of historical literature on the matter. Orthodox histories do not deny that the United States has witnessed the appearance of various nativist and racist movements, but the latter, it is argued, have been infrequent and generally short-lived. Similarly, ethnic violence is traditionally depicted as an aberration of the American Creed, the occurrence of which can largely be isolated to specific groups in specific locations at specific times. Ethnic intimidation has not, therefore, been either a commonplace or widespread phenomenon (Wade, 1969, p. 7; Hofstadter, 1970, pp. 4–5). According to orthodox historians, even slavery, an institution usually associated with cruelty and violence, assumed a mild and paternalistic form in the United States. Ulrich B. Phillips, whose work epitomized conventional interpretations, intimated that "injustice, oppression, brutality and heart-burning" were no more commonplace within southern slavery than they were in modern American society (1959 [1918], p. 514). Contrasting the antebellum plantation with the latifundia of classical times, Phillips asserted: "There was plenty of coercion in the South; but in comparison with the harshness of the Roman system the American regime was essentially mild" (ibid., p. 342). Phillips, it should be noted, subscribed wholeheartedly to the theory of black racial inferiority that was so prevalent among Americans during the early twentieth century (ibid., pp. 291, 339, 341–3). Moreover, as a Southerner, Phillips was clearly motivated by a desire to defend his native region's record on race relations. "Every plantation of the standard Southern type", he wrote, "was, in fact, a school constantly training and controlling pupils who were in a backward state of civilization". It is hardly surprising, therefore, that Phillips found southern slavery to be characterized by "paternalism rather than repression" (ibid., p. 342). This view held sway within the historical profession throughout the first half of the twentieth century.

The Revisionist Stress on Intimidation

During the 1950s, the orthodox perspective on ethnic violence was totally and irrevocably discredited by the publication of two seminal revisionist works. The first book, Higham's *Strangers in the Land*, demonstrated that, not only were deep-seated nativist and racist hostilities persistently simmering below the surface of American society, but that they regularly manifested themselves in the form of violence during the period 1860–1925. Higham revealed that Italian, Jewish, and German immigrants had all at one time or another been on the receiving end of "anti-foreign" violence, including public floggings, tar-and-featherings, lynchings, and full-scale riots (1955, pp. 48, 89–92, 169, 184–6, 208–9, 264, 429). However, Higham readily conceded that "[n]o variety of anti-European sentiment . . . ever approached the violent extremes to which anti-Chinese agitation went in the 1870s and 1880s" (ibid., p. 25). The second book, Kenneth Stampp's *The Peculiar Institution: Slavery in the Ante-Bellum South*, showed that African-American bondage rested funda-mentally upon the constant threat and frequent use of violence. Stampp claimed that "cruelty was endemic in all slaveholding communities" and that on the large plantations – where the "typical overseer seemed to have little confidence in the use of incentives as a method of governing" and "had a decided preference for physical force" – the slave system was characterized by "brutality" (1956, pp. 183, 185). Stanley Elkins, in his highly controversial book *Slavery: A Problem in American Institutional and Intellectual Life* (1959), took the revisionist interpretation a step further by drawing parallels between the experiences of the southern plantation slave and the Nazi concentration camp inmate. According to Elkins, the southern plantation system was so harsh that it virtually dehumanized black slaves and stripped them of their personalities. As already noted (see Chapter 1), Elkins's interpretation attracted criticism from a variety of directions (see also Fredrickson, 1988, pp. 112–24). Robert Fogel and Stanley Engerman pulled the debate in completely the opposite direction with their two-volume work, *Time on the Cross* (1974). Making much of the scientific methods used in their research, such as computer-assisted analyses of plantation records, Fogel and Engerman reduced the slave-owners' use of force against the slaves to the level of a statistic showing the average number of whippings dealt out per slave per year and then declared that these whippings were nowhere near as common as previously believed. The response to these claims was swift and the criticisms withering. Traditionalists questioned the appropriateness of evaluating slavery's severity principally in statistical terms, whereas critics more au fait with "cliometric" methodology convincingly demonstrated that Fogel and Engerman's findings were frequently based upon an unsound handling of both quantitative and qualitative materials (David, et al., 1976).

Subsequent revisionist studies have shown that violent intimidation at the hands of the dominant society has been a characteristic of many an ethny's historical experience, as well as being a phenomenon that has materialized in most regions of the United States and periods of its history. In an exploratory essay that noted the "extraordinary frequency" and "sheer commonplaceness" of violence in American history and identified riots as "the most important single form of domestic violence", Richard Hofstadter asserted that "by far the greatest number of riots have arisen out of ethnic-religious or racial antagonisms" (1970, pp. 7, 13). Hofstadter argued not only that ethnic and racial conflict had "overshadowed" class conflict in the nation's history, but that "class war", when it had "flared up" in the United States, had "seldom taken place in a clear atmosphere, unclouded by our racial-ethnic antagonisms and by our complex hierarchy of status based upon religious-ethnic-racial qualities" (ibid., p. 13). Nonetheless, Hofstadter also emphasized the "circumscribed character and the small scale of the typical violent incident" (ibid., p. 7). Richard C. Wade made a similar observation in a probing essay on urban violence: "Attacks on immigrants seldom produced an encore, though they might have an analogue in some other city in the same month or year" (1969, pp. 21–2). Moreover, Wade contended that ethnic violence had minimal long-term impact. "Though the immigrants suffered a good deal at the hands of nativists", wrote Wade, "the bitterness engendered by riots and disorders . . .

did not slow down for long the process of their incorporation into American life" (ibid., p. 23). However, Wade took pains to point out that "race riots", by which he meant primarily white attacks on blacks, "were almost always different from other kinds of disorders": "[t]heir roots went deeper", "they broke out with increasing frequency", "their intensity mounted rather than declined" and "between major disorders the incidence of small-scale violence was always high" (ibid., p. 24). Interestingly, Hofstadter, Wade, and other revisionist writers, inspired as they were by the urban race riots erupting around them during the "long hot summers" of the 1960s, reminded a forgetful public that anti-black violence, though typified by the southern practice of lynching, was in the early twentieth century equally likely to take the form of a race riot in a northern city (Boskin, 1976; Rudwick, 1964; Sandburg, 1969; Shogan and Craig, 1964; Tuttle, 1972). Studies by William Ivy Hair (1976), Robert Haynes (1976), and Scott Ellsworth (1982), have also drawn attention to early twentieth-century race riots in southern cities. Subsequent scholarship has also provided a more detailed analysis of such neglected topics as ante-bellum nativist violence (Feldberg, 1975) and the fairly widespread and severe anti-German violence that occurred during World War I (Luebke, 1974). Similarly, revisionism has drawn attention to the experiences of nonwhite ethnies, like Asian Americans and Mexican Americans, who, though frequently the targets of ethnic violence, had largely been overlooked in historical treatments of the subject. Acknowledging this oversight in the preface to the second edition of *Strangers in the Land*, John Higham conceded that earlier he had "regarded opposition to certain non-European peoples, such as the Chinese and, to a lesser extent, the Japanese, as somewhat separate phenomena, historically tangential to the main currents of American nativism" (1963, p. vii). As noted above, Alexander Saxton has been one of the pioneers in the task of integrating the Asian-American experience into the mainstream of American ethnic history. As well as showing how the policy of "abatement by violence" promulgated by California labor leaders fueled a "series of pogroms which resulted in the dispossession and murder of Chinese and the leveling of small town ghettoes from San Diego to Seattle" during the 1880s, Saxton's *The Indispensable Enemy* demonstrated a direct link between the anti-Chinese movement in the West and the later nation-wide hostility toward immigrants from southern and eastern Europe (1971, p. 268). Despite the frequency of anti-Asian violence in late nineteenth- and early twentieth-century America and the regularity with which scholars refer to the phenomenon, it is surprising that, with the exception of numerous article-length case studies, no in-depth analysis of the topic has yet to appear (Karlin, 1948 and 1954; Carranco, 1961; Hallberg, 1973; Tanaka, 1978; De Witt, 1979; Showalter, 1989; Laurie, 1990a and 1990b). F. Arturo Rosales recently contended that while "large-scale outbursts against immigration began in the nineteenth century when Anglo-Americans reacted first to the influx of Catholic Irish and German newcomers and then to Asians and southern and eastern Europeans", during the twentieth century "Mexicans have been the main recipients of such antipathy" (1999, p. 1). According to Rosales's estimates, there were at least 157 incidents of civilian violence toward Mexicans, ranging from lynchings to riots, during the period 1900–30 (pp. 100–15). Moreover, the revisionist perspective initiated a re-interpretation of United States military actions against Native Americans and Mexicans, which came to be viewed by many scholars, particularly those influenced by internal-colony theory, as cases of legally sanctioned ethnic intimidation (Acuña, 1972; Barrera, 1979; Blauner, 1972; Drinnon, 1980; Limerick, 1987; Matthiessen, 1983; Slotkin, 1973; Utley, 1984).

Revisionism and the Debate over the Origins of Ethnic Violence

Having successfully repudiated the orthodox view that ethnic intimidation has been an infrequent occurrence in American history, revisionist scholarship has in recent decades mostly focused upon uncovering the causes of the phenomenon. Initially, this task largely involved disproving the theory that attacks on ethnies were usually motivated by a specific and genuine grievance against the targeted group. For instance, it was long believed that lynching was a direct response to the raping of white women by black men, an assertion that revisionist scholarship has demonstrated to be entirely spurious. To be fair, anti-lynching campaigners and social scientists largely accomplished the task of debunking these myths long before historians began to show a serious interest in the subject in the late 1970s (Brundage, 1997, pp. 5–10). In recent decades, the search for an underlying cause of ethnic violence – a search, it might be added, that has largely focused upon racial violence, especially the lynching of blacks, in the South – has produced three broad types of study: those that emphasize socio-economic factors, those that emphasize cultural factors, and those that draw upon both of these sets of factors (see Brundage, 1993, pp. 1–16, and 1997, pp. 1–20). The first approach has been more favored by social scientists than historians, so it is only fitting that the book which best exemplifies it – Stewart Tolnay and E. M. Beck's *A Festival of Violence: An Analysis of Southern Lynchings, 1882–1930* (1995) – was written by two sociologists. Tolnay and Beck identified correlations between trends in the level of lynching and fluctuations in such factors as the economy and the ethnic composition of the population. The second type of approach, the preferred choice among historians until recently, tended to see white attacks on blacks in the South as very much an outgrowth of one or more of the region's cultural peculiarities; deep-seated racism, an anachronistic code of honor, psychosexual anxieties, or rigid patriarchal attitudes (Ayers, 1984; Brown, 1983; Hall, 1979; Williamson, 1984). Clearly, each of these approaches has its strengths and weaknesses: while the former affords an easily comprehensible overview but downplays local variations, the latter lends itself readily to explaining individual case studies but not so well to making usable generalizations. Consequently, W. Fitzhugh Brundage alerted scholars to the need for studies which displayed "an understanding of both variations in the salience of racist ideologies from era to era and the specific historical circumstances of racially inspired violence" (1993, p. 13). In short, historians should approach the study of lynching in a way that combines the advantages of the socio-economic and cultural perspectives but avoids their respective pitfalls.

Interpretations of the origins of anti-black riots in the urban North have also undergone revisions similar to those on the causes of lynching. Comparing the three most serious race riots of the early twentieth century – East St Louis in 1917, Chicago in 1919, and Detroit in 1943 – Elliott Rudwick dismissed the traditional view that these were triggered by black provocation and argued instead that they originated in the "status struggle between Negroes and whites" (1964, p. 232). "In the three cities", noted Rudwick,

> the racial violence resulted from: threats to the security of whites brought on by the Negroes' gains in economic, political, and social status; Negro resentment of the attempts to "kick him back into his place"; and the weakness of the "external forces of constraint" – the city government, especially the police department (ibid., p. 217).

Rudwick concluded his study with the observations that "the last major race riot took place over two decades ago" and that the contemporaneous civil rights movement "has thus far occurred without a major race riot" (ibid., p. 233). Ironically, in the very same year that Rudwick's study was published Harlem became the site of the first major race riot since the Detroit disturbances and set a pattern of African Americans responding with violence to a combination of police brutality and white indifference to black poverty that was replicated in cities across the United States during the second half of the 1960s.

Redressing Revisionism's Biases and Limitations

While deserving credit for debunking the myth of America as a country historically immune to ethnic violence, revisionist scholarship has engendered, albeit largely unintentionally, an equally over-simplified view of history as that which prevailed during the early twentieth century. Whereas orthodox historians turned a blind eye to the tradition of ethnic intimidation that invalidated their interpretation of American ethnic history, many modern scholars are apt to assign more importance to the phenomenon than the evidence before them supports. For instance, scholars commonly characterize the United States as a country long plagued by ethnically motivated violence and yet back up their assertions with little more than a brief reference to some of the nation's most well-known nativist and racist movements. A notable example of this uncritical approach is the mythical status often ascribed to the Ku Klux Klan, the mere mention of which is regularly deemed sufficient proof in itself of the existence of ethnically motivated violence. Nowhere is this tendency more evident than in early historical treatments of the 1920s Ku Klux Klan revival. During the late 1950s, a string of eminent historians provided brief but influential portraits of the second Klan that characterized it as essentially nativist – that is, anti-Catholic, anti-Semitic, and anti-immigrant, as opposed to racist and anti-black – and "inherently violent" (Moore, 1993, pp. 21–2). William Leuchtenburg (1958, p. 211) reflected the opinions of historians like Richard Hofstadter (1955, pp. 291–5, 297, 299), John Higham (1955, pp. 294–5), and John D. Hicks (1960, p. 95), when he wrote: "Wherever the Klan entered, in its wake came floggings, kidnappings, branding with acid, mutilations, church burnings, and even murder". Robert Moats Miller took this theme further by placing the second Klan in the same category as the European fascist movements of the interwar period and, with reference to the organization's apparent "predilection for violence", commented: "Contemporary observers tended to exaggerate the extent of Klan violence, but perhaps recent scholarship has swung too far in its minimization of it" (1968, p. 238). Nancy MacLean's *Behind the Mask of Chivalry* also draws the comparison with European fascism (1994, pp. 179–84). This image of the second Klan, as an organization preoccupied with terrorizing racial and ethnic minorities, still appears in many of the standard surveys of American ethnic history (Barkan, 1996, p. 19; Heinze, 2003, pp. 145–6). However, recent studies of the 1920s Ku Klux Klan reveal not only that the movement was largely peaceful but that when it did take a violent form ethnic minorities were less likely to be the targets than gamblers, bootleggers, adulterers or other persons deemed to be engaged in immoral activity. As Shawn Lay has noted, virtually all of the numerous new case studies that have appeared since the late 1970s tended to support the view that the second Klan "rarely engaged in violent vigilantism" (1994, p. 668). In contrast to the debate surrounding the nature of the second Klan, it is virtually beyond dispute that the first Klan was essentially a white supremacist organization that freely resorted to terrorism in the pursuit of its aims (Chalmers, 1987, pp. 424–5; Trelease, 1995 [1971], pp. xli–xlviii).

More generally, while scholars freely wax lyrical about the ignominious episodes in America's past, few care to mention the fact that dominant group intimidation of ethnic minorities has been steadily decreasing throughout the nation's history. Major outbreaks of ethnic violence directed at European immigrants, for example, although commonplace during the antebellum period, had become a rarity by the early twentieth century. As Richard Wade has observed, "[e]ven when people organized on a large scale against minority groups – such as the Americans' Protective Association in the 1890s or the Ku Klux Klan in the 1920s – they have seldom been able to create major riots or disorders" (1969, pp. 23–4). Moreover, in hindsight it is even possible to reject Wade's more pessimistic view about future trends in racial violence – writing in the late 1960s he feared that "the summers will remain long and hot" – in favor of the more sanguine prediction of one of his contemporaries, Richard Hofstadter. Recognizing that black ghetto riots were "tapering off", Hofstadter implied that one day the 1960s might be viewed as just "another peak period, rather more pronounced than many, which is followed by relative calm" (1970, pp. 40, 42). If racial violence in the United States is indeed cyclical, as Hofstadter stated was the case for American violence generally, then the evidence from the period since the late 1960s would suggest that the cycle is following a downward spiral.

To be fair, the major problem with modern scholarship on ethnic violence is not its bias but it scarcity. No single aspect of American ethnic history is in need of more comprehensive and detailed investigation than that of dominant society intimidation of minorities. Admittedly, recent decades have witnessed the publication of some excellent monographs, especially on the subject of southern lynching. Indeed, it is creditworthy that a field, which was aptly described in the early 1990s as having "only recently moved beyond its infancy", had matured immensely by the end of the same decade (Brundage, 1993, p. 8). However, the abundance of recent studies on anti-black violence is matched by a dearth of works on most other ethnies. Moreover, this imbalance makes the possibility of achieving a fully comparative view of ethnic violence, which the topic is desperately in need of, all the more remote.

SUMMARY

Clearly, scholarship on ethnicity demonstrates that American society has throughout its history been inconsistent in adhering to its professed principles of freedom and equality. However, the heavy emphasis upon victimization in many revisionist works implies that ethnies exercised little agency or control over their destinies. As we will see in subsequent chapters, only recently have significant advances been made in challenging and transcending what Alex M. Saragoza aptly labeled the "them-versus-us" perspective on American ethnic history (1988–90, p. 8).

FIVE

Ethnic Incorporation

INTRODUCTION

As the previous chapter demonstrated, the controversies over integration and equality, which together constitute the inclusion/equality–exclusion/inequality dichotomy, clearly pose questions that are central to our understanding of American ethnic history. How easily and at what levels have ethnic and racial minorities been incorporated, if at all, into the social and economic structures of the United States? Has incorporation been a uniform process or has it varied from ethny to ethny? To gain a deeper insight into these debates and the issues they raise it is worth examining three topics, each of which is the subject of hotly contested inquiry, that are closely related to the general discussion of ethnic incorporation: residential patterns, educational provision, and economic opportunities.

RESIDENTIAL PATTERNS

At first glance, the issue of ethnic spatial separation seems to be more relevant to the inclusion-exclusion dichotomy than the equality-inequality one, but this impression is misleading. Scholarly investigation of ethnic residential patterns is not merely confined to determining who lived where and then making judgments on whether levels of separation were low or high, it also addresses the question of why spatial separation existed at all. Is residential concentration something that ethnies voluntarily opted for or was it forced upon them by the dominant society? If the latter, what was the motivation behind using residential segregation as a means of ethnic exclusion and to what extent, if any, did it produce inequality?

Origins of the Ghetto Model

Ethnic residential concentration is treated in orthodox accounts as a phenomenon that was, if not uncommon, then at least temporary in duration and, if not entirely voluntary, then at least accidental in origin. That said, ethnic residential patterns is a subject that for a long time was generally either ignored or accorded cursory examination by historians. Writing during the post-World War I era, the first generation of immigration historians, like most other scholars of American history at the time, were greatly influenced by the Turnerian view of the frontier as an ethnic melting pot and consequently focused their attention upon the erosion rather than consolidation of group boundaries (Blegen, 1940; Hansen, 1964 [1940]; Stephenson, 1926; Wittke, 1939: see also Berthoff, 1953, pp. 210–11). This trend was compounded by the "old" immigration bias in immigration scholarship, because few historians examined the experiences of the "new" immigrants who were less likely to settle in rural areas and consequently more likely to reside in urban ethnic neighborhoods (Hansen, 1964 [1940]). Although some orthodox perspective historians did eventually identify the tendency among urban-based immigrants to reside in ethnic ghettos, no attempt was made to study the phenomenon in greater detail. In 1901, Frederick Jackson Turner perceived the "congestion of foreigners in localities in our great cities" as both a characteristic of the "new" immigration of the late nineteenth century and as an impediment to the assimilation process that had apparently proceeded apace among the "old" immigrants on the agrarian frontier (Saveth, 1965 [1948], pp. 128–30). By the time of his death, Turner was attributing the same characteristics of congregation in cities, links with the rise of slum conditions, and a challenge to assimilation to the antebellum wave of immigration, mostly composed of Irish and Germans (1935, pp. 43, 93–6, 579, [608]).

The task of formulating a framework for the understanding of ethnic residential patterns in American cities was left to several generations of social scientists who, inspired by the pioneering work of Chicago School sociologists like Robert Ezra Park and Ernest W. Burgess, embarked upon a multitude of studies from the 1920s onwards. In his seminal essay "The Growth of the City", Burgess portrayed the modern city as composed of a series of concentric zones. At the heart of the city, in the zone of "transition" or "deterioration", expanding commercial and manufacturing districts competed with "slums" for urban space. These slums, noted Burgess, were "crowded to overflowing with immigrant colonies – the [Jewish] Ghetto, Little Sicily, Greektown, Chinatown" and the more impoverished parts of the "Black Belt" (1925, pp. 50–1, 54, 56). This zone was encircled by one of relatively stable working-class neighborhoods, which was itself ringed by areas of progressively more affluent middle-class residences, many of which were located in "restricted" districts that excluded some ethnic groups. Ongoing migration created a pattern of ethnic neighborhood "invasion" and "succession", with each new influx of migrants having the

> effect of a tidal wave inundating first the immigrant colonies, the ports of first entry, dislodging thousands of inhabitants who overflow into the next zone, and so on until the momentum of the wave has spent its force on the last urban zone (ibid., pp. 50, 57–8).

The zone of "workingmen's homes", therefore, was "an area of second immigrant settlement", the "region of escape from the slum" largely inhabited by second-generation ethnics (ibid., p. 56). Nonetheless, early social science studies still implied that the long-term trend was towards residential dispersion, because they depicted inner-city ethnic ghettos as places where newly-arrived immigrants settled in order to gain a footing in the United States and use as a base from which to enter into mainstream society (Cressey, 1938, pp. 65–9). This tradition, as Stanley Lieberson's *Ethnic Patterns in American Cities* (1963) exemplifies, long persisted in sociological scholarship. Most of this social science research focused upon the experiences of white immigrants residing in the great industrial urban centers of the East and Midwest; nonwhite and rural-based ethnies were largely ignored. Scholars were not only slow in turning their attention to nonwhite city-dwellers, like African Americans, for example, but they failed to view the concentration of Native Americans on rural reservations as linked to the wider picture of ethnic spatial separation. That said, social scientists had produced a sizeable and valuable body of work on the lives of African-American city-dwellers – ranging from W. E. B. Du Bois's pioneering *The Philadelphia Negro* (1996 [1899]) to St Clair Drake and Horace Cayton's classic *Black Metropolis* (1945), focusing on Chicago – a full two decades before historians made any significant contribution to the field (see Kusmer, 1986; Trotter, 1995).

Oscar Handlin incorporated much of the Chicago School theory of urban ecology into his various treatments of immigrant city life. In *Boston's Immigrants, 1790–1865*, Handlin equated economic mobility with geographic mobility, arguing that the low economic status of most Irish immigrants meant that they did not generally participate in the "centrifugal movement [that] winnowed the well-to-do from the impoverished". The dispersal of the city's French, German, and English immigrant populations, which Handlin attributed to these groups' more varied economic activities and greater affluence, "consequently segregated the great mass of Irish within the narrow limits of old Boston" (1941, pp. 94–7). In a chapter of *The Uprooted* entitled "The Ghettos", Handlin observed how the "immigrants find their first homes in quarters the old occupants no longer desire", noting that "the available housing gave the districts to which the immigrants went the character of slums" (1951, p. 146). Although Handlin viewed the ethnic ghetto as the product of chance rather than design, he devoted considerable space to detailing the squalor and misery endured by its inhabitants (1941, pp. 106–27; 1951, pp. 144–64). Handlin was also fairly pessimistic about the efficacy of the immigrants' resettlement in outlying but adjacent zones which he viewed as only a temporary escape from the conditions of the ever-encroaching ghetto (1951, pp. 164–9).

Handlin (1951, pp. 146, 164) and other orthodox historians (Cole, 1963, pp. 109–12; Rischin, 1962, pp. 79, 92–4), like Burgess (1925, pp. 54, 56) and the urban ecologists before them, also viewed the ethnic ghetto as a temporary phase in the life of immigrant groups. As Robert Ernst wrote in his study of immigrant life in antebellum New York:

> The immigrant community, like a decompression chamber,
> represented a place and a time of adjustment from one atmosphere to
> another. The psychological transition from alien to American was
> slow, lasting over several generations, but the first and most important
> stage occurred in the immigrant settlement, where there was a
> constant struggle between the old and the new (1979 [1949], p. 46).

However, Ernst, noting the importance of both "[n]ative prejudice against foreigners" and ethnic "group consciousness", maintained that the initial location and subsequent consolidation of ethnic neighborhoods were determined by more than merely impersonal economic factors. Foreshadowing by many decades some of the arguments of revisionist scholars, Ernst claimed that "[o]nce a nucleus was established toward which later arrivals were attracted, the cohesive bond resulting from consciousness of similarity tended to replace the magnetic forces of cheap shelter and ready employment" (ibid., pp. 37, 40: see also Cole, 1963, p. 153; Rischin, 1962, p. 79). According to Ernst, the existence of multiple ethnic districts, especially in Lower Manhattan, gave New York City the "aspect of a polyglot boardinghouse" (1979 [1949], p. 47). Although Ernst depicts a pluralistic ethnic landscape in urban New York, this observation is by no means a contradiction of the assimilationist bent of orthodox scholarship. The orthodox model of urban ecology first mapped out by Burgess clearly portrays ethnic residential patterns as characterized by initial concentration followed by ever-increasing dispersal, a pattern that supposedly mirrored the immigrant's passage along the socio-cultural continuum that began in pluralism and ended in assimilation. It was possible, therefore, for orthodox scholars to equate ethnic residential segregation with cultural pluralism and residential dispersal with assimilation without undermining the essentially assimilationist basis of their argument.

Challenging the Ghetto Model

Since the late 1960s, however, numerous researchers have argued that traditional scholarship exaggerated both the extent to which migrants to the city
congregated in distinct ethnic enclaves and also the role that cultural bonds
played in determining settlement patterns (Conzen, 1979; Warner and Burke,
1969; Chudacoff, 1973). David Ward, for instance, claimed that "the Irish and
German immigrants who arrived in American cities before the Civil War found
housing in almost every section of the city" (1971, p. 120). Moreover, Ward
attributed the "proportionately greater concentration of new arrivals from
southern and eastern Europe" in the late nineteenth century less to cultural
factors than to changes in the urban environment – such as the growth of intra-
urban transportation, which permitted middle-income groups to relocate to the
commuter belt, and the increasing centralization of urban employment, which
gave the relatively less skilled and lower-paid new arrivals an incentive to
remain close to the main sites of employment in the inner city (ibid., pp. 120–1).
Indeed, Humbert Nelli contended that the "size", "cohesiveness" and "unity"
of early residential concentrations among even the "new" immigration groups,
like Italians, had traditionally been "exaggerated" (1970, p. 53). In *Mobile
Americans* (1972), Howard Chudacoff also identified substantial residential
mobility but minimal ethnic clustering in Omaha during the period 1880–1920.
Prior to the 1920s, asserted Nelli, "no set, rigid, and unchanging Italian colony
existed" in Chicago and Italians not only "exhibited a high degree of residential
mobility" but from the onset of the group's settlement in the city many
immigrants had established themselves in areas outside of the central district
(1970, p. 53). Similarly, Ward stated that the "boundaries of ethnic ghettoes
were seldom fixed or well defined and mixed ethnic populations lived in many
immigrant districts" (1971, p. 121). Moreover, he claimed that "[e]ven the
largest and most stable immigrant groups were unable . . . to establish
enduring ghettoes in central fringe areas" close to the business district and
that the lifecycle of ethnic neighborhoods was determined not by the "sentiments and values of the occupants" but by "the timing, scale, and direction of
the expansion of adjacent non-residential land uses and on the appropriateness
of the original housing for multi-family occupancy or a higher density of single-
families" (ibid., pp. 118, 119, 121). The various works that emerged in the late
1970s and early 1980s from the monumental and renowned Philadelphia Social
History Project (PSHP), which utilized computer analysis of statistical sources,
tended to lend support to many of Ward's arguments (Burstein, 1981; Greenberg, 1981) and, though he was reluctant to admit it, Dean Esslinger's findings
also seemed to suggest that occupation exerted a stronger influence than
ethnicity upon residential patterns in late nineteenth-century South Bend,
Indiana (1975, pp. 45–68).

Revisionist Perspectives on Ethnic Residential Patterns

In contrast to the orthodox position, revisionists view ethnic residential concentration as extensive, durable, and in many cases the deliberate outcome of dominant society policies and practices. As early as the 1930s, Grant Foreman's pioneering studies of Native-American history examined the forced relocation of eastern tribes during the antebellum period, charting the origins of a policy that culminated in the Indian reservation system and produced extremely high levels of ethnic spatial separation, not to mention "demoralization and impoverishment" (1934, p. viii: see also Foreman, 1932 and 1946; Young, 1958). More recently, Donald Fixico's *Termination and Relocation* demonstrated how federal efforts to dissolve the trust status of tribal communities and disband the reservations led to the dispersal and urbanization of large segments of the Native-American population from the 1950s onwards (1986, pp. 134–57). However, these works were not set within the context of wider ethnic residential segregation and cannot be viewed as heralding the onset of a major revisionist challenge to orthodoxy, which was not to occur until the early 1960s. Once again, revisionism originated in the social sciences, with the publication of Karl and Alma Taeuber's path-breaking demographic study, *Negroes in Cities* (1965). The Taeubers found that, in contrast to the traditional picture of ever-decreasing levels of ethnic residential segregation the situation for urban-based African Americans was exactly the reverse, with the group tending to become more segregated throughout the course of the twentieth century. The Taeubers based their finding on an index of dissimilarity that used the city block as the unit of measurement and ranked levels of ethnic residential segregation on a scale of 0 to 100, with figures below 30 representing minimal segregation and figures over 90 representing almost total segregation (ibid., pp. 203–4, 223–38). Interestingly, the Taeubers used virtually the same methodology as Stanley Lieberson (1963, pp. 30–40) did in his earlier study, but while he discovered a downward trend in levels of spatial separation for white ethnics they found an upward one for blacks.

This pioneering sociological work was soon followed by Gilbert Osofsky's *Harlem: The Making of a Ghetto* (1966) and Allan H. Spear's *Black Chicago: The Making of a Negro Ghetto, 1890–1920* (1967), two books which stimulated a burgeoning of historical research into ethnic residential patterns that was not just restricted to the case of African Americans (see also Kusmer, 1976; Connolly, 1977; Trotter, 1985, pp. 264–82). By the early 1970s, discussions of ethnic spatial separation featured prominently in scholarship influenced by internal-colony theory, which regularly compared the experiences of different nonwhite ethnies and emphasized their similarity and interconnectedness. While the works of Osofsky, Spear and others described the "ghettoization" of black urbanites, Albert Camarillo coined the term "barrioization" to refer to "the formation of residentially and socially segregated Chicano barrios or neighborhoods" in the urban Southwest (1979, p. 53). Camarillo presented this process as a Mexican retreat into a "closed Mexican social universe" when "confronted by a hostile outside world" dominated by Anglos. The confinement in barrios had a twofold effect: it protected the cultural heritage of the Mexican community but it also facilitated their further marginalization socially, economically and politically (ibid., pp. 53–4, 117–26: see also Griswold del Castillo, 1979; Romo, 1983). As Stanford Lyman pointed out, another ethnic ghetto, the ubiquitous "Chinatown", seemed to originate in similar circumstances and perform similar functions to the Mexican urban barrio: "Chinatown acted as a partial buffer against the prejudices, hatreds, and depredations of hostile whites" and was a place where the urban Chinese "attempted to build a secure if not prosperous life" (1970, pp. 78, 98).

Another body of revisionist scholarship revisited the issue of residential consolidation among European immigrants. Exploring in greater depth themes that had earlier been touched upon by Robert Ernst, scholars like Josef Barton (1975), John Briggs (1978), Caroline Golab (1977a), and Virginia Yans-McLaughlin (1977), and more recently Dino Cinel (1982), Donna Gabaccia (1984), and Ewa Morawska (1985), all emphasized the role that immigrant networks played in determining ethnic residential patterns. While acknowledging the influence of external and impersonal factors, these scholars drew attention to the cultural capital possessed by and agency exercised by the immigrants. "Their coming to America", asserted Caroline Golab, "their settling in its cities; their settling in a particular city, region or neighborhood . . . these were not random or haphazard events", but the products of "[d]emographic and cultural as well as economic forces" (1977a, p. 7). "Work", Golab observed, "was the original impetus for the creation and location of the neighborhood", but "[i]n its maturity the ethnic neighborhood represented a balance of work, geography and ethnicity" (ibid., p. 164). Virginia Yans-McLaughlin (1977, p. 118) was even more forthright in her exposition of the revisionist viewpoint:

> . . . economics and prejudice by themselves fail to explain residential segregation into low-income neighborhoods. The process of chain migration also helped to perpetuate it. The personal rewards reaped by living close to relatives and townsmen who shared one's own language, culture, and class experience were very meaningful. Life in the Italian quarter provided a coherence and familiarity which drew immigrants irresistibly toward it.

Although they differ in various ways, these revisionist works all place an emphasis on the agency exercised by immigrants in the process of creating ethnic neighborhoods that the traditional "ghetto" school, as exemplified by Handlin, rarely acknowledged.

In subsequent years, scholarly interest in ethnic residential patterns was kept alive by, among other things, the ongoing debate over the origins and character of the so-called "second ghetto" which some historians argue exists today in many large American cities. This second ghetto – generally inhabited by poor African Americans – is differentiated from the first ghetto which took shape during the first half of the twentieth century by its more persistent and severe social deprivation and by its greater social and economic isolation from mainstream America. According to Arnold Hirsch, the "reasons for making a distinction between the 'first ghetto' of the World War I era and the 'second ghetto' of the post-World War II period are quantitative, temporal, and qualitative" (1983, p. 2). Using Chicago as a case study, Hirsch demonstrated that the quantitative and temporal differences between the first and second ghettos derived from the facts that the black population was ten times larger and constituted a much higher proportion of the city's total population (30 per cent as opposed to 4 per cent) in the 1960s than in the 1920s and that this demographic shift had largely occurred after 1945 (ibid., p. 3). However, the qualitative, and "most distinguishing feature of the post-World War II ghetto expansion", was "that it was carried out with government sanction and support", largely through "urban redevelopment and renewal policies, as well as a massive public housing program" (ibid., pp. 9–10). Despite some subtle differences, Hirsch's interpretation does not depart significantly from the pattern established by Osofsky, Spear, and other "ghetto synthesis" scholars, of portraying residential segregation as something that urban blacks had imposed upon them rather than opted for voluntarily.

Key Themes in Revisionism

By the early 1980s, the revisionist perspective on ethnic residential patterns was largely centered on a fairly coherent set of beliefs. To begin with, revisionists tended to believe that ethnic enclaves were not short-lived but very durable entities. Not surprisingly, scholars found that the longevity of ethnic neighborhoods varied from group to group. For instance, it is generally acknowledged that, among the European immigrants, Italians displayed a pronounced tendency for establishing durable urban ethnic communities. As Gary Mormino remarked about St Louis's long-established Italian-American neighborhood known as the "Hill":

Early residents, after a period of settlement, erected communal institutions that have continued to sustain and maintain individual and family allegiance. Immigrants on the Hill clustered together in an isolated and exclusively Italian enclave where most inhabitants sank tenacious roots, refusing to leave the colony despite limited economic prospects (1986, p. 5).

Challenging the orthodox model of high residential mobility and rapid "succession", Mormino claimed that the Hill was not an ethnic ghetto sustained by "successive waves of new faces", but a "community" built by "[s]uccessive generations of the same families" (ibid., p. 81). "Assimilationists", noted Mormino, "long argued that immigrant neighborhoods would disappear in time, happy victims of the Melting Pot. But the Hill stubbornly has refused to disappear, its loyal inhabitants defiantly resisting the temptation of the American dream of suburbia" (ibid., p. 82). While Mormino unassumingly avoided making grandiose claims about the applicability of his findings to the experience of Italians in American cities generally, studies by other historians indicate that the Hill was far from atypical (ibid., p. 5, Barton, 1975, pp. 59–63, 64–90; Briggs, 1978, pp. 118–19, 138–62; Cinel, 1982, pp. 103–21; Gabaccia, 1984, pp. 74–85). However, revisionist scholarship has also suggested that residential concentration was both more widespread and long-lasting than was previously believed to be the case among groups, such as the Germans, who were traditionally depicted as fairly broadly dispersed throughout the cities in which they settled. Kathleen Conzen's portrayal of ethnic residential patterns in antebellum Milwaukee, for example, contrasts sharply with the one of Boston during the same era previously offered by Handlin (1941, pp. 94–106):

> Milwaukee's two main immigrant groups were certainly segregated. For the great majority of Germans, particularly, residence involved minimal neighborhood contact with either natives or Irish. The new city permitted its major immigrant group [the Germans] to carve out an entire sector for itself, large enough to provide for internal variations in residential status. There was little sign among either Germans or Irish of the type of movement predicted by the classic ghetto hypothesis – movement from central receiving ghetto to more middle-class but still ethnically-defined fringe neighborhoods. In a city like Milwaukee, where primitive transportation placed a premium on central location, the newer immigrants developed the outer areas while the areas of first settlement improved in status as their residents gained greater security (Conzen, 1976, p. 152).

Similarly, in his study of New York's "Little Germany", Stanley Nadel recently argued that "the linguistically isolated Germans appear to have displayed a strong tendency toward self-segregation nearly everywhere they settled" (1990, p. 39).

Another important tenet of revisionist thought is the belief that government agencies frequently played a key role in bringing about the residential isolation of some ethnies, particularly nonwhites and especially Native Americans and

African Americans. In this respect, revisionists are clearly following in the footsteps of the scholars, already mentioned above, who pioneered the study of such topics as Indian removal, black ghettoization and Latino barrioization. More recent treatments of these topics, however, tend to place greater emphasis upon the cultural adaptations and institutional supports that the ethnic minorities developed in response to their enforced spatial isolation (Green, 1982; McLoughlin, 1993; Phillpott, 1978; Sánchez, 1993; Trotter, 1985).

Additionally, revisionist works frequently contend that ghettoization and its Latino corollary, barrioization, were generally not accidental in origin but the products of policies designed to control ethnic minorities and prevent them from achieving upward mobility. A large body of scholarship testifies to the fact that residential segregation has been used in all regions of the United States, North and South, East and West, during most periods of the nation's history, to perpetuate the social, economic and political subordination of African Americans. For instance, Howard Rabinowitz (1978, pp. 103–6) showed that levels of residential segregation increased rapidly in the urban South during the late nineteenth century largely due to a white desire to exclude blacks from white neighborhoods and also to limit the political power of African Americans by confining them to carefully gerrymandered political wards. David Katzman's *Before the Ghetto* (1973, pp. 67–80), which covers virtually the same time period as Rabinowitz's study, revealed that residential segregation performed comparable functions in a northern city, Detroit, where white racism was the chief factor contributing to the confinement in one district of over four-fifths of the black population. Likewise, Albert Broussard's study of San Francisco's black community during the early twentieth century demonstrated similar forces at work. According to Broussard, municipal and federal policy makers created segregated public housing developments for African Americans "under the pretext of preserving the racial and ethnic integrity of neighborhoods". When combined with an influx of black migrants during World War II, this policy, which essentially served the interests of the real estate business, "laid the groundwork for the black ghetto in the postwar era" (1993, p. 179). Consequently, many revisionist studies still tended to typify inner-city ethnic ghettos as pathological social environments. This was the picture, for instance, of African-American enclaves in both northern and southern cities, antebellum and postbellum eras, that had emerged by the early 1980s from the works of historians like Gilbert Osofsky (1966), Allan Spear (1967), Kenneth Kusmer (1976), Leonard Curry (1981), and Howard Rabinowitz (1978).

Furthermore, while accepting that ethnic group members frequently displayed a preference for residing in their own segregated neighborhoods, revisionists have often attributed this to the fact that the ethnic enclave tended to act as a refuge or haven from the prejudice and intimidation that were

widespread in mainstream society. Ricardo Romo, for example, while acknowledging that "most [Mexicans] were prevented from moving to White
neighborhoods by restrictive real estate covenants and prejudices", argued in
his history of the East Los Angeles barrio that "the majority of Mexican
immigrants, for reasons of language, kinship, and folk customs chose to live
together in barrios" (1983, pp. 9–10). In her study of New York Jews,
Deborah Dash Moore makes a similar claim for that European immigrant
group, asserting that "anti-Semitism shaped Jewish housing patterns less
decisively than did associational networks" (1981, p. 38). Likewise, Jeffrey
Gurock observed of Harlem's Jewish enclave: "It was that certain joy and
certain security felt by immigrants living among their own kind and experiencing the 'Jewish atmosphere' that permeated the immigrant settlement"
(1979, p. 59). In response, therefore, to the ghetto model's characterization of
urban ethnic enclaves as neighborhoods largely inhabited by "losers and
sinners", revisionist historians contended that these communities actually
sustained varied and vibrant economic activities, as well as sophisticated
networks of cultural, social and political institutions (Romo, 1983, p. 9: see
also Blassingame, 1973; Kwong, 1979).

Finally, implicit in the revisionist interpretation is the view that persistently
high levels of ethnic spatial separation justify the characterization of the
United States as historically a fragmented society, composed of fairly
autonomous rural and urban ethnic communities. This has major implications
for the broader discussion over the nature of American ethnic history. As
Olivier Zunz (1982a, p. 46) has noted, this concentration-versus-dispersion
debate among historians studying ethnic residential patterns is intrinsically
linked to the wider assimilation-versus-pluralism one:

> The "ghetto" and the "residential melting pot" have been very
> powerful concepts because they correspond to two different . . .
> visions of American society. Finding a residential melting pot
> suggests that ethnic conflicts were never very strong, at least not
> strong enough to be translated into conflicts for space . . . Finding
> the ghetto suggests great ethnic differences in American society, but
> it also implies that they are temporary . . .

As contentious as the closing statement about the ephemerality of ethnicity may
appear, even revisionist scholars like Romo readily concede that ethnic enclaves
"essentially acted as an acculturation way station where the recently arrived
immigrants could work out their own social and economic adjustment to
American life at a pace that suited them rather than that favored by Americanization programs and 'cultural custodians'" (1983, p. 12). However, revisionists also tend to agree that for one group, African Americans, ethnic

concentration has not been followed by rapid or even gradual dispersion and that the black ghetto has become a permanent rather than temporary phenomenon (Hershberg, et al., 1981; Zunz, 1982a, pp. 45–6; Bodnar, et al., 1982).

New Directions in Research on Ethnic Clusters: Agency, Community, Rural Isolation

In recent decades, numerous historians have adopted a modified version of the revisionist viewpoint that de-emphasizes the pathological effects of the ghetto and stresses the agency exercised by its inhabitants. Exponents of this "agency" school of thought argue that residential segregation, even when imposed upon an ethny by the dominant society, can have beneficial effects. One of the pioneers of this approach, James Borchert, argued that even the most lowly and apparently powerless newcomers to the city – in this case the rural black migrants who came to reside in the alleyways of Washington, DC – managed to "create strategies which enabled them to survive the often harsh and difficult urban experience". In fact, according to Borchert the migrants "'remade' their urban environment, both physically and cognitively, to fit their needs" (1980, p. xii). Other scholars of the African-American experience have shown how residential concentration has promoted communal spirit and ethnicization among urban blacks. The concept of "community building" – defined, in rather broad and not altogether elucidating terms, by Richard W. Thomas as "the sum total of the historical efforts of black individuals, institutions, and organizations to survive and progress as a people and to create and sustain a genuine and creative communal presence" (1992, p. xi) – has influenced many of the studies of African-American urban life that have appeared since the early 1990s (Taylor, 1993; Phillips, 1997; Trotter, 1998b; Phillips, 1999).

As well as reinterpreting the urban ghetto experience, scholars have in recent years revisited the long-neglected topic of ethnic segregation in rural areas. The picture emerging from a variety of studies is of a rural landscape dotted with small and medium-sized townships inhabited predominantly and in some cases almost entirely by members of the same ethnic group (Gjerde, 1985; Ostergren, 1988; Hamilton, 1991; Matsumoto, 1993; González, 1994). The fact that rural ethnic communities enjoyed higher levels of both homogeneity and isolation from assimilatory influences than their urban counterparts appears to have facilitated the survival of ethnic attachments and practices for a longer period and in a less diluted form than in the cities. While few contemporary historians would challenge the assertion that residential concentration – whether in rural or urban areas – does assist cultural retention, debate continues over the role that culture plays in determining the residential patterns of ethnic groups. The findings of the PSHP have done much to fuel this controversy. One of the project's researchers, Stephanie Greenberg, claimed that her study of German, Irish, and black residential patterns in late nineteenth-century Philadelphia demonstrated that, "in terms of community formation, industrial affiliation seems to have been the primary organizing factor, with ethnicity emerging as a secondary factor" (1981, p. 225). Ethnic residential clusters, claimed Greenberg, were "not simply the product of either the abstract, natural laws put forth by the classical ecologists or the desire of people with a common heritage to live close to one another", but were instead "linked to decisions made in the local, regional, and national economies that determine the location of industries" (ibid., p. 226). This interpretation has also more recently been applied to ethnic separation in the rural setting, as Kenneth Marvin Hamilton's observations about the establishment of all-black communities during the postbellum era illustrate: "Economic motives, rather than racism, led to the inception of western black towns. Their founders were speculators aiming to profit by fostering a migrant population's quest for social equality and financial security" (1991, p. 1). This perspective, however, has not been without it detractors and Olivier Zunz, for one, has been vociferous in criticizing the "economic determinism" of scholars who relegate cultural factors to a subordinate role in the historical process (1982b, p. 468).

That said, one of the most interesting historiographical developments of recent decades has been the appearance of numerous works suggesting that residential segregation has in some cases fostered the growth of ethnic economic enclaves, which can later provide ethnic group members with the means to enter the mainstream economy at a higher level than would previously have been possible. One the starkest examples of this pattern is the experience of Japanese Americans, who prior to 1945 suffered from exclusion and discrimination at the hands of the dominant society, but during the post-World War II era became one of the nation's most affluent ethnic groups. John Modell, in his highly influential study of urban-based Japanese in California during the interwar years, contended that "[a]lthough Japanese gave more than adequate proof that they wished to move away from their cramped areas, residential segregation was in fact crucial to the support of an ethnic isolation that made the Los Angeles Japanese-American community such a 'success' in parochial economic terms" (1977, p. 67). However, a more serious criticism of revisionism points to statistical data suggesting that levels of spatial separation are decreasing for virtually all ethnies and in the case of some groups, most notably white ethnics, have been doing so for some time. This point has been made by scholars, mostly social scientists, drawn from a variety of ideological backgrounds (Lieberson, 1963; Omi and Winant, 1986).

EDUCATION: "THE GREAT EQUALIZER"?

The antebellum reformer Horace Mann's belief in universal education as "the great equalizer of the conditions of men, the balance wheel of the social machinery" has become as integral a part of the American Creed as the words of Thomas Jefferson or Emma Lazarus. "To this day", observed the sociologist Stephen Steinberg more than a century after Mann's statement was made, "it is an article of faith in American society that education is the key to material success, and the key to eliminating social inequalities as well" (1989, pp. 128–9). With regards to the issue of public education, therefore, scholars of American ethnic history are faced with two main questions. First, to what extent was the promise of universal education intended to encompass children from all ethnies? And second, how successful was the American education system at providing individual ethnic group members with a gateway to upward mobility?

Unlike most other aspects of American ethnic history, where the historiographical trend over the last half century has generally been one of a violent swing from an extreme assimilationist orthodox position in the 1950s to an extreme pluralist revisionist position in the 1970s, and then a gradual settling down to a position somewhere between these two extremes by the 1990s, the discussion of historical educational opportunities for ethnies has remained consistently polarized since the first revisionist critiques of the public school system appeared in the late 1960s and early 1970s. The orthodox view that American public education had historically provided ethnies with true equality of opportunity was staunchly defended by many contemporaries of the revisionist historians, whose allegations were quickly rebuffed. There is, therefore, no strong generational dimension to the orthodox–revisionist divide over the historical efficacy of public education for ethnic minorities, because the orthodox position, although hotly contested, has never really gone out of fashion.

Orthodoxy: Ethnic Opportunity through Public Education

The orthodox perspective on the correct relationship between ethnicity and education dates back at least as far as the Progressive Era and is based upon the assumption that the public education system facilitates the assimilation of ethny members and creates the basis for social unity and harmony. As early as 1890, Francis Parkman asserted: "The common schools are crucibles in which races, nationalities, and creeds are fused together till all alike became American" (quoted in Saveth, 1965 [1948], p. 109). For Parkman, a crucial role of the public schools was to ameliorate inter-denominational strife. "The expectation of cultural harmony", Oscar Handlin has observed, "was also linked with the promise of social mobility". In Handlin's opinion, "[i]t was not a bad deal that the schools offered – occupational and social advancement at the price of cultural acquiescence; and whatever the immigrants thought, their children, by and large, responded positively, or wished to" (1982, p. 11: see also Smith, 1969). Moreover, orthodox historians maintain that there are ample historical examples of ethny members using the open access to numerous levels of education available in the United States as a vehicle for upward mobility. American Jews, for instance, have traditionally been held up as a paragon of this phenomenon, as have, more recently, Japanese Americans. Moses Rischin (1962), Milton Gordon (1964), Nathan Glazer and Daniel Patrick Moynihan (1963) have all explained East European Jews' impressive social advancement in the United States as largely the product of American educational opportunities, while a similar interpretation of Japanese Americans' success has been given by Harry Kitano and Stanley Sue (1973).

The orthodox position has two main weaknesses. First, for every paragon of success, there are countless instances of ethnies whose members, although accorded full access to the public education system, have not achieved either full assimilation or significant levels of upward mobility. To demonstrate this point, critics of the orthodox perspective regularly draw attention to the case of Italian immigrants, who despite arriving in the United States at almost exactly the same time and settling in the very same places as East European Jews, did not derive the same benefits from the American education system. Salvatore LaGumina asserted that "Italians did not have a positive school experience" and attributed much of the blame for this to "the negative reception accorded these people by a host society whose actions were prompted by nativist prejudice and the requirements of the industrial order" (1982, p. 74: see also Briggs, 1978, pp. 191–244). The public schools, it is argued, failed in their objective. Comparisons of Italian Americans' educational achievement with that of other European immigrant groups are provided by Richard Gambino (1974) and Michael Olneck and Marvin Lazerson (1974). However, neither of these works, it is worth noting, advanced the view that the public school system was primarily to blame for Italian Americans' relatively lower levels of scholastic attainment. In fact, both placed emphasis upon the role played by cultural factors, particularly Italian immigrants' mistrust of public education and their undervaluing of formal education.

Second, as specialists in the history of nonwhite ethnies and internal-colony theorists have frequently shown, some ethnies were deliberately excluded from the mainstream education system, either through de facto and de jure segregation or in extreme cases the complete absence of provision. School segregation, which affected numerous nonwhite groups, most particularly African Americans, Mexican Americans and Asian Americans, was an irrefutable negation of the American Creed, as the United States Supreme Court famously admitted in the 1954 case of *Brown* v. *Board of Education, Topeka*: "We conclude that in the field of public education the doctrine of 'separate but equal' has no place. Separate educational facilities are inherently unequal" (Martin, 1998, p. 174: see also Bullock, 1967; González, 1990; San Miguel, 1987; Weinberg, 1977; Wollenberg, 1976).

Revisionism: Education as Socialization

The revisionist perspective originated in a number of left-wing historical studies that, although they examined numerous ethnic experiences in detail, were more interested in offering a critique of conventional views about the American education system in general than in exploring the issue of ethnic inequality in education. In works with such telling titles as *The Great School Legend* (Greer, 1972), *Education and the Rise of the Corporate State* (Spring, 1972), and *Schooling in Capitalist America* (Bowles and Gintis, 1976), radical historians characterized American educational reformers as capitalist lackeys and the public schools as factories for supplying American industry with compliant workers (see also Katz, 1968; Feinberg and Rosemont, 1975; Feinberg, 1975). Nonetheless, these revisionist studies of American education history inspired scholars working in the field of American ethnic history to examine more closely the way that public schools historically treated ethnic minorities. More a by-product of his decades-long involvement in the struggle for equality of educational provision in Chicago than an outgrowth of the contemporaneous historiographical debate over public education, Meyer Weinberg's *A Chance to Learn* (1977) stands as a landmark in the history of ethnic groups' encounters with the US education system. Examining the experiences of African Americans, Mexican Americans, Native Americans, and Puerto Ricans, Weinberg concluded that "[s]ince its earliest beginnings, the American public school system has been deeply committed to the maintenance of racial and ethnic barriers". "The most devout defenders of the common school", noted Weinberg, "from Horace Mann to John Dewey held their tongues when the subject of minority – especially black – children became an issue" (ibid., p. 1). In the time since Weinberg's book was published the class-based theories of revisionist education historians have gradually exerted a more noticeable influence over scholarship on ethnic inequality in education, especially that focusing upon the experiences of nonwhite minorities. For instance, James D. Anderson's critique of traditional interpretations of black education reform in the South was unmistakably radical in tone. In an essay entitled "Education as a Vehicle for the Manipulation of Black Workers", Anderson challenged the view expounded by scholars like Louis Harlan, C. Vann Woodward, Horace Mann Bond, John

Hope Franklin, and Henry Bullock, that northern and southern white patrons of black education in the postbellum South were essentially motivated by humanitarian and egalitarian impulses and that "public schooling in the black South functioned historically as an institution of social, economic, and moral elevation". In contrast, Anderson viewed "the institution of 'Negro education' as a system deemed socially necessary for the development and maintenance of a particular form of economic order and white rule in the postwar South". According to Anderson, therefore, black education was "rooted mainly in exploitative economic and racial interests instead of in any humanitarian movement" and was "forged from the interests and views of the industrial philanthropists of the Northeast and the reformers and emerging businessmen of the New South, who held corresponding interests in the industrial conquest and white dominance of the American South" (1975, p. 18).

Revisionists argued that the public education system was designed, first and foremost, to serve the interests of the predominantly white, Anglo-Saxon, Protestant and pro-capitalist, American middle classes. This Radical/New Left characterization of public education as the servant of elitist, racist and nativist interests originates in Michael Katz's *The Irony of Early School Reform*, which highlighted anti-black discrimination in the antebellum North, and Colin Greer's *The Great School Legend*, which focused upon the experiences of the so-called "new" immigrants during the late nineteenth and early twentieth centuries. Rather than acting as a route to upward mobility for ethnic minorities, therefore, the purpose of the public schools was to turn the nation's ethnically diverse lower classes into an acculturated, skilled and compliant workforce. In their detailed examination of the Gary, Indiana, public school system, whose curriculum and timetable innovations influenced practices across the United States during the early twentieth century, Ronald Cohen and Raymond Mohl came to the following conclusion: "Traditional middle class WASP values determined school programs and policies. The schools sought to shape the behavior of the students, wipe out ethnic backgrounds, turn immigrants into Patriotic Americans, and socialize children for the workplace" (1979, p. 98). It was in pursuance of these aims, revisionists claim, that the policy-making elite in numerous states sanctioned the establishment of segregated schools for nonwhite ethnies. As we have already seen, James Anderson argued that the education of Southern blacks was imbued with this rationale. In his study of the segregated education that was the norm for ethnic Mexican children across the Southwest during the first half of the twentieth century, Gilbert González claimed this practice "grew out of policy decisions corresponding to the economic interests of the Anglo community" and "reproduced a socioeconomic bifurcation in society" (1990, pp. 27, 157). "However", González added, the mere segregation of children by itself could never lead to these consequences; it needed certain techniques to accomplish its politico-economic goal. Americanization, testing, tracking into vocational education, and slow-learner and mentally retarded classes, provided the internal machinery that made segregation an effective tool (ibid., p. 157).

Furthermore, the emphasis upon Americanization in the public school curriculum, which from the Progressive Era onwards became a more deliberate facet of education policy, is described by revisionists as cultural imperialism on a grand scale. In his broad study of the subject, Robert Carlson claimed that, while the Americanization movement exerted its greatest influence over school curricula during the period 1900–25, the urge to "educate Americans for homogeneity" has been a constant theme in public education since Puritan times (1975, pp. 14–15: on Americanization in public education, see Adams, 1995; Anderson, 1988; Appel and Appel, 1982; Elson, 1964; González, 1990; Isser and Schwartz, 1985; McClymer, 1982; Prucha, 1979; Riney, 1999; Trennert, 1988). Rejecting the view that Americanization education sprang from essentially humanitarian impulses, Carlson contended that the effort to "stamp the individual American into groups norms" was "intellectually inconsistent with the US ideal of a free society", "unnecessary for national unity" and demonstrated that "Americanizers lacked confidence in the very institutions they claimed to be upholding". While conceding that "Americanizers did help to overcome demands for harsher measures, including genocide", he maintained that "their efforts for homogeneity from Puritan times to the present . . . [were] no more and no less than attempts at cultural genocide" (1975, p. 15). As a recent work by Guadalupe San Miguel, Jr (2004), demonstrates, the homogenizing impulse is still a potent force in American society and lately succeeded in shifting federal educational policy from support of to opposition to bilingual instruction for schoolchildren not proficient in English.

Revisionists also dismiss as a mere cover for assimilationism the "immigrant gifts" version of ethnic pluralism expounded by some Progressive reformers. In his detailed study of the intercultural education movement that flourished briefly during the 1930s, Nicholas Montalto concluded: "Despite a kind of rhetorical celebration of diversity, many liberals saw the ethnic group as a breeding ground of narrowness and bigotry, and ethnic consciousness as a contaminant of American individualism" (1982a, p. 281). According to Montalto, liberal educationalists gave only "conditional support for ethnic studies" and did so because they thought it would, on the one hand, prevent a resurgence of previous decades' rampant nativism and, on the other hand, render semi-acculturated American-born children more amenable to the guidance of their immigrant parents (ibid., pp. 280–1). In other words, liberals were motivated by "a desire to maintain national unity and social control" rather than a genuine commitment to pluralism (ibid., p. 281: see also Montalto, 1982b; Mohl, 1982).

With reference to the ethnies traditionally viewed as paragons of educational achievement, many revisionists attribute the success of these groups to their Old World cultures rather than New World opportunity structures. In the case of East European Jews, this argument could not be more clearly stated than in the following words of Leonard Dinnerstein:

> When one studies what the 2,000,000 or so Jewish immigrants who arrived in this country between 1880 and 1930, and their children, accomplished . . . there can be no doubt that educational endeavors must be regarded as a significant, if not prime, cause of their social mobility. And the reason that education played this role was the high regard for learning that had for centuries pervaded the Jewish culture.
>
> No other European immigrant group valued learning more than the East European Jews (1982, pp. 454, 464–5, 472–7: see also Olneck and Lazerson, 1974, pp. 454, 464–5, 472–7; Gordon, 1964, pp. 186–7; Glazer, 1958).

Likewise, some prominent Italian-American scholars have conceded that Italian immigrants – whose children comprised the second-largest ethnic group after Jews in the New York City public schools at the beginning of the twentieth century and consequently are regularly compared, usually unfavorably in terms of academic performance, with Jewish children – did not share anything like the enthusiasm for education of East European Jews (LaGumina, 1982, pp. 62–72). However, Timothy Smith has challenged the view that East European Jews' respect for education was significantly greater than that of Greek Orthodox, Roman Catholic or Protestant immigrants also arriving from east, south and central Europe during the period 1880–1930 (1969, pp. 532–4).

Curiously, studies arguing that ethnic culture determined academic achievement have originated from a combination of usually incongruous ideological perspectives. For instance, left-leaning exponents of ethnic agency assert that the phenomenon of some ethnies spending prolonged periods in education was actually a consequence not a cause of upward mobility, as Charles Hirschman and Morrison Wong (1986, p. 23) contended with regards to Asian Americans:

> An important factor behind the educational progress of the second generation of Asian-Americans in the early decades of the [twentieth]

century was the economic progress of their parents. Asian workers were unable to penetrate the higher echelons of the occupational ranks nor were they allowed to participate in the relatively well-paid skilled craft occupations of industrial work. Left to their own resources, Asians developed an ethnic economy that created an increasing number of jobs in trade and services . . . [and] this development was a major factor behind the educational gains of Asian-American children in the decades prior to World War II.

Similarly, Sherry Gorelick claimed that traditional explanations of Jewish educational achievement in New York City contain almost as many myths as they do truths:

A never-never land has been imagined in which docile Jews, living in safe slums, gratefully, respectfully, obediently lap up the gifts of Anglo-Saxon culture to the admiration and love of their teachers. In this never-never land democratic and free institutions open gladly and bountifully to receive the hopes and passions of their eager entrants . . . The East European Jews were not welcomed, and they were not docile . . . The educational ladder that the Jews are said to have climbed was not there when the East European Jews reached North America, and it was not created for them (1981, p. 9: see also Berrol, 1976).

In contrast to these interpretations, Thomas Sowell and other right-leaning exponents of cultural-capital theory draw attention to the high academic performance achieved by ethnies, notably Asian Americans, formerly excluded from mainstream educational opportunities (1981, pp. 282–5, 291, 293–4: see also Glazer, 1975; Kitano, 1976).

"The Revisionists Revised"

The weaknesses of the revisionist interpretation have been pointed out by various scholars from both the pluralist and assimilationist perspectives. Many pluralists maintain that due to ethnic resilience the public schools failed to Americanize ethnies. Probably the most extreme example of public education deliberately being used to eradicate ethnic culture, for instance, is the case of the forced Americanization that Native-American children underwent in federal off-reservation boarding schools from the late 1870s onward. The "main goal" of these Indian schools, as Robert Trennert stated in his pathbreaking study of one of them, "was to remove Indian youngsters from their traditional environment, obliterate their cultural heritage, and replace that background with the values of white middle-class America" (1988, p. xi). However, it is now the prevailing view among scholars of Native-American history that the boarding schools generally failed in their mission of forced acculturation, not least because of the defiance of the children made to attend them. "Indian students", David Wallace Adams asserted in his book *Education for Extinction*, "were anything but passive recipients of the curriculum of civilization":

> When choosing the path of resistance, they bolted the institution,
> torched buildings, and engaged in a multitude of schemes to
> undermine the school program. Even the response of accommodation
> was frequently little more than a conscious and strategic adaptation
> to the hard rock of historical circumstance, a pragmatic recognition
> that one's Indianness would increasingly have to be defended and
> negotiated in the face of relentless hegemonic forces (1995, p. 336:
> see also Trennert, 1988, p. 210; Riney, 1999, pp. 217–18; Hoxie,
> 1984, pp. 189–210, 243–4; Lomawaima, 1994, pp. xii–xiii).

As might be expected, historians writing about European immigrant children's public school experiences would not attempt to suggest that they were as harrowing as those of pupils in federal Indian schools, but they do claim that similar signs of resistance to acculturation were displayed by students from a wide variety of European ethnic backgrounds and that ethnic cultures were not completely obliterated. This argument, for example, is expressed quite strongly by John Briggs (1978, pp. 191–244), Josef Barton (1975, pp. 117–46), and Carol Coburn (1992, pp. 60–80, 152, 154, 157, 161–2), and in a modified form by John Bodnar (1982, pp. 90–1), Victor Greene (1982, pp. 201–3), and Salvatore LaGumina (1982, pp. 72–3), who see some transformation as well as survival of traditional culture emerging from the ethnic encounter with public education. In their examinations of schooling for Mexican-American pupils, Richard Garcia (1991, pp. 175–203), Lynne Marie Getz (1997, pp. 2, 10–12, 123), Gilbert González (1990, p. 25) and Guadalupe San Miguel, Jr (1987, pp. 64–90, 216) also offer assessments of Americanization education that suggest it had a limited impact upon ethnic culture.

Another criticism of revisionism is that it tends to homogenize the experiences of nonwhite ethnies, which in reality were very varied, with some groups enjoying high levels of access to equal educational opportunities. For instance, Charles Hirschmann and Morrison Wong demonstrated that widespread discrimination against Asians during the early twentieth century "did not diminish the ability of Japanese- and Chinese-American families to support the education of their American-born children at levels comparable to or above that of the majority population" (1986, p. 16). In contrast, the types of discrimination that African Americans and Mexican Americans faced in education during the same time period made it impossible for either group to match let alone exceed white/Anglo rates of high school completion and college attendance. Indeed, as various works by Thomas James (1985 and 1987) showed, even the children of Japanese-American internees during World War II enjoyed greater access to higher education than the average African American or Mexican American serving in the armed forces could have dreamed of for his or her child. Moreover, recent research suggests regional variations in conditions were also very important and often produced geographical differences of experience among members of the same ethny. Nowhere is this more noticeable than in the case of African Americans during the Jim Crow era. Not only was there a divergence between the North and South in that education for blacks in the latter region was generally more segregated and – in both absolute and relative terms – more inferior to what whites received (Cohen and Mohl, 1979, pp. 83–122; Perlmann, 1988), but modern studies show that there were significant differences between cities and states within the same regions in terms of African Americans' educational opportunities and experiences (Bullock, 1967, pp. 177, 180–1; Ment, 1983). Having said that, Hirschmann and Wong found that regional differences were virtually insignificant in explaining Asian Americans' educational achievement, which highlights the pitfalls not only of looking for all-encompassing generalizations about the ethnic experience in the United States but also of emphasizing the similarities between Asian Americans and other nonwhite ethnies in the realm of public education (1986, pp. 12–16).

Assimilationists put forward an even longer list of revisionism's shortcomings. First, revisionists generally overlook the fact that differences in ethnic educational performance have largely evened out, particularly since World War II and especially among white ethnics. Richard Alba has shown, for example, that while rates of college attendance and graduation for Americans born during the period 1916–25 were considerably above average for those of solely British ancestry and commensurately below average for those of southern and eastern European ancestry, for the cohort of Americans born between 1956 and 1965 the differences between the two groups are negligible (1995, pp. 6–8). Ironically, Rudolph Vecoli, the don of the pluralist school of immigration historians, made the same point back in the early 1970s when he noted how "[s]ince World War II, with the boom in higher education, the walls of ethnic exclusion around the groves of academe have come tumbling down" (1970, p. 81).

Second, the emphasis revisionists place upon the theme of cultural imperialism is at best exaggerated and at worst downright spurious, as is demonstrated by studies of parochial schools which show that the latter were often more effective agents of Americanization than the public schools. In his study of Catholic education in Chicago, James Sanders found that during the early twentieth century the Church authorities succeeded in reining in the particularist tendencies of the various nationality-based parochial schools and imposing a considerable degree of uniformity and cohesion upon what was previously a very loose network. Sanders claimed that Catholic educators brought about "a fusion of diverse cultural strands into a new social whole" and that even Americanizers "had to admit that the Catholic school eased the immigrants' transition from the Old World to the New" (1977, p. 55). Curiously, the scholarly literature on this topic all seems to confirm the view that, while parochial education originated in an antebellum attempt to counter what was viewed as the Protestant and secular biases of the burgeoning public school system, Catholic educational institutions – both in their conception and their influence – adhered far more strongly to American ideals than to religious or ethnic particularism (Lannie, 1968; Gleason, 1982; Fass, 1989, pp. 189–228, 234–5). Moreover, recent research shows that Americanization had a positively beneficial effect on some previously isolated ethnies, such as Jews, Mexican Americans, Native Americans, and Asian Americans, because it opened up access to mainstream opportunities. Stephan Brumberg (1986, pp. 2, 10, 200, 210–11, 214–15, 220–1, 224–5), Richard Garcia (1991, p. 177–8, 202, 203), Donal Lindsey (1995, pp. 267–70), and Thomas James (1985, pp. 160–1, 163, 171) all present an argument along these lines, albeit with varying degrees of stress upon the need for qualification.

Third, revisionists, when confronted by the blatant ethnocentrism displayed in the past by educational reformers, are often so blinded by their own moral outrage that they neglect to acknowledge that the latter were frequently motivated by a genuine, albeit misguided, humanitarianism. In *The Revisionists Revised: A Critique of the Radical Attack on the Schools*, which provides virtually a point by point refutation of the New Left perspective on the education of ethnic and racial minorities in the United States, Diane Ravitch asserted that while "liberals . . . describe educational failures as the result of errors, of good intentions gone unpredictably wrong", the "radical historians . . . offer moralistic condemnation instead of understanding, and hindsight instead of insight" (1978, pp. 36, 56). "It is easy, with hindsight", averred Ravitch,

> to recognize error and shortsightedness. It is more difficult, but no less significant, to document how and why people made certain choices, not only in terms of the limitations imposed by their values and perceptions, but also in terms of the influence of historic forces that they could neither foresee nor control (ibid., p. 56).

Ravitch's admonition is unquestionably salutary. However, in summarizing the findings of his detailed, thorough and generally commendable comparison of Irish, Italian, Jewish, and African-American schoolchildren in Providence, Rhode Island, between 1880 and 1935, Joel Perlmann provided a perfect example of how a scholar attempting to tackle highly contentious historiographical issues in an impartial way can arrive at almost indisputably accurate and yet, particularly from the reader's standpoint, entirely baffling conclusions:

> One generalization will not serve to describe or explain the ethnic differences found in American social history. Many groups behaved in similar ways; others differed for a range of special reasons. Neither culture nor discrimination nor class origins in the American city can alone provide a credible summary. Rather, ethnic groups are products of distinct histories. We need not seek the single, consistently primary factor creating ethnic distinctiveness, nor even a single generalization that will cover the relationships among several factors; far better, with a comparative perspective and an eye on theory, to explore the individual ethnic histories (1988, p. 219).

It is apt to conclude this discourse on ethnic education with an examination of a book whose argument is as bold as the above one is timid and whose subject is the most important court ruling in twentieth-century American ethnic history. In *The Burden of Brown: Thirty Years of School Desegregation* (1984), Raymond Wolters argued that, while the Supreme Court's famous 1954 decision and subsequent supplementary ones succeeded in desegregating many school districts in southern and border states, the differences in educational achievement between black and white children had remained virtually unchanged. According to Wolters school desegregation has fallen short of its pedagogic objectives because it fails to address the economic and cultural factors which lay at the root of disparities in educational performance (ibid., pp. 280–7). While they might claim with some justification that Wolters's argument is merely a variant of the conservative cultural-capital theory, liberal and radical historians still find it difficult – and to date have not seriously attempted – to counter the charge that school integration has not turned out to be, as it was originally heralded, the panacea for black underachievement in education. In fairness, Wolters's opponents could claim that thirty, or even fifty years as it is now, is too short a period in which to measure the success or failure of school desegregation, but such a response is cold comfort to the bulk of the African-American pupils still being poorly served by the American public school system. Whereas many historiographical debates bear little import outside of academia, this one has major policy implications and, for the public good, deserves to be promptly resolved.

SOCIAL MOBILITY: THE "LAND OF OPPORTUNITY"?

Although the matter of social mobility in the new republic was left open to broad interpretation by Jefferson's fairly indistinct phrase "the pursuit of Happiness", America's leading thinkers had, within only a dozen years of the signing of the Declaration of Independence, clarified this issue by expressing a firm preference for meritocracy. "There are strong minds in every walk of life", observed Alexander Hamilton in number 36 of *The Federalist*, "that will rise superior to the disadvantages of situation, and will command the tribute due to their merit, not only from the classes to which they particularly belong, but from the society in general. The door ought to be equally open to all . . .". Was the door of opportunity opened so wide in the United States that it was possible for the members of any ethnic group to turn, through their own efforts, the dream of upward mobility into a reality? This is the question Hamilton's statement poses for scholars of American ethnic history.

Orthodoxy: Individualism and Upward Mobility

According to the orthodox view which originated in the late nineteenth century and dominated the field of American ethnic history up until the 1960s, ethnies generally experienced rates of upward mobility proportionate to their stock of human capital (see Saveth, 1965 [1948], pp. 87–8, 127–30, 133–5, 182–3, 190, 203, 213). While Progressive historians generally agreed upon the superiority of the American social and economic system, they differed over the ability of the various ethnic groups to benefit from it. Indeed, chauvinistic views of immigrants commonly appeared in the writings of otherwise serious scholars well into the twentieth century, as is evidenced by Frederick Jackson Turner's statement that "the idea of America as the land of freedom and opportunity to rise" had taken hold "even in the dull brains of [the] great masses of . . . unfortunates from southern and eastern Europe" (1962 [1920], p. 34). Nonetheless, traditional and especially assimilationist texts were generally imbued with faith in economic individualism. Orthodox historians depicted the United States as a classless society which operated an open economy that was entirely conducive to ethnic enterprise and upward mobility. Whether it was the agrarian frontier or the industrial city, the American environment was depicted as one in which even groups entering on the lowest rung of the economic ladder could and did work their way up it. Such is how Marcus Hansen viewed the social structure of the typical manufacturing centre, "with the Irish displacing, or at least taking the place of, the Yankees; the French Canadians succeeding the Irish; and they in turn followed by the Greeks and Slavs" (1927, pp. 507–8: see also Turner, 1962 [1920], pp. 9–22, 23–4). Conventional histories typically showed how American history abounds with examples of both individual and collective ethnic success stories. "[I]n spite of all the difficulties", wrote Robert Ernst, moving to America – in this case New York City – "offered chances of advancement to the immigrant":

> Through hard work and extremely frugal living, the building trades' employee could become a contractor, the clothing worker a shopkeeper or manufacturer, and the cabinet-maker a dealer. Many a newcomer started from scratch, toiled to save every penny, and later set up a small business of his own, hiring his more recently arrived countrymen, who started the process anew (1979 [1949], p. 83).

With slight modifications, this version of events was reproduced in successive decades by such scholars as: Oscar Handlin (1941, pp. 59–92; 1959; pp. 68–77, 118–19), Rowland Berthoff (1953, pp. 107–21), Edward P. Hutchinson (1956, pp. 153–6, 191–6, 214–18, 265–7, 273–8), Donald Cole (1963, pp. viii, 129–30), Moses Rischin (1962, pp. 51–75), Andrew Rolle (1968, pp. 9–11), Howard Chudacoff (1972, pp. 102–3), Kathleen Conzen (1976, pp. 63–125), Arcadius Kahan (1978), Thomas Kessner (1977, pp. 165–77), James Lemon (1972, pp. 218–27), Humbert Nelli (1970, pp. 55–87), and numerous others (Doyle, 1985; Nadel, 1990, pp. 62–90; Toll, 1984, pp. 3–7, 8–41, 191–5). Even Native-American tribal societies were perceived to have experienced economic improvements as a result of contact with whites, whose methods and technology the former adapted to their own needs. As the anthropologist and pioneer of "ethnohistory", John C. Ewers, claimed in *The Horse in Blackfoot Indian Culture*:

> The use of horses not only enriched the material culture of the tribes who acquired them but it altered their habits of daily life, served to develop new manual and motor skills, changed their concepts of their physical environment and the social relationships of individuals (1955, p. 338).

Ewers also pointed out that

> the adaptation of horses to the Plains Indian economy brought about a change from a relatively classless society to a society composed of three classes, which graded almost imperceptibly into one another, and in which membership was determined largely upon the basis of horse ownership (ibid.).

But he failed to explore the question of whether this stratification counteracted in any way what he implied was for Native Americans the largely beneficial economic impact of this particular aspect of the innovations initiated in the Americas by Europeans (ibid., p. 338). Similarly, Francis Paul Prucha (1962) has taken a fairly benign view of the intent, though not the impact, of early US policy towards Native Americans, particularly with regards to the preservation of their traditional economic activities.

Revisionism: Ethnic Stratification in the American Economy

While not entirely inaccurate, the picture of ethnic economic progress in the United States painted by orthodox scholars was idealized and incomplete. The major weakness of the human-capital model is that it largely ignores the role that structural factors play in determining the rates of ethnic upward mobility, an inexcusable oversight to make in the case of the United States, which has a long history of legalized ethnic subordination, taking such forms as racial slavery and whites-only citizenship. Scholars like Kenneth Stampp (1956, pp. 5–6, 34–85, 383–418), Eugene Genovese (1974, pp. 4–25, 295–309), and Ronald Lewis (1979, pp. 81–103, 111–39, 179–209), for instance, have demonstrated the central role that economic exploitation played in southern slavery. Numerous historians examining the plight of the free black in the antebellum South have also drawn conclusions similar to Marina Wikramanayake's that "the restrictions imposed on him by virtue of his color gave him less than complete access to the opportunity for free enterprise afforded the white man" (1973, pp. 93–4: see also Franklin, 1995 [1943]; Berlin, 1974). Similarly, studies of southern sharecropping by Joel Williamson (1965), James Roark (1977), Roger Ransom and Richard Sutch (1977), Lawrence Powell (1980), Ronald Davis (1982), Gerald Jaynes (1986), and Jay Mandle (1992), while differing in opinions about the origins of the system are in agreement upon the point that in their economic relationship with the former slaves the planter class still had the upper hand. Likewise, Thomas Bailey (1932), Spencer Olin (1966), and Robert Higgs (1978), have drawn attention to the way California legislators during the early twentieth century took advantage of the alien-ineligible-for-citizenship status of Asian immigrants to pass laws banning this group from owning land and designed specifically to eliminate Japanese competition in agriculture. The economic consequences of federal Indian policy since the 1830s – which can briefly be summarized as removing tribes from areas of growing white settlement, confining them to ever-shrinking reservations of communally-held land, splitting these reservations up into nuclear-family-owned plots, and encouraging private corporations to exploit the natural resources on Indian reservations – are examined in detail by historians like Lawrence Kelly (1968), H. Craig Miner (1976), Leonard Carlson (1981), Frederick Hoxie (1984), Donald Fixico (1986), Janet McDonnell (1991), and Jane Lancaster (1994). While not all of these scholars would subscribe to every element of the dependency theory that informs Richard White's work, few if any of them would disagree with his overall assessment of federal policy's economic impact on Native Americans:

> The collapse of their subsistence systems and their integration into world markets brought increasing reliance on the capitalist core [and] lack of economic choice . . .
>
> Although they had once been able to feed, clothe, and house themselves with security and comfort, Indians gradually resorted to whites for clothing and food. Initially they obtained clothing and other manufactured items as the result of various exchanges . . . whose terms and methods were not beyond their control. Increasingly, however, the terms of these exchanges were literally dictated by whites. In the end, whites specified what was to be exchanged, how it was to be exchanged, what the Indians were to receive, and how they were to use it. At its most extreme, the process rendered the Indians utterly superfluous – a population without control over resources, sustained in its poverty by payments controlled by the larger society . . . (1983, p. xix).

Clearly, the combined examples of the African-American, Asian immigrant, and Native-American experiences provide a compelling case against the traditional argument that the United States has been a land of equal economic opportunity for all ethnic groups.

Moreover, the idea that, for white ethnics at least, easy and rapid upward mobility had been a historical reality in the United States was shown to be a myth by the numerous "mobility studies" that appeared during the 1960s and 1970s. This new direction in historical investigation was pioneered by Stephan Thernstrom in *Poverty and Progress* (1964), which used census reports to trace the occupational careers of sample groups in Newburyport, Massachusetts, during the period 1850–80. On social mobility in general, Thernstrom's data suggested that the "climb into a nonmanual occupation was not impossible for the unskilled workman, but it was achieved by only a tiny minority" (ibid., p. 103). However, the "immigrant workman", noted Thernstrom, "was markedly less successful than his native counterpart in climbing out of the ranks of the unskilled" and "up the occupational ladder" (ibid., pp. 99, 109). Using four broad occupational categories – unskilled, semiskilled, skilled, and nonmanual – Thernstrom found that in successive censuses "the foreign-born [samples] remained concentrated at the bottom of the occupational scale". In explaining these differences, Thernstrom dis-counted the immigrants' relative lack of skills and attributed most of the blame to employers' preferences for hiring native workers, even if only to perform unskilled tasks, which meant that "immigrants had particularly restricted access to employment in the occupations most open to the ambitious common laborer" (ibid., p. 101). Although "ethnic differences in mobility opportunities narrowed somewhat in the post-Civil War years", Thernstrom found that the "sons of Yankee laborers obtained high status employment . . . much more easily than [the] sons of foreign-born workmen" and while "a high proportion [of the latter] found semiskilled positions in local factories" the "upper levels of the factory hierarchy were completely closed to them" (ibid., pp. 109–11).

Thernstrom's book inspired a multitude of similar studies of occupational mobility in American cities and the attention paid to ethnic differentials grew appreciably as the field developed. Appearing nearly ten year's after *Poverty and Progress*, Thernstrom's *The Other Bostonians* examined a much larger city and a greater variety of ethnic groups across a wider timespan than his earlier study. It also summarized and drew comparisons with the various other mobility studies that had appeared during the intervening period. As will be shown later, Thernstrom's view by this time on the fluidity of the American class system was more optimistic than it had been in the previous decade. However, his conception of the ethnic differences in occupational mobility was largely unchanged, finding as he did both "sharp ethnic differences in economic opportunity" and "important variations between particular national groups" (1973, p. 250). Claiming that these "variations [were] as striking as the overall differences between immigrants, second-generation men, and Yankees", Thernstrom suggested that northern and western Europeans and Jews "found their way into the higher occupational strata with exceptional speed", southern and eastern Europeans and the Irish "moved ahead economically only sluggishly and erratically", but African Americans, far from being "'the last of the immigrants' . . . were instead on another spectrum altogether" and found it virtually impossible to achieve even a small degree of inter-generational mobility (ibid., pp. 250–1). Although he implied that discrimination was a more salient factor in explaining the situation of African Americans, Thernstrom did not emphasize this factor as much in explaining the differences between natives and immigrants as he did in his earlier book (ibid., pp. 251–5). The pattern of ethnic differentials in occupational mobility outlined in *The Other Bostonians* was broadly replicated – with varying degrees of emphasis upon the role of ethnic discrimination as a causal factor – in subsequent works by, among others, Dean Esslinger (1975, pp. 119–21), Josef Barton (1975, p. 110), John Bodnar (1977, pp. 71–5; Bodnar, et al., 1982, pp. 113–48), Peter Decker (1978, pp. 80–5), and Clyde and Sally Griffen (1977, p. 255). Over recent decades a body of scholarship has emerged which expands upon and refines the idea of what might be termed black exceptionalism in the area of occupational mobility. Covering various periods of African-American history – from Leonard Curry's (1981, pp. 15–48) and Theodore Hershberg's (1981) studies of antebellum free blacks, to Joe Trotter's (1985, pp. xi–xii, 226–38) and Albert Broussard's (1993, pp. 38–58, 143–65, 205–20) examinations of the early twentieth century, and on through to assessments of the post-World War II era by Thomas Sugrue (1996, pp. 91–123), Hershberg and others (Hershberg, et al., 1981) – all of these works seem to be describing, albeit some more explicitly than others, what Trotter (1985, pp. xi–xii, 226–38) refers to as the "proletarianization" of African Americans. A similar portrayal of ethnic occupational patterns is given, once again with varying degrees of emphasis on the concept of proletarianization, in the works on Mexican Americans by Albert Camarillo (1979, pp. 79–80, 89, 98–9, 126–8, 140, 165–77, 182), Richard Griswold del Castillo (1979, pp. 51–61), and Kenneth Stewart and Arnoldo De León (1993, pp. 21–37).

The utility of these mobility studies, it is worth noting, is not universally accepted among historians. Not only do traditionalists question the premise that historical truths can be derived from the quantitative analysis of sources, but some researchers used the same or similar methodologies as those named above yet arrived at very different and sometimes even entirely opposite conclusions. For example, the mobility studies produced by Clyde Griffen (1972, pp. 324–5) and Suzanne Model (1988) both stressed the fluidity rather than rigidity of the nineteenth-century American class structure. Similarly, Gordon Kirk and Carolyn Tyirin Kirk found that, as well as ethnicity, "community characteristics such as age, regional location, changes in occupational structure, population size and rate of growth" played important roles in determining patterns of immigrant occupational mobility in numerous locations (1978, pp. 226–7). Consequently, the whole idea of actually examining occupational change has been challenged. According to James Henretta, "the entire conceptual framework of the analysis of social mobility is predicated upon the universality of the values and goals of this white, upwardly-mobile, Quaker or Protestant middle-class". "The inevitable result" claimed Henretta, "is to distort the meaning of the life-experience of other ethnic, racial, or class groups" (1977, p. 173).

Structuralism: Ethnic Proletarianization, Middleman Minorities

In contrast to the emphasis orthodox accounts place upon economic individualism, revisionism generally stresses the importance of structural factors, particularly the existence of what is variously known as the dual, split or segmented labor market. In a seminal exposition of this concept, the sociologist Edna Bonacich explained that "[t]o be split, a labor market must contain at least two groups of workers whose price of labor differs for the same work, or who would differ if they did the same work" (1972, p. 549). Sociological and historiographical discussion of labor market segmentation centers around three aspects of this phenomenon: its origins, its form, and its extent. In terms of its origins, for a long time left-wing scholars viewed the dual labor market as the product of the divide-and-rule tactics capitalists used against America's ethnically diverse workforce. This is typically how orthodox Marxist, also known as "Old Left", historians writing during the 1930s explained both the origins of ethnic conflict and the absence of class consciousness among American proletarians. For example, Roger Shugg argued that a tiny slave-owning planter class was able to maintain its economic and political hegemony in Louisiana during the antebellum era and even regain it after the Civil War and Reconstruction by exploiting the black–white racial divide within the proletariat. "It is not hard to understand", asserted Shugg, "why labor . . . made little progress toward organization", because "[i]t was composed of jealous elements, white and colored, native and foreign, slave and free, divided among themselves" and "completely submerged in a slaveholding society which regarded status rather than contract as the normal basis of its labor supply" (1939, p. 116). Ideological differences aside, Shugg's vague definition of class and his lumping together of virtually all non-planter whites under the label "proletarian" provoked, with good reason, strong criticism from his contemporaries.

This Old Left perspective was frequently based upon supposition and empirical studies suggest that employers were usually forced into the abandonment of laissez-faire under pressure from the white workforce, the latter regularly acting with the full backing of organized labor. According to Edna Bonacich, the major flaw in both Old and New Left explanations for labor market segmentation is their assumption that the phenomenon was essentially prompted by "racial and cultural differences" rather than the "economic processes" that she believed to be "more fundamental" (1972, p. 548). "In split labor markets", Bonacich explained, "conflict develops between three key classes: business, higher paid labor, and cheaper labor" (ibid., p. 553). Refuting the "Marxist argument that the capitalist class purposefully plays off one segment of the working class against the other", she declared that

Business . . . rather than desiring to protect a segment of the working class supports a liberal or laissez faire ideology that would permit all workers to compete freely in an open market. Such open competition would displace higher paid labor. Only under duress does business yield to [the establishment of a] labor aristocracy . . . (ibid., p. 557).

Labor market segmentation along ethnic lines, therefore, was a victory for the "higher paid labor" group (who in the American case generally happened to be white workers), not for business (ibid., pp. 554–6). The most detailed and influential exploration of this phenomenon has been the body of scholarship devoted to the study of the anti-Chinese and anti-Japanese movements that appeared on the West Coast in the late nineteenth and early twentieth centuries. One of the earliest versions of this model appeared in Ping Chiu's *Chinese Labor in California, 1850–1880.* "Contemporary observers", noted Chiu, "tended to assume there was but one single labor market . . . and that there was perfect labor mobility". However, Chiu perceived "several labor markets co-existing in time and space": "Chinese labor was concentrated in the low-price, low-wage fields, primarily in agriculture and import-competing industries", while "[t]he majority of white workers were in the high-price, high-wage fields and in non-import-competing industries" (1967 [1963], p. xi). The labor-led anti-Chinese movement in California, Chiu asserted, played a pivotal role in creating this ethnic division of labor (ibid., pp. 134–5: see also Saxton, 1971; Kwong, 1979, pp. 35–6; Mei, 1984; Yim, 1984; Boswell, 1986; Ichioka, 1990, pp. 2–3, 91–145). Albert Camarillo (1979, pp. 126–7, 172) and, more recently and with greater emphasis upon the role played by Anglo workers and labor unions, Emilio Zamora (1993, pp. 6, 110–32) have shown how most Mexican workers were confined to lower-paid occupations in the Southwest. Similarly, Edna Bonacich (1975 and 1976) has provided a split labor market perspective on the economic position of African Americans.

Early expositions of the dual labor market theory focused upon its most obvious form: the division of employment opportunities along ethnic lines into higher-paid skilled and lower-paid unskilled jobs, with the former being reserved for members of the dominant society and the latter for subordinated minorities. This trend is most noticeable in, although not restricted to, studies of Mexican-American employment patterns, as evidenced by such works as Mario Barrera's *Race and Class in the Southwest*, Albert Camarillo's *Chicanos in a Changing Society*, and Richard Griswold del Castillo's *The Los Angeles Barrio*, which all appeared in 1979, and Mario T. García's *Desert Immigrants* (1981), and even to a certain extent in later works like Kenneth L. Stewart and Arnoldo De León's *Not Room Enough* (1993) and Emilio Zamora's *The World of the Mexican Worker in Texas* (1993). However, it was not long before scholars suggested that the dual economy could take a variety of forms, such as the ethnic sub-economies which commonly develop among ethnies that are excluded from mainstream economic opportunities. Faced by a combination of strong competition from better qualified native-born jobseekers and ethnic discrimination in hiring practices, immigrants regularly looked to self-employment as a means of securing affluence and status. Traditionally, the resulting over-representation of the foreign born among the ranks of small retail merchants was explained partly by the pressure of discrimination in the job market but also by the inability of native-born merchants to cater for the "special consumer demands", particularly with regards to food products, of immigrant populations (Light, 1972, pp. 4–5, 11–14).

Research on the ethnic sub-economy also originated the concept of the "middleman minority", an ethny composed of small-scale capitalists, such as Jews and Asians, that acted as a buffer between the dominant society and more rigidly excluded ethnies, like African Americans. In her article "A Theory of Middleman Minorities", Edna Bonacich offered the following summary of this kind of group's status and economic role:

> In contrast to most ethnic minorities, they occupy an intermediate rather than low-status position. They tend to concentrate in certain occupations, notably trade and commerce, but also other "middleman" lines such as agent, labor contractor, rent collector, money lender, and broker. They play the role of middleman between producer and consumer, employer and employee, owner and renter, elite and masses (1973, p. 583).

Citing Jewish, Greek, Chinese, and Japanese immigrants as examples of middleman minorities in the United States, Bonacich claimed that a "hall-mark" of such groups was not only "concentration" in but "domination" of certain occupations and markets (ibid., p. 587). Although middleman busi-nesses were typically "labor-intensive", they managed to reduce labor costs through a combination of "thrift" and "ethnically-based paternalism", that is by only hiring laborers from within the ranks of their own ethny. However, according to Bonacich, "the epitome of efficient distribution of resources" was "found in the vertical organization of a particular line, where one set of firms feeds another, within the ethnic community". This position was thought to have been achieved by East European Jews in New York's garment business, "where Jewish manufacturers sold to Jewish wholesalers who used Jewish retail outlets" (ibid., p. 586). Despite its apparent applic-ability to American Jews, the middleman image has most regularly been evoked in historical scholarship in studies of Asian immigrant communities, such as in works by James Loewen (1971), June Mei (1984) and Sucheng Chan (1986) on the Chinese, and Harry Kitano (1974), John Modell (1977) and Edna Bonacich (Bonacich and Modell, 1980) and Nobuya Tsuchida (1984) on the Japanese. In his study of the Japanese in Los Angeles during the first four decades of the twentieth century, John Modell claimed that "however wronged they were, they are certainly a group to which the category 'downtrodden' cannot be applied" (1977, pp. 15–16). Modell found that the economic success of the Japanese earned them a degree of influence in the wider community that was denied to other nonwhites. Local whites recognized a "color line separating them [the Japanese] from black and brown people" and even considered exempting Asians from prescriptive practices – such as restrictive covenants in residential areas – that were unwaveringly applied to African Americans and Mexicans (ibid., pp. 14–15).

However, more contentious than the debates over the origins and form of labor market segmentation, is the one over its extent. Although the concept was originally proposed with the historical division between white and nonwhite labor in mind, it soon became common currency in works comparing the differences in economic opportunity between old-stock whites and ethnies originating from southern and eastern Europe. In the late 1970s, economic historians devoted much attention to the issue of wage differentials between the so-called "old" northern and western European immigrant groups and the "new" southern and eastern ones. While scholars like Robert Higgs (1971) and Peter Hill (1975) found little evidence of discrimination against southern and eastern European immigrants, studies by Robert Shergold (1976), Paul McGouldrick and Michael Tannen (1977), and Francine Blau (1980) suggested that differences in economic opportunity did exist between these ethnic groups and that discrimination, while not the only cause, was a major factor. Recently, Joseph Ferrie (1995, 1997 and 1999) has examined the relatively neglected topic of social mobility among immigrants during the early to mid-nineteenth century and found that immigrants as a whole and Irish immigrants in particular did not enjoy the same levels of advancement as native-born Americans. Blau found that by the early twentieth century the Irish pattern of employment was more akin to that of the new European immigrants than it was the native-born or old European immigrant ones (1980, p. 37). From the late 1970s onwards, social historians, focusing primarily upon the period 1880–1940, also began to depict a two-tier opportunity structure based upon ethnicity – or the "cultural division of labor" as they are apt to call it – among workers in the United States, with skilled occupations being dominated by the native born and old European immigrants, and new European immigrants being confined to less skilled, lower-paid jobs. In northern industrial cities where African Americans or Mexicans were present in large numbers, this became a three-tier ethnic hierarchy among workers, with nonwhites at the bottom. Such is the picture drawn of Pennsylvania steelworkers in John Bodnar's (1977, pp. 74–5) study of Steelton and Ewa Morawska's (1985, pp. 161–70) one of Johnstown, as well as in James Barrett's (1987, pp. 36–63, 272–3) examination of Chicago meat-packing workers.

The concept of an internally segmented white workforce – with southern and eastern European immigrants experiencing exclusion similar to that of nonwhites – has been criticized by various groups of scholars, most notably adherents of the racial formation perspective, who argue that historically the overriding motivation behind and characteristic of the segmented labor market in the United States has been the exclusion of nonwhites by whites. Yuji Ichioka gives a clear exposition of this viewpoint in *The Issei: The World of the First Generation Japanese Immigrants, 1885–1924*:

> Many European immigrants faced formidable obstacles upon their arrival in America. Italians, Poles, Greeks, Armenians, Jews, and others experienced great hardship adjusting and adapting to an alien and often hostile land. Japanese immigrants shared much in common with their European counterparts . . . During the rapid expansion of industrial capitalism after the Civil War, non-English-speaking immigrants, chiefly of eastern- and southern-European origin, filled the ranks of the unskilled labor force required by American industry. In the western United States, Japanese immigrants entered the urban service trades and the agricultural, railroad, mining, lumber, and fishing industries (1990, pp. 1–2).

"Yet", noted Ichioka, "every European group, regardless of national origin, had the right of naturalization" and this created important differences between European and Asian immigrants in the economic sphere, because the latter were open to legalized forms of discrimination, such as the "alien land laws enacted by most western states [which] prohibited aliens ineligible to citizenship from purchasing and leasing land" (ibid., pp. 1–2). A similar assessment is offered by Stanley Lieberson in *A Piece of the Pie: Blacks and White Immigrants since 1880*:

> The early living conditions of the new Europeans after their migration to the United States were extremely harsh and their point of entry into the socioeconomic system was quite low. However, it is a non sequitur to assume that new Europeans had it as bad as did blacks . . . The situation for new Europeans in the United States, bad as it may have been, was not as bad as that experienced by blacks at the same time. Witness, for example, the differences in the disposition to ban openly blacks from unions at the turn of the century . . . the greater concentration of blacks in 1900 in service occupations and their smaller numbers in manufacturing and mechanical jobs . . . and even the greater segregation of blacks with respect to the avenues of eminence open to them. It is a serious mistake to underestimate how far the new Europeans have come in the nation and how hard it all was, but it is equally erroneous to assume that the obstacles were as great as those faced by blacks or that the starting point was the same (1980, p. 383).

The differences between white and nonwhite economic experiences in the United States are also accentuated when account is taken of historical studies of conditions for rural workers. As is demonstrated in such works as William Cohen's *At Freedom's Edge* (1991) on southern blacks, Ronald Takaki's *Pau Hana* (1983) on Asians in Hawaii, Sucheng Chan's *This Bittersweet Soil* (1986) on the Chinese in California, and David Montejano's *Anglos and Mexicans in the Making of Texas* (1987), nonwhite agrarian workers experienced well into the twentieth century varieties of semi-feudal conditions and relations with employers and landowners that their European-immigrant counterparts almost never encountered.

Communalism: Attempting to Reconcile Structuralism with Ethnic Agency

Along with structuralism, another dominant theme in revisionist scholarship has been communalism. For instance, when addressing the question of why some ethnies, in spite of the constraints placed upon them by the dominant society, have made remarkable progress in the economic realm, revisionists generally attribute this success to the groups' adaptive skills, such as a strong spirit of collectivism and co-operation. Once again, Japanese Americans are the group that scholars have focused upon most when exploring this phenomenon. In an influential study of Japanese-American small businesses, Edna Bonacich and John Modell suggested that white hostility in itself does not explain the rapidity and regularity with which Japanese immigrants established small businesses, because many anti-Asian policies, such as the Alien Land Laws, were actually designed to discourage Issei entrepreneurship (1980, pp. 251–3). In contrast, Bonacich and Modell argued there was "a good deal of positive evidence" pointing towards "cultural and situational explanations" of Issei enterprise: "The immigrants did come with some cultural baggage that encouraged concentration in small business, most notably their strong bonds of ethnic solidarity" (ibid., p. 253). From this perspective, ethnicity – and particularly group cohesion – is itself a source of economic strength. Moreover, as Bonacich and Modell noted, "ethnic solidarity interacts significantly with small business in such a way that each sustains the other" (ibid., p. 257). Strong community identification formed the basis for the pooling of resources that enabled the establishment of the ethnic sub-economy and, once established, the sub-economy provided an economic incentive for maintaining ethnic allegiance and ties. Valerie Matsumoto has recently identified the same link between ethnic solidarity and economic activity among the Japanese-American population in the small rural community of Cortez, California. In *Farming the Home Place*, Matsumoto claimed that the ethnic community's ability to survive both the Great Depression and internment during World War II was due to "the maintenance of the effective economic cooperative association that has constituted the backbone of Cortez agriculture, in conjunction with a constellation of social groups that have provided material assistance and cultural affirmation since the 1920s" (1993, p. 12).

Explaining Ethnic Differences: Dead Ends and Loose Ends in Recent Theorizing

Despite dispelling the myth of unimpeded upward mobility, revisionism has fallen short of providing a definitive explanation of the historical relationship between ethnicity and economic attainment in the United States. The dual labor market theory, for instance, has a number of weaknesses. First, like most pluralistic models, it tends to subsume class within ethnicity, thereby ignoring the possibility that differentials in ethnic economic status may actually be mere by-products of American class relations. In an assessment of white workers' animosity towards and collaboration in discrimination against non-white workers, Mario Barrera advanced a persuasive case for viewing race – but the argument appears equally applicable to ethnicity and thereby to relations between old-stock whites and the so-called new European ethnies – as playing a subordinate role to class in the economic realm:

> [A] careful historical examination reveals that Anglo workers have been reacting to the racially segmented labor system created by employers precisely to undercut the wage standards, organizing efforts, and unity of workers as a whole. To the extent that employers have been successful in these efforts, Anglo workers have seen their enemies as the manipulated minority workers, rather than the manipulators. This misperception, essentially a type of false consciousness, has been encouraged by the racial ideologies developed to support the system, and by the general obscuring of class relations created by the hegemony of capitalist ideology (1979, p. 213).

Curiously, Barrera did not take this argument the next apparently logical step further by viewing race and ethnicity in all their manifestations, and not just in the economic sphere, as mere derivations of underlying class relations. Instead, he opts for a more hybrid perspective which allows independent roles for cultural and economic variables alike. This is unfortunate because it compromises the very clarity and coherency which make his statement above so creditable.

By emphasizing the economic origins of ethnic inequality, split labor market theorists also frequently overlook the important part that the state played in the racialization of minorities. Mario Barrera (1979, pp. 157–73) and Terry Boswell (1986, pp. 353–4), with reference to Mexicans and the Chinese, respectively, have both been critical of this oversight in revisionist scholarship. The state, they argued, far from playing a neutral role in society, generally advanced the interests of the capitalist elite and through the passage of immigration, naturalization, and other laws played a fundamental role in creating the context for economic discrimination against ethnic minorities. To be fair, it is worth noting that these criticisms of early descriptions of the split labor market were aimed not at demolishing the theory but at further refining it.

A further flaw in the revisionist case, as exponents of both the assimilationist and pluralist-integration models are apt to point out, is that since World War II most of the barriers to economic advancement have been removed and upward mobility has been the reality for many previously excluded groups, especially white ethnics of southern and eastern European ancestry. This optimistic viewpoint is expressed in Stephan Thernstrom's assessment of social mobility in modern American cities:

> It is true that the climb up the class ladder was harder for men of
> foreign stock than for Yankees, and harder for some immigrant
> groups than for others . . . [Nonetheless,] all of the major immigrant
> groups, however dismal their plight when they first arrived,
> experienced substantial upward mobility in subsequent years. The
> only group that could be considered a truly permanent proletariat
> was the blacks, and even they have found new opportunities for
> advancement in recent decades (1973, pp. 257–8).

Writing from a more leftist ideological position, William Julius Wilson seems to be in agreement with Thernstrom when he contends in *The Declining Significance of Race* that "as the influence of race on minority class-stratification decreases" in the post-civil rights era, "class takes on greater importance in determining the life chances of minority individuals" (1980, p. x: see also Barrera, 1979, pp. 217–18). However, while they agree on the point of racial discrimination's decline in recent decades, Thernstrom and Wilson disagree over how open the American class system is, the former believing that it is now very fluid, the latter that it has become increasingly more rigid. In contrast, Thomas Sowell (1981, pp. 290–4), who like Thernstrom believed that America's capitalist economy provides ethnies with ample opportunity for economic advancement, was apt to downplay the beneficial impact of the anti-discrimination legislation of the 1960s, because to emphasize the state's role in determining social mobility is anathema to his belief in the greater influence of human capital and individual effort. Similarly, Robert Higgs found no clear link between discrimination and black poverty in the post-bellum era and argued that the influence of the state upon the economic plight of African Americans was minimal but mostly beneficial (1977, pp. 125–7, 129–33). Despite their differences, all three of these positions challenge the revisionist emphasis on the persistence of discrimination as the key determinant of ethnic differences in economic achievement.

The revisionist emphasis on communalism has likewise attracted a certain amount of criticism. First, most evidence suggests that ethnic collectivism in the economic sphere declines over time and eventually gives way to individualism. For instance, Edna Bonacich and John Modell found that the Japanese-American propensity for operating small businesses became less pronounced over time as each new generation found the expanding opportunities for individual advancement in the mainstream economy after World War II, which partly resulted from a decline in anti-Asian prejudice and discrimination, to be more enticing than remaining in the ethnic sub-economy. Moreover, these economic changes appeared to have had a deleterious effect upon ethnic solidarity: "Those who moved into the corporate economy had less material reason for retaining close ethnic ties than did those who ran small businesses, and they behaved accordingly". Bonacich and Modell concluded, therefore, that while "[e]thnic affiliation is a resource that may be called upon to support certain economic interests", the case of Japanese Americans suggested that "[w]hen those economic interests are no longer present, ethnicity is likely to subside in importance", which implies that it is appropriate to view ethnicity as "not an eternal verity but a variable that is responsive to societal conditions" (1980, p. 257).

Second, scholars who stress the importance of communal adaptive techniques appear at times to be following a line of argument that is little more than a collectivist version of human-capital theory, a position which is completely at odds with structuralist explanations of ethnic economic inequality. An example of this tendency can be found in Ivan Light's pioneering and influential *Ethnic Enterprise in America*. The historical context in which Light's study originated is illuminating. As with so many other subjects in the field of American ethnic history, the racial disturbances of the 1960s were the impetus for this scholarly investigation. While the riots in Los Angeles, Detroit, and other major cities "differed in intensity", Light observed that "wherever they occurred they usually involved attacks by local blacks on white-owned stores in their neighborhoods" (1972, p. 2). Noting how the targeted businesses were "owned disproportionately by Jews and by foreign-born whites", Light was struck by the fact that "[i]n this scenario of American rioting, the conspicuously missing figure is the black retail proprietor who does business in a black neighborhood and specializes in appliances, furniture, clothing, liquor, or groceries" (ibid., pp. 2–3). Light was thus inspired to investigate the virtual absence of this economic class among African Americans. In his search for an explanation of this phenomenon, Light rejected the simple argument that it originated in the more severe discrimination faced by African Americans due to racial prejudice:

> These cruel disadvantages explain many differences between blacks and foreign-born whites, but they do not explain why the latter have been regularly active in business proprietorships (even in black neighborhoods) whereas the blacks themselves have not. On the contrary, the extra disadvantages of blacks ought, strictly speaking, to have stimulated them to more extensive self-employment than the foreign-born whites.

Indeed, Light argued that the experiences of two other nonwhite ethnies, Chinese Americans and Japanese Americans, provided "empirical illustration of the manner in which poverty, discrimination, and ethnic visibility stimulated business proprietorship among some disadvantaged immigrants" (ibid., p. 5). Light also challenged the traditional view that the "lack of special consumer demands and the consequent presence of inhibiting white competition" primarily explained black under representation in small business activity, noting how Asian immigrant small businessmen relied heavily upon their trade with non-Asian customers (ibid., pp. 12, 15–18). Another explanation for the scarcity of African-American small businesses was that, discriminated against by mainstream banks and money-lending institutions, blacks lacked access to the credit necessary for entrepreneurial activity. However, Light claimed that foreign-born white and Asian immigrants were similarly discriminated against by mainstream financial institutions but this did not prevent them from setting up small businesses (ibid., pp. 19–21). In fact, Light argued that probably the key factor in explaining differences in levels of small-scale entrepreneurship among African Americans and Asian immigrants was the latter's ability to generate their own supply of capital through involvement in rotating credit associations, a tradition they had imported from Asia and which American-born blacks lacked. This made Asian immigrants less dependent than African Americans on mainstream sources of credit and, combined with their "penchant for partnerships rather than solo entrepreneurships", gave them a distinct advantage over blacks in the field of small business activity (ibid., pp. 18, 36). In short, Light believed that "culturally-derived differences" were more important determinants of entrepreneurship than the structural factors emphasized in the "consumer-demands" and "discrimination-in-lending" theories (ibid., pp. 18–19).

Light's argument lends itself too easily to appropriation by exponents of the "model minority" theory, who use the example of Asian-American economic success to herald the veracity of the "land of opportunity" ideal and draw disparaging comparisons with other less successful nonwhite groups, like African Americans and Puerto Ricans. As Bonacich and Modell (1980, pp. 7–8) point out, the model minority viewpoint implicitly raises the question: "If the Japanese Americans can overcome racial discrimination, why can't you?" Indeed, both Sowell (1981, pp. 282–4, 291) and Higgs (1977, p. 127) have suggested that cultural factors explain the relatively low levels of economic achievement among some racial minorities. However, just as Stanley Lieberson criticized the practice of drawing parallels between the experiences of European immigrants and African Americans on the grounds that it was not comparing like with like, Edna Bonacich and John Modell have pointed out that the same is true in the case of blacks and Asian immigrants, because the latter were not as a group, either before or after the abolition of slavery, as ruthlessly exploited as the black population long tied to the agrarian economy of the American South (1980, p. 8).

SUMMARY

What light then do these discussions of residential patterns, education, and social mobility shed up the subject of the inclusion/equality–exclusion/inequality dichotomy? In the debate over residential patterns, the orthodox picture of an open society does not stand up well against revisionist critiques buttressed by countless examples of ethnies experiencing high levels of segregation. Moreover, this alternative picture of ethnic exclusion and inequality is further strengthened by the evidence showing that residential segregation was more usually involuntary than voluntary and that the advantages ethnies derived from ghettoization were more than outweighed by the drawbacks. Similarly, the traditional image of an education system that provided all groups with equal access to opportunity is seriously compromised by the fact that, as revisionists have shown, nonwhites were frequently denied access to public education or, at best, provided with a palpably inferior version of that available to whites. However, revisionist historians have been less successful in demonstrating that the public schools served old-stock children much better than they did newcomers from southern and eastern Europe. Nonetheless, the debate over social mobility renders moot the education controversy, because few historians would now challenge the revisionist contention that, as a direct result of discrimination, most immigrant groups at one time or another and virtually all nonwhite ethnies for much of the time, no matter what level of education they had attained, were prevented from enjoying the same degree of economic opportunity as native-born, old-stock whites.

Clearly, in terms of the ease with which ethnic and racial minorities have been incorporated into the social and economic structures of the United States and the heights to which they have been able to rise, the revisionist argument of exclusion and inequality does seem to carry more weight than the orthodox one of inclusion and equality. However, exponents of the orthodox interpretation can and do take solace from the fact that in all three of the areas examined in this chapter – residential patterns, education, and social mobility – the overall historical trend (albeit one punctuated by occasional reversals) has been one of increasing levels of ethnic inclusion combined with decreasing levels of ethnic inequality. As to whether incorporation has been a uniform process or one that varied from ethny to ethny, the historical literature can be summarized as pointing to a single broad pattern that seems to apply to all three topics. That pattern being a clear white–nonwhite divide in the histories of American ethnic groups, with the nonwhite experiences generally being characterized by exclusion and inequality, and the white ethnic experiences by inclusion and equality. Moreover, by identifying the variations of group experience that exist within these broad racially defined categories, the historical scholarship suggests that the different group experiences appear to be plotted at intervals along a spectrum ranging from inclusion and equality at one end to exclusion and inequality at the other and that skin color seems to be the only consistent determinant of the position occupied by any particular group. The lighter the skin color, the closer an ethny is to the inclusion-equality end of the spectrum. The darker the skin, the further they are away from it.

A crucial difference between the issues covered in this chapter and those in the previous one is that, while dominant society perceptions and policies are still the main focus, considerations of ethnic agency come into play much more in scholarly discussions of residential patterns, education, and upward mobility than they do in those on more central aspects of the American Creed. It is only appropriate, therefore, that in the next chapter we continue with this shift towards emphasis upon minority group viewpoints and behavior by turning to the topic of ethnic collective action.

PART IV

Minority Group Responses to American Life

SIX

Ethnic Collective Action

INTRODUCTION

Ethnic collective action is one of the most written-about topics in the field of American ethnic history, but also probably the least understood. The historiography of the subject is complex and not easily accessible to the novice. The reasons for this are twofold. First, scholarship on ethnic collective action encompasses a multiplicity of debates, each addressing questions that relate to different facets of the phenomenon. How frequently does ethnic collective action occur? What causes it – are the stimuli to group activity mostly internal or external in origin? What forms does ethnic collective action take and what are the outcomes typically connected to each of these forms? These are only the key questions posed by an examination of how ethnies respond to the dominant society, a multitude of others arise when the issue of interethnic relations is explored. Second, the debates generated by these questions regularly cut across the main theoretical divisions in American ethnic history. The main schools of thought on ethnic collective action do not, for instance, neatly correspond to the alignments of the assimilation–pluralism dichotomy.

The picture is further complicated by the problems associated with defining ethnic collective action. Scholars not only use both broad and narrow definitions of the term, but also refer to it by other names, such as ethnic politics, ethnic protest, and so on. There are a variety of narrow definitions of ethnic collective action, which each associate the term with only one of the following distinct activities: defending the ethny's culture; promoting its material interests; or championing the wider cause of ethnic tolerance and equality. In its broader sense, the term and its synonyms relate to a combination of any or all of these types of activity. This broader definition of ethnic collective action is the one most commonly subscribed to, albeit implicitly in many cases, by scholars working in the field of American ethnic history.

This chapter provides a structured analysis of historical writing on ethnic collective action. Three key issues are examined: the causes of ethnic collective action; its main forms and outcomes; and interethnic relations. In addition to outlining the main contours of the debates surrounding these topics, the relationship of the latter to broader historiographical discussions are also explored.

CAUSES OF ETHNIC COLLECTIVE ACTION

Before examining the forms of ethnic collective action, it is necessary to outline the two main schools of thought on the causes of the phenomenon. As with so many other aspects of American ethnic history, the academic debate on this subject centers upon a major dichotomy, in this case the "external–internal" one, and a single question: Is ethnic collective action produced by internal forces, that is forces emanating from within the ethny itself, or external ones, emanating from outside of the group, such as from the dominant society or another ethny? Once again, scholarly opinion is not divided into two opposing viewpoints that maintain that the stimuli for ethnic collective action are either all external or all internal, but rather into theoretical perspectives that recognize the presence of both internal and external forces but place more emphasis on one set of factors than the other.

Orthodoxy: Ethnies as Reactive Entities

For a long time, historians typically portrayed ethnic collective action as a reactive rather than proactive phenomenon. Ethnies were conventionally depicted as the supporting cast in the drama of American history, with the leading roles being played by members of the dominant ethny. Or to use another analogy, ethnies were viewed as pawns in a game of chess played between opponents of white, Anglo-Saxon, Protestant ancestry. Like pawns, ethnies were considered not to have played any part in either devising the rules of the game or determining its outcome, other than when serving as a tool in one of the players' strategies. A telling example of this tendency is the treatment of Native Americans in the fields of North American diplomatic and military history, which, along with political history, were the chief areas of interest to professional historians until well into the twentieth century. Wars, alliances, and treaties with indigenous peoples have long figured prominently in studies of post-Columbian military and diplomatic events in North America, largely because it would be impossible to write about such topics, particularly with reference to the seventeenth, eighteenth, and early nineteenth centuries, without mentioning Native Americans, but the latter were not credited in traditional scholarship with playing roles equal in importance to those of the European imperialists or American colonists (for fairly representative examples of this ethnocentric perspective on North American diplomatic history, see Kellogg, 1925 and 1935; Peckham, 1961; Leach, 1958). Similarly, immigrants were typically depicted as the sheep-like minions of corrupt urban political bosses who derived their power from the ability to mobilize ethnic voting blocs. Consequently, the ethnic influence on mainstream politics, where it was acknowledged at all by historians and social scientists, was generally characterized as being a deleterious one (Saveth, 1965 [1948], pp. 150–78: see also Hall, 1906; Ross, 1914; Commons, 1907; Fairchild, 1926). A notable exception to the traditional practice of discounting Native-American agency was Max Farrand's (1905) study of the boundary line established in 1763 by the British to separate white and indigenous settlements in North America, while George Hunt (1960 [1940]) offered an early critique of the conventional depiction of Native Americans as unworldly and irrational. Similarly, George Stephenson (1926) made a serious attempt at providing a balanced analysis of immigrants' influence upon American politics. Despite these voices of dissent, the traditionally very narrow outlook on the causes of ethnic collective action dominated historical thinking during the first half of the twentieth century. Moreover, some ethnies were viewed as more pawn-like than others. This was particularly the case in historical treatments of collective action among nonwhite ethnies. Asian immigrants, for instance, were rarely accredited with playing an active, let alone prominent role in resisting and overturning the anti-Asian discriminatory practices and laws of the late nineteenth and early twentieth centuries (see, for example, Konvitz, 1946; Daniels, 1962). However, as will be shown, from the 1950s onwards, the traditional view increasingly came under attack and was criticized for being ethnocentric and patronizing.

The Revisionist Emphasis on Ethnic Agency

Early revisionist studies did not generally abandon the view that ethnic collective action was essentially reactive, but they accredited ethnies with historically exercising far more agency than was suggested in orthodox works. Revisionism did not place the ethnies at center stage, but it did acknowledge that they were not the mere tools of the main players and could on occasion impose their will upon events in a way that influenced the wider course of American history. The causes of ethnic collective action, therefore, were still external to the ethny, but the ethny was not external to the processes that created those causes (Stephenson, 1926; Du Bois, 1935; Hunt, 1960 [1940];

Downes, 1940; Handlin, 1941; Ernst, 1979 [1949]). Indeed, one of the most important achievements of the first generation of immigration historians was to secure recognition for the mere fact that ethnicity and ethnic groups had played a role in American politics. For instance, neither of the two dominant theoretical perspectives in the field of sociology during the early twentieth century acknowledged ethnicity as being a cause of collective action in its own right. Classical Marxism viewed virtually all incidents of collective action as manifestations of the ongoing class struggle between the broad economic interest groups created by the modernization process of urbanization, industrialization, and bureaucratization. Marxists viewed ethnic collective action as an anomaly in modern society and a phenomenon that would eventually disappear due to the inevitable growth of class consciousness and its transcendence of culturally-defined allegiances like ethnicity. Likewise, the functionalist perspective being developed at the University of Chicago during the early twentieth century interpreted collective action as essentially irrational and originating in the sense of alienation felt by groups who were marginalized by their own inability to adapt to modernization. For the influential Chicago school scholars, therefore, the ethnic dimension evident in some collective action was merely viewed as further proof that the phenomenon was nothing more than the dysfunctional behavior of unassimilated elements of the urban population and that such occurrences would cease once these groups had been fully assimilated (see Hirsch, 1990, pp. 171–219). In *The Immigrant in American History*, Marcus Lee Hansen presented a modified version of these perspectives on ethnic collective action. Hansen argued that nineteenth-century European immigrants were rarely highly politicized, let alone radical in their politics, and consequently had little impact on American political ideals and institutions, which remained virtually unchanged during the period of mass immigration. Political practices were influenced by immigration to the extent that the main parties had to cater to emerging ethnic voting blocs, but Hansen saw the latter as transitory phenomena. In fact, Hansen believed that, due to the political conservatism and pro-capitalist sentiments of most immigrants and their offspring as well as to the salience of ethnic voting blocs, immigration had an essentially conservative influence upon American politics and actually delayed the emergence of European-style class-based politics (1964 [1940], pp. 77–96). Hansen's successor as the don of American immigration history, Oscar Handlin, agreed that the immigrants generally shied away from radicalism and were even unmoved by the major home-grown reform movements, such as Populism and Progressivism. However, for Handlin ethnic political behavior was essentially neither irrational nor rooted in pre-modern sensibilities but motivated rather by a keen awareness of group self-interest. In *The Uprooted*, Handlin emphasized the links between the appearance of formidable ethnic voting blocs and the rise of political machines, like New York's notorious Tammany Hall, during the nineteenth century. According to Handlin, urban political bosses maintained the loyalty of ethnic voters not just because of a shared ethnic heritage, but because they catered to the material needs of their constituents. Corrupt as the spoils system may have been, it gave immigrant workers access to secure blue-collar employment and for talented individuals an alternative route into white-collar employment and middle-class status. Nonetheless, Handlin viewed ethnic voting blocs and the political machines and bosses they sustained as ephemeral phenomena whose disappearance occurred virtually in tandem with the assimilation of the immigrants' descendants (1951, pp. 201–26).

Although both Hansen and Handlin rather uncritically assumed that ethnic groups possessed a higher degree of homogeneity than is probably warranted by the facts, their interpretations of ethnic politics are not incompatible with the "situational" view of ethnicity discussed in Chapter 1. According to this perspective, ethnies are traditionally very heterogeneous and diffuse entities and it requires the appearance of an outside threat for them to be galvanized into a unified group and mobilized into taking collective action.

The situational interpretation of ethnic collective action comes in three varieties. One of these variants, the "instrumental" perspective, considers ethnic collective action to be a response by subordinate ethnies to the prejudice, discrimination and maltreatment they experience at the hands of dominant ethnies. This viewpoint can be found in the treatments of ethnic politics by historians like George Stephenson (1926, pp. 118, 126) and Oscar Handlin (1951, p. 219), both of whom suggested that immigrants took refuge in bossism at the local level and the Democratic Party at state and national levels in response to the nativism of first the Whigs and then later the Republicans. The main weakness of this viewpoint is that it depends upon ethnic group members consistently putting collective interests before personal ones, which critics argue does not reflect reality. According to exponents of "incentive" theory, participants in collective action are usually motivated more by self-interest than altruism, the latter being insufficient in itself to mobilize ethnies. However, incentive theory, which originated in the social sciences, has found few converts among scholars studying the history of collective action among American ethnic groups.

Other variants of the situational perspective are the numerous class-based or structural theories which consider capitalist exploitation to be the cause of ethnic collective action. One such example is the "cultural division of labor" concept that underpins classic versions of the internal–colony model (Hechter, 1975 and 1978). According to Michael Hechter, Debra Friedman, and Malka Appelbaum,

[t]his theory assumes that when the members of ethnic groups occupy distinctive positions in the class or occupational structures, or in the labor market (especially disadvantaged positions), and when they become aware of their common plight, it will be only a matter of time before collective action ensues (1982, p. 413).

This view can be criticized on the grounds that concentrated depravation and inequality is rarely the trigger for specific instances of ethnic collective action. Indeed, ethnic political mobilization has occurred far less frequently than structural theories suggest ought to be the case, because the level of ethnic segmentation in the American economy has rarely been matched by the incidence of ethnic collective action directed at challenging discrimination. Moreover, there are countless periods of American history when ethnic collective action did not occur but when, if structural theories about the conditions giving rise to it are to be believed, it should have done. As Hechter, Friedman, and Appelbaum pointed out:

A theory that explains the occurrence of ethnic collective action solely by the existence of a common interest in change – and the collective benefits this would bring – cannot account for its nonoccurrence in the face of outright exploitation. Nor can it explain variation in the incidence and form of ethnic collective action among groups having the same interest in seeking political change. Such a theory can only explain the desirability of collective action rather than its actual occurrence (1982, p. 415).

The third main variant of the situational perspective is the "competition" model, which suggests that ethnic collective action is triggered by demographic changes which intensify the struggle for resources among ethnies. The most comprehensive and influential exposition of this perspective is Susan Olzak's *The Dynamics of Ethnic Competition and Conflict*, which analyzed "the causes of racial and ethnic confrontations, protests, riots, and attacks" in America's largest seventy-seven cities during the period 1877 to 1914 (1992, pp. 1, 11). According to Olzak, the competition model "represents a shift in emphasis away from considering static conditions" because it "focuses instead on processes of change that ignite racial and ethnic strife". Arguing that "changes in inequality foster ethnic conflicts and protests", Olzak claimed that "efforts to explain racial and ethnic conflicts need to move beyond consideration of static conditions of inequality and political repression as primary causal factors". Criticizing both the instrumental and structural perspectives for their inability to "explain patterns of ethnic violence that have varied over time and across targets", Olzak asserted:

"Explaining such patterns demands theories that directly take the dynamics of changing conditions into account". Olzak believed she had accomplished this feat in arriving at her central argument that "ethnic conflicts and protests erupt when ethnic inequalities and racially ordered systems begin to break down" (ibid., p. 13). Olzak's theory is based and to a certain degree dependent upon her utilization of a very broad and far from orthodox definition of ethnic collective action:

> *Ethnic collective action* is a public action of two or more persons that articulates a distinctly ethnic (or racial) claim, expresses a grievance, or attacks members of another ethnic group (or their property). Such actions include protests involving proactive claims of one group as in civil rights' activity. They also include conflicts, as when members of two or more ethnic populations confront one another (ibid., p. 6).

Olzak readily acknowledged that this definition permitted even collective action involving the "white majority" and nativist/racist groups like the Ku Klux Klan to be classified as ethnic protest events (ibid., p. 9). While the logic of Olzak's reasoning is hard to dispute, her broad definition of ethnic collective action is not one that previously had been commonly used by scholars working in the field of American ethnic history (for whom "ethnic" invariably meant groups who did not belong to the majority population or dominant society), nor has it become so subsequently.

In recent decades, it has become more common for historians to view ethnic collective action as proactive rather than reactive. This trend reflects the greater emphasis placed upon "agency" in the work of the New Social History school that emerged out of the 1960s (Kessler-Harris, 1990, p. 165). According to this view, all ethnies in the United States have adopted associational activity as a means of ensuring the group's survival. As Josef Barton observed in a study of ethnic leadership among southern and eastern European immigrants:

> If one surveys the emergence of ethnic leadership in American cities, one is confronted with a bewildering picture of diverse institutional responses to what, for all its variations in outward form, is essentially a common problem: the construction of collective means of coming to terms with the realities of urban life (1978, p. 160).

During the period 1890–1950, claimed Barton, the "laggard response of public institutions to urban problems" made the development of voluntary associations virtually a matter of necessity for urban ethnic communities (ibid., pp. 156–7). Moreover, the numerous exponents of "resource mobilization" theory who have appeared since the early 1970s maintain that the more organized an ethny is the greater the likelihood there is of it engaging in collective action (Jenkins, 1983; McAdam, 1982; Morris, 1984). However, this line of argument immediately raises the question of why some ethnies are more likely to mobilize politically than others. Two main types of answer have been given to this question. Numerous scholars claim that cultural factors account for ethnic differences in levels of collective action. Some ethnies, it is argued, have stronger traditions of protest, radicalism, political awareness, and so on, which accounts for their higher rates of activism. In *Beyond the Melting Pot*, Nathan Glazer and Daniel Patrick Moynihan characterized Puerto Rican migrants in New York City as an "island-centered community" more interested in the politics of their homeland than of their adopted home. This outlook, claimed Glazer and Moynihan, explained why "relatively few Puerto Ricans, compared with Negroes in the city, or with the non-Puerto Rican white groups, register and vote" and accounted for the "relative weakness of community organization and community leadership among them" (1963, pp. 99–101). The absence of detailed historical studies on Puerto Rican New Yorkers meant that the observations in social science studies like *Beyond the Melting Pot* occupied a prominent place in the historiography of ethnic collective action until the early 1980s. Similarly, as Arnoldo De León (1991, pp. 20–9) has noted, Mexican Americans in the Southwest, when referred to at all in the works of professional historians, were at least until the mid-1960s typically characterized as a group who for cultural reasons were lacking in community organization and effective political mobilization. The conventional histories rested upon a specious argument because it is hard to find an ethnic culture that does not possess a protest tradition to be drawn upon should the need arise. Indeed, as Virginia Sánchez Korrol demonstrated in her revisionist study of Puerto Ricans in New York City, Glazer and Moynihan's failure to locate the existence of developed organizational activity and political leadership among this ethny largely derived from the fact that they were looking in the wrong places. According to Korrol, Glazer and Moynihan's focus on the post-World War II migration meant that they overlooked the pioneer migrants of the late nineteenth and early twentieth centuries who established traditions of community organization and leadership that culminated in an eruption of high profile political activity during the decade following the first publication of *Beyond the Melting Pot* (Korrol, 1994, pp. 4–5, 132–5, 162–3, 184, 199–200, 224–35). Furthermore, due to their neglect of working-class and hometown organizations, Glazer and Moynihan failed to recognize the very institutions which had laid the foundations for Puerto Rican political activism, which is ironic because these types of institutions were widely credited with performing exactly the same historical role among other ethnic groups in New York City.

   Alternatively, another group of scholars places more emphasis on a group's social capital, asserting that affluence is an essential prerequisite for political activity (Jenkins, 1983, pp. 531–2). However, American history is replete with cases of impoverished ethnies mobilizing for political action and sustaining such efforts over a long period of time. Furthermore, the most famous examples of ethnic collective action have usually involved the most marginalized ethnies protesting against the introduction of discriminatory laws and practices, that is external stimuli.

VARIETIES OF ETHNIC COLLECTIVE BEHAVIOR

Although the debate over its origins continues, the main historiographical discussion about ethnic collective action centers on its form and outcomes. Two main questions are the focus of this discourse. What form has ethnic collective action most commonly taken in the United States and which has been the most effective? In order to address these questions it is first necessary to outline the main types of ethnic collective behavior, which can be grouped into four categories: passive participation, passive non-participation, active participation, and active non-participation. The labels "passive" and "active" refer to strategy, "participation" and "non-participation" to objectives. While the terms relating to strategy are fairly self-explanatory, those referring to objectives deserve further explanation. "Participation" means working within mainstream American politics, whereas "non-participation" means the opposite, that is challenging, rejecting or undermining the political culture, structure and institutions of the United States. The four category headings, therefore, can be defined as follows: passive participation is a form of collective action that pursues a strategy of accommodation to achieve integration; passive non-participation seeks ethnic autonomy through legal and political separation from the United States; active participation involves the pursuit of integration through involvement in mainstream politics; and active non-participation uses revolutionary tactics to overthrow one or more element of the American system of social, economic and political organization.

Passive Participation

Historians have traditionally implied, if only occasionally explicitly stated, that ethnic collective action in the United States has generally taken the form of passive participation, more commonly known as "accommodationism". Scholars have adhered to this orthodox position for a variety of reasons. Most have done so because they discount ethnicity as a variable in American politics. When refuting nineteenth-century historians' claims that immigrants introduced radical and corrupting influences into American politics, Edward

Saveth probably went too far in asserting that "[t]here were other phases of American life in which the immigrant played a greater role" (1965 [1948], p. 178). Other historians argue that accommodationism has been the prevalent form of ethnic collective action merely because it was the only option available to many ethnies for much of the time. The acknowledged embodiment of this type of accommodationism is Booker T. Washington, who in his famous Atlanta Compromise speech of 1895 urged his fellow African Americans to resist the temptation to agitate for either social or political equality and instead to channel their energies into economic improvement as a means of gradually earning the respect and acceptance of whites. As historians like August Meier (1963) and Louis Harlan (1972 and 1983) have suggested, to pursue any other course during an era of spiraling lynchings and federal indifference to the plight of blacks might have proved at best futile and at worse disastrous.

Origins of Accommodationism: Voluntarism

Passive participation, therefore, appears to come in two forms: voluntary and involuntary. Scholars who perceive accommodationism as essentially voluntary tend to do so because they assume that most groups, because they are generally treated well by the dominant society, have no need for engaging in more extreme forms of ethnic politics. "The bulk of naturalized voters in the nineteenth century", asserted Marcus Lee Hansen, "never grasped the fine points involved in public policy; but they comprehended the basic character of American democracy and usually made its maintenance without essential change their principal political objective" (1964 [1940], p. 95).

Origins of Accommodationism: Discrimination

In contrast, scholars who emphasize the involuntary nature of passive participation identify the reasons why groups are regularly forced to adopt this approach to power relations. First, passively conforming to the expectations of the dominant society leads to more ready acceptance of an ethny, which eases the group's incorporation into mainstream social and economic activity and, hence, individual mobility. According to Thomas Sowell, this strategy of "quiet persistence" was adopted by and "proved successful" for the Chinese, Japanese, and East European Jews (1981, p. 294). Second, avoidance of politics enables an ethny's members to concentrate on economic activities, possibly creating a niche that will be the base for later upward mobility. As a result of its "conscious economic motive", claimed John Modell, the Issei (first-generation Japanese immigrant) population of Los Angeles laid the foundations during the early twentieth century for the phenomenal success of their children and grandchildren, the Nisei and Sansei, respectively, during the post-World War II era (1977, p. 126). Modell described this "accommodation" as "a group response to external pressures born partly of white resentment of Japanese resourcefulness in exploiting local opportunities" that nonetheless was "a responsible strategy" and "not an unrewarded pattern" (ibid., p. ix). Third, accommodationism, with its emphasis on keeping a low profile, can prevent ethnies from attracting unwanted attention and hostility. As Naomi Cohen has shown in her book *Encounter with Emancipation*, the German Jews who settled in the United States from the 1830s onwards successfully pursued such a strategy of conforming to their new surroundings in an attempt to "win acceptance and integration within the larger society" and achieve "rapid economic mobility" in the process (1984, pp. xi, xii).

Over recent decades, the assumptions and arguments that the orthodox perspective is founded upon have increasingly been challenged. Revisionists claim that accommodationism perpetuates rather than undermines the marginal status of ethnies. Accommodationism, state its critics, makes an ethny appear weak and therefore an easy target for further mistreatment and discrimination. Grant Foreman early argued that the removal from the South of 60,000 Cherokees, Creeks, Chickasaws, Choctaws, and Seminoles during the 1830s and their resettlement in what later became the state of Oklahoma – a trek which included the infamous "Trail of Tears" that cost the lives of 4,000 Cherokees – was greatly facilitated by the strides these so-called "Five Civilized Tribes" had made over the preceding half century in conforming to white patterns of thought and behavior:

> In proportion as these Indians improved in intelligence and culture, wealth, and enterprise, did the white man covet their country in the South. Individually and in concert, by law and without law, he oppressed these owners of the soil and depredated upon their country until they were driven forth to find refuge in the wilderness west of the Mississippi River (1934, p. vii).

In the case of the Cherokee, noted William McLoughlin, the "rebirth of that people in the image of the United States" during the period 1794–1833 was to no avail, because the simultaneous "transition in Western culture from the world view of the Enlightenment to the world view of Romanticism" had effected "a redefinition of what it meant to be an American" (1986, pp. xv, xvi, xix). In Thomas Jefferson's late eighteenth-century Enlightenment-influenced vision of the United States, based as it was upon a belief in the "unity of the human race", there was a place for assimilated Native Americans, but in Andrew Jackson's early nineteenth-century Romanticism-influenced vision, which presupposed a "hierarchy of races", there was not (ibid., pp. xv–xvi). Moreover, revisionist historians contend that while only meager benefits are derived from pursuing passive participation, those that are generally fall to the ethny's elite, so the strategy is inherently divisive because it creates cleavages between the more and the less disadvantaged elements within a group. In his introduction to the collection of essays entitled *Ethnic Leadership in America*, John Higham, observing how "[t]he alternatives of protest or accommodation arise when a group faces a choice in its relations with the surrounding society", claimed that the contributions by Nathan Glazer, Roger Daniels, Frederick Luebke, and Nathan Huggins, on Jews, Japanese, Germans, African Americans, and Native Americans, respectively, revealed how in the past all of these groups' ethnic leaderships had been divided along such lines (1978, p. 8). Despite Higham's suggestion that this division was an almost natural phenomenon, many of the very essays that he referred to provided telling examples of the deleterious effect that struggles between pro- and anti-accommodation factions can have upon a group's ability to respond effectively to discrimination and persecution by the dominant society. Moreover, studies of Native Americans' responses to the removal crisis generally attest to the fact that the Five Civilized Tribes were severely weakened by internal wrangles between the parties of appeasement and resistance, the former mainly representing the more assimilated and wealthier tribesmen and the latter the traditionalist, less affluent elements (Young, 1958; Wilkins, 1970). Similarly, Louis Harlan, in his relatively sympathetic appraisal of Booker T. Washington, readily admitted that the eminent black leader's own experience of the Progressive Era stood in stark contrast to those he claimed to represent: "What was for Washington personally the best of times was for most blacks the worst – the most discouraging period since the freeing of the slaves", characterized by the "loss of voting rights in the South, segregation, economic exploitation, and a nationwide atmosphere of white racial hatred and violence" (1983, pp. viii–ix). Washington, commented Harlan, "found it impossible to accommodate to the system of white supremacy and at the same time to challenge or change it" (ibid., p. ix).

Passive Non-Participation

Prior to the 1960s, few historians would have stated that there was a significant tradition of ethnic separatism in the United States, despite, in the case of some ethnies, stark and abundant evidence of its existence. However, the rise of the pluralist school prompted an upsurge in interest in passive non-participation as a pattern of ethnic collective action. Passive non-participation has appeared in two main forms: movements that seek some form of separatism within the political and/or geographic boundaries of the

United States; and those that have an external locus, such as an ancestral homeland. Because of the distinctive nature of these phenomena they require separate analysis.

Separatism: Reactive or Proactive?

The first of these two forms of passive non-participation appears to have emerged as a response to discrimination and exclusion suffered at the hands of the dominant society, which forced ethnies to establish separate institutions – such as businesses, mutual aid societies, educational establishments, political organizations, and so on – in order to survive and prosper in the United States. These separatist inclinations reach their most complete expression in the form of full-blown nationalist movements. In their introduction to *Black Nationalism in America*, John Bracey, August Meier, and Elliott Rudwick pointed out that "nationalist sentiment, although present throughout the black . . . experience in America, tends to be most pronounced when . . . [African Americans'] status has declined, or when they have experienced intense disillusionment following a period of heightened but unfulfilled expectations" (1970, p. xxvi). While Bracey, Meier, and Rudwick approached the topic of black nationalism in an objective manner, Howard Brotz's (1970), Alphonso Pinkney's (1976), and Tony Martin's (1976) pioneering monographs on the topic were somewhat dogmatic. As well as accounting for the emergence during the late 1960s of the separatist Black Power movement out of the integrationist civil rights movement, this interpretation was early advanced by Alvin Josephy (1971, pp. 13–14) to explain the rise of the contemporaneous Native-American Red Power movement and, more recently, by Carlos Muñoz (1989, pp. 12, 15–16) with reference to the Chicano movement. Josephy's book, like the Bracey, Meier, and Rudwick volume on black nationalism, is only a collection of documents, but early and sympathetic narratives of the Red Power movement were provided by D'Arcy McNickle (1973) and Peter Matthiessen (1983), and a more skeptical one by Francis Paul Prucha (1985). While Meier and Rudwick argued that "the dominant thrust of black ideologies has been the desire for inclusion in the broader American society" and viewed the "ebb and flow in the popularity of nationalist doctrines" as evidence of their subordinate status, Bracey and others have viewed black nationalism as a response to African Americans' status as an internal colony and contend that the movement continually gains momentum over time (Bracey, et al., 1970, pp. liv–lv, lvi, lix). The case for continuity in nationalist sentiment among ethnies has also been argued by John Chávez (1984) and Sterling Stuckey (1987). Whereas Bracey's judgment, like that of many other historians writing on the topic, seems to have been clouded by his own enthusiasm for the nationalist movements of the 1960s, in hindsight it appears as though Meier's and Rudwick's assessment of the longevity of such groups was closer to mark. As Frederick Luebke's studies of German Americans have revealed, it was not just nonwhites who have sought solace in nationalism as a response to perceived mistreatment. During the decades prior to World War I, many Germans "labored mightily to erect a complex of institutions that served to sustain ethnic culture" and, in the face of declining immigration from Germany, "ethnic leaders sought to inhibit the inevitable disintegration of the group by espousing a new cultural chauvinism" (1978, p. 65: see also Luebke, 1974).

Having witnessed the spectacular rise and rather sudden fall of numerous militant nationalist groups during the 1960s and 1970s, many scholars came to view such separatist movements as a temporary but nonetheless important stage in the adaptive process. Separatist activities appeared to perform useful functions. Passive non-participation permitted groups to develop strong cultural, social, economic, and political institutions that would be a resource to draw upon in the future, even after external prejudice decreased and incorporation became easier. For instance, studies of groups who formed ethnic subeconomies suggest that their members achieved higher levels of mobility in later generations. As María Cristina García shows in her book *Havana USA*, the Cuban community in South Florida conforms to this model. Perceiving themselves as "exiles, not immigrants", Cubans established a "viable economic enclave" and, intent on "preserving *cubanidad* ('Cubanness', or Cuban identity)", "created a cultural enclave as well" (García, 1996, pp. 1–2). While the Cuban émigrés have yet to realize their dream of returning to a Castro-free Cuba, they have succeeded through their enterprise in placing the US-born Cuban-American generation in a fortuitous economic and social position.

Homeland Focus: Help or Hindrance to Integration?

The second form of passive non-participation, most pronounced among groups possessing a strong sojourner mentality, is one in which ethnies displayed a keener interest and involvement in the politics of their ancestral homeland than they did in those of the United States. Sometimes, ethnies retained this concern over homeland politics because their country of origin was involved in a struggle to cast off colonial rule. As H. Brett Melendy (1977), Kinsley Lyu (1977a and 1977b), and Bong-youn Choy (1979) have shown, for Asian immigrants, particularly the Koreans involved in the struggle to end Japanese colonial rule, this sentiment usually took concrete form in the provision of direct aid and assistance to the homeland nationalist movement, rather than in attempts to influence US foreign policy. Jewish immigrants' homeland focus, as illustrated in the works of Gary Best (1982),

Naomi Cohen (1972), Henry Feingold (1970), and Melvin Urofsky (1975 and 1978), has gradually shifted in emphasis away from their eastern and central European sending regions, where the concern was over Tsarist and Nazi persecutions of Jews, towards Palestine and concern over the fate of the fledgling Jewish settlements there and the ensuing new state of Israel.

In the case of some groups, these nationalist energies were later channeled, very successfully, into mainstream American politics. Indeed, for various ethnic groups, the desire to influence US foreign policy toward or harness it to gain independence for the ancestral homeland prompted some of their earliest forays into American politics. This was true of a number of the groups attempting to influence Woodrow Wilson's contribution to the Versailles peace settlement at the end of World War I, as is demonstrated in a multi-authored collection of essays on the topic edited by Joseph O'Grady (1967). Nonetheless, scholars debate the extent to which ethnies have either possessed an interest in or exerted any influence over US policy towards their ancestral homelands. Laurence Halley, for example, has argued that Greek, Irish, and Polish Americans have all "successfully, for a time, held the rest of the nation to ransom" by putting their, in the words of Woodrow Wilson, "ancient affections" before the best interests of the United States (1985, p. 5). In contrast, Irving Horowitz summarized the contributions in *Ethnicity and US Foreign Policy* as suggesting that "the actual amount of impact has been minimal; far less than one would predict given the large number of immigrant peoples involved in gross aggregate terms". Indeed, some of the papers, observed Horowitz, came "perilously close to suggesting that the independent and dependent variables should be reversed: that US foreign policy serves to galvanize ethnic sentiments as much, if not more, than the other way around" (1977, p. 175). Broadly similar conclusions were earlier drawn in Louis Gerson's *The Hyphenate in Recent American Politics and Diplomacy* (1964). O'Grady arrives at similar conclusions, stating that "only two of the immigrant groups studied really influenced Wilson, and in neither case was the principal means the operation of public opinion" (1967, p. 28).

The process by which an ethny's homeland interest is transformed into political power in the United States was first explored, with reference to the Irish, by Thomas Brown (1966) and Edward Levine (1966), but was most neatly summarized in the following decade by Joseph O'Grady in his book *How the Irish Became Americans*. O'Grady believed that "minority groups in America function as successful pressure groups only when they possess a cause around which they can rally their people" and for the Irish this issue was the struggle for Ireland's independence from Great Britain (1973, p. [vi]). The seminal role that the Irish played in the development of modern American politics is beyond doubt. They were the first ethnic group to turn a bloc vote into the possession of political power. From humble beginnings in the antebellum era, Irish politicians had by the early twentieth century monopolized power in many of the nation's major cities and were important power brokers in most of the others. As O'Grady noted of this impressive feat: "They were able to achieve it because they possessed the basic characteristics – adequate leadership, large numbers, and an issue to unite both – that made a pressure group politically successful in America" (ibid., p. 158: see also Shannon, 1963). Although Ireland's securing of autonomy in the 1920s removed the unifying cause for Irish Americans, they held on to political power for a further three, four and sometimes more decades in various parts of the United States. Yonathan Shapiro found that Zionism performed a similar function among American Jews during the period 1897–1930 (1971, p. 5). An interesting perspective on this phenomenon is given by Armando Navarro (2000) in his study of La Raza Unida Party, a third-party challenge, sired by the Chicano nationalist movement, that enjoyed some success and caused not inconsiderable alarm to the Democrats in Texas during the 1970s.

On other occasions, ethnies maintained strong ties with their homeland government because they looked to it for protection against discrimination and mistreatment in the United States. Some studies suggest that calling upon assistance from the homeland government was often more effective than seeking redress through the American political system. This appears to have been true for Japanese immigrants, at least until Pearl Harbor. However, as Roger Daniels has shown, the Issei's reliance on Japan's intervention in cases of discrimination was far from voluntary. Not only were they barred from naturalizing and therefore prevented from participating in American politics, but Japanese immigrants were carefully vetted by their own government prior to departure and closely supervised by it after their arrival in the United States. While the imperial government provided much protection for its subjects residing in the United States, Daniels maintains that this interest in the immigrants grew out of Japan's desire to preserve its national prestige and "should not be interpreted as stemming from a humanitarian concern for their welfare" (1978, p. 39).

More generally, it has been claimed that nationalist movements not only raised awareness among Americans of various ethnies' problems, but also helped legitimize the nation's ethnic pluralism. For instance, Zionist leaders in the United States, by "accommodating their movement and its message to the realities of the American and American Jewish scenes", created during the early twentieth century, according to Naomi Cohen, "an *Americanized* Zionism, a movement that was as much American as it was Zionist" (2003, p. 1). This syncretism, notes Cohen, had implications not just for how the ethny viewed itself but also for how the wider society viewed the ethny and its attachment to a perceived ancestral homeland:

The results of Zionist activity in the United States ultimately served to modify the identity of the Jewish community. No longer merely another religious denomination, Judaism enriched by Zionism made Jews, synagogue affiliated or not, into a recognizable ethnic group. When a wave of ethnicity swept America in the last third of the twentieth century, early Zionist efforts at instilling a national consciousness laid the groundwork that permitted Jewish ethnic loyalties to emerge full blown, now recognized as perfectly legitimate, in their American setting (ibid., p. 217).

The emergence of scholarship emphasizing the advantages of passive non-participation was soon followed by a critique of its main tenets. First, critics argued that all attempts at achieving some form of separatism within the boundaries of the United States were doomed to failure because the federal government had never allowed any ethny to set up an autonomous political unit. An essential element of the "American orientation to ethnic difference" established at the birth of the republic, wrote Nathan Glazer in the wake of the nationalist movements of the 1960s, was that "no separate ethnic group was to be allowed to establish an independent polity in the United States". It had at an early stage become one of the "major tendencies of American thought and political action", claimed Glazer, that the United States "was to be a union of states and a nation of free individuals, not a nation of politically defined ethnic groups" (1975, p. 5). Second, as has been demonstrated by studies of German-American opposition to the Allies during World War I and Korean-American neglect of American politics until well into the post-World War II era due to absorption with homeland issues, nationalist preoccupations often retarded an ethny's acculturation, assimilation, and integration in America (Child, 1970 [1939]; Luebke, 1974 and 1978; Lyu, 1977a and 1977b; Choy, 1979). Moreover, not all ethnies managed to channel nationalist energies into mainstream American politics in the same way as, for example, the Irish did. Edward Kantowicz has shown that Polish Americans in Chicago, despite constituting a solid, sizeable and for the Democrats a very reliable voting bloc, were generally not as successful in translating votes into offices as other immigrant groups arriving in the city at the same time as them. Ironically, the internal unity of the Polish-American community proved to be its downfall in Chicago's multi-ethnic political arena and Kantowicz concluded that "Polish-American political leaders might have achieved more had they moved beyond solidarity to bridge-building, broker politics" (1975, p. 219). Third, cultural nationalists' condemnation of the more acculturated, assimilated, and integrated, that is "successful", members of an ethny created internal divisions and weakness. In *Poor Cousins*, Ande Manners revealed the "hostility" that long characterized relations between the more established and assimilated German Jews and the recently-arrived Russian Jews, who typically responded with "rebellion, indignation, and mockery" to the former's attempts to Americanize them (1972, pp. 115, 301). As Frederick Luebke (1978) has shown, the chauvinism and extremism of their ethnic leadership during the interwar years alienated so many German Americans that they mostly shunned ethnic politics and all the more readily embraced assimilation. Fourth, many ethnies had no homeland state to appeal to for assistance and, even if they did, weak foreign governments were generally ineffectual in fighting discrimination in the United States. Barred from entering the country, denied the opportunity to naturalize, targeted by racist rioters, and excluded from many mainstream institutions, the Chinese in the United States during the period 1868–1911, according to Shih-shan Henry Tsai, "felt the disadvantages of belonging to a weak nation and attributed the discrimination and maltreatment they suffered to this weakness" (1983, p. 144). Like Delber McKee (1977) before him, Tsai concluded that even able and energetic representatives of the Chinese government "could accomplish little through diplomatic channels when China was weak and her prestige low" (1983, p. 143). For similar reasons, claimed Gilbert González (1999) and Francisco Balderrama (1982), Mexican immigrants residing in the Southwest could expect only limited help from local Mexican consuls in protesting harsh working conditions or avoiding deportation during the Depression. However, as Francis Paul Prucha has indicated, the situation was even direr for Native-American tribes because after the establishment of the United States they had no external protector to turn to and "by the early decades of the twentieth century had become politically subordinate to and almost completely dominated by the federal government" (1985, p. 29). In this state of "dependency", Native Americans became increasingly reliant upon "paternalistic responses on the part of the federal government", but that "paternalism in turn caused still greater dependence" (ibid., p. 28).

Active Participation

While the burgeoning of scholarship on American ethnic history has in recent decades produced many important studies of both accommodationism and separatism, the form of ethnic collective action that has attracted by far the greatest amount of interest from historians is that of active participation, also known as "reformism". From the 1960s onwards, revisionist studies began to appear indicating that ethnocultural factors had long played an important role in mainstream American politics, influencing allegiances to and the policies of political parties and reform movements alike. In his pathbreaking book *The Concept of Jacksonian Democracy*, Lee Benson boldly declared:

The present study rejects the economic determinist interpretation that Frederick J. Turner and Charles A. Beard impressed upon American political historiography. It also rejects the proposition that American political differences are random in character, that they reflect not group patterns, but the clashing ideas held by individual voters about the "community interest". And it rejects the proposition that socioeconomic cleavages are the obvious place to begin a study of American voting behavior. A counterproposition is advanced here: that at least since the 1820s, when manhood suffrage became widespread, ethnic and religious differences have tended to be *relatively* the most important sources of political differences (1964 [1961], p. 165).

Benson's findings, based upon a case study of antebellum New York, gained support from Ronald Formisano's (1971) study of political parties in antebellum Michigan, Paul Kleppner's (1970) detailed analysis of late nineteenth-century Midwestern politics, and John Allswang's (1971) examination of ethnic politics in Chicago during the period 1890–1936.

The Liberal Defense of Reformism

Most of the recent research into ethnies' active participation in American politics has tended to extol the benefits derived from such activity. Scholars argue that ethnies that participated fully in American politics were more likely to form effective voting blocs, which in turn increased the likelihood of their gaining representation in government. As John Allswang contended, when "ethnic groups increased in number and became larger and more acculturated to American political mores" they became "more important . . . and more hearkened to". While the immigrant generation, lacking large numbers of naturalized voters, "were a rather passive force and one which politicians tended to take for granted", later generations of "ethnics were well organized, largely naturalized and thus able to vote, and . . . accustomed to being recognized as specific groups, with individual interests of their own and the power to reciprocate if those interests were not met" (1971, p. 205).

A common assumption among historians writing about ethnic politics – and a view that can be found, for instance, in studies of such diverse groups as Norwegians in the Midwest (Soike, 1991; Wefald, 1971) and Mexicans in the Southwest (García, 1998; Garcia, 1991) – is that ethnic mobilization is both natural and beneficial for the groups concerned, particularly when it results in one or more group member's election to public office. Following this path, say historians, has rewarded ethnies with greater influence and the ability to secure greater social acceptance of the group and its culture, alleviate material problems, like poverty, and defend the group and its institutions against prejudice. It came to be accepted that this pattern, though perfected by the Irish (Shannon, 1963; Wittke, 1956), was replicated with greater and lesser degrees of success among virtually all ethnic groups (Handlin, 1951, pp. 209–17). Moreover, by working within and defending mainstream institutions, is it often argued, an ethny reduces prejudice against itself. Irish Catholics, it has frequently been noted, rose within the span of a little more than a century from being a despised group suspected of, at best, divided loyalties, to an ethny whose allegiance to the United States was so widely accepted that one of its number could even be elected to the highest political office in the land.

Groups that have opted for ethnic over class politics, it is regularly contended, have also been viewed as affirming the American way of life, with its traditional avoidance of and disdain for the internecine class warfare that characterized politics in most European nations for much of the nineteenth and twentieth centuries. A fascinating exploration of this issue can be found in David Gerber's impressive study of politics in Buffalo during the period 1825–60. According to Gerber, "the need to forge coalitions led politicians to keep class grievances and prescriptions for radical change in the ownership or relations of production out of politics" (1989, p. 329). As a result of immigration, politicians were provided with the means of accomplishing this feat by the formation of distinct ethnic neighborhoods, the consolidation therein of voting blocs, and the appearance of ethnic leaders capable of delivering those votes to the party offering the best rewards. By accommodating themselves to the immigrant presence and the expansion of the franchise, political leaders ensured that party affiliation would be determined by ethnic rather than class divisions. "The political parties", observed Gerber, "purposefully managed the process by which groups bargained on behalf of individuals for patronage and public resources" and "they guided the process of group empowerment by determining where, when, and how ethnic leadership was brought into decision-making positions in both party and government" (ibid., pp. 327–8).

Scholars maintain that even groups who experienced varying degrees of exclusion from mainstream politics have generally found that working within the system created an opportunity to reform it. The overturning of discriminatory laws in the United States, historians note, has invariably been achieved through mainstream ethnic political mobilization, in the forms of lobbying, protest, and legal test cases, to name but a few. The African-American civil rights movement is undeniably the most famous example of ethnic reformism being practiced (see Meier and Rudwick, 1973; Kluger, 1976; Garrow, 1978; Hine, 1979; Zangrando, 1980; Tushnet, 1987). Nonetheless, a wide range of other ethnies have adopted the strategy and enjoyed success with it at one time or another, including Asian Americans (Chuman, 1976; Gioia, 1984; McClain, 1994; Riggs, 1950), Mexican Americans (García, 1989; Griswold del Castillo and Garcia, 1995; San Miguel, 1987), Jewish Americans (Dinnerstein, 1987), and Native Americans (Washburn, 1971).

The Radical Critique of Reformism

A more radical interpretation of reformist collective action, although one that neither all nor only radical historians subscribe to, finds much to be wanting in this strategy for ethnic advancement. First, critics of reformism contend that America's institutions have traditionally been controlled by white, Anglo-Saxon, Protestants who are not responsive to ethnic challenges to their dominant position. Consequently, reform regularly meets with failure or takes a very long time to achieve. Many of the same works which charted the successes of ethnic civil rights movements also emphasized the frustratingly slow pace at which progress was made and the ultimately limited impact that legislation and legal rulings had upon ethnic inequality (Burk, 1984; Garrow, 1978; McClain, 1994; Navasky, 1971; San Miguel, 1987; Tushnet, 1987; Washburn, 1971; Whalen and Whalen, 1985; Wilkinson, 1979). Moreover, Susan Olzak's competition model seems to suggest that ethnic mobilization could prompt the dominant ethny to mobilize in response, leading to severe backlashes and even violent attacks. Olzak claimed that civil rights protests and desegregation are key triggers of ethnic violence and that such violence directed against African Americans was usually effective in quelling further agitation for racial equality (1992, pp. 9, 210–11, 220–2). "For immigrants", noted Olzak, "organizations flourish in environments of turmoil" and white ethnic newspapers, for example, "evidently *thrived* during periods of massive antiforeigner attacks". In contrast, "the effect of hostility on [African Americans] . . . depressed the creation of black newspapers" and resulted in "the stagnation of growth in organizational resources in African-American communities" (ibid., p. 221). The difference in the two responses, explained Olzak, was accounted for by the greater severity of attacks on blacks. However, two case studies of this "backlash" phenomenon – one by Steven Reich (1996) examining the suppression of black protest in one southern state after World War I and the other by Michael Klarman (1994) analyzing the white South's persecution of black civil rights organizations in the wake of the *Brown* decision – both indicated that attacks on African Americans, while reducing the level of protest activity in the short term, actually gave rise to more radical forms of protest and hence increased the likelihood of militancy in the long term.

Second, reformism is criticized for lacking durability and impact, even in instances where its stated aims had been achieved. Ethnic mobilization has often been short-lived because protest movements generally disintegrated soon after their goals were met. Indeed, it would seem as though it were in the very nature of things for reformism to be a short-lived phenomenon, because only out-groups seeking an end to exclusion engage in protest and their reason for mobilizing is removed once they achieve in-group status. John Higham alluded to this truism when commenting upon the accommodation-versus-protest dilemma faced by various ethnic leaderships in the United States:

> In one way or another the choice between protest and
> accommodation has ceased to be a live option for Jews, Germans,
> and Japanese. All three groups have attained a relatively favorable
> status in America, and that has greatly lightened the tasks of
> leadership. It is among underprivileged groups, such as blacks and
> Indians – groups which must continue to try to overcome historic
> injustices – that the tension between protest and accommodation
> remains urgent (1978, p. 6).

As revealed by countless studies of the civil rights movement, the number of African Americans participating in protest, or any form of political activity for that matter, gradually declined after the passage of legislation during the 1960s outlawing racial discrimination and disenfranchisement. Moreover, mainstream reform rarely eliminated the underlying causes of ethnic inequality, such as poverty and inadequate educational provision. Scholars like William Julius Wilson (1980) and Manning Marable (1984) have shown how the civil rights revolution enabled the nascent bourgeois segment of the African-American population to achieve rapid upward mobility yet left the economic status of the black masses virtually unchanged. This weakness of moderate reform movements also meant that they regularly became radicalized, which could be counter-productive because it created internal divisions and also attracted increased hostility from the dominant ethny. In his study of the Student Non-violent Coordinating Committee (SNCC), for instance, Clayborne Carson (1981) revealed how growing disillusionment with conventional politics led this civil rights organization to adopt increasingly more radical policies and tactics as the 1960s progressed. Stokely Carmichael, who became chairman of SNCC in 1966, gave voice to these frustrations in the book he co-authored with Charles Hamilton, *Black Power*: "Voting year after year for the traditional party and its silent representatives gets the black community nowhere; voters then get their own [that is, black] candidates, but these may become frustrated by the power and organization of the machines". *Black Power* challenged the traditional assumptions that "a viable coalition can be effected between the politically and economically secure and the politically and economically insecure", that real change can be brought about by "appeals to conscience", that "the best . . . way for black people to win their political and economic rights is by forming coalitions with liberal, labor, church and other kinds of sympathetic organizations or forces, including the 'liberal left' wing of the Democratic Party", and even that the existing political system was capable of bringing an end to racism (1967, pp. 58, 60). "If the political institutions do not meet the needs of the people", concluded Carmichael and Hamilton, "if the people finally believe that those institutions do not express their own values, then those institutions must be discarded" (ibid., p. 176). The historiographical significance of *Black Power* cannot be overstated, because it was more than just a political treatise, it was a seminal exposition of the internal-colony interpretation of American ethnic history.

Another criticism of reformism is that the avoidance of more radical, class-based politics limited the opportunities for coalitions with other ethnies. David Gerber's *The Making of an American Pluralism* clearly demonstrated that the two-party system in the United States encouraged the development of vertical alliances between out-group leaders and in-group elites, rather than horizontal ones between various ethnic out-groups. American political practices, observed Gerber, "continually impeded the consolidation of an independent working-class movement by luring its leadership into party and government" (1989, p. 328). In other words, the up-and-coming leaders of ethnic out-groups, the very individuals upon whom a prospective working-class movement would depend for the creation of an effective organization, were continually co-opted by political parties that represented the interests of capital not labor.

Active Non-Participation

The category of active non-participation includes forms of collective action in which the participants reject the value system of the dominant society and have as their objective the overthrow of that system in either a part of the country or all of it. The latter variety of active non-participation includes radical movements aimed at bringing down the entire capitalist order, the former includes irredentist movements, like the Native-American and Mexican-American struggles for self-determination.

Historians' Rediscovery of Irredentism and Ethnic Radicalism

As a form of ethnic collective action, irredentism is as old as European colonization of North America and the first violent resistance that settlers encountered from Native Americans. Although it has reduced in scale and intensity over the centuries, Native-American irredentism has never died out and continues to this day. Strangely, this is one of the most undervalued manifestations of ethnic collective action, because the 500-year conflict between Europeans and Indians over territory, which has always figured very prominently in studies of American history, has traditionally been viewed from the perspective of the colonizers instead of the colonized (see, for example, Kellogg, 1925 and 1935; Peckham, 1961; Leach, 1958). Consequently, the focus on whites' inexorable expansion across North America has obscured the indigenous population's equally long struggle to resist this expansion and reclaim lost lands. During the course of the twentieth century, this trend in scholarship was gradually reversed, with scholars like Randolph Downes (1940), George Hunt (1960 [1940]), Mari Sandoz (1953), Alvin Josephy (1961), and Robert Utley (1963), pioneering the method of viewing the red–white territorial struggle from the Native-American perspective. Modern studies reveal that Native Americans were not merely passive or at best unthinking participants in the process of white expansion, but fully aware of its long-term implications and entirely capable of developing sophisticated means of resisting it (see Edmunds, 1980 and 2001). Indeed, the power of Native Americans was so great, asserted Francis Jennings, that "Indian *cooperation* was the prime requisite for European penetration and colonization of the North American continent" (1984, p. 367).

Mexican-American resistance to Anglo conquest and domination of the American Southwest has traditionally been viewed in similar ways to that of Native-American irredentism. For instance, Anglo scholars depicted Mexican folk heroes like Juan Cortina and Gregorio Cortez as mere criminals rather than legitimate symbols of resistance to oppression (Webb, 1935; Richardson, 1943; Woodman, 1950). This current in historical thought has also been challenged in recent decades, with studies like Robert Rosenbaum's *Mexicano Resistance in the Southwest* revealing how so-called "border troubles" were far more organized and ideologically charged than conventional accounts admitted. Defining "self-preservation" as an attempt to "preserve a traditional way of life, particularly its economic forms and spheres of activity", Rosenbaum asserted:

From the Treaty of Guadalupe Hidalgo until well after the turn of the century, *mexicanos* resisted Anglo domination with violence. Violent efforts at self-preservation ranged from the individual outbursts of social bandits to planned and coordinated uprisings by groups like Las Gorras Blancas [the White Caps], but whatever their form, all incidents originated from and were carried out by *los pobres* . . . [A]lthough *mexicanos* across the Southwest shared a hostility toward Anglos and a willingness to use violence, their common resentment found expression in independent and isolated revolts. The separate, local nature of the revolts kept them from having anything more than a delaying effect, but the fact that *mexicanos* in California, Texas, and New Mexico resisted violently demonstrated their dissatisfaction with the Anglo regime and their active commitment to do something about it (1981, pp. 140, 153: see also Paredes, 1958; Thompson, 1994).

In addition to their historiographical contribution, revisionist studies like Rosenbaum's strike at the heart of some of the most cherished American myths about the frontier West.

As the studies of irredentism reveal, ethnies have not been the passive objects of hostility they are usually portrayed as in traditional studies of ethnic and racial violence (Higham, 1955, pp. 25, 48, 84, 90–3, 169, 264–5). Contrary to conventional opinion, oppressed ethnies, particularly nonwhite ones, have regularly taken up arms to defend themselves from or take revenge for violent attacks, or simply to further their interests. In recent decades, scholarship on ethnic violence has undergone major revision, a development most visible in the field of African-American history. Traditionally, African Americans have nearly always been portrayed as the victims of violence, whether in the form of whippings and other kinds of brutality under slavery, lynchings in the postbellum South, or race riots in modern urban centers (see above, pp. 84–90). However, black resistance to white violence was generally overlooked or underestimated. Nineteenth-century historians, influenced by pseudo-scientific racism and its stereotyping of blacks as innately docile, suggested that slave unrest and rebellion were conspicuously absent from American history (Fiske, 1897, p. 196; Schouler, 1882, pp. 238–9). This viewpoint was first challenged in the early twentieth century by African-American scholars. Carter G. Woodson, for example, took issue with the image of black contentment portrayed in *American Negro Slavery* by Ulrich Phillips and criticized the author for either ignoring or failing to recognize the importance of various major slave insurrections (1919, pp. 480–1). Subsequent revisionist scholarship has shown that there is a long tradition of African-American resistance to and retaliation against white violence, stretching from slavery through the Jim Crow era to the late twentieth century. Scholars like Harvey Wish (1937 and 1939) and Herbert Aptheker (1943 and 1947) demonstrated the frequency with which slave revolts had taken place during the colonial, antebellum and Civil War eras, with Aptheker even contending that such occurrences were revolutionary in the Marxist meaning of the word. More recently, Kevin Mulroy (1993) has provided a detailed examination of Maroons, the runaway slaves who set up independent communities beyond areas of white settlement. Rejecting Aptheker's idea of a "revolutionary tradition", Eugene Genovese offered a modified version of the

Marxian interpretation. Slave insurrections in the United States, noted Genovese, "did not compare in size, frequency, intensity, or general historical significance with those of the Caribbean or South America" and never posed a serious threat to the South's peculiar institution (1974, p. 588). However, the explanation for this was not to be found in the docility attributed to African Americans by racists like Phillips:

> The slaves of the United States had always faced hopeless odds. A slave revolt anywhere in the Americas, at any time, had poor prospects and required organizers with extraordinary daring and resourcefulness. In the United States those prospects, minimal during the eighteenth century, declined toward zero during the nineteenth . . . As time went on those conditions became steadily more discouraging: the hinterland filled up with armed whites; the population ratios swung against the blacks; creoles replaced Africans; and the regime grew in power and cohesion (ibid., 1974, p. 588: see also Genovese, 1979).

Elliott Rudwick's *Race Riot at East St Louis* was one of the earliest studies to emphasize the importance of black self-defense against urban violence, noting as he did that white mobs would avoid attacking African Americans if the latter appeared capable of putting up a strong fight (1964, pp. 226–7). This theme was later explored in greater breadth and detail by Herbert Shapiro in *White Violence and Black Response: From Reconstruction to Montgomery* (1988).

Orthodox scholarship on the other form of active non-participation, radicalism, has traditionally ignored the influence of ethnicity on and the significant role various ethnies have played in this kind of collective action. This is particularly true of conventional studies of organized labor in the United States. At the beginning of the twentieth century, the pioneering labor historian, John R. Commons, believed that it was impossible to unionize recent immigrants and thought their main impact on organized labor was to weaken it by undermining class solidarity (Commons, et al., 1918, vol. 1, pp. 9–10, 412, 597, vol. 2, pp. 372–3). This characterization of ethnic groups as being marginal to the American labor movement survived in historical writing into the second half of the twentieth century. Joseph Rayback's *History of American Labor* (1959), for instance, provided no discussion on the importance of ethnicity and only a brief, superficial one on race.

A contradictory, but no less persistent stereotype in historical writing was that of the radical immigrant. This originated in the popular belief – a belief regularly based more upon assumption than fact – that immigrants played a prominent role in such events as: the Molly Maguires' terrorist campaign against Pennsylvania mine owners during the 1870s; the bomb thrown at police during a workers' rally at Chicago's Haymarket Square in 1886; and the assassination of President McKinley in 1901. From the late nineteenth century onwards, immigrants were typically characterized by historians as agents of political extremism (Saveth, 1965 [1948], pp. 171–2, 174, 189–90, 197–8). This conception of the immigrant was not seriously challenged until the interwar period, when Marcus Hansen argued that most immigrants demonstrated an aversion to rather than penchant for involvement in radical politics (1964 [1940], pp. 84–95). Hansen's interpretation was developed further by Oscar Handlin (1951), but according to Sally Miller, having "undermined the stereotype of the radical immigrant", these scholars "created a contrasting stereotype which resulted once more in a warped view of the so-called typical immigrant". This new stereotype of an essentially conservative immigrant, averred Miller, "did not fit all immigrant groups" and overlooked the fact that "some of the strengths immigrants developed as a result of their adversities, such as group consciousness . . . sometimes became direct routes to non-conservative actions" (1974, pp. 19–20). Another theme in traditional thinking on ethnic radicalism is that the significant number of African Americans who joined the American Communist Party during the interwar period were essentially the dupes of an organization seeking to exploit the race issue in the United States for the benefit of the Soviet Union (Record, 1951 and 1964).

Revisionist research has revealed that ethnic groups had a major influence on American radicalism, at all stages of its development and in all its guises – unionism, socialism, communism, and so on (Gutman, 1976b; Hoerder, 1983; Asher and Stephenson, 1990). In fact, some labor and leftist organizations made strident efforts to increase their ethnic membership. At its founding in 1905, Melvyn Dubofsky informs us, the radical Industrial Workers of the World (IWW) – often referred to as the "Wobblies" – "opened membership to all workers", "native and immigrant", "black, white, and even yellow", and thereafter concentrated on organizing "those workers neglected by the main-stream of the labor movement": "exploited eastern and southern European immigrants, [and] racially excluded Negroes, Mexicans, and Asian Americans" (1969, pp. 86, 148). Revisionist scholars also argue that ethnies derived important benefits from engaging in radical movements. As Dan Carter (1969), Charles Martin (1976), Mark Naison (1983), Gerald Horne (1988), and Robin Kelley (1990) have demonstrated, the American Communist Party not only actively recruited African-American members, but it also provided financial and legal support in civil rights cases, such as the famous Scottsboro trial. Scholars like Philip Foner (1977) and Sally Miller (1974 and 1996) have revealed that, in contrast to the communists, the Socialist Party, while recruiting many European immigrants, displayed little interest in reaching out to African Americans. Recent studies have also shown how a commitment to left-wing politics constituted a major source of identity. For instance, a strong commitment to radicalism was one of the major sources of identity and unity among some of the very groups that Handlin characterized as conservative, southern and eastern European immigrants like Finns (Karni and Ollila, 1977; Kostiainen, 1983), Italians (Avrich, 1991; Cannistraro and Meyer, 2003; Gabaccia, 1988), and Jews (Buhle, 1980; Howe, 1976; Leviatin, 1989). Likewise, in a comparative study of immigrant radicalism, Richard Oestreicher (1986) described how a wide range of ethnies contributed to the development of class consciousness and solidarity in a Detroit neighborhood during the late nineteenth century.

Questioning the Significance of Active Non-Participation

Naturally, as with all of the forms of ethnic collective action examined so far, active non-participation does, as scholars have pointed out, have it drawbacks. Irredentism, for instance, has invariably met with failure. Michael Green (1982) and Daniel Richter (1992), in the cases of the Creeks and the Iroquois League, respectively, have shown how even highly organized efforts by Native Americans failed to resist loss of territory to the encroaching whites. Moreover, violent movements generally have shown a tendency to prompt retaliation by the dominant ethny and a subsequent intensification of oppression. A notable example of this is the suppression of Mexicans in South Texas following the discovery of the 1916 Plan of San Diego, which envisaged a violent uprising in the Southwest that would expel the Anglos and reclaim the region for Mexico (Johnson, 2003). The adoption of violent tactics has also been shown to create divisions within ethnies, with moderates distancing themselves from controversial activities. In *Urban Revolt*, Eric Hirsch showed how Chicago's German-dominated anarchist movement – the "most highly mobilized in the country", encompassing "seventeen political clubs with a total of one thousand members and five or six thousand sympathizers" and a coalition of twenty-two labor unions, "including the eleven largest in the city" – rapidly disintegrated after the Haymarket affair of 1886 (1990, p. xiv). Thereafter, the city's ethnic workers, alienated by the use of violence, generally displayed an aversion to all forms of radicalism and not just the extreme varieties.

Although it has been more common and fared much better than irredentism, ethnic radicalism has still enjoyed only limited success in the United States. Scholarship reveals that the weakness of ethnic radicalism stems from two sources: (1) the nature of American radicalism and (2) the attitudes of ethnies towards radical movements. Numerous studies demonstrate that, for a variety of reasons, American radicalism traditionally had very little to offer ethnic workers. First, American radicalism and unionism were generally riven with internal divisions and have always been relatively weak and poorly supported. Critics also say that American radicalism has not always been very radical and regularly degenerated into reformism (Hirsch, 1990; Miller, 1996; Mink, 1986; Rosenblum, 1973). Second, when the members of ethnic minorities attempted to join labor unions or radical political groups they were often excluded or faced prejudice and discrimination within the organizations. Early examinations of labor unions excluding or discriminating against ethnic workers include studies by Robert Asher (1982) on southern and eastern European immigrants; Sterling Spero and Abram Harris (1931), and Philip Foner (1974) on blacks; Alexander Saxton (1971) on Asians; and Juan Gómez-Quiñones (1994) and Emilio Zamora (1993) on Mexicans. Gwendolyn Mink has persuasively argued that the "massive immigration of workers from eastern, central, and southern Europe . . . insinuated a very deep race problem within the American working class at the very moment that the trade union movement was taking off" (1986, p. 46). Exploring the "split between union and nonunion, old and new immigrant workers", and the roles that "nativism and racism" played in creating or deepening these divisions (ibid., p. 10), Mink concluded:

> Organized labor, in adopting a protectionist stand against newer, cheaper labor, joined anticapitalist economic action [strikes, boycotts, and so on] with anti-immigrant economic and political action in an effort to limit the movement of newer and cheaper labor into the orbit of American capitalism. Significantly, exclusionist unionism in the United States not only was racist, but became increasingly conservative as well[;] . . . old-stock workers . . . aligned *with* classes above to struggle against new immigrant masses below [and] . . . trade unionists regarded their campaign to create barriers to immigration as part of a group struggle to curtail expansion of the class beneath and thereby to consolidate trade-union autonomy at work and over the labor movement (ibid., pp. 47–8).

Immigration, therefore, and organized labor's nativist response to it, contributed to the development of an American labor movement that represented only a very narrow section of the industrial workforce.

With regards to ethnies' attitudes towards and involvement in American radical movements and labor organizations, research reveals that the former played a key role in undermining and reducing the effectiveness of radicalism as a form of collective action. While historians now reject John Commons's ethnocentric view that the peasant mind set and vehemently anti-radical Old World cultures of many immigrants made them both unsuitable and unlikely recruits for radical or worker organizations, some scholars do believe that the sojourner mentality and ethnic fixation of immigrants did veer them away from identification with or involvement in revolutionary movements (Commons, 1907, pp. 10–11). In seeking to explain "the conservatism of the American labor movement when contrasted with those in Europe", exemplified by the hegemony of the pro-capitalist, business unionism of organizations like the American Federation of Labor (AFL) over the anti-capitalist, revolutionary unionism of the IWW, Gerald Rosenblum assigned a major role to the attitudes and behavior of immigrants. According to Rosenblum, "immigrant orientations to American society were confined to a limited segment of it" (1973, p. 173):

> Their focus, both in coming and after their arrival, had to do with economic conditions surrounding the job. Operating, as they did, within the boundaries of an ethnic subsystem, the scope of their orientations remained narrowly trained on these issues while broader societal attachments were sustained to their area of origin. It is on this basis that it is argued that the immigrant was a far more ready recruit for conservative business unions than for revolutionary unionism and/or political activity (ibid., p. 167).

Hence, the "organizing success of the radical Industrial Workers of the World among immigrants" derived not from the latter's rejection of capitalism but from the fact that, in such instances as the famous textile workers' strike over pay cuts at mills in Lawrence, Massachusetts, in 1912, "the IWW provided an instrument in obtaining goals which were, in effect, of a business union character". The "transitory nature of immigrant membership, confined largely to periods of strike activity", averred Rosenblum, was demonstrated by the rapid decline of IWW membership in Lawrence after the strike succeeded in achieving its objectives (ibid., p. 176).

Moreover, even unionized and politically-active workers, it has been argued, often displayed an unwillingness to loosen their ethnic allegiances and adhere to a more class-based agenda. As demonstrated by David Corbin (1981), Peter Rachleff (1984), Ronald Lewis (1987), Eric Arnesen (1991), and others, for example, the racism of white workers was the chief impediment to the emergence of a unified and powerful labor movement in the South during the late nineteenth and early twentieth centuries. In their detailed examination of African Americans' involvement in the rise of the United Automobile Workers (UAW) union in Detroit, August Meier and Elliott Rudwick concluded:

> The UAW was one of the most racially egalitarian labor organizations in the country, yet prejudice among its white rank and file simply would not disappear. As a result blacks were compelled to

continue their battle for access to better jobs; and while substantial advances were registered during the [Second World] war and post-war period, virtual exclusion from the higher-status and best-paying positions . . . lasted for a score of years. Some Negroes could be officers of locals and salaried International representatives, but not very many. Nor was the elevation of a black to the International Executive Board possible as long as the rank-and-file majority remained overwhelmingly racist (1979, pp. 207–8).

Peter Friedlander, in his study of a UAW local, found that part of the explanation for the conservatism of labor unions lay in the fact that, in expanding their membership during the 1930s to include workers from groups with "prepolitical subcultures", these ostensibly leftist organizations were de-radicalized to an extent by their new members (1975, p. 131). In contrast to this viewpoint, the works of historians like Gary Gerstle (1989), Thomas Gobel (1988), Lizabeth Cohen (1990), Sean Wilentz (1984), and James Barrett (1992) suggest that union membership and radicalization actually undermined ethnic bonds in favor of class consciousness, and an Americanized version of it at that. It is probably less important to discover which of these two interpretations is correct than to note that, either way, ethnicity and radicalism appear to be anathema to each other: the strength of one creates weakness in the other.

THE CHARACTER OF INTERETHNIC RELATIONS IN THE USA

Having examined the four types of ethnic collective action, it is now necessary to turn to the related topic of interethnic relations to see if the option of interethnic cooperation often referred to by academics really did exist. A major problem encountered in discussing the historiography of interethnic relations in the United States is the paucity of works dealing specifically with this subject. Whereas ethnic collective action is one of the most written-about topics in American ethnic history, interethnic relations is one of the least thoroughly explored. Most studies of interethnic relations focus on the interaction between a minority ethny and the dominant ethny; very few systematically examine relations between two or more ethnic minorities. Consequently, few of the statements scholars make about interethnic relations are grounded in solid empiricism and many are speculative or anecdotal at best.

Explaining Amity and Cooperation

One historiographical tradition perceives interethnic relations in the United States to have been essentially cordial. Some scholars find the root of this amity in the promise of American opportunity, which encouraged ethnies to drop old enmities and foster a harmonious environment in which all groups could prosper. This perspective is exemplified in Oscar Handlin's *Boston's Immigrants*:

> Consciousness of identity particularized groups; but mere pluralism evoked no conflict in Boston society. Those coherently welded by circumstances of origin, economic status, cultural variations, or color differences often moved in distinct orbits, but were part of a harmonious system. In some instances, native Bostonians adopted newcomers; in others, they adapted themselves to the existence of aliens in their community. But whatever friction arose out of the necessity for making adjustments produced no conflict, until the social order and the values upon which it rested were endangered (1941, p. 184).

This blissful state of affairs lasted from the 1790s to the 1830s and was only shattered, according to Handlin, by Irish Democrats' opposition to the strong reform and abolitionist movements in New England.

An alternative interpretation is that common experiences of prejudice, discrimination and mistreatment at the hands of the dominant ethny have been the more usual reason behind empathy and cooperation between ethnic minorities. Hasia Diner (1977), for instance, has examined the much celebrated tradition of African-American and Jewish collaboration in advancing the cause of civil rights in the United States. Similarly, numerous studies have revealed the Italian-American tendency to find common cause with other ostracized ethnies, like Jews, blacks, and Latinos (Cunningham, 1965; Scarpaci, 1975; Mormino and Pozzetta, 1987). Sometimes it has been the similarity of cultures and backgrounds which has brought ethnies together to work in close alliance. The growth of pan-ethnic groupings is a good example of this kind of coalition building. For example, white territorial encroachment, the Indian boarding school experience, and even Commissioner of Indian Affairs John Collier's "Indian New Deal", have all been attributed with giving rise to pan-Indian sentiment and political activity (Edmunds, 1984; Hertzberg, 1971; Taylor, 1980; Merrell, 1989; Dowd, 1992). A variety of historical studies also suggest that pan-African cultural elements constitute a major ingredient of the black identity and sense of solidarity forged under slavery (Blassingame, 1979; Levine, 1977). Likewise, Richard Alba's *Ethnic Identity: The Transformation of White America* (1990) and William Wei's *The Asian American Movement* (1993) chart the development of pan-ethnicity among European Americans and Asian Americans, respectively (see also Espiritu, 1992; Fox, 1996). Other times it has been a similarity of experience, such as racial oppression, religious persecution, or class exploitation that has moved ethnies of often very different cultures and backgrounds to form coalitions (Fraser, 1986; Friday, 1994; Kelley, 1990; Naison, 1983; Oestreicher, 1986). One of the most famous and successful examples of this phenomenon is the alliance between the native Seminoles and runaway black slaves that proved to be a major hindrance to white settlement in Florida during the antebellum period. Indeed, the Second Seminole War (1835–42) turned out to be the most costly, in both lives and money, of the United States' many military conflicts with Native Americans (Porter, 1971 and 1996). According to some scholars, groups do not need to have entered into formal alliances for us to detect the existence of amity between them, because there are instances of ethnies merely emulating the behavior of a more successful counterpart in their efforts to overcome the same barriers imposed by the dominant society. Rudolf Glanz's (1971) study of Jewish-Italian relations fits very much into this mould, with Italian immigrants evidently following in the footsteps of their more successful Jewish neighbors.

Explaining Discord and Conflict

The other main historiographical tradition is one that characterizes interethnic relations in the United States as fundamentally antagonistic. According to this perspective, multiethnic coalitions and pan-ethnic formations are essentially expedient measures and even the most successful of them are usually tinged with antagonism (Arnesen, 1991; Kellogg, 1925 and 1935; Meier and Rudwick, 1979; Rachleff, 1984). A much publicized manifestation of this phenomenon that has come under considerable scrutiny in recent decades is the often acrimonious relationship between blacks and Jews (Foner, 1975; Salzman, et al., 1992; Bracey and Meier, 1993; Salzman and West, 1997; Franklin, et al., 1998). Moreover, the more common pattern, it is argued, has been for ethnies to compete with and even exploit each other, or at best to maintain a wary distance between themselves (Bayor, 1988; Foner, 1975; Franklin, et al., 1998; Halliburton, 1977; Hirsch, 1983; Hirsch, 1990; Littlefield, 1976, 1977, 1978 and 1980; Perdue, 1979; Salzman and West, 1997; Stack, 1979).

Scholars offer varying interpretations on the reasons behind interethnic hostility and conflict. Some researchers suggest that a "perceived sense of threat" and competition over resources are inherent parts of group relations in multiethnic societies like the United States (Bayor, 1988, p. xi). Ronald Bayor, in his pathbreaking study, *Neighbors in Conflict*, contended that "[r]acial and ethnic conflict . . . derive from . . . a sense of real or imagined threats to group interests and values based largely on competitive and explosive issues" (ibid.: see also Capeci, 1977; Capeci and Wilkinson, 1991; Formisano, 1991;

Higham, 1955; Jackson, 1967; Olzak, 1992; Rieder, 1985; Senechal, 1990; Stack, 1979). An alternative view is that the specific cultural, social, economic, and political conditions of the United States are the actual cause of interethnic hostility and conflict. One factor that many scholars have focused upon is American capitalism, which it is argued possesses an innate tendency to intensify competition between groups. As Eric Hirsch has observed:

> The mistake so many analysts make is assuming that capitalist markets are characterized by free competition; in fact, such markets are more commonly dominated by groups able to successfully limit competition. Ethnic, racial, gender, or other social differences are not made irrelevant by the rise of industrial capitalism. Instead, such differences are often utilized by those with power in labor markets (employers and craft unions) to exclude outsiders from the rewards of the system (1990, p. 198).

According to Hirsch, this situation engenders conflict between excluded ethnies and the ethnies above and below them in the labor market. Moreover, the virtual omnipotence of capitalist culture in the United States means that class consciousness is generally too weak to overcome ethnic subcultures and divisions (see Chapter 7, pp. 191–8).

Scholars have also detected various social mechanisms which bolster the capitalist order by perpetuating ethnic conflict. One mechanism is the "cultural division of labor" identified by internal-colony theorists, which often generates conflict between ethnies. By accentuating the demarcation between colonized and colonizing ethnies, the cultural division of labor attenuates class differences and tensions within the latter group which might otherwise destabilize the capitalist order. "The most important aspect" of the internal colonial economic system, asserted Mario Barrera in *Race and Class in the Southwest*, "has to do with the divisions that are created among the workers as a whole, since this allows capitalists to promote what is after all their ultimate interest, the perpetuation of class society itself" (1979, pp. 212–13). Another mechanism is the "middleman minority" (see Chapter 5, p. 123), in which the go-between group is the target of hostility for both the dominant society and other subordinate ethnies. Numerous studies suggest that much of the past conflict between African Americans and groups like Jews (Diner, 1997; Foner, 1975; Greenberg, 1991; Lewis, 1991; Trotter, 1998a) and Asians (Abelmann and Lie, 1995) fits into this pattern. The latter two ethnies have often been perceived by blacks as being exploitative middleman groups that monopolized landlord and retail business in black ghettos and then used this position to impose high rents and prices on the neighborhoods' inhabitants. More recently, affirmative action for ethnic minorities has been identified as a mechanism which assists the nation's capitalist elite in maintaining the white-nonwhite divide among the masses and thereby preventing the development of strong class consciousness (Formisano, 1991; Lind, 1995; Rieder, 1985). Similarly, a large number of scholars subscribe to the view that, like class, race is another yet entirely separate cause of inter-group hostility and conflict. Research shows that a peculiar feature of race's impact on inter-group relations is that potentially excluded ethnies go to great lengths to avoid being associated with existing pariah (that is nonwhite) groups and to secure acceptance as "white" (Chuman, 1976, p. 70; García, 1989, p. 48; Haney-López, 1996 and 2003, p. vii; Ignatiev, 1995; Kelley, 1990, pp. 27–8; Konvitz, 1946, pp. 80–96; Modell, 1977, pp. 14–15, 172). However, the contention that race is an entirely independent cause of ethnic conflict rather than a mechanism for facilitating class exploitation appears less and less convincing in an age when legalized forms of racial discrimination no longer exist and informal ones are steadily disappearing.

SUMMARY

Despite the complexity of the historiography of ethnic collective action in the United States, it is possible to outline four main trends in scholarship on the subject. First, historians have displayed a growing acceptance of the important role played in American politics by ethnicity, which previously was grossly underestimated. Second, historical scholarship has shown an increasing understanding of the diversity of ethnic collective action, particularly the long-overlooked topics of separatism, irredentism and radicalism. Third, with regards to opinion on what form of ethnic collective action has historically been the most common and/or successful, the majority view among historians, on both counts, has shifted over the course of the twentieth century from an emphasis on accommodationism to one on reformism. Finally, in terms of determining the precise nature of interethnic relations in the United States, all that can be said is that much more investigation into this topic needs to be carried out before historians should venture to make definitive statements about it.

SEVEN

Confronting Challenges to Ethnic Allegiance

INTRODUCTION

So far this book has examined various issues relating to how ethnies have been viewed and treated in the United States and how they have interacted with both mainstream society and other ethnies, but only tangential reference has been made to the internal dynamics of ethnies. This topic has not been left to the last because it is the least important of all those covered in this book. In fact, the very opposite is true. Intraethnic dynamics not only exert a powerful influence upon interethnic relations, but they also determine whether ethnic identities and boundaries can withstand the challenges posed by either American society's strong assimilatory pressures or potent competing allegiances like class and gender. If ethnies have proved incapable of sustaining strong identities and boundaries over the long duration, then the discussion of all other issues and debates relating to American ethnic history is purely academic. Studying the issue of intraethnic dynamics, therefore, takes us to the heart not the periphery of American ethnic history.

Scholarly debate on intraethnic dynamics tends to focus upon determining the potency or otherwise of two sets of factors: (1) those that are generally perceived to be agents of ethnic particularism, such as distinctive culture, language, or religion, separate ethnic institutions, and closely-knit social networks; and (2) those that appear to be anathema to ethnic particularism, such as class formation, gender divisions, and exogamy. The frequent invocation of ethnicity, class, and gender in multiculturalist tracts makes an exploration of the exact relationship between these three factors all the more pressing. Do ethnicity and gender stand on a par with class in importance as determinants of social stratification and identification, or was John Higham correct when he asserted: "Class typically cuts across ethnicity and gender, since endowment groups generally occupy more than one class level" (1993, p. 196). In historical discourse it is not uncommon for class, gender and ethnicity to be likened to the suits in a deck of playing cards, with the debate revolving around which variable trumps the others. Clearly, these debates are closely related, indeed central to those surrounding the assimilation–pluralism dichotomy. Evidence pointing to the permeability and impermanence of ethnic boundaries lends support to the assimilationist perspective, while proof of their inviolability and resilience buttresses the pluralist perspective.

ETHNIC BOUNDARIES

Before exploring issues related to particularist influences in American history, it is first necessary to examine the varying perspectives on the precise nature of ethnic identities and boundaries. Are they fixed or impermanent? If the latter, do they disappear entirely or are they transformed into new, perhaps composite, entities?

Orthodoxy: Impermanence of Boundaries

Originating in the late nineteenth and early twentieth centuries, the conventional scholarly view of ethnic boundaries portrayed them as impermanent. Influenced by classical modernization theory, social scientists and historians foresaw longstanding ethnic customs, identities and boundaries rapidly eroding as life in urban-industrial society undermined traditional living patterns. The historian Frederick Jackson Turner and sociologist Robert Ezra Park both suggested that the American environment, whether in the shape of the frontier or the city, was peculiarly efficient at actuating rapid and complete cultural homogenization and social integration. The first generation of professional immigration historians continued this tradition. Prominent scholars like Carl Wittke (1939), Theodore Blegen (1940), Marcus Lee Hansen (1964 [1940]), George Stephenson (1932), and Robert Ernst (1979 [1949]) predicted that ethnic distinctiveness and boundaries, rooted as they were in Old World beliefs and customs, would not long survive the passing of the immigrant generation. In *The Religious Aspects of Swedish Immigration*, Stephenson claimed that "the fight to preserve a distinctive Swedish culture was . . . a losing one". "Transplanted to American soil", he asserted, "the Swede was placed in an inexorable environment" and "found himself in . . . a society so strong . . . that is must inevitably dominate him" (1932, p. v). This viewpoint was buttressed by the activities of early twentieth-century Progressive "reformers" who energetically sought to eradicate all remnants of foreign culture, which they saw as impediments to acculturation and assimilation. Regardless of whether they originated in egalitarian or elitist impulses, or used persuasive or coercive tactics, the Americanization initiatives which mushroomed during the early twentieth century – and coincided with the era of immigration restriction, which presaged a reduction in the foreign-born proportion of the total population – no doubt persuaded many scholars that immigrant cultures and the ethnic boundaries that they helped to maintain would soon disappear (Carlson, 1975). Even later scholars, like Oscar Handlin (1951), John Higham (1984) and, more recently, Elliott Barkan (1995), who have viewed ethnicization (that is, the creation of an ethny, a process also sometimes referred to as "ethnogenesis") as a product partly of the American environment and not simply the transferal of Old World loyalties to the United States, still suggested that ethnicization was merely an intermediate level of or the necessary precursor to assimilation. This interpretation actually dates back at least as far as the disorganization-reorganization model used by the Chicago School sociologists William I. Thomas and Florian Znaniecki in their pioneering study *The Polish Peasant in Europe and America* (1927 [1918–20]).

Revisionism: Permanence of Boundaries

Faith in conventional interpretations which emphasized the fragility and impermanence of ethnic boundaries was shattered by the ethnic revival of the 1960s and 1970s. In the early 1960s, a new generation of scholars discovered that ethnic identities and boundaries had not succumbed to decades of Americanization pressure and immigration restriction but were still an important feature of American life. Scholarly attention now shifted to explaining the survival rather than the demise of ethnic identification and demarcations (Glazer and Moynihan, 1963; Vecoli, 1964; Vecoli, 1970; Holli and Jones, 1977). As the African-American civil rights movement increasingly drew attention to the proscribed status of nonwhite ethnies in the United States, even assimilationists found it hard to deny that the nation's historic racial exclusivism had contributed to the creation and perpetuation of rigid ethnic demarcations. More and more studies lent weight to the view that persecution reinforced ethnic boundaries, both from without and within (see Chapter 5, pp. 9–10, 58–60). Various studies depicted ethnicity as a mechanism for coping with the constraints and challenges facing proscribed groups in America. For individuals, the ethnic subculture seemed to be a haven from the scorn and hostility of the dominant society. In an early essay entitled "On Culture", Juan Gómez-Quiñones claimed that while the ethnic Mexican population contained a variety of "culture and identity groups", there were only two cultural poles: "Mexicano versus Anglo" (1977, p. 39). Equating assimilation into Anglo society with both acquiescence to cultural domination and acceptance of economic exploitation, Gómez-Quiñones asserted that for Mexicans "to acculturate is not merely to exercise a cultural preference but to go to other side" (ibid., p. 35). As studies of African-American folk culture and festivals by Lawrence Levine (1977), William Wiggins (1987), Richard White (1993), and Shane White (1994) have shown,

> even in the midst of the brutalities and injustices of the antebellum and postbellum racial systems black men and women were able to find the means to sustain a far greater degree of self-pride and group cohesion than the system they lived under ever intended for them to be able to do (Levine, 1977, p. xi).

Perry Duis discovered that in urban centers like Boston and Chicago a more unexpected establishment provided an "ethnic space" and refuge from mainstream society, because many migrants to the city – including "old" and "new" European immigrants, as well as African Americans – "found the saloon to be a comfortable complement to their ethnicity" (1983, p. 146). Thus, persecution gave rise among marginalized groups to the kind of oppositional culture, or reactive ethnicity, alluded to in early expositions of internal-colony theory (see Chapter 1, p. 10). Moreover, revisionists claimed that strong group boundaries were visible among white as well as nonwhite ethnies and originated in resilient Old World cultures as well as persecution. The ethnic revival among various European-ancestry groups seemed to suggest that ethnic identities and boundaries could survive the onslaught of mass culture and consumerism (Gambino, 1974; Novak, 1973; Weed, 1973). More recent revisionist studies have shown that ethnic boundaries regularly coincided with a distinctive group niche in the labor market, a phenomenon noticeable among nonwhites and whites alike (see Chapter 5, pp. 117–26).

The difference between revisionist and conventional scholarship was as much moral as it was theoretical. While traditional studies had largely lamented the survival of ethnic demarcations, revisionists generally saw this as a cause for celebration. However, some revisionist works took a less optimistic view and saw ethnic survival as a reversion to tribalism and the harbinger of a dangerous Balkanization of the American nation. This juxtaposition first took shape at the height of the white ethnic revival, with writers like Richard Gambino (1974) and Michael Novak (1973) representing the former viewpoint and Harold Isaacs (1975) and Orlando Patterson (1977) the latter.

Beyond the Permanent–Impermanent Dichotomy

Clearly, the relationship between the traditional and revisionist perspectives on ethnic boundaries is one of thesis and antithesis. The two positions are diametrically opposed on certain, fundamental points. Traditionalists consider America's mainstream culture to be more influential, particularly as far as the individual is concerned, than the various sidestream ethnocultures, whereas revisionists believe that sidestream ethnocultures are more potent than mainstream American culture. Traditionalists perceive ethnic identities to be fragile and boundaries impermanent, whereas revisionists view the former as strong and the latter durable. In true Hegelian fashion, this dialectic has given rise in recent decades to a synthesis in which ethnic boundaries are afforded a greater complexity than either the traditionalist or revisionist interpretations allow for. This synthesis originated in a critique of the revisionist perspective which revealed that the latter is just as inflexible and at odds with reality as conventional interpretations. First, numerous findings have cast doubt over the role homeland identities played in maintaining ethnic boundaries. For instance, it has been pointed out that many Old and New World "national" identities were not properly formed at the time that the sending regions witnessed their highest rates of emigration. This is particularly true of immigration from places like Central Europe and Mexico during the late nineteenth and early twentieth centuries. These areas did not at the time have well-defined national identities for the immigrants to transplant to America and use as the basis for ethnic boundary formation (Sánchez, 1993, p. 9; Conzen, et al., 1992, p. 22). Even where ethnic boundaries did form around strong homeland identities they were frequently undermined by the ethnies' own efforts to enter into the American mainstream. The filiopietism which flourished among ethnies in the late nineteenth and early twentieth centuries, for example, was intended to improve a group's standing in American eyes in the hope that this would lead to greater acceptance and eventual assimilation (see Saveth, 1965 [1948], pp. 202–15). Moreover, the revived ethnic interest noticeable since the 1960s, which inspired much revisionist research, has been shown in subsequent studies to be largely "symbolic" and not strong enough to sustain ethnic boundaries for more than a few generations (Gans, 1979; Alba, 1985; Waters, 1990).

Second, numerous post-revisionist studies reveal that even the more ascriptive ethnic boundaries, such as the racial ones established by the dominant society, are not as impermeable as previously believed. The boundaries of ascribed ethnies are often artificial and not compatible with the identities of the group members. The group known as "Indians", for example, is actually a very heterogeneous collection of ethnies whose disparate identities are just as likely to undermine as to bolster the boundaries established by the dominant society (see Chapter 1, p. 9). Moreover, there is even evidence of ethnies switching between racial boundaries in order to secure advantages for the group from changing circumstances. Mexican Americans, for instance, campaigned to be recognized as white during the era of Jim Crow, but later claimed the status of deprived minority after legal segregation had been dismantled and affirmative action programs introduced (De León, 1989, pp. x, 140, 164–5, 185–9, 207–9; García, 1989, pp. 46, 48, 301–2; Haney-López, 2003, pp. vii–x).

Admittedly, many of these criticisms of the revisionist perspective came from traditionalist scholars, but the synthesis emerging during the 1980s and 1990s was not merely a modified version of the conventional interpretation. Post-revisionist scholarship emphasized the complexity of ethnic identities and boundaries in the United States (Zunz, 1982a; Gerber, 1989). Whereas traditionalists saw the demise of smaller ethnic units as evidence of assimilation, post-revisionist studies revealed that the members of disappearing ethnies were merging not into an undifferentiated "American" group but into trans-ethnic yet sub-national racial groupings. Numerous scholars, for instance, identified the emergence during the post-World War II era of a unified European-American, or white, collectivity (Hirsch, 1983; Alba, 1990). Similarly, while revisionists viewed ethnicity as something transplanted to America, post-revisionist works demonstrated that ethnic identities were actually created in the United States and that group boundaries were not dependent upon the existence of strong or unifying homeland cultures. According to the post-revisionist perspective, ethnicization was an ongoing and complex process in which old identities and boundaries could be transformed and new ones created. The "Finns, South Slavs, Swedes, Cornish, and Italians" working in Minnesota's iron mining industry, it has been noted, "developed a strong identity and solidarity out of shared hardships and struggles": "A strong commitment to labor unionism and liberal politics, kinship networks resulting from extensive intermarriage, and a common culture, of which the sauna, bocce, pasties, potica, deerhunting, and hockey became emblematic, denoted an emergent 'Iron Range' ethnicity" (Conzen, et al., 1992, p. 15). Similar claims have been made for an "ethnicity of the Appalachians" (Abramson, 1980, p. 157), an ethnicity of the American South (Tindall, 1976), and a "common identity" as "Latins" among Italians, Spaniards, and Cubans, in South Florida (Mormino and Pozzetta, 1987, p. 319). Likewise, scholars like J. Leitch Wright, Jr, have demonstrated how numerous pre-Columbian peoples, devastated by the impact of early European incursions, "were forced to relocate, merge with, or settle among neighboring tribes, perhaps repeating the process again and again" until they "developed a new culture and economy" and a new tribal identity as well (1986, pp. xi–xii: see also Hudson and Tesser, 1994). Studies showing that individuals possessing multiple ethnic allegiances and capable of traversing supposedly inviolable group demarcations were commonplace in American society further accentuated the need for a more nuanced approach to the study of ethnic identities and boundaries. As we will see in the discussion below of intermarriage, it is frequently claimed that the experiences of persons of mixed ethnic, and even racial, ancestry often fit this description. However, the post-revisionist synthesis might justifiably be labeled neo-orthodox because in the final analysis it does emphasize the breaking down of smaller ethnic collectivities and their merging into larger ones, an interpretation which essentially constitutes a slowed-down version of the traditional assimilationist model (see Chapter 3, pp. 65–6).

PARTICULARIST TENDENCIES IN AMERICAN LIFE

The maintenance of marked ethnic identities and boundaries is dependent upon the effects of various agents of particularism, that is influences that promote group solidarity, distinctiveness, and separation. Among the most commonly noted agents of particularism are culture, language, group institutions, religion, family patterns, and social networks. Historians disagree about how powerful each or all of these factors are. Assimilationists tend to view particularizing agents as being essentially weak, while pluralists believe they exert a powerful and durable influence.

Distinctive Cultures and Languages: The Traditional Emphasis on Fragility

Conventional scholarship has generally portrayed the physical incorporation of ethnies into American society, whether through conquest or forced or voluntary immigration, as accompanied by a mental and emotional transformation from traditional to modern ways of thinking. Moreover, assimilationist historians suggested that the promise of American opportunity gave the members of ethnies an incentive to abandon their traditional cultures and undergo rapid acculturation. The loss of distinctive group customs, therefore, has generally been viewed as the first stage of the assimilation process (Morawska, 1994, pp. 81–2). The spatial dispersion of ethnies that generally accompanied upward mobility, it has been argued, further undermined their cultural homogeneity (Zunz, 1982a, pp. 399–403 and 1985). Carl Wittke cited the demise of ethnic newspapers in the decades after World War I as an example of the deleterious effect American life has had upon ethnic cultures. "The struggle for the survival of the fittest", observed Wittke, "has been especially severe in the ranks of the foreign-language press". Although ethnic newspapers mushroomed during the late nineteenth and early twentieth centuries, Wittke noted how the "mortality rate in the ranks of the foreign-language press had been very high" and "directly affected by the ebb and flow of the immigrant tide" (1973 [1957], p. 2). However, the fate of the ethnic press was not ultimately determined by immigration patterns. According to Wittke, the ethnic press, by the very nature of the functions it performed, unavoidably contributed to its own demise:

> There can be no doubt that journalists of the immigrant press are in a position to exercise considerable leadership in the political field and significant influence among immigrant groups in preserving the cultural heritage of their people . . . In the long run, however – and the run often is no longer than one generation, as many publishers of foreign-language journals have discovered to their dismay – the forces of assimilation have proved far stronger than those that make for national or cultural separatism. If the foreign-language newspaper acts as a centripetal force for a time by making its readers more conscious of their national origins, it also functions as a centrifugal force by introducing them to the life of their new community, thus helping them to break down their cultural and social isolation (ibid., pp. 4–5).

For Wittke, the survival of the German-language press in the United States, despite its being "the most numerous, the most influential, and the best edited of all the foreign-language newspapers published in this country", was somewhat surprising and appeared to be the exception that proved the rule (ibid., p. v). Linked to this phenomenon is the demise of ethnic languages and the shift to English monolingualism, which some scholars argue is completed among most groups within two or three generations. "The almost complete break in language transmission between the second and third generations", Stephen Steinberg has asserted, "marks a decisive stage in the assimilation process, and it means that the fourth generation is the first generation to be reared by parents who, except in rare circumstances, cannot speak the native tongue of their ethnic group" (1989, p. 46).

Distinctive Cultures and Languages: The Revisionist Stress on Resilience

As might be expected, pluralists have strenuously criticized the conventional view of ethnic cultural and language retention. Many immigrant ethnies, it has been stated, possessed a strong sojourner mentality that made acculturation appear unnecessary and unattractive to individual group members. As Gunther Barth wrote of the Chinese immigrants arriving in California from the 1850s onwards:

> The newcomers came with a vision; they would make money to return to China with their savings for a life of ease, surrounded and

honored by the families which their toil had sustained. Their goal
kept the Chinese apart from the flood of other immigrants who came
to America as permanent residents. The vast majority of arrivals
from the Middle Kingdom were merely sojourners and they shaped
the initial encounter with Americans, molding the impact made by all
Chinese newcomers . . . The sojourners' pursuit of their limited goal
influenced the reception of the Chinese in the United States who
were, as a result, excluded from the privileges and obligations of
other immigrants (1964, p. 1).

In response to Californians' attempts at Americanization, Chinese immigrants, claimed Barth, "clung tenaciously to their culture and rejected the new
standards", or at best "hesitantly entered into the process of assimilation"
(ibid., pp. 5, 7). Various studies have also shown that even among immigrant
groups whose settlement in the United States was intentionally permanent it
is still possible to detect a persistent concern over and interest in the ancestral
homeland (O'Grady, 1967; Halley, 1985). Indeed, some historians claim that
ethnic symbols and celebrations have frequently been given greater prominence in the United States than they ever had in immigrants' homelands and
constituted a conscious effort to perpetuate the ethnies' historic memories; a
point demonstrated by the "American origins" of America's most prominent
and widely celebrated ethnic festival, St Patrick's Day parades (Miller, 1985,
p. 7). This is doubly ironic for the fact that in Northern Ireland it is the
Loyalists not the Nationalists for whom parades play a conspicuous role in the
maintenance of ethnicity. According to revisionist scholars, the physical
isolation of ethnies often increased the level of their cultural isolation.
Sometimes, this isolation was voluntary, as in the case of the Amish
(Hostetler, 1980), or Hasidic Jews (Poll, 1962). Other times it was involuntary, caused by rural isolation or ghettoization (see Chapter 5, pp. 96–103).
Some scholars argue that pluralism was a product of the American milieu,
because ethnies could maintain their cultural heritage without being barred
from citizenship, nor was cultural retention incompatible with loyalty to and
participation in the activities of US institutions. Interestingly, Carl Wittke,
who is generally regarded as being aligned with the assimilation perspective,
provided one of the earliest post-World War II expositions of this viewpoint:
"Americanization is concerned . . . with the development of a unique
American pattern of civilization in which political unity is based on cultural
diversity, and with the breeding of a new loyalty by blending an old heritage
with the best of the new" (1973 [1957], p. 3). Moreover, when attempts were
made to Americanize ethnic minorities, revisionists claim that these were
strenuously resisted by the targeted groups. Echoing Barth's observations
about the Chinese, Juan Gómez-Quiñones (1977), Richard Gambino (1974),

and Michael Novak (1973) were early exponents of the argument that immigrants frequently resented and responded negatively to Americanization initiatives.

Revisionist scholarship has frequently focused on the particularizing effects of language. The language barrier caused by lack of proficiency in English, it has been argued, has prevented some groups from integrating into American society, which in turn prevented them from acquiring proficiency in English, and so on, in a self-perpetuating cycle. It has been shown that in various parts of the Southwest the authorities took advantage of the language barrier issue to segregate Mexican school children. The schools for non-English-speaking pupils set up for this purpose have been depicted by revisionist scholars as a pointed example of the failure of organized efforts to eliminate a group's ancestral language through a program of Americanization (García, 1981; San Miguel, 1987; González, 1990; Getz, 1997). Revisionists insist that ethnies made strenuous efforts to maintain their language, which in many cases culminated in the establishment of foreign-language newspapers, ethnic organizations, and schools which avoided the use of English. In *Language Loyalty in the United States*, Joshua Fishman provided a classic exposition of this viewpoint:

> While admitting the centrality of de-ethnicization and acculturation in American history and in American national awareness, it must be pointed out that its opposite has also been a part of the continental American scene from the very beginning . . . [T]he efforts of ethnic minorities to maintain themselves . . . have always been underway . . . Language maintenance, prompted by one or another variety of language loyalty, has frequently been a component – and, at times, a catalyst – in these efforts (1966, p. 21).

Moreover, Fishman noted that in the mid-1960s "[e]thnic groups and ethnicity, language loyalty and language maintenance, still exist[ed] on the American scene" (ibid., p. 31). Subsequent studies have shown that virtually every American ethnic group has had its own press and, in the case of non-English language publications, this institution made a significant contribution to the continuation of language diversity in the United States (Miller, 1987; Hoerder and Harzig, 1987; Andersen, 1990; Kanellos and Martell, 2000). While some ethnic presses, such as those serving the African-American (Suggs, 1983 and 1996; Hutton, 1993), Irish-American (Joyce, 1976; Hueston, 1976), and Native-American (Murphy and Murphy, 1981) populations, did not perform a strictly language maintenance role, they still helped sustain a distinctive ethnic culture and identity among their readers.

The revisionist perspective has been criticized in recent decades on a number of counts. First, it tends to exaggerate the linguistic and cultural homogeneity of ethnies, which are frequently composed of diverse elements. As John Higham wrote:

> Pluralism encourages the further illusion that ethnic groups typically have a high degree of internal solidarity. Actually many of them are unstable federations of local or tribal collectivities, which attain only a temporary and precarious unity in the face of a common enemy.
> On top of sharp local differences, an ethnic group is likely to be split along religious, class, and political lines (1984, p. 236).

Moreover, critics of the pluralist position claim that even the invented traditions around which new ethnies usually form are no guarantee of group survival, as is evidenced by the case of the English, Scots, and various other immigrants who have rapidly disappeared as distinct entities. Despite finding plenty of evidence of ethnic cultural and organizational activity among British immigrants, Rowland Berthoff still felt obliged to conclude that, unlike some other ethnies, "the British-Americans had no 'second generation', no ill-adjusted class, like the children of less fortunate foreigners, without firm roots in either the old or the new culture":

> In effect their children were simply Americans, neither better nor worse adapted to the normal life of the country than were the children of old-stock parents. They seldom thought of themselves as anything but Americans (1953, p. 210).

Second, the formulation and projection of the group's historic memory has often been a hotly contested issue within many ethnies: a point frequently made by pluralists themselves, but usually without subsequently exploring the obvious assimilatory potential of such internal debates (Gerber, 1989; Gómez-Quiñones, 1977; Higham, 1978; Kelley, 1994; Manners, 1972; Márquez, 1993; Trotter, 1985).

This critique of revisionism has given rise to a more interactive interpretation of ethnic culture, which is viewed as displaying signs of both change and continuity, and being the product of both ancestral and American influences. As Kathleen Neils Conzen, David Gerber, Ewa Morawska, George Pozzetta, and Rudolph Vecoli stated in their influential essay "The Invention of Ethnicity":

> Internal debates and struggles over the nature of the group's emerging ethnicity were inevitable. One of the purposes of invented traditions was to provide symbols and slogans which could unify the

group despite such differences. The symbolic umbrella of the ethnic culture had to be broad and flexible enough to serve several, often contradictory, purposes: provide the basis for solidarity among the potential members of the group; mobilize the group to defend its cultural values and to advance its claims to power, status, and resources; and, at the same time, defuse the hostility of the mainstream ethnoculture by depicting the compatibility of the sidestream ethnoculture . . . with American principles and ideals (1992, pp. 5–6).

"Ethnic group boundaries", according to these scholars, "must be repeatedly renegotiated, while expressive symbols of ethnicity (ethnic traditions) must be repeatedly reinterpreted" (ibid., p. 5). Nonetheless, this interaction between mainstream and sidestream ethnocultures was not thought to be unidirectional. In *Adapting to Abundance*, Andrew Heinze showed how, on the one hand, "[a]s consumers, Jews sought important elements of American identity", but on the other, "[a]s entrepreneurs in consumer-oriented trade, they . . . enriched the potent environment of urban consumption which had become such a distinctive feature of American society" (1990, p. 4). In the "immigrants' pursuit of the American standard of living", noted Heinze, they created a "new identity [that] depended on the fusion of Jewish habits from eastern Europe with urban American ways" (ibid., p. 5). Among the German-American Catholics of Stearns County, Minnesota, Kathleen Neils Conzen (1991) even found an example of the sidestream ethnoculture playing the dominant role in this dynamic relationship between cultures, with the mainstream culture being changed more by the minority group culture than vice versa.

Ethnic Institutions: The Traditional Depiction as Agents of Americanization

Institutions are far more tangible than culture and consequently have attracted a lot more attention from scholars of American ethnic history. That said, some ethnies have displayed virtually no independent organizational life, a fact which has traditionally been regarded as evidence of assimilation (Gordon, 1964). However, some scholars argued that the growth of ethnic institutions was curtailed more by dominant society hostility than by ethnies' ready admission into mainstream society (Olzak, 1992, pp. 208, 220–1). Whatever the case, conventional studies regularly paid little attention to ethnic organizational activity or else viewed it as something likely to accelerate rather than impede assimilation. Traditionalist scholarship has unearthed countless examples of ethnic organizations actually facilitating acculturation and integration. The creation of ethnic institutions, it has been argued, is an adaptive strategy which enables groups and individuals to gain a foothold in American society, thereby aiding their incorporation. As Oscar Handlin argued with reference to ethnic institutions:

> [T]he societies, the schools . . . the press, [and] the theater . . . [were] means through which the immigrants came to know each other . . . The man who joined a mutual aid association, who took a newspaper or went to the theater, was adjusting thereby to the environment of the United States. These were not vestiges of any European forms, but steps in his Americanization (1951, p. 185).

Chicago school sociologists viewed ethnic institutions as an important element in the "disorganization–reorganization" process, by which a conscious effort was made to salvage as much traditional group life as possible from the social upheaval caused by modernization and immigration (Kazal, 1995, p. 443). Religious institutions seemed to typify this pattern, because conventional studies suggested that rather than distancing ethnies from American life they actually acted as a vehicle for greater involvement in it. The fact that the United States has no official religion, due to the separation of church and state in the Constitution, led traditionalist scholars to believe that membership of ethnic religious institutions was not an impediment to assimilation (Handlin, 1951, pp. 125–6). Indeed, some ethnic religious groups were characterized as being not only openly integrationist but decidedly hostile to the concept of ethnic pluralism. Colman Barry's characterization of the Irish-dominated Catholic Church in the United States as an Americanizing force that stressed conformity and taught its multiethnic flock "to love and to understand American political and civic ideals" represented the standard view of historians up until the 1960s (1953, p. 276–7: see also Ellis, 1965, pp. 102–3; Commager, 1950, p. 193). In the higher education sector, concluded Philip Gleason, "Catholic colleges, although firmly attached to traditional Catholic faith and culture, have nonetheless both experienced a process of Americanization themselves and acted as agencies of Americanization for the students who passed through them" (1982, p. 168). Needless to say, the numerous Christian denominations conducting missionary work among the nation's various indigenous peoples pursued an unmistakably assimilationist agenda (Prucha, 1976 and 1979). That said, William McLoughlin has shown in his studies of the Cherokees that missionaries often had to settle for "a syncretic form of Christianity among their converts that allowed the old and the new religion to coexist in ways comfortable to the Cherokees" (1990, p. 6). "Much that the missionaries did, and tried to do, for the Cherokees deserves more credit than has been given", asserted McLoughlin, while still concluding that "what the Cherokees took from the missionaries they took on their own terms and adapted to their own needs and perspectives" (1984, p. 12).

Another type of organization which seemed to facilitate assimilation was the ethnic labor union, which typically admitted members from other ethnies, cooperated with other unions, and eventually affiliated with either the American Federation of Labor (AFL) or the Congress of Industrial Organizations (CIO). Two good examples of this phenomenon are the International Ladies Garment Workers Union (ILGWU) and the Amalgamated Clothing Workers of America (ACWA), both of which started off in the early twentieth century with predominantly Jewish and Italian immigrant memberships but rapidly incorporated large numbers of other ethnic workers (Dubofsky, 1961; Perlman, 1952; Howe, 1976; Fraser, 1986), and later Latinos (Durón, 1984; Ortiz, 1990). Ethnic organizations, therefore, have been depicted as a sort of "compression chamber" between sidestream and mainstream cultures (Buenker and Ratner, 1992, p. 249). The institutions appeared to unify heterogeneous groups by eroding old loyalties and creating new ones, with each step of the process leading individuals away from narrowly-focused identities, such as the village or region, towards broader ones, such as the ancestral nation and ethny (Handlin, 1951, pp. 186–9). The transition from local to ethnic to hyphenate (that is, Irish-American, Japanese-American, and so on) identity appeared to prepare the ground for eventual sole identification with the multiethnic American nation.

Many ethnic institutions were weak particularizing agents because they willingly embraced assimilationist ideology. Indeed, Kathleen Conzen has pointed out that the term "*Schmelztiegel*" – that is, "melting pot" – was used in German immigrants' discussions about assimilation as early as 1857, "a good half-century before it became current in English" (1985, p. 138). Another reason why ethnic institutions have been viewed as ineffective agents of particularism is their diversity. All ethnies contained a variety of competing organizations, representing stark ideological differences or deep religious divisions, all of which worked against the achievement of complete institutional unity. And as John Higham has indicated, "No American ethnic group . . . has created an organized community capable of speaking for all its members" (1984, p. 237).

Ethnic Institutions: The Revisionist Depiction as Agents of Particularism

Revisionists have stressed the durability of ethnic institutional life, which they have shown frequently survives the decline of other particularizing agents, such as language and customs. According to this perspective, ethnic organizations are flexible and easily adjust to changing circumstances. In recent decades, virtually every revisionist study charting the history of specific ethnic communities, particularly if they are urban-based ones, has included an examination of organizational activity and drawn a link between this and ethnic resilience. Josef Barton's *Peasants and Strangers* (1975) was probably the earliest revisionist historical work to adopt both this practice and perspective. Those who have done so since are too numerous to mention. Moreover, pluralists argue that ethnic institutions touch every aspect of group life, such as religion, education, community relations, politics, economic activity, and so on, and as a result help perpetuate ethnic language, culture, and solidarity. Of all the varieties of formal ethnic organization, the ethnic press is frequently given a special mention in this regard. According to Sally Miller, ethnic newspapers were "a necessary element in the lives of their respective peoples": 'The press gave its readership information that it wanted and needed. It embodied its public's point of view and values as it did so, and it expressed its essence when it spoke to the outside world" (1987, p. xix). As well as being "informational", the ethnic press "expressed a group's values, heritage, and changing sense of identity", and "promoted group pride as well as economic and political power" (ibid., pp. xv–xvi). Many scholars argue that religious institutions played a particularly important role in ethnic community life, encompassing as they did such areas as education, social welfare, the family and even politics (Dolan and Hinojosa, 1994; Dolan and Vidal, 1994; Greene, 1975; Hayashi, 1995; Jalkanen, 1972; Lincoln and Mamiya, 1990; Liptak, 1989; Martin, 1978; Orsi, 1985; Parot, 1981; Wallace, 1970). More importantly, revisionists challenge the view that religious institutions facilitated Americanization. Without questioning the characterization of American Catholicism's Irish-dominated hierarchy as pro-assimilationist, scholars like Rudolph Vecoli (1969 and 1977), Josef Barton (1977), and Jay Dolan (1977) claimed that Italian, Czech, German, and other non-Irish co-religionists resisted, some more successfully than others, the Church's attempts to Americanize them during the late nineteenth and early twentieth centuries. Indeed, Polish immigrants' resistance to the church hierarchy's Americanizing tendencies threatened the very unity of the Catholic community in various locales, even prompting some Poles to secede and form their own alternative congregation, the Polish National Catholic Church (Galush, 1977; Greene, 1975; Parot, 1981; Orton, 1981; Kuzniewski, 1980). However, Richard Linkh questioned whether the Catholic Church possessed either the will or the way to Americanize its flock: "Opting as it did for the melting pot theory and for a gradual assimilation of the newcomer, it failed to satisfy either cultural pluralists or those favoring hasty Americanization" (1975, p. 195). American Catholicism was "too ambivalent toward 'Americanization' to be an effective agency" and its work among immigrants "too meager" to have much influence prior to World War I (ibid., p. 191). After the war, it is true that "Catholics became a major factor in immigrant welfare work and in 'Americanization' programs designed to teach new arrivals the English language and the rudiments of American government", but immigration in general and from Europe in particular declined precipitously following the passage of restrictive immigration laws (ibid., p. 194).

According to revisionists, ethnic organization was often prompted by prejudice or discrimination experienced in encounters with mainstream society. Revisionists contend that ethnic institutions regularly spearheaded the opposition to Americanization programs. Many ethnies, for example, established their own schools because they viewed the public schools as agents of cultural imperialism. The large network of Catholic parochial schools is one of the best studied examples of this phenomenon. In *The Education of an Urban Minority*, James Sanders contended that in Chicago – which "boasted the largest Catholic school system in the United States", enrolling 30 per cent of the city's schoolchildren – "Catholic education largely originated from and fed on reaction to unfavorable aspects of the public schools and the city's other public and private institutions" (1977, pp. xii–xiii, 5). According to Sanders, the parochial schools were far more conducive to ethnic pluralism than the public education system:

> The public school, as a symbol of established mores – not merely
> Protestant in original orientation, but Anglo-Saxon and middle class
> as well – stood to a degree as a truly organized effort by the
> established to impose their values on those they saw as deviant . . .
> But Catholic schools, as expressions of the deviant, originated from
> and thrived on rejection of that belief, first in its religious dimension,
> and then in its broader cultural and socioeconomic ramifications.
> Thus, as public schools centralized to secure cultural homogeneity,
> Catholic schools, as an early expression of counter-culture rights and
> beliefs, deliberately reveled in hopeless – or glorious – diversity.
> Further, in catering to the culturally diverse, the parochial school
> appears to have functioned in sympathetic vibration with the
> Catholic, immigrant, alien poor, whereas the public school, as the
> increasingly bureaucratic agent of the dominant culture, could not
> (ibid., pp. 226–7).

Revisionists claim that opposition to religious bigotry frequently acted as a rallying point for ethnic solidarity. The Protestantism of American culture, it has been argued, alienated many ethnies, making religion an extremely divisive influence in US society. David Gerber, for instance, has shown that the focus of Irish Catholic ethnicity in antebellum Buffalo was the defense of their religious faith and institutions against attacks from the Protestant majority (1989, pp. 120–62). Catholic ethnies were not the only ones whose levels of ethnic identification were enhanced by the prevalence of religious bigotry in the United States. As Leonard Dinnerstein argued in *Antisemitism in America*, "most Protestants regarded Catholics and Jews as inferior and adherents of these faiths often perceived themselves as outsiders in a Protestant nation, at best tolerated but not embraced" (1991, p. x: see also Dinnerstein, 1987). These contentions appear to be borne out by the fact that intolerance and hatred of non-Protestants was one of the defining characteristics of all major eruptions of nativism in the United States and regularly spilled over into many aspects of public life, particularly politics (Lichtman, 1979; Gerlach, 1982; Bennett, 1988; Knobel, 1996).

Another and more famous example of institutional activity emerging as a response to prejudice and discrimination is the body of African-American organizations commonly known as the civil rights movement. C. Eric Lincoln and Lawrence Mamiya have summarized the black church's role in the 1960s civil rights movement thus:

> Black churches were the major points of mobilization for mass meetings and demonstrations, and black church members fed and housed the civil rights workers from SNCC, CORE, and other religious and secular groups. Most of the local black people, who provided the bodies for the demonstrations, were members of black churches acting out of convictions that were religiously inspired. Black church culture also permeated the movement from oratory to music, from the rituals and symbols of protest to the ethic of nonviolence (1990, pp. 211–12).

Revisionists claim that religious conviction has frequently empowered and inspired ethnic protest movements, and not just peaceful ones like the black crusade for civil equality but also violent ones, such as slave rebellions (Wilmore, 1972) and the Native-American Ghost Dance movement (Utley, 1963).

Some debate exists over whether the ethnic institutions established in the United States, particularly those by immigrants, were recreations of traditional bodies or innovations prompted by American conditions; if the latter, then the organizational activity might be viewed as an early stage of ethnicization and eventual assimilation. In his examination of an early twentieth-century Jewish movement, the Kehillah, Arthur Goren provided a model of the typical pattern of institutional development among immigrant groups: "A loose network of communal agencies evolved – part transplanted, part indigenous – which supplied the immigrant settlement with social and welfare services, and above all with an ethnic identity" (1970, p. 1). Goren's study suggested that, while movements like the Kehillah were successful in that they "eased the immigrant's adjustment to the alien environment", their lifespan was destined to be short, because "even as immigrants built institutions to preserve the solidarity of their particular group and to provide a measure of personal security, they [also] endeavored to fit these institutions into the American social landscape". Consequently, ethnic institutions ultimately succumbed to the "[p]owerful assimilatory forces" which operated in American society (ibid., p. 2). In contrast, Michael Weisser's study of one of the most popular Jewish immigrant organizations in America, a benevolent society known as a *landsmanshaft*, depicts a transplanted institution that facilitated "the conscious recreation of Old World activities, relationships, and patterns" (1985, p. 4). Weisser claimed that the "people who joined a landsmanshaft and kept it at the psychic core of their existence were at the same time rejecting the larger society and resisting its opportunities for assimilation" (ibid., p. 5). However, there is no evidence to suggest that transplanted ethnic organizations like the *landsmanshaftn* ever survive much beyond the immigrant generation. Other weaknesses in the revisionist case include the fact that many ethnic organizations, especially the protest ones, were only set up to achieve specific short-term objectives and soon went into decline once these had been attained (see Chapter 6, pp. 155–6). Recent research has also shown that the Great Depression destroyed many ethnic institutions in the United States: first, by draining them financially as they sought to alleviate the plight of the rising number of destitute among their membership and, second, by ushering in the New Deal labor reforms and welfare state that rendered them redundant. As Lizabeth Cohen has argued in *Making a New Deal*, "[w]hen their welfare capitalist employers and ethnic communities who had promised to take care of them in the 1920s let them down in the crisis of the Great Depression, workers found a new protector in the state" (1990, p. 289). A more enduring force which acts to undermine ethnic institutions is the ongoing secularization of American society, which poses a major threat to what has long been perceived as one of the most powerful agents of particularism – traditional religion. Ironically, East European Jews, one of the few American ethnies whose appellation directly derives from an ancestral religion, were, according to Lloyd Gartner, "overwhelmed" in early twentieth-century New York by "modern secular culture" and deserted Judaism in their droves (1969, p. 10). However, various studies suggest that the particularizing effects of religion may well have been exaggerated by scholars in the past. Parochial schools, for example, appear to have been equally as effective agents of Americanization as the public school system; probably more so, if we consider the fact that Italian Americans, who have often been viewed as the European immigrant group with the slowest rate of assimilation, were also the Catholic ethny least likely to establish or patronize parochial schools and hence most likely to have its younger generations educated in the public schools (Sanders, 1977, p. 16). For all its tolerance of ethnic diversity, admitted James Sanders, the Catholic education system failed to prevent the "de-ethnicization" and "progressive assimilation of the Church's ethnic groups", while the number and proportion of children attending parochial schools rapidly declined following the upward mobility and suburbanization of the main European ethnic groups in the post-World War II era (ibid., pp. 17, 227–30).

Ethnic Family Structure: The Traditional Emphasis on Change

Orthodox and revisionist historians would agree that the family is the most influential of all ethnic institutions. However, conventional scholarship suggested that even this fundamental social unit was shattered by the process of modernization and experience of immigration. Early sociological studies concluded that modernization and immigration led to demoralization and individualization, which in turn led to the destruction of the traditional extended family (Thomas and Znaniecki, 1927 [1918–20]). Immigration historians agreed that in the New World traditional family patterns collapsed and were replaced by modern, individualist values. The relationship between the immigrant generation and their second-generation offspring, therefore, was characterized as one of alienation and conflict. Family breakdown was depicted as a regular accompaniment of immigrant adjustment. In the early twentieth century, contemporary observers, like the famous journalist Jacob Riis, frequently noted how newly-arriving immigrants brought with them patriarchal family patterns. "Yet where wordly-wise children guided their elders", commented historian Moses Rischin on the Jewish generation growing up amidst the "turmoil" and "agitation" of New York's Lower East Side, where "all life's conventions and expectations seemed topsy-turvy", "adult patterns, shaken in their equilibrium, trembled beneath pitiless scrutiny, and filial affection often vanished". According to Rischin, "[c]hasms of misunderstanding embittered family relations" (1962, pp. 144–5: see also Handlin, 1951, pp. 227–58). The same fate was attributed to the victims of involuntary immigration and slavery. Scholars argued that slavery, as well as destroying traditional family patterns, also prevented the family from functioning as a meaningful and effective social unit (Stampp, 1956; Elkins, 1959).

Ethnic Family Structure: The Revisionist Stress on Continuity

Revisionist studies suggested that traditional family patterns were not only transported to the United States by immigrants – or, in the case of indigenous groups, survived the experience of conquest – but actually dominated group and individual responses to education, gender roles, economic imperatives, and so on, to the event that they undermined acculturation and even mobility. The family was depicted as the hub of a network of interdependent relations, a resilient institution that provided emotional and economic support, and reinforced ethnic culture. Revisionists claimed that these primary group ties were the most enduring and always remained within the ethny. The ethnic family appeared capable of surviving all circumstances, including industrialization, slavery, or even the decline of ethnic culture and institutions. A work which epitomizes the revisionist perspective emerging in the late 1960s and early 1970s is Virginia Yans-McLaughlin's article "Patterns of Work and Family Organization: Buffalo's Italians". Finding "little evidence of family disorganization", Yans-McLaughlin claimed that, "contrary to general descriptions of European immigrant adjustment, Buffalo's Italians suffered no immediate or radical disruption in family life" and the Italian family "did not develop a characteristic frequently associated today with lower-class life – a female-headed family system" (1971, p. 313). In an essay that was contemporary and complimentary to Yans-McLaughlin's, Caroline Golab asserted that "rather than obliterating or homogenizing the immigrant family, the industrial experience, at least in America, enabled new forms and responses to evolve" and "these new forms and responses constitute the essence of ethnic persistence in the United States today" (1977b, p. 32: see also Modell, 1968; Alvarez, 1987). However, the family was closely associated in revisionist works with two other supposed bulwarks of ethnicity, religion and the ethnic neighborhood, which suggests that it may not have been quite the independent variable Yans-McLaughlin originally claimed it to be (1971, pp. 299–300).

At around the same time as Yans-McLaughlin and Golab were writing, a reinterpretation of the African-American family was being spearheaded by Herbert Gutman. In *The Black Family in Slavery and Freedom*, Gutman asserted:

> Enslavement was harsh and constricted the enslaved. But it did not destroy their capacity to adapt and sustain the vital familial and kin associations and beliefs that served as the underpinning of a developing Afro-American culture . . . Their household arrangements do not mean that such persons were without "problems". A vast and painful record documents the economic and social – as well as the psychological – costs extracted from poor rural and urban blacks in the decades between the general emancipation and the Great Depression. But that record is not evidence that the black family crumbled or that a "pathological culture" thrived (1976a, p. 465).

In a similar vein, John Blassingame wrote: "Although it was weak, although it was frequently broken, the slave family provided an important buffer, a refuge from the rigors of slavery . . . [and] was, in short, an important survival mechanism" (1972, p. 103). While scholars like Gutman and Blassingame identified black resistance to oppression as the primary cause of family stability among slaves, other historians suggested that an important role was actually played by the slaveowners. Robert Fogel and Stanley Engerman claimed that "it was to the economic interest of planters to encourage the stability of slave families and most of them did so" because a contented workforce was a more productive one (1974, vol. 1, p. 5). Works by Eugene Genovese (1974), and Ira Berlin and Leslie Rowland (1997), have also helped solidify this image of stability and continuity in African-American family patterns.

Critiques of the revisionist perspective have generally called for modifications to rather than a complete rejection of its treatment of the ethnic family. Tamara Hareven provided an early and perceptive appraisal of the revisionists' claim that "the immigrant family actually controlled its own destiny and charted the careers of its members":

Unfortunately, the studies that have reversed the stereotype of family passivity and breakdown in the industrial process have carried the reversal to the other extreme. The new filiopietism that has been emerging recently attributes seemingly unlimited strength to the immigrant or working-class family and tends to exaggerate its autonomy as an institution. Thus, this neoromantic interpretation of the role of the family could easily result in yet another stereotype, as removed from historical reality as the earlier image of social breakdown (1977, p. 49).

An even more scathing critique of the revisionist depiction of the black family has recently been offered by Wilma Dunaway:

In their haste to celebrate the resilience and the dignity of slaves, scholars have underestimated the degree to which slaveholders placed families at risk. Taken to its extremes, the search for individual agency shifts to the oppressed the blame for the horrors and inequalities of the institutions that enslaved them. If, for example, we push to its rhetorical endpoint the claim of Berlin and Rowland that slaves "manipulated to their own benefit the slaveowners' belief that regular family relations made for good business", then we would arrive at the inaccurate conclusion (as some have) that the half of the US slave population who resided in single-parent households did so as an expression of their African-derived cultural preferences, not because of any structural interference by owners (2003, p. 5).

"Notions like 'windows of autonomy within slavery' ", Dunaway contests, "seriously overstate the degree to which slaves had control over their own lives, and they trivialize the brutalities and the inequities of enslavement" (ibid., p. 4).

Many of these criticisms have been taken on board by revisionists, whose work is now more fairly characterized as emphasizing both change and continuity in family patterns, depicting the ethnic family as pragmatic and flexible. In *Family and Community*, for instance, Virginia Yans-McLaughlin expressed an awareness of "both the continuities and the incongruities that exist in transitional cultures" (1977, p. 23). Over recent decades, such statements have become the norm in works examining ethnic family adaptation. While rejecting the view that Mexican-American families were "relatively static, tradition bound, and dysfunctional in the American environment", for example, Richard Griswold del Castillo still believed that they were "ethnically identifiable and maintain important links with the past" (1984, p. 132). In her study of Italian and Jewish immigrants in early twentieth-century Providence, Judith Smith arrived at a similar conclusion: "Immigrant families were not doomed in American cities, nor did they remain unchanged by the world they found there" (1985, p. 166: see also Bodnar, 1985; Cohen, 1993; di Leonardo, 1984; Gabaccia, 1984; Morawska, 1985; Yoo, 2000). According to this viewpoint, traditional ways did not dictate modern ethnic family patterns, but nor did they disappear entirely, as was suggested in conventional studies.

COMPETING PARTICULARISMS

Having examined factors like culture, institutions, and kin networks, each of which is usually viewed as demonstrating at least some particularist tendency, it is now appropriate to consider the influence of the competing particularisms of class and gender. Class and gender constitute competing particularisms because it is possible to argue that in certain circumstances both or either of them can trump ethnicity as a cause of social division or locus of personal identification.

Conflict Perspective: Class and Americanization

Class is one of the most neglected issues in American history. Admittedly, virtually every modern historian makes the obligatory reference in his or her work to the importance of class, but on the whole the subject is dealt with in a perfunctory and superficial manner. Among contemporary scholars, avowedly multiculturalist (and, hence, supposedly "radical") ones are probably the worst offenders in this respect, because they regularly make the most allusions to but display the least understanding of class stratification in the United States (Higham, 1993, pp. 201–3). However, the practice of belittling the significance of American class divisions actually originates in the assimilationist tradition. Many, but not all, assimilationist historians have subscribed to the view that the United States has from the outset been a classless society, in the sense that upward mobility was easy and rapid, and that class consciousness was virtually non–existent because most workers and immigrants embraced individualism. This interpretation was clearly adhered to by John Commons and other pioneers of US labor history (Commons, et al., 1918, vol. 1, pp. 9–10, 14–19 and 1935, vol. 4, p. 622). The Commons school's thinly-veiled bias against southern and eastern European immigrant workers, who were portrayed as peculiarly lacking in class consciousness, shaped attitudes for many decades and was not seriously challenged until Victor Greene (1968) argued that Slavic workers were often more militant than native-born and old-stock immigrant workers (see also Pula and Dziedzic, 1990). That said, Progressive historians like Charles Beard argued from early in the twentieth century that the essential dynamic in American history was the struggle between competing class interests. As we have already seen, Progressive historians paid little attention to ethnicity. They believed that the experience of economic exploitation by capitalists, plus the promulgation of class ideology by socialist movements and labor unions, inculcated workers with class consciousness. Like most other versions of modernization theory, the Progressive perspective assumed that ethnic loyalties were quickly replaced by occupational and class ones (Benson, 1960; Stephenson, 1926; Hansen, 1964 [1940]). This tradition resurfaced in the late 1960s, when the so-called "New Labor History" scholars endeavored to unearth what they believed was a previously overlooked tradition of interethnic and interracial cooperation among American workers. Herbert Gutman fired the signaling shot by claiming that in the late nineteenth century the United Mine Workers (UMW) "functioned as a viable, integrated trade union and quite possibly ranked as the most thoroughly integrated voluntary association in the United States" (1968, pp. 114–15: see also Brier, 1977; Corbin, 1981).

Subsequent generations of scholars have found that, even if ethnic loyalties were not completely obliterated by class ones, every ethny was indeed divided internally by class. A common pattern, for example, has been one of employer versus worker divisions within an ethny. The contours of this class stratification within ethnies have usually been outlined in works by exponents of the pluralist model, but the authors invariably failed to delve into the deeper meaning of this type of intraethnic division. Although it is at variance with what most of the individual authors intended, because the pluralist perspective privileges ethnicity over class, collectively these works suggest that differences in economic roles have long been a cause of internal division within ethnies. This pattern of inadvertently emphasizing the salience of class cleavages is most pronounced in the large number of works which examine a single ethnic group in a single urban location, because in order to produce what their peers would consider a reasonably comprehensive treatment of their chosen subject they have little choice other than to address the issue of class (see, for example, Cinel, 1982; Garcia, 1991; Mei, 1984; Sheridan, 1986; Trotter, 1985). More recent investigation into the subject of proletarianization has shown that working-class elements develop a separate, often oppositional, ethnic culture to middle-class members of the same ethny. Robin Kelley's innovative book, *Race Rebels* (1994), is the most prominent example of this trend. Similarly, numerous studies have demonstrated how middle-class elements have regularly held contempt for and attempted to distance themselves from working-class members of their own ethny, usually in an effort to gain acceptance from and entry into mainstream society. Immigrant communities, as John Bodnar has pointed out, were "arenas in which people sorted themselves out into workers and owners, leaders and followers, traditionalists and modernizers" and "in this arena a new middle class emerged which in many ways owed its status to premigration experiences and which was frequently ambivalent about its relationship to the mass of immigrant workers, alternating between separateness and involvement" (1985, p. 142).

Various suggestions have been made about when and how the shift from a predominantly ethnic to predominantly class consciousness among workers occurred, and the dates vary depending upon the ethnies concerned. Labor historians contest that the Depression era constituted a turning point for workers of eastern and southern European ancestry. During this period the New Deal's pro-union policies accelerated the pace of class formation, a process which not only radicalized but also Americanized ethnic workers. In his case study of New England textile workers, Gary Gerstle contended that a workforce previously divided along ethnic lines was unified by a local labor union through the latter's "elaboration of a working-class Americanism" (1989, p. 5). Roger Horowitz suggested in *"Negro and White, Unite and Fight!"* (1997) that from the New Deal era onwards the American labor movement also made significant progress towards overcoming racial divisions among meatpackers by espousing an ideology that emphasized the common class interests of black and white workers. Indeed, these studies suggest that the proletarianization which took place during the 1930s was a more successful agent of assimilation than the Americanization initiatives vigorously pursued in earlier decades. In his pioneering article "Americanization from the Bottom Up", James Barrett rejected the traditional narrow conception of "Americanization" as "something the native white middle class did to immigrants, a coercive process by which white elites pressed WASP values on immigrant workers, a form of social control" (1992, p. 997). Barrett contended that "class formation" was itself another, parallel form of Americanization, originating among the masses rather than the elite. As Barrett explained:

> . . . by "Americanization from the bottom up", I mean the gradual acculturation of immigrants and their socialization in working-class environments and contexts – the shop floor, the union, the radical political party. These settings provided immigrants with alternatives to the world view and the values advocated in programs sponsored by employers and the government (ibid., p. 998).

For nonwhite ethnies the civil rights revolution of the 1960s is viewed by some scholars as constituting a watershed, because the demise of racial oppression meant that class became the primary cause of inequality in American society (Wilson, 1980). Similarly, numerous studies have revealed that internal class divisions regularly came to the fore in ethnic protest movements once they succeeded in their objective of eliminating ethnic discrimination (Márquez, 1993).

Pluralist Critiques of the Emphasis on Class

The pluralist critique of the Progressive perspective on class began in the post-World War II era, when the "consensus" school of history emerged. While not all consensus historians were pluralists, in fact many if not most were staunchly assimilationist, they did agree that there was little evidence of class consciousness or solidarity in American history (Boorstin, 1965). By the 1960s, some consensus historians had adopted an openly pluralist position, arguing that, along with social mobility, ethnic diversity had traditionally served as one of the main impediments to the development of class cleavages in the United States. "Since the United States is highly heterogeneous, and has high mobility", explained Lee Benson, "I assume that men tend to retain and be more influenced by their ethnic and religious group membership than by their membership in economic classes or groups" (1964 [1961], p. 165). Various studies suggested that upward mobility had traditionally thwarted class formation yet permitted ethnicity to persist (Rolle, 1968; Nelli, 1970; Lemon, 1972; Chudacoff, 1972; Conzen, 1976; Kessner, 1977).

Since the 1960s, various radical interpretations of American history have emerged which contend that while class and ethnic status and consciousness are often intertwined they are not always complimentary to each other. New Left historians like Gabriel Kolko, whose future dream was a socialist America, felt compelled to discover why in the past "the American labor movement, unique to the world, failed to develop a commitment to one of the several historical socialist ideologies and the goal of sharing in the operational control of social power" and why "in a society where the working class is an objective reality it fails to develop a consciousness, even from its structurally common experience, comparable to that of virtually every other capitalist society" (1976, p. 67). Studies of labor history suggested that the American working class lacked unity because it had always been divided into separate ethnic subcultures. In *Roots of the American Working Class*, Susan Hirsch contended that "[w]orkers' attempts to use the political system for economic ends foundered . . . because of the vitality of ethnic conflict and the belief that class politics was un-American" (1978, p. 130). According to Hirsch this lack of class unity originated in the fact that, since the onset of industrialism in the United States, "the main focus of working-class life remained the attempt to retain preindustrial and ethnic values within the urban, industrial world", a pattern accentuated by "the constant influx of immigrants of diverse nationalities and religions, many of whom came from preindustrial cultures" (ibid., p. 135). Various scholars conceded – or exclaimed, if they were ideologically committed to the concept of pluralism – that ethnicity appeared to cut across class lines, rather than vice versa (Rosenblum, 1973; Friedlander, 1975; Rosenzweig, 1983; Bukowczyk, 1984; Miller, 1990). An increasing number of studies pointed to labor market segmentation as a cause of ethnic formation. Hiring practices which produced ethnic niches in certain industries and occupations seemed to promote emergent ethnicity more than they did trans-ethnic class consciousness (Bodnar, 1977; Barrera, 1979; Bodnar, et al., 1982; Rosenzweig, 1983). Further research suggested that nativism and racism within working-class and radical movements spurred ethnic formation and strengthened group boundaries (Spero and Harris, 1931; Saxton, 1971; Foner, 1974; Mink, 1986; Lane, 1987; Glickman, 1993). Herbert Hill's critique of the New Labor History, which he dubbed "romanticized popular front leftism", instigated one of the most acrimonious exchanges – generally referred to as the Gutman-Hill debate (although Gutman had already passed away before the controversy began) – between competing schools of historians ever to be witnessed in the field of American history (Hill, 1988, p. 133). In an article entitled "Myth-Making as Labor History: Herbert Gutman and the United Mine Workers of America", Hill asserted:

Denial of the central role of race and the relegation of race consciousness to class consciousness in labor history has resulted in a representation and interpretation of the black workers' experience with white organized labor that cannot be sustained by the historical record. The tendency to deny race as a crucial factor, to permit questions of class to subsume racial issues, is based on a perspective that ignores racism as a system of domination, as it ignores the role of racist ideology in working-class history (ibid., pp. 191–2).

The recent wave of "whiteness" studies generally lends weight to this viewpoint (Saxton, 1990; Roediger, 1991; Roediger, 1994; see also Kolchin, 2002). In *The Wages of Whiteness: Race and the Making of the American Working Class*, David Roediger, emphasizing the "construction of identity through otherness" – with blacks and the "slave labor" they were associated with being the "other" – argued that "whiteness was a way in which white workers responded to a fear of dependency on wage labor and to the necessities of capitalist work discipline" in the newly emerging commercial and industrial order (1991, pp. 13–14). Various studies uncovering evidence of labor militancy originating at the grass-roots level among black (Harris, 1977), Asian (Yu, 1992), and Latino workers (Almaguer, 1984), have in recent decades overturned a core myth of organized labor's traditional whites-only ideology – the belief that nonwhite laborers were incapable of developing class consciousness or displaying worker solidarity.

The internal-colony paradigm made an important contribution to pluralist perceptions of the relationship between class and ethnicity. According to early internal-colony theorists, the so-called "cultural division of labor" played a major role in the appearance of ethnic groups in modern societies. One influential version of the internal-colony model, that put forward by Mario Barrera, suggests that class formation among colonized nonwhites was virtually the inverse of that among the colonizing whites, with the latter ethnies possessing sizeable middle classes and a relatively small working class and the former ethnies vice versa (1979, pp. 214–16). The split-labor-market and middleman theories also seem to support the view that while class structures may have contributed towards ethnic formation, ethnicity did not usually promote a broader trans-ethnic class consciousness. Among middleman minorities, class and ethnic interests, especially for the bourgeois stratum, appeared to be curiously intertwined. Societal discrimination, suggested Edna Bonacich and John Modell, which excluded both Japanese immigrant workers and entrepreneurs from the mainstream economy, strengthened reciprocal ties between the two. "New immigrants", observed Bonacich and Modell, "were forced to take jobs wherever they could get them, and the fact that fellow ethnics offered them an opportunity to establish themselves was bound to produce loyalty" (1980, pp. 251–2). Likewise, because Japanese entrepreneurs were restricted to small-scale activities and excluded from the more lucrative sectors of the wider commercial economy, "the precapitalist form of their businesses deemphasized internal class divisions and produced an especially loyal and hardworking labor force" (ibid., p. 251).

In recent decades, an increasing number of scholars have emphasized the point that working-class culture appears to have been more ethnic than middle-class culture. In fact, it is frequently implied that only working-class culture is ethnic. In an essay on the "Immigrant Foundations" of the American working class, Gabriel Kolko pointed out "a large proportion of all who came to America were marginal, increasingly dispossessed men and women in their own homelands, they were rarely carriers of the deeper culture of their own nations" and "[v]ery few intellectuals or bearers of 'high culture' migrated to America" (1976, p. 95: see also Hirsch, 1978; Rosenzweig, 1983). According to Kolko, not only did most southern and eastern European immigrants fail to rise out of the working class but they also made up the majority of its white members for most of the twentieth century, lending a distinctively ethnic flavor to American working-class culture. This interpretation is evocative of Milton Gordon's identification of what he called "ethclass" subgroups (1964, p. 51). Many pluralist scholars now perceive this apparent confluence of ethnicization and proletarianization as the answer to the old conundrums about whether class and ethnicity are mutually antagonistic forms of identity or which of the two types of allegiance is the most potent. Various works suggest that a resolution of the race–class dichotomy at the centre of the Gutman–Hill debate might be found by proceeding in this direction. Historians like Ronald Lewis (1987), Daniel Rosenberg (1988), Joe Trotter (1990), and Eric Arnesen (1993 and 1994), have developed a more "refined and nuanced" understanding of the relationship between class and race, showing that "the racial policies of organized labor in the early twentieth century were far from monolithic" and black workers' relationships with their white co-workers were "less antagonistic and far more complex than previously assumed" (Halpern, 1994, pp. 75–6). Recent works exploring the phenomena of "oppositional culture" and "infra-politics" – the "daily, unorganized, evasive, seemingly spontaneous . . . acts of resistance" that characterized "urban black working-class opposition" in the Jim Crow South – also seem to suggest that it is not necessary to make such comparisons between class and ethnicity but rather to understand the relationship between the two (Kelley, 1993, pp. 76–7, 79). However, there is a major flaw in this perspective. Working-class culture may well be more ethnic than middle-class culture, but extensive evidence of upward mobility suggests that this working-class ethnic culture has continually been undermined in the United States. Indeed, Benjamin Márquez's observation that in the post-Civil Rights era "[i]ncreased levels of education and economic mobility have broken the lower-class/ethnic bond" that held Mexican Americans together during their earlier struggle for equal rights might equally be applied to numerous other ethnic and racial minorities (1993, p. 109). Ethnic culture, therefore, would appear to belong to an ever-decreasing proportion of the US population. Nonetheless, the current state of the field is that most scholars manifestly shy away from offering a definitive answer on the question of whether class trumps ethnicity, or vice versa, in American history.

Conflict Perspective: Gender and Intraethnic Discord

Gender differences would appear on the face of it to be more likely to undermine than buttress ethnic boundaries. A stark male–female divide existed within virtually every ethny and this invariably took the form of patriarchy. Traditional ethnic gender roles usually afforded women little or no autonomy outside of certain roles and settings. In contrast, mainstream society, with its individualistic values and relatively more progressive attitudes to female emancipation, appeared to offer ethnic women a variety of options denied them within their own ethny. Women's opportunity, therefore, would seem to have been inhibited more by the patriarchy of their own ethnic groups than ethnic discrimination by the dominant society. Consequently, various studies have suggested that ethnic women's growing awareness of gender inequality created tensions within ethnies (Krause, 1978; Martinelli, 1978; Ichioka, 1980; González, 1983; Bloom, 1985; Yung, 1995; Glenn, 1986; Helmbold, 1987; Monroy, 1990; Pickle, 1996). At school, in the workplace, or through the mass media, girls and women were continually open to influences that reminded them how the mainstream culture's conception of gender roles differed to that of their ethny. For "young immigrants [who] . . . needed to learn at least surface conformity to American styles of dress, speech, and behavior", asserted Leslie Tentler in *Wage-Earning Women*, "[t]he work group could provide them with an authentically contemporary model of adolescent culture, as opposed to the formal, excessively middle-class model of the schoolroom or the outdated expectations of parents" (1979, pp. 67–8). According to Tentler,

> . . . [O]pen and disruptive ethnic conflict among working women was rare. The bonds of age and sex usually served to transcend the divisions of ethnicity. For as young women of various national groups pursued as fellow workers their common goals of a thoroughly American personal style and unprecedented freedom from parental control, they often had reason to feel that they had more in common with one another than with the older generation. Through their work experience, reinforcing as it did a heightened identification

with mass popular culture, these young women were creating for themselves a common identity that we can call working-class (ibid., p. 71).

A number of factors compounded the extent to which ethnic girls and women were exposed to acculturating influences. Numerous scholars have found evidence of Americanization initiatives deliberately targeting the female population of ethnies, whose traditional role as child-carers and primary transmitters of culture to the next generation seemed to make them the ideal agents of acculturation. As Elizabeth Ewen noted in *Immigrant Women in the Land of Dollars*, "[s]ocial workers and other agents of assimilation aimed much of their assault at those aspects of life which were the customary provinces of women", because "[t]he household, and particularly the mother, was seen as the linchpin holding an anachronistic way of life together" (1985, p. 266: see also Juliani, 1978; Seller, 1978b; Webster, 1978; Mohl, 1982; Trennert, 1982; Yung, 1995; Mihesuah, 1993; Ruiz, 1998). During the 1960s and 1970s, the tensions created by the competing demands of ethnic loyalty and female emancipation came to a head for many of the women involved in the various ethnic protest movements. As Ramón Gutiérrez has shown, this conflict was particularly pronounced in the Chicano movement:

> Within the Chicano student movement, women were denied leadership roles and were asked to perform only the most traditional stereotypic roles – cleaning up, making coffee, executing the orders men gave, and servicing their needs. Women who did manage to assume leadership positions were ridiculed as unfeminine, sexually perverse, promiscuous, and all too often, taunted as lesbians (1993, p. 47).

Women activists openly criticized the male chauvinism that permeated the ideologies, structures and practices of the Chicano movement, as in countless other ethnic protest groups and organizations (Riddell, 1974; Ling, 1989; Orozco, 1990; Collins, 1990; Mills, 1994; García, 1997).

Pluralist Emphasis on Gender as a Particularizing Agent

An alternative viewpoint to the one outlined above offers an entirely different interpretation of what is virtually the same set of facts. Pluralist scholars concede that ethnic gender patterns were frequently patriarchal, but they argue that customary beliefs about female roles were usually applied in a pragmatic and flexible way, thereby permitting women a great deal of freedom in and control over their family roles. A representative example of this interpretation is provided by Susan Glenn in her study of East European Jewish immigrants, *Daughters of the Shtetl*:

> The evolving nature of Jewish New Womanhood seems paradoxical. Teenage girls came to this country, worked in the garment industry, went out on strike, briefly became involved in union activities, married, and settled into domestic life. Such a trajectory was typical, containing all of the compelling experiences of immigrant women's lives – work, the labor movement, marriage, motherhood. This life course pulled Jewish daughters in seemingly contradictory directions. On the one hand, the labor movement expanded the female sphere, giving women a greater (one might say an official) role in the civic life of the Jewish community. And work, traditionally conferred upon immigrant daughters a sense of competence and, for some, a feeling of self-worth that came from knowing they could earn a living if they had to. At the same time, however, young women aspired to a romantic version of marriage (1990, p. 238: see also Seller, 1978a and 1981; Smith, 1978; Yang, 1984; Ewen, 1985; Peiss, 1986; Weinberg, 1988; Cohen, 1993; Shoemaker, 1995; Ruiz, 1998; Perdue, 1998).

Revisionist historians also claim that, despite coming into contact with acculturating influences, women were more likely to function as guardians of ethnic culture than agents of Americanization. Studies reveal that ethnic women maintained a strong attachment to traditional religious allegiances and group customs, which they kept alive within the home. The dynamics of this process were described by Donna Gabaccia:

> First as community activists and later as socializers of children and organizers of family and religious rituals, immigrant women reproduced and transformed cultural traditions through their labors. Men at first sought women's help in reproducing ethnicity and then abandoned it increasingly to women and their domestic roles. It is scarcely surprising that women, more than men, continue to view ethnicity and their immigrant "roots" as an important influence on their lives (1994, p. 131: see also Seller, 1981; Jones, 1985; Coburn, 1992; Higginbotham, 1993; Korrol, 1994; Shoemaker 1995; Pickle, 1996; Schwalm, 1997; Perdue, 1998).

Various studies suggest that women, as well as holding onto their ethnicity longer, were generally slower than men to adopt the individualist values of American society. Irish immigrant women's willingness to migrate on their own and fend for themselves economically once in America, Hasia Diner has noted, should not be interpreted as demonstrating their "autonomy and independence":

> Their actions stemmed from family loyalties. They reckoned that they could support and succor brothers, sisters, and parents better from America than on the "ould sod". Their actions represented a commitment to Irish Catholic culture and to its way of life. The move to America did not represent a search for a new identity, nor did it constitute a break with the past (1983, p. xiv).

With regards to their treatment by mainstream society, it is claimed that far from encountering greater acceptance and opportunity than from within their own ethny, ethnic women were customarily the victims on account of their ethnicity and gender of a double oppression (or triple, if class is included). This concept of double oppression is most typically used with reference to the experiences of nonwhite women, as was the case in one its earliest expositions, penned in the early 1970s by the civil rights campaigner Lourdes Miranda King:

> The Puerto Rican woman in the United then is caught between two forces. On the one hand, she is entrapped within the bleak economic and political powerlessness affecting the Puerto Rican population in general. On the other hand, she suffers from the socialization of sex roles which causes her to have guilt feelings about the fulfillment of her potential and its expression in a society which looks down its aquiline Anglo nose at her and her people . . .
> The Puerto Rican woman in the mainland United States feels the impact of double discrimination as a woman and as a Puerto Rican – often as a woman, a black, and a Puerto Rican (1974, p. 25).

In acknowledgment of the fact that ethnic women have historically been subject to the most extreme forms of negative stereotyping and exploitation, the theme of "double discrimination", or variations of it, and the focus upon intersections of race/ethnicity, gender, and class, have since been utilized in countless studies of the Latino, African-American, and Asian-American, but also on occasion European-American females' experiences (see, for example, Cheng, 1979; Dickinson, 1980, p. 209; Cheng and Bonacich, 1984, p. 367; Jones, 1985, p. 3; Deutsch, 1987; Chato and Conte, 1988; Guy-Sheftall, 1990; Segura, 1990; Yung, 1995, p. 5; Anderson, 1996, p. 7; Ruiz, 1998, p. xvi; Bao, 2001, p. 3; Glenn, 2002). The dominant society's treatment of ethnic women is therefore viewed as a factor that strengthens rather than weakens ethnic boundaries.

Finally, the prominent role that ethnic women have traditionally played in ethnic protest movements is pointed to as evidence that gender issues have had little impact on ethnic unity. The fame of Rosa Parks alone attests to the fact that African-American women made a significant contribution to the civil rights movement and recently this has begun to be reflected in historical scholarship (see, for example, Robinson, 1987; Thompson, 1990; Yee, 1992; Crawford, et al., 1993). Similarly, ethnic Mexican women have been shown to have played a major and frequently leading role not just in the Chicano movement, but in countless labor struggles throughout the twentieth century (see, for example, Vásquez, 1980; Monroy, 1980; Durón, 1984; Ruiz, 1990; Ruiz, 1987). Moreover, as Kathleen Blee's *Women of the Klan* demonstrated, ethnic women – in this case White Anglo-Saxon Protestant ones – were not above actively participating in organizations that represented their own "reactionary political views on race, nationality, and religion" (1991, p. 3). In some cases, women activists even withheld their criticisms of male chauvinism in order to prevent gender disputes from becoming a cause of disunity within ethnic protest organizations, thereby allowing the struggle for ethnic equality to take priority over that for sexual equality (Robinson, 1987; Terborg-Penn, 1983). Conversely, American feminism, according to Elinor Lerner (1986), has a long tradition of ignoring the interests of ethnic women. However, probably the most striking and best documented example of American females putting ethnicity or race before gender is the support southern white women, including feminists, lent first to slavery and then to Jim Crow (Hooks, 1982; Lebsock, 1984; Janiewski, 1985; White, 1985; Fox-Genovese, 1988; Hine, 1989; Bynum, 1992; Morton 1996; Gilmore, 1996). For other ethnic women, such as the Jewish garment worker union activists examined by Alice Kessler-Harris, "the class struggle was preeminent" (1976, p. 23: see also Gabaccia, 1994).

Clearly, there is a strong case for classifying gender as both a category that undermines ethnic boundaries and one that strengthens them, and it has undoubtedly performed both roles in the past. However, it is too early to offer a judgment on which function gender has most consistently performed in relation to ethnic boundary maintenance. Women's history has long been neglected by scholars and, while important strides have been made in recent years to redress the balance, especially in the field of American ethnic history, a great deal more research needs to undertaken before it will be possible to arrive at more concrete conclusions about the issues discussed above.

INTERMARRIAGE

Before examining the range of views relating to the effects intermarriage may have had upon ethnic boundaries in the United States, it is first necessary to make a few observations about scholarly perspectives on the nature and extent of the phenomenon. Miscegenation – sexual intercourse and interbreeding between different "races" – while not quite a taboo subject in American society, has traditionally been viewed as condemnable and its mixed-ancestry human products as pitiable. In an article entitled "The Beginnings of the Miscegenation of Whites and Blacks", Carter G. Woodson claimed that whites in colonial America "disowned their offspring by slave women, leaving these children to follow the condition of their mother" (1918, pp. 338–9). Moreover, compared with other colonized parts of the New World, Woodson observed, there was

> not so much less miscegenation among the English but there remained the natural tendency so to denounce these unions as eventually to restrict the custom, as it is today, to the weaker types of both races, the offspring of whom in the case of slave mothers became a commodity in the commercial world (ibid., p. 339).

It is only since the 1970s that historians have begun to seriously examine the topic of interracial sex first explored by Woodson around the time of World War I. However, recent studies revealing the severe social and legal consequences faced by those who breached the anti-miscegenation code suggest that it was not a course of action one might advise to be undertaken by the "weaker types" of any race (Johnston, 1970; Fowler, 1987; Pascoe, 1996; Mumford, 1997; Hodes, 1999; Wallenstein, 2002; Robinson, 2003; Romano, 2003; Rothman, 2003; Lubin, 2005). Negative attitudes towards race mixing have long held sway among professional historians in the United States and are only slowly giving way to a more enlightened, humanistic perspective. For instance, one article which appeared not too long ago in the *Journal of American Ethnic History* referred to mixed-race individuals as "victims of miscegenation", the assumption being that monoethnic relationships and ancestry are inherently preferable to multiethnic ones (Collier-Thomas and Turner, 1994, p. 9). However, in recent decades a growing number of scholars have openly condemned the disparaging way in which miscegenation and mixed-ancestry people have traditionally been treated in historical studies (Root, 1992a). Moreover, some leading historians have called upon their peers to finally acknowledge the full extent of ethnic and racial amalgamation in the United States, which has continually been either overlooked or underestimated in the past. In an article entitled "The Hidden History of Mestizo America", Gary Nash asserted:

> The silence in our history books on the topic of multiraciality reflects the antimiscegenist attitudes supported by the law. In fact, about

three-quarters of African Americans today are multiracial, and perhaps one-third have some Indian ancestry. Virtually all Latino Americans are multiracial, so are almost all Filipino Americans, so are a large majority of American Indians, and millions of whites have multiracial roots (1995, p. 949).

Numerous studies suggest that ethnic and racial interbreeding has, since the very beginning of American history, been extensive, involving all ethnies, regardless of the region or time period under investigation. As Paul Spickard pointed out in his study of intermarriage, *Mixed Blood*:

> [A] pattern of mixing is especially prominent in the American past. People came to America from all over the world. They bore every conceivable color, religion, and national heritage. Within a generation or two after arriving here, most socialized and mated with people who were not like them – who did not share their color, their religion, or their national heritage (1989, p. 4).

Some ethnies are so intermixed that the majority of their members have mixed ancestry. Ruby Jo Reeves Kennedy's seminal study of marriage patterns among European Americans in New Haven between 1870 and 1940 led her to conclude that the "different nationalities are merging" (1944, p. 331: see also Bernard, 1980). As the title of Joel Williamson's book *New People* (1980) suggests, he believed that African Americans are predominantly of mixed racial ancestry. Indeed, levels of mixed ancestry are much higher than many historians would care to admit. The "kind of multiculturalism that insists on studying self-contained and absolutized groups", according to Gary Nash, is threatened by and is, indeed, "the enemy of *mestizaje*", because the very existence of mixed ancestry people seriously calls into question the premise that "racial difference is the alpha and omega of intellectual discourse and politics, and therefore, of social action" (1995, p. 961).

Amalgamation and Assimilation

Ethnic intermarriage has traditionally been viewed as a factor which breaks down group boundaries and aids acculturation. It is for this reason that members of the dominant society frequently welcomed intermarriage. There is evidence of many ethnies being rapidly accepted by and marrying into the dominant ethny. "Among whites", Richard Alba has noted, "a long-term trend of increasing intermarriage, which dates at least to the immediate post-World War II period and probably earlier, has made marriage across ethnic lines now the rule rather than the exception" (1990, p. 12). Some leading American politicians and intellectuals even envisioned widespread intermarriage taking place between whites and nonwhites. Indeed, Thomas Jefferson not only expressed his desire that white and Native-American communities "meet and blend together, to intermix, and become one people", but he even had a prolonged, yet furtive, relationship with an African-American woman and sired numerous children by her (Nash, 1995, p. 943: see also Graham, 1961; Lewis and Onuf, 1999; Neiman, 2000). The first generation of professional sociologists and historians to examine American ethnic patterns also believed that group boundaries would eventually be obliterated by intermarriage. Amalgamation, a manifestation of primary-level contact between the members of different ethnies, has conventionally been viewed as part of an intermediate stage of assimilation, being preceded by secondary-level contacts in the initial stage and followed by identification with the mainstream culture in the final stage. Scholars generally agreed that exogamy hindered the maintenance of distinct ethnic cultures and strong group boundaries. Expressing an opinion with which his eminent predecessor, Robert Park, would most likely have concurred, the sociologist Milton Gordon asserted: "If marital assimilation takes place fully, the minority group loses its ethnic identity in the larger host or core society" (1964, p. 80). Various studies have suggested that ethnic interbreeding also created internal divisions within ethnies, setting single- and mixed-ancestry groups against each other. Moreover, this internal conflict and competition frequently worked to the advantage of the dominant society, for whom the mixed-ancestry faction appeared to function as a buffer against the usually less amenable unmixed element, a situation which appeared to have made ethnies even less capable in the long term of resisting assimilatory influences. A traditional view on this issue can be found in Mary Young's depiction of the internecine conflict evident within the various "Civilized Tribes" prior to the removal crisis of the 1830s:

> Long-term contact between the southeastern tribes and white traders, missionaries, and government officials created numerous half-breeds. The half-breed men acted as intermediaries between the less sophisticated Indians and the white Americans. Acquiring direct or indirect control of tribal politics, they often determined the outcome of treaty negotiations. Since they proved to be skillful bargainers, it became common practice to win their assistance by thinly veiled bribery. The rise of the half-breeds to power, the rewards they received, and their efforts on behalf of tribal reform gave rise to bitter opposition (1958, p. 32).

Similarly, Gary Mills (1977) has argued that mulattoes often distanced themselves from and were reluctant to cooperate politically with darker-skinned African Americans in the nineteenth-century South, adopting the practice of identifying themselves as "Creole" rather than "Negro".

Exogamy and Pluralism

Upon closer examination, it is clear that ethnic interbreeding did not always have a corrosive effect on ethnic boundaries. A multitude of studies have shown how mixed-ancestry individuals, rather than being welcomed into mainstream society, were customarily ascribed by the dominant ethny to membership of the minority ethny. This was particularly true in the case of marginalized, nonwhite ethnies. Ethnic interbreeding, therefore, effectuated an enlargement of the marginalized ethny's population rather than the undermining of the boundaries that separated it from the dominant and other ethnies. This practice is most evident in the history of African Americans, who under racial slavery, Jim Crow laws, and even modern-day census practices have arbitrarily been categorized as black or nonwhite even in cases where an individual's ethnic ancestry is incontestably more European or non-African than African. In *Roll, Jordon, Roll*, Eugene Genovese contended that "the two-caste system in the Old South drove the mulattoes into the arms of the blacks, no matter how hard some tried to build a make-believe third world for themselves" (1974, p. 431: see also Degler, 1971; Mencke, 1979; Williamson, 1980). More recent research has drawn attention to the occasions upon which ethnic interbreeding has resulted in the formation of entirely new ethnies with hybrid cultures and identities. For instance, the Seminoles, due to the extent of intermarriage between tribal members and runaway slaves, are regularly portrayed as siring a fusion of Native-American and African-American genes and cultures (Littlefield, 1977; Mulroy, 1993; Porter, 1996). Another example of this hybridity is the "biethnic Punjabi-Mexican community" created in Southern California during the early twentieth century when many male immigrants from India, prevented by state anti-miscegenation laws from marrying whites, married and raised families with women of Mexican nationality and ancestry (Leonard, 1992, p. 3). Many of these studies also reveal that relations between mixed and unmixed ancestry elements were not always antagonistic and did not always undermine the ethny's ability to maintain a distinctive culture and boundaries. Mixed ancestry elements may well have been more acculturated, but they frequently utilized their greater knowledge and understanding of American society to devise more effective strategies for maintaining group boundaries and resisting further assimilation. Theda Perdue, for instance, has recently provided a revisionist interpretation of both the identity and role of "mixed blood" Indians in the life and trials of the southeastern tribes before and during the removal era:

By the nineteenth century, many southern Indians were . . . "both white and red" in terms of ancestry and culture. In our [modern] accounts, however, the white often obscures the red. We are blinded by the spectacle of Indians living in mansions, owning plantations and African-American slaves, sending their children to school, worshipping in Christian churches, governing themselves under constitutions and written laws. In our analysis of "mixed blood" Indians, we have privileged whiteness, and as a result, we have underestimated the power and persistence of the culture into which they were born and chose to live (2003, pp. 68–9).

Perdue points out that the "mixed bloods" who dominated lawmaking bodies of the southeastern tribes even instituted, and on occasion carried out, the death penalty for selling tribal lands to whites. As Perdue asserts,

Perhaps more than anything else, the determination of national leaders to preserve their nations demonstrates the fallacy of characterizing "mixed bloods" as different from other Indians in the Southeast. "Mixed bloods" as well as "full-bloods" understood the deep bond between their people and the land on which they lived in the Southeast (ibid., pp. 66–7: see also Peterson, 1988).

Mixed ancestry individuals appeared to be ideally suited for rising to positions of leadership or acting as role models to less acculturated group members. According to Joel Williamson the mulatto offspring of white planters, who afterwards intermarried with blacks, "move[d] into the vanguard of their people" in the post-emancipation era and are the ancestors of the "mulatto elite" who throughout the twentieth century have dominated African-American intellectual and political leadership (1980, pp. 56, 145).

SUMMARY

As the discussion in this chapter has demonstrated, the issues surrounding ethnic identity and boundary maintenance are complex and not as clear-cut as they often appear in many of the conceptual models utilized by scholars, assimilationist and pluralist alike. Despite the existence of various particularizing agents, ethnic identity and boundaries are clearly more susceptible to erosion than pluralists have generally been willing to concede. Likewise, class, gender and intermarriage do not appear to have been as effective at undermining ethnic identities and boundaries as many assimilationists would like to think.

Bibliography

Abelmann, N., and J. Lie (1995), *Blue Dreams: Korean Americans and the Los Angeles Riots*, Harvard University Press, Cambridge, MA.

Abramson, H. (1980), "Assimilation and Pluralism", in S. Thernstrom (ed.), *Harvard Encyclopedia of American Ethnic Groups*, Harvard University Press, Cambridge, MA, pp. 150–60.

Acuña, R. (1972), *Occupied America: The Chicano's Struggle Toward Liberation*, Canfield Press, San Francisco.

Acuña, R. (1988), *Occupied America: A History of Chicanos*, HarperCollins, New York, 3rd edn.

Acuña, R. (2004), *Occupied America: A History of Chicanos*, Pearson-Longman, New York, 5th edn.

Adams, D. (1995), *Education for Extinction: American Indians and the Boarding School Experience, 1875–1928*, University Press of Kansas, Lawrence.

Alba, R. (1985), "The Twilight of Ethnicity among Americans of European Ancestry: The Case of Italians", *Ethnic and Racial Studies*, vol. 8, January, pp. 134–58.

Alba, R. (1990), *Ethnic Identity: The Transformation of White America*, Yale University Press, New Haven, CT.

Alba, R. (1995), "Assimilation's Quiet Tide", *The Public Interest*, spring, pp. 3–18.

Alexander, C. (1965), *The Ku Klux Klan in the Southwest*, University Press of Kentucky, Lexington.

Allen, R. (1970), *Black Awakening in Capitalist America*, Doubleday, Garden City, NY.

Allswang, J. (1971), *A House for All Peoples: Ethnic Politics in Chicago, 1890–1936*, University Press of Kentucky, Lexington.

Almaguer, T. (1984), "Racial Domination and Class Conflict in Capitalist Agriculture: The Oxnard Sugar Beet Workers' Strike of 1903", *Labor History*, vol. 25, summer, pp. 325–50.

Alvarez, R. (1987), *Familia: Migration and Adaptation in Baja and Alta California, 1800–1975*, University of California Press, Berkeley.

Andersen, A. (1990), *Rough Road to Glory: The Norwegian-American Press Speaks Out on Public Affairs, 1875 to 1925*, Balch Institute Press, Philadelphia, PA.

Anderson, G. (1980), "Early Dakota Migration and Intertribal War: A Revision", *Western Historical Quarterly*, vol. 11, January, pp. 17–36.

Anderson, J. (1975), "Education as a Vehicle for the Manipulation of Black Workers", in W. Feinberg and H. Rosemont (eds), *Work, Technology, and Education: Dissenting Essays in the Intellectual Foundations of American Education*, University of Illinois Press, Urbana, pp. 15–40.

Anderson, J. (1988), *The Education of Blacks in the South, 1860–1935*, University of North Carolina Press, Chapel Hill.

Anderson, K. (1996), *Changing Woman: A History of Racial Ethnic Women in Modern America*, Oxford University Press, New York.

Appel, J., and S. Appel (1982), "The Huddled Masses and the Little Red Schoolhouse", in B. Weiss (ed.), *American Education and the European Immigrant, 1840–1940*, University of Illinois Press, Urbana, pp. 17–30.

Aptheker, H. (1943), *American Negro Slave Revolts*, Columbia University Press, New York.

Aptheker, H. (1947), "Additional Data on American Maroons", *Journal of Negro History*, vol. 32, October, pp. 452–60.

Arnesen, E. (1991), *Waterfront Workers of New Orleans: Race, Class, and Politics, 1863–1923*, Oxford University Press, New York.

Arnesen, E. (1993), "Following the Color Line of Labor: Black Workers and the Labor Movement before 1930", *Radical History Review*, vol. 55, winter, pp. 53–87.

Arnesen, E. (1994), " 'Like Banquo's Ghost, It Will Not Down': The Race Question and the American Railroad Brotherhoods, 1880–1920", *American Historical Review*, vol. 99, December, pp. 1601–33.

Asher, R. (1982), "Union Nativism and the Immigrant Response", *Labor History*, vol. 23, summer, pp. 325–48.

Asher, R., and C. Stephenson (1990), (eds), *Labor Divided: Race and Ethnicity in United States Labor Struggles, 1835–1960*, State University of New York Press, Albany.

Avrich, P. (1991), *Sacco and Vanzetti: The Anarchist Background*, Princeton University Press, Princeton, NJ.

Ayers, E. (1984), *Vengeance and Justice: Crime and Punishment in the 19th Century South*, Oxford University Press, New York.

Bailey, T. (1932), "California, Japan, and the Alien Land Legislation of 1913", *Pacific Historical Review*, vol. 1, March, pp. 36–59.

Balderrama, F. (1982), *In Defense of La Raza: The Los Angeles Mexican Consulate and the Mexican Community, 1929 to 1936*, University of Arizona Press, Tucson.

Balderrama, F., and R. Rodríguez (1995), *Decade of Betrayal: Mexican Repatriation in the 1930s*, University of New Mexico Press, Albuquerque.

Bao, X. (2001), *Holding Up More Than Half the Sky: Chinese Women Garment Workers in New York City, 1948–92*, University of Illinois Press, Urbana.

Barkan, E. (1992), *The Retreat of Scientific Racism: Changing Concepts of Race in Britain and the United States Between the World Wars*, Cambridge University Press, Cambridge.

Barkan, E. (1995), "Race, Religion, and Nationality in American Society: A Model of Ethnicity – From Contact to Assimilation", *Journal of American Ethnic History*, vol. 14, winter, pp. 38–75.

Barkan, E. (1996), *And Still They Come: Immigrants and American Society, 1920 to the 1990s*, Harlan Davidson, Wheeling, IL.

Barrera, M. (1979), *Race and Class in the Southwest: A Theory of Racial Inequality*, University of Notre Dame Press, Notre Dame, IN.

Barrett, J. (1987), *Work and Community in the Jungle: Chicago's Packinghouse Workers, 1894–1922*, University of Illinois Press, Urbana.

Barrett, J. (1992), "Americanization from the Bottom Up: Immigration and the Remaking of the Working Class in the United States, 1880–1930", *Journal of American History*, vol. 79, December, pp. 996–1020.

Barrett, J., and D. Roediger (1997), "Inbetween Peoples: Race, Nationality and the 'New Immigrant' Working Class", *Journal of American Ethnic History*, vol. 16, spring, pp. 3–44.

Barry, C. (1953), *The Catholic Church and German Americans*, Catholic University of America Press, Washington, DC.

Barth, G. (1964), *Bitter Strength: A History of the Chinese in the United States, 1850–1870*, Harvard University Press, Cambridge, MA.

Barton, J. (1975), *Peasants and Strangers: Italians, Rumanians and Slovaks in an American City, 1890–1950*, Harvard University Press, Cambridge, MA.

Barton, J. (1977), "Religion and Cultural Change in Czech Immigrant Communities, 1850–1920", in R. Miller and T. Marzik (eds), *Immigrants and Religion in Urban America*, Temple University Press, Philadelphia, PA, pp. 3–24.

Barton, J. (1978), "Eastern and Southern Europeans", in J. Higham (ed.), *Ethnic Leadership in America*, Johns Hopkins University Press, Baltimore, MD, pp. 150–75.

Bayor, R. (1988), *Neighbors in Conflict: The Irish, Germans, Jews, and Italians of New York City, 1929–1941*, University of Illinois Press, Urbana, 2nd edn.

Beard, C. (1914), *An Economic Interpretation of the Constitution of the United States*, Macmillan, New York.

Bennett, D. (1988), *The Party of Fear: From Nativist Movements to the New Right in American History*, University of North Carolina Press, Chapel Hill.

Benson, L. (1960), *Turner and Beard*, Free Press, Glencoe, IL.

Benson, L. (1964 [1961]), *The Concept of Jacksonian Democracy: New York as a Test Case*, Atheneum, New York.

Berkhofer, R. (1979), *The White Man's Indian: Images of the American Indian from Columbus to the Present*, Vintage, New York.

Berlin, I. (1974), *Slaves without Masters: The Free Negro in the Antebellum South*, Pantheon, New York.

Berlin, I., and L. Rowland (eds) (1997), *Families and Freedom: A Documentary History of African-American Kinship in the Civil War Era*, New Press, New York.

Bernard, R. (1980), *The Melting Pot and the Altar: Marital Assimilation in Early Twentieth-Century Wisconsin*, University of Minnesota Press, Minneapolis.

Berrol, S. (1976), "Education and Economic Mobility: The Jewish Experience in New York City, 1880–1920", *American Jewish Historical Quarterly*, vol. 65, March, pp. 257–71.

Berry, M., and J. Blassingame (1982), *Long Memory: The Black Experience in America*, Oxford University Press, New York.

Berthoff, R. (1953), *British Immigrants in Industrial America, 1790–1950*, Harvard University Press, Cambridge, MA.

Best, G. (1982), *To Free A People: American Jewish Leaders and the Jewish Problem in Eastern Europe, 1890–1914*, Greenwood Press, Westport, CT.

Billington, R. (1938), *The Protestant Crusade, 1800–1860: A Study of the Origins of American Nativism*, Macmillan, New York.

Blassingame, J. (1972), *The Slave Community: Plantation Life in the Antebellum South*, Oxford University Press, New York.

Blassingame, J. (1973), *Black New Orleans, 1860–1880*, University of Chicago Press, Chicago.

Blassingame, J. (1979), *The Slave Community: Plantation Life in the Antebellum South*, Oxford University Press, New York, rev. edn.

Blau, F. (1980), "Immigration and Labor Earnings in Early Twentieth Century America", *Research in Population Economics*, vol. 2, pp. 21–41.

Blauner, R. (1972), *Racial Oppression in America*, Harper & Row, New York.

Blee, K. (1991), *Women of the Klan: Racism and Gender in the 1920s*, University of California Press, Berkeley.

Blegen, T. (1940), *Norwegian Migration to America: The American Transition*, Norwegian-American Historical Association, Northfield, MN.

Bloom, F. (1985), "Struggling and Surviving: The Life Style of European Immigrant Breadwinning Mothers in American Industrial Cities, 1900–1930", *Women's Studies International Forum*, vol. 8, no. 6, pp. 609–20.

Bodnar, J. (1977), *Immigration and Industrialization: Ethnicity in an American Mill Town, 1870–1940*, University of Pittsburgh Press, Pittsburgh, PA.

Bodnar, J. (1982), "Schooling and the Slavic-American Family, 1900–1940", in B. Weiss (ed.), *American Education and the European Immigrant, 1840–1940*, University of Illinois Press, Urbana, pp. 78–95.

Bodnar, J. (1985), *The Transplanted: A History of Immigrants in Urban America*, Indiana University Press, Bloomington.

Bodnar, J., R. Simon, and M. Weber (1982), *Lives of Their Own: Blacks, Italians, and Poles in Pittsburgh, 1900–1960*, University of Illinois Press, Urbana.

Bonacich, E. (1972), "A Theory of Ethnic Antagonism: The Split Labor Market", *American Sociological Review*, vol. 37, October, pp. 547–59.

Bonacich, E. (1973), "A Theory of Middleman Minorities", *American Sociological Review*, vol. 38, October, pp. 583–94.

Bonacich, E. (1975), "Abolition, the Extension of Slavery, and the Position of Free Blacks: A Study of Split Labor Markets in the United States, 1830–1863", *American Journal of Sociology*, vol. 81, November, pp. 601–28.

Bonacich, E. (1976), "Advanced Capitalism and Black/White Relations in the United States: A Split Labor Market Interpretation", *American Sociological Review*, vol. 41, February, pp. 34–51.

Bonacich, E., and J. Modell (1980), *The Economic Basis of Ethnic Solidarity: Small Business in the Japanese American Community*, University of California Press, Berkeley.

Boorstin, D. (1965), *The Americans: The National Experience*, Random House, New York.

Borchert, J. (1980), *Alley Life in Washington: Family, Community, Religion, and Folklife in the City, 1850–1970*, University of Illinois Press, Urbana.

Boskin, J. (1976), *Urban Racial Violence in the Twentieth Century*, Glencoe Press, Beverly Hills, CA.

Boswell, T. (1986), "A Split Labor Market Analysis of Discrimination against Chinese Immigrants, 1850–1882", *American Sociological Review*, vol. 51, June, pp. 352–71.

Bowles, S., and H. Gintis (1976), *Schooling in Capitalist America: Educational Reform and the Contradictions of Economic Life*, Basic Books, New York.

Bracey, J., and A. Meier (1993), "Towards a Research Agenda on Blacks and Jews in United States History", *Journal of American Ethnic History*, vol. 12, spring, pp. 60–7.

Bracey, J., A. Meier, and E. Rudwick (eds) (1970), *Black Nationalism in America*, Bobbs-Merrill, Indianapolis, IN.

Brier, S. (1977), "Interracial Organizing in the West Virginia Coal Industry: The Participation of Black Mine Workers in the Knights of Labor and the United Mine Workers, 1880–1894", in G. Fink and M. Reed (eds), *Essays in Southern Labor History*, Greenwood Press, Westport, CT, pp. 18–43.

Briggs, J. (1978), *An Italian Passage: Immigrants to Three American Cities, 1890–1930*, Yale University Press, New Haven, CT.

Brotz, H. (1970), *The Black Jews of Harlem: Negro Nationalism and the Dilemmas of Negro Leadership*, Schocken Books, New York.

Broussard, A. (1993), *Black San Francisco: The Struggle for Racial Equality in the West*, University Press of Kansas, Lawrence.

Brown, B. (1983), *Southern Honor: Ethics and Behavior in the Old South*, Oxford University Press, New York.

Brown, D. (1971), *Bury My Heart at Wounded Knee: An Indian History of the American West*, Holt, Rinehart, & Winston, New York.

Brown, T. (1966), *Irish-American Nationalism, 1870–1890*, J. B. Lippincott, Philadelphia, PA.

Brumberg, S. (1986), *Going to America, Going to School: The Jewish Immigrant Public School Encounter in Turn-of-the-Century New York*, Praeger, New York.

Brundage, W. (1993), *Lynching in the New South: Georgia and Virginia, 1880–1930*, University of Illinois Press, Urbana.

Brundage, W. (ed.) (1997), *Under Sentence of Death: Lynching in the South*, University of North Carolina Press, Chapel Hill.

Buenker, J., and L. Ratner (eds) (1992), *Multiculturalism in the United States: A Comparative Guide to Acculturation and Ethnicity*, Greenwood Press, Westport, CT.

Buhle, P. (1980), "Jews and American Communism: The Cultural Question", *Radical History Review*, vol. 23, spring, pp. 9–33.

Bukowczyk, J. (1984), "The Transformation of Working-Class Ethnicity: Corporate Control, Americanization, and the Polish Immigrant Middle Class in Bayonne, New Jersey, 1915–1925", *Labor History*, vol. 25, winter, pp. 53–82.

Bullock, H. (1967), *A History of Negro Education in the South, From 1619 to the Present*, Harvard University Press, Cambridge, MA.

Burgess, E. (1925), "The Growth of the City: An Introduction to a Research Project", in R. Park, E. Burgess, and R. McKenzie, *The City*, University of Chicago Press, Chicago, pp. 47–62.

Burk, R. (1984), *The Eisenhower Administration and Black Civil Rights*, University of Tennessee Press, Knoxville.

Burstein, A. (1981), "Immigrants and Residential Mobility: The Irish and Germans in Philadelphia, 1850–1880", in T. Hershberg (ed.), *Philadelphia: Work, Space, Family, and Group Experience in the Nineteenth Century*, Oxford University Press, New York, pp. 174–203.

Bynum, V. (1992), *Unruly Women: The Politics of Social and Sexual Control in the Old South*, University of North Carolina Press, Chapel Hill.

Camarillo, A. (1979), *Chicanos in a Changing Society: From Mexican Pueblos to American Barrios in Santa Barbara and Southern California, 1848–1930*, Harvard University Press, Cambridge, MA.

Cannistraro, P., and G. Meyer (eds) (2003), *The Lost World of Italian American Radicalism: Politics, Labor, and Culture*, Praeger, Westport, CT.

Capeci, D., (1977), *The Harlem Riot of 1943*, Temple University Press, Philadelphia, PA.

Capeci, D., and M. Wilkinson (1991), *Layered Violence: The Detroit Rioters of 1943*, University Press of Mississippi, Jackson.

Carlson, L. (1981), *Indians, Bureaucrats, and Land: The Dawes Act and the Decline of Indian Farming*, Greenwood Press, Westport, CT.

Carlson, R. (1975), *The Quest for Conformity: Americanization Through Education*, J. Wiley and Sons, New York.

Carmichael, S., and C. Hamilton (1967), *Black Power: The Politics of Liberation in America*, Random House, New York.

Carranco, L. (1961), "Chinese Expulsion from Humboldt County", *Pacific Historical Review*, vol. 30, November, pp. 329–40.

Carroll, P. (2003), *Felix Longoria's Wake: Bereavement, Racism, and the Rise of Mexican American Activism*, University of Texas Press, Austin.

Carson, C. (1981), *In Struggle: SNCC and the Black Awakening of the 1960s*, Harvard University Press, Cambridge, MA.

Carter, B., M. Green, and R. Halpern (1996), "Immigration Policy and the Racialization of Migrant Labour: The Construction of National Identities in the USA and Britain", *Ethnic and Racial Studies*, vol. 19, January, pp. 135–57.

Carter, D. (1969), *Scottsboro: A Tragedy of the American South*, Louisiana State University Press, Baton Rouge.

Chalmers, D. (1965), *Hooded Americanism: The First Century of the Ku Klux Klan*, Doubleday, Garden City, NY.

Chalmers, D. (1987), *Hooded Americanism: The History of the Ku Klux Klan*, Duke University Press, Durham, NC, 3rd edn.

Chan, S. (1986), *This Bittersweet Soil: The Chinese in California Agriculture, 1860–1910*, University of California Press, Berkeley.

Chan, S. (1990), "European and Asian Immigration into the United States in Comparative Perspective, 1820s to 1920s", in V. Yans-McLaughlin (ed.), *Immigration Reconsidered: History, Sociology, and Politics*, Oxford University Press, New York, pp. 37–75.

Chan, S. (ed.) (1991), *Entry Denied: Exclusion and the Chinese Community in America, 1882–1943*, Temple University Press, Philadelphia, PA.

Chapman, M., M. McDonald, and E. Tonkin (eds) (1989), *History and Ethnicity*, Routledge, London.

Chato, G., and C. Conte (1988), "The Legal Rights of American Indian Women", in L. Schlissel, V. Ruiz, and J. Monk (eds), *Western Women: Their Land, Their Lives*, University of New Mexico Press, Albuquerque, pp. 229–46.

Chávez, J. (1984), *The Lost Land: The Chicano Image of the Southwest*, University of New Mexico Press, Albuquerque.

Cheng, L. (1979), "Chinese Immigrant Women in Nineteenth-Century California", in C. Berkin and M. Norton (eds), *Women of America: A History*, Houghton Mifflin, Boston, MA, pp. 223–44.

Cheng, L., and E. Bonacich (eds) (1984), *Labor Migration Under Capitalism: Asian Workers in the United States before World War II*, University of California Press, Berkeley.

Child, C. (1970 [1939]), *The German-Americans in Politics, 1914–1917*, Arno Press, New York.

Chiu, P. (1967 [1963]), *Chinese Labor in California, 1850–1880: An Economic Study*, State Historical Society of Wisconsin, Madison.

Choy, B. (1979), *Koreans in America*, Nelson-Hall, Chicago.

Chudacoff, H. (1972), *Mobile Americans: Residential and Social Mobility in Omaha, 1880–1920*, Oxford University Press, New York.

Chudacoff, H. (1973), "A New Look at Ethnic Neighborhoods: Residential Dispersion and the Concept of Visibility in a Medium-Sized City", *Journal of American History*, vol. 60, June, pp. 76–93.

Chuman, F. (1976), *The Bamboo People: The Law and Japanese-Americans*, Publisher's Inc., Del Mar, CA.

Cinel, D. (1982), *From Italy to San Francisco: The Immigrant Experience*, Stanford University Press, Stanford, CA.

Coburn, C. (1992), *Life at Four Corners: Religion, Gender, and Education in a German-Lutheran Community, 1868–1945*, University Press of Kansas, Lawrence.

Cohen, L. (1990), *Making a New Deal: Industrial Workers in Chicago, 1919–1939*, Cambridge University Press, Cambridge.

Cohen, M. (1993), *Workshop to Office, Two Generations of Italian Women in New York City, 1900–1950*, Cornell University Press, Ithaca, NY.

Cohen, N. (1972), *Not Free to Desist: The American Jewish Council, 1906–1966*, Jewish Publication Society of America, Philadelphia, PA.

Cohen, N. (1984), *Encounter With Emancipation: The German Jews in the United States, 1830–1914*, Jewish Publication Society of America, Philadelphia, PA.

Cohen, N. (2003), *The Americanization of Zionism, 1897–1948*, Brandeis University Press/University Press of New England, Hanover, NH.

Cohen, R., and R. Mohl (1979), *The Paradox of Progressive Education: The Gary Plan of Urban Schooling*, Kennikat Press, Port Washington, NY.

Cohen, W. (1991), *At Freedom's Edge: Black Mobility and the Southern White Quest for Racial Control, 1861–1915*, Louisiana State University Press, Baton Rouge.

Cole, D. (1963), *Immigrant City: Lawrence, Massachusetts, 1845–1921*, University of North Carolina Press, Chapel Hill.

Collier-Thomas, B., and J. Turner (1994), "Race, Class and Color: The African American Discourse on Identity", *Journal of American Ethnic History*, vol. 14, fall, pp. 5–31.

Collins, P. (1990), *Black Feminist Thought: Knowledge, Consciousness, and the Politics of Empowerment*, Unwin Hyman, Boston, MA.

Commager, H. (1950), *The American Mind: An Interpretation of American Thought and Character since the 1880s*, Yale University Press, New Haven, CT.

Commons, J. (1907), *Races and Immigrants in America*, Macmillan, New York.

Commons, J., D. Saposs, H. Sumner, E. Mittelman, H. Hoagland, J. Andrews, and S. Perlman (1918), *History of Labour in the United States*, vols 1 and 2, Macmillan, New York.

Commons, J., S. Perlman, and P. Taft (1935), *History of Labor in the United States, 1896–1932*, vol. 4, Macmillan, New York.

Connolly, H. (1977), *A Ghetto Grows in Brooklyn*, New York University Press, New York.

Conzen, K. (1976), *Immigrant Milwaukee, 1836–1860: Accommodation and Community in a Frontier City*, Harvard University Press, Cambridge, MA.

Conzen, K. (1979), "Immigrants, Immigrant Neighborhoods, and Ethnic Identity: Historical Issues", *Journal of American History*, vol. 66, December, pp. 603–15.

Conzen, K. (1985), "German-Americans and the Invention of Ethnicity", in F. Trommler and J. McVeigh (eds), *America and the Germans: An Assessment of a Three-Hundred-Year History*, vol. 1, University of Pennsylvania Press, Philadelphia, pp. 131–47.

Conzen, K. (1991), "Mainstreams and Side Channels: The Localization of Immigrant Cultures", *Journal of American Ethnic History*, vol. 11, fall, pp. 5–20.

Conzen, K. (1996), "Thomas and Znaniecki and the Historiography of American Immigration", *Journal of American Ethnic History*, vol. 16, fall, pp. 16–25.

Conzen, K., D. Gerber, E. Morawska, G. Pozzetta, and R. Vecoli (1992), "The Invention of Ethnicity: A Perspective from the USA", *Journal of American Ethnic History*, vol. 12, fall, pp. 3–41.

Corbin, D. (1981), *Life, Work, and Rebellion in the Coal Fields: The Southern West Virginia Miners, 1880–1922*, University of Illinois Press, Urbana.

Corwin, A. (1978), "Early Mexican Labor Migration: A Frontier Sketch, 1848–1900", in A. Corwin (ed.), *Immigrants – and Immigrants: Perspectives on Mexican Labor Migration to the United States*, Greenwood Press, Westport, CT, pp. 25–37.

Costo, R., and J. Costo (eds) (1987), *The Missions of California: A Legacy of Genocide*, Indian Historian Press, San Francisco.

Crawford, V., J. Rouse, and B. Woods (eds) (1993), *Women in the Civil Rights Movement: Trailblazers and Torchbearers, 1941–1965*, Indiana University Press, Bloomington.

Cressey, P. (1938), "Population Succession in Chicago: 1898–1930", *American Journal of Sociology*, vol. 44, July, pp. 59–69.

Crosby, A. (1971), *The Columbian Exchange: Biological and Cultural Consequences of 1492*, Greenwood Press, Westport, CT.

Crosby, A. (1976), "Virgin Soil Epidemics as a Factor in Aboriginal Depopulation in America", *William and Mary Quarterly*, 3rd series, vol. 33, April, pp. 289–99.

Cunningham, G. (1965), "The Italian, a Hindrance to White Solidarity in Louisiana, 1890–1898", *Journal of Negro History*, vol. 50, January, pp. 22–36.

Curry, L. (1981), *The Free Black in Urban America, 1800–1850: The Shadow of the Dream*, University of Chicago Press, Chicago.

Curtin, P. (1969), *The Atlantic Slave Trade: A Census*, University of Wisconsin Press, Madison.

Daniel, G. (1992), "Beyond Black and White: The New Multiracial Consciousness" in M. Root (ed.), *Racially Mixed People in America*, Sage Publications, Newbury Park, CA, pp. 333–41.

Daniels, R. (1962), *The Politics of Prejudice: The Anti-Japanese Movement in California and the Struggle for Japanese Exclusion*, University of California Press, Berkeley.

Daniels, R. (1974), "American Historians and East Asian Immigrants", *Pacific Historical Review*, vol. 43, November, pp. 449–72.

Daniels, R. (1978), "The Japanese", in J. Higham (ed.), *Ethnic Leadership in America*, Johns Hopkins University Press, Baltimore, MD, pp. 36–63.

Daniels, R. (1991), *Coming to America: A History of Immigration and Ethnicity in American Life*, HarperCollins, New York.

Daniels, R. (1997), "No Lamps Were Lit for Them: Angel Island and the Historiography of Asian American Immigration", *Journal of American Ethnic History*, vol. 17, fall, pp. 3–18.

David, P., H. Gutman, R. Sutch, P. Temin, and G. Wright (1976), *Reckoning with Slavery: A Critical Study in the Quantitative History of American Negro Slavery*, Oxford University Press, New York.

Davidson, B. (1970), *The African Slave Trade*, Little, Brown, & Co., Boston, MA.

Davis, D. (1966), *The Problem of Slavery in Western Culture*, Oxford University Press, New York.

Davis, F. (1991), *Who is Black? One Nation's Definition*, Pennsylvania State University Press, University Park.

Davis, R. (1982), *Good and Faithful Labor: From Slavery to Sharecropping in the Natchez District, 1860–1890*, Greenwood Press, Westport, CT.

Debo, A. (1934), *The Rise and Fall of the Choctaw Republic*, University of Oklahoma Press, Norman.

Debo, A. (1940), *And Still the Waters Run: The Betrayal of the Five Civilized Tribes*, Princeton University Press, Princeton, NJ.

Debo, A. (1941), *The Road to Disappearance: A History of the Creek Indians*, University of Oklahoma Press, Norman.

Decker, P. (1978), *Fortunes and Failures: White-Collar Mobility in Nineteenth Century San Francisco*, Harvard University Press, Cambridge, MA.

Degler, C. (1959), "Slavery and the Genesis of American Race Prejudice", *Comparative Studies in Society and History*, vol. 2, October, pp. 49–66.

Degler, C. (1971), *Neither Black Nor White: Slavery and Race Relations in Brazil and the United States*, Macmillan, New York.

De León, A. (1983), *They Called Them Greasers: Anglo Attitudes toward Mexicans in Texas, 1821–1900*, University of Texas Press, Austin.

De León, A. (1989), *Ethnicity in the Sunbelt: A History of Mexican Americans in Houston*, University of Houston, Houston, TX.

De León, A. (1991), "Texas Mexicans: Twentieth-Century Interpretations", in W. Buenger and R. Calvert (eds), *Texas Through Time: Evolving Interpretations*, Texas A&M University Press, College Station, pp. 20–49.

Deloria, V. (1992), "American Indians", in J. Buenker and L. Ratner (eds), *Multiculturalism in the United States: A Comparative Guide to Acculturation and Ethnicity*, Greenwood Press, Westport, CT, pp. 31–52.

Deutsch, S. (1987), *No Separate Refuge: Culture, Class, and Gender on an Anglo-Hispanic Frontier in the American Southwest, 1880–1940*, Oxford University Press, New York.

De Witt, H. (1979), "The Watsonville Anti-Filipino Riot of 1930: A Case Study of the Great Depression and Ethnic Conflict in California", *Southern California Historical Quarterly*, vol. 61, fall, pp. 291–302.

Dickinson, J. (1980), *The Role of the Immigrant Women in the US Labor Force, 1890–1910*, Arno Press, New York.

di Leonardo, M. (1984), *The Varieties of Ethnic Experience: Kinship, Class, and Gender Among California Italian-Americans*, Cornell University Press, Ithaca, NY.

Diner, H. (1977), *In the Almost Promised Land: American Jews and Blacks, 1915–1935*, Greenwood Press, Westport, CT.

Diner, H. (1983), *Erin's Daughters in America: Irish Immigrant Women in the Nineteenth Century*, Johns Hopkins University Press, Baltimore, MD.

Diner, H. (1997), "Between Words and Deeds: Jews and Blacks in America, 1880–1935", in J. Salzman and C. West (eds), *Struggles in the Promised Land: Toward a History of Black–Jewish Relations in the United States*, Oxford University Press, New York, pp. 87–106.

Dinnerstein, L. (1982), "Education and the Advancement of American Jews", in B. Weiss (ed.), *American Education and the European Immigrant, 1840–1940*, University of Illinois Press, Urbana, pp. 44–60.

Dinnerstein, L. (1987), *Uneasy at Home: Antisemitism and the American Jewish Experience*, Columbia University Press, New York.

Dinnerstein, L. (1991), *Antisemitism in America*, Oxford University Press, New York.

Dinnerstein, L., R. Nichols, and D. Reimers (1996), *Natives and Strangers: A Multicultural History of Americans*, Oxford University Press, New York.

Dittmer, J. (1977), *Black Georgia in the Progressive Era, 1900–1920*, University of Illinois Press, Urbana.

Divine, R. (1957), *American Immigration Policy, 1924–1952*, Yale University Press, New Haven, CT.

Dobyns, H. (1973), *Their Number Become Thinned: Native American Population Dynamics in Eastern North America*, University of Tennessee Press, Knoxville.

Dolan, J. (1977), "Philadelphia and the German Catholic Community", in R. Miller and T. Marzik (eds), *Immigrants and Religion in Urban America*, Temple University Press, Philadelphia, PA, pp. 69–83.

Dolan, J., and G. Hinojosa (eds) (1994), *Mexican Americans and the Catholic Church, 1900–1965*, University of Notre Dame Press, Notre Dame, IN.

Dolan, J., and J. Vidal (eds) (1994), *Puerto Rican and Cuban Catholics in the US, 1900–1965*, University of Notre Dame Press, Notre Dame, IN.

Dowd, G. (1992), *A Spirited Resistance: The North American Indian Struggle for Unity, 1745–1815*, Johns Hopkins University Press, Baltimore, MD.

Downes, R. (1940), *Council Fires on the Upper Ohio: A Narrative of Indian Affairs in the Upper Ohio Valley until 1795*, University of Pittsburgh Press, Pittsburgh, PA.

Doyle, R. (1985), "Wealth Mobility in Pella, Iowa", in R. Swierenga (ed.), *The Dutch in America: Immigration, Settlement, and Cultural Change*, Rutgers University Press, New Brunswick, NJ, pp. 125–71.

Drake, S., and H. Cayton (1945), *Black Metropolis: A Study of Negro Life in a Northern City*, 2 vols, Harcourt, Brace & World, New York.

Drinnon, R. (1980), *Facing West: The Metaphysics of Indian-Hating and Empire Building*, University of Minnesota Press, Minneapolis.

Dubofsky, M. (1961), "Organized Labor and the Immigrant in New York City, 1900–1918", *Labor History*, vol. 2, spring, pp. 182–201.

Dubofsky, M. (1969), *We Shall Be All: A History of the Industrial Workers of the World*, Quadrangle, Chicago.

Du Bois, W. (1935), *Black Reconstruction: An Essay Toward a History of the Part Which Black Folk Played in the Attempt to Reconstruct Democracy in America, 1860–1880*, Harcourt, Brace & Co., New York.

Du Bois, W. (1970 [1896]), *The Suppression of the African Slave-Trade to the United States of America, 1638–1870*, Dover Publications, New York.

Du Bois, W. (1996 [1899]), *The Philadelphia Negro: A Social Study*, University of Pennsylvania Press, Philadelphia.

Du Bois, W. (1997 [1904]), "The Development of a People", in W. Du Bois, *The Souls of Black Folk*, ed. by D. Blight and R. Gooding-Williams, Bedford Books, Boston, MA, pp. 238–54.

Duis, P. (1983), *The Saloon: Public Drinking in Chicago and Boston, 1880–1920*, University of Illinois Press, Urbana.

Dunaway, W. (2003), *The African-American Family in Slavery and Emancipation*, Cambridge University Press, Cambridge.

Durón, C. (1984), "Mexican Women and Labor Conflict in Los Angeles: The ILGWU Dressmakers' Strike of 1933", *Aztlán*, vol. 15, spring, pp. 145–62.

Eby, C. (1973), *"That Disgraceful Affair": The Black Hawk War*, W. W. Norton & Co., New York.

Edmunds, R. (1984), *Tecumseh and the Quest for Indian Leadership*, Little, Brown, & Co., Boston, MA.

Edmunds, R. (1995), "Native Americans, New Voices: American Indian History, 1895–1995", *American Historical Review*, vol. 100, June, pp. 717–40.

Edmunds, R. (ed.) (1980), *American Indian Leaders: Studies in Diversity*, University of Nebraska Press, Lincoln.

Edmunds, R. (ed.) (2001), *The New Warriors: Native American Leaders since 1900*, University of Nebraska Press, Lincoln.

Elkins, S. (1959), *Slavery: A Problem in American Institutional and Intellectual Life*, University of Chicago Press, Chicago.

Eller, J., and R. Coughlan (1993), "The Poverty of Primordialism: The Demystification of Ethnic Attachments", *Ethnic and Racial Studies*, vol. 16, April, pp. 183–202.

Ellis, J. (1965), *American Catholicism*, University of Chicago Press, Chicago.

Ellsworth, S. (1982), *Death in a Promised Land: The Tulsa Race Riot of 1921*, Louisiana State University Press, Baton Rouge.

Elson, R. (1964), *Guardians of Tradition: American Schoolbooks of the Nineteenth Century*, University of Nebraska Press, Lincoln.

Erickson, C. (1990 [1972]), *Invisible Immigrants: The Adaptation of English and Scottish Immigrants in Nineteenth-Century America*, Cornell University Press, Ithaca, NJ.

Ernst, R. (1979 [1949]), *Immigrant Life in New York City, 1825–1863*, Octagon Books, New York.

Espiritu, Y. (1992), *Asian American Pan-Ethnicity: Bridging Institutions and Identities*, Temple University Press, Philadelphia, PA.

Esslinger, D. (1975), *Immigrants and the City: Ethnicity and Mobility in a Nineteenth-Century Midwestern Community*, Kennikat Press, Port Washington, NY.

Ewen, E. (1985), *Immigrant Women in the Land of Dollars: Life and Culture on the Lower East Side, 1890–1925*, Monthly Review Press, New York.

Ewers, J. (1955), *The Horse in Blackfoot Indian Culture, with Comparative Materials from Other Western Tribes*, Smithsonian Institution, Washington, DC.

Ewers, J. (1975), "Intertribal Warfare as the Precursor of Indian-White Warfare on the Northern Plains", *Western Historical Quarterly*, vol. 6, October, pp. 397–410.

Fairchild, H. (1926), *The Melting-Pot Mistake*, Little, Brown, & Co., Boston, MA.

Farrand, M. (1905), "The Indian Boundary Line", *American Historical Review*, vol. 10, July, pp. 782–91.

Farrand, M. (1913), *The Framing of the Constitution of the United States*, Yale University Press, New Haven, CT.

Fass, P. (1989), *Outside In: Minorities and the Transformation of American Education*, Oxford University Press, New York.

Feinberg, W. (1975), *Reason and Rhetoric: The Intellectual Foundations of Twentieth Century Liberal Educational Policy*, J. Wiley & Sons, New York.

Feinberg, W., and H. Rosemont (eds) (1975), *Work, Technology, and Education: Dissenting Essays in the Intellectual Foundations of American Education*, University of Illinois Press, Urbana.

Feingold, H. (1970), *The Politics of Rescue: The Roosevelt Administration and the Holocaust, 1938–1945*, Rutgers University Press, New Brunswick, NJ.

Feldberg, M. (1975), *The Philadelphia Riots of 1844: A Study of Ethnic Conflict*, Greenwood Press, Westport, CT.

Ferrie, J. (1995), "Up and Out or Down and Out? Immigrant Mobility in the Antebellum United States", *Journal of Interdisciplinary History*, vol. 26, summer, pp. 33–55.

Ferrie, J. (1997), "The Entry into the US Labor Market of Antebellum European Immigrants, 1840–1860", *Explorations in Economic History*, vol. 34, July, pp. 295–30.

Ferrie, J. (1999), *Yankeys Now: Immigrants in the Antebellum United States, 1840–1860*, Oxford University Press, New York.

Fields, B. (1982), "Ideology and Race in American History", in J. Kousser and J. McPherson (eds), *Region, Race, and Reconstruction*, Oxford University Press, New York, pp. 143–77.

Fischer, D. (1989), *Albion's Seed: Four British Folkways in America*, Oxford University Press, New York.

Fishman, J. (1966), *Language Loyalty in the United States: The Maintenance and Perpetuation of Non-English Mother Tongues by American Ethnic and Religious Groups*, Mouton & Co., The Hague.

Fiske, J. (1897), *Old Virginia and Her Neighbors*, Houghton Mifflin, Boston, MA.

Fixico, D. (1986), *Termination and Relocation: Federal Indian Policy, 1945–1960*, University of New Mexico Press, Albuquerque.

Fogel, R. (1989), *Without Consent or Contract: The Rise and Fall of American Slavery*, W. W. Norton & Co., New York.

Fogel, R., and S. Engerman (1974), *Time on the Cross: The Economics of American Negro Slavery*, 2 vols, Little, Brown, & Co., Boston, MA.

Fogelman, A. (1998), "From Slaves, Convicts, and Servants to Free Passengers: The Transformation of Immigration in the Era of the American Revolution", *Journal of American History*, vol. 85, June, pp. 43–76.

Foner, P. (1974), *Organized Labor and the Black Worker, 1619–1973*, Praeger, New York.

Foner, P. (1975), "Black-Jewish Relations in the Opening Years of the Twentieth Century", *Phylon*, vol. 36, winter, pp. 359–67.

Foner, P. (1977), *American Socialism and Black Americans: From the Age of Jackson to World War II*, Greenwood Press, Westport, CT.

Foreman, G. (1932), *Indian Removal: The Emigration of the Five Civilized Tribes of Indians*, University of Oklahoma Press, Norman.

Foreman, G. (1934), *The Five Civilized Tribes: Cherokee, Chickasaw, Choctaw, Creek, Seminole*, University of Oklahoma Press, Norman.

Foreman, G. (1946), *The Last Trek of the Indians*, University of Chicago Press, Chicago.

Formisano, R. (1971), *The Birth of Mass Political Parties, Michigan, 1827–1861*, Princeton University Press, Princeton, NJ.

Formisano, R. (1991), *Boston against Busing: Race, Class, and Ethnicity in the 1960s and 1970s*, University of North Carolina Press, Chapel Hill.

Fowler, D. (1987), *Northern Attitudes towards Interracial Marriage: Legislation and Public Opinion in the Middle Atlantic and the States of the Old Northwest, 1780–1930*, Garland, New York.

Fox, G. (1996), *Hispanic Nation: Culture, Politics, and the Constructing of Identity*, Carol Publishing Group, Secaucus, NJ.

Fox-Genovese, E. (1988), *Within the Plantation Household: Black and White Women of the Old South*, University of North Carolina Press, Chapel Hill.

Franklin, J. (1986), "On the Evolution of Scholarship in Afro-American History", in D. Hine (ed.), *The State of Afro-American History: Past, Present, and Future*, Louisiana State University Press, Baton Rouge, pp. 13–22.

Franklin, J. (1995 [1943]), *The Free Negro in North Carolina, 1790–1860*, University of North Carolina Press, Chapel Hill.

Franklin, V., N. Grant, H. Kletnick, and G. McNeil (eds) (1998), *African Americans and Jews in the Twentieth Century: Studies in Convergence and Conflict*, University of Missouri Press, Columbia.

Fraser, S. (1986), "*Landslayt* and *Paesani*: Ethnic Conflict and Cooperation in the Amalgamated Clothing Workers of America", in D. Hoerder (ed.), *Struggle a Hard Battle: Essays on Working Class Immigrants*, Northern Illinois University Press, DeKalb, pp. 280–303.

Fredrickson, G. (1981), *White Supremacy: A Comparative Study in American and South African History*, Oxford University Press, New York.

Fredrickson, G. (1987 [1972]), *The Black Image in the White Mind: The Debate on Afro-American Character and Destiny, 1817–1914*, Wesleyan University Press, Middletown, CT.

Fredrickson, G. (1988), *The Arrogance of Race: Historical Perspectives on Slavery, Racism, and Social Inequality*, Wesleyan University Press, Middletown, CT.

Fredrickson, G., and D. Knobel (1980), "Prejudice and Discrimination, History of", in S. Thernstrom (ed.), *Harvard Encyclopedia of American Ethnic Groups*, Harvard University Press, Cambridge, MA, pp. 829–47.

Friday, C. (1994), *Organizing Asian American Labor: The Pacific Coast Canned-Salmon Industry, 1870–1942*, Temple University Press, Philadelphia, PA.

Friedlander, P. (1975), *The Emergence of a UAW Local, 1936–1939: A Study in Class and Culture*, University of Pittsburgh Press, Pittsburgh, PA.

Fuchs, L. (1990), *The American Kaleidoscope: Race, Ethnicity and the Civic Culture* University Press of New England, Hanover, NH.

Gabaccia, D. (1984), *From Sicily to Elizabeth Street: Housing and Social Change Among Italian Immigrants, 1880–1930*, State University of New York Press, Albany.

Gabaccia, D. (1988), *Militants and Migrants: Rural Sicilians Become American Workers*, Rutgers University Press, New Brunswick, NJ.

Gabaccia, D. (1994), *From the Other Side: Women, Gender, and Immigrant Life in the US, 1820–1990*, Indiana University Press, Bloomington.

Gabaccia, D. (2002), *Immigration and American Diversity: A Social and Cultural History*, Blackwell, Oxford.

Galenson, D. (1981), *White Servitude in Colonial America: An Economic Analysis*, Cambridge University Press, Cambridge.

Galush, W. (1977), "Faith and Fatherland: Dimensions of Polish-American Ethnoreligion, 1875–1975", in R. Miller and T. Marzik (eds), *Immigrants and Religion in Urban America*, Temple University Press, Philadelphia, PA, pp. 84–102.

Gambino, R. (1974), *Blood of My Blood: The Dilemma of the Italian-Americans*, Doubleday, Garden City, NY.

Gans, H. (1979), "Symbolic Ethnicity: The Future of Ethnic Groups and Cultures in America", in H. Gans, N. Glazer, J. Gusfield, and C. Jenks (eds), *On the Making of Americans: Essays in Honor of David Riesman*, University of Pennsylvania Press, Philadelphia, pp. 193–220.

García, A. (ed.) (1997), *Chicana Feminist Thought: The Basic Historical Writings*, Routledge, New York.

García, J. (1980), *Operation Wetback: The Mass Deportation of Mexican Undocumented Workers in 1954*, Greenwood Press, Westport, CT.

García, M. (1981), *Desert Immigrants: The Mexicans of El Paso*, Yale University Press, New Haven, CT.

García, M. (1989), *Mexican Americans: Leadership, Ideology, and Identity, 1930–1960*, Yale University Press, New Haven, CT.

García, M. (1996), *Havana USA: Cuban Exiles and Cuban Americans in South Florida, 1959–1994*, University of California Press, Berkeley.

García, M. (1998), *The Making of a Mexican American Mayor: Raymond L. Telles of El Paso*, Texas Western Press, El Paso.

Garcia, R. (1991), *Rise of the Mexican American Middle Class: San Antonio, 1929–1941*, Texas A&M University Press, College Station.

Gardner, J., and G. Adams (eds) (1983), *Ordinary People and Everyday Life: Perspectives on the New Social History*, American Association for State and Local History, Nashville, TN.

Garrow, D. (1978), *Protest at Selma: Martin Luther King, Jr, and the Voting Rights Act of 1965*, Yale University Press, New Haven, CT.

Gartner, L. (ed.) (1969), *Jewish Education in the United States: A Documentary History*, Teachers College Press, New York.

Geertz, C. (1973), *The Interpretation of Cultures*, Basic Books, New York.

Genovese, E. (1974), *Roll, Jordan, Roll: The World the Slaves Made*, Pantheon, New York.

Genovese, E. (1979), *From Rebellion to Revolution: Afro-American Slave Revolts in the Making of the Modern World*, Louisiana State University Press, Baton Rouge.

Gerber, D. (1989), *The Making of an American Pluralism: Buffalo, New York, 1825–60*, University of Illinois Press, Urbana.

Gerber, D. (ed.) (1986), *Anti-Semitism in American History*, University of Illinois Press, Urbana.

Gerlach, L. (1982), *Blazing Crosses in Zion: The Ku Klux Klan in Utah*, Utah State University Press, Logan.

Gerson, L. (1964), *The Hyphenate in Recent American Politics and Diplomacy*, University Press of Kansas, Lawrence.

Gerstle, G. (1989), *Working-Class Americanism: The Politics of Labor in a Textile City, 1914–1960*, Cambridge University Press, Cambridge.

Gerstle, G. (1993), "The Limits of American Universalism", *American Quarterly*, vol. 45, June, pp. 230–35.

Getz, L. (1997), *Schools of Their Own: The Education of Hispanos in New Mexico, 1850–1940*, University of New Mexico Press, Albuquerque.

Gilmore, G. (1996), *Gender and Jim Crow: Women and the Politics of White Supremacy in North Carolina, 1896–1920*, University of North Carolina Press, Chapel Hill.

Gioia, J. (1984), "A Social, Political and Legal Study of *Yick Wo v. Hopkins*", in G. Lim (ed.), *The Chinese American Experience*, Chinese Culture Foundation/Chinese Historical Society of America, San Francisco, pp. 211–20.

Gjerde, J. (1985), *From Peasants to Farmers: The Migration from Balestrand, Norway, to the Upper Middle West*, Cambridge University Press, Cambridge.

Glanz, R. (1971), *Jew and Italian: Historic Group Relations and the New Immigration, 1881–1924*, Klau, New York.

Glazer, N. (1958), "The American Jew and the Attainment of Middle Class Rank: Some Trends and Explanations", in M. Sklare (ed.), *The Jews: Social Patterns of an American Group*, Free Press, Glencoe, IL, pp. 138–46.

Glazer, N. (1975), *Affirmative Discrimination: Ethnic Inequality and Public Policy*, Basic Books, New York.

Glazer, N., and D. Moynihan (1963), *Beyond the Melting Pot: The Negroes, Puerto Ricans, Jews, Italians and Irish of New York City*, MIT Press/Harvard University Press, Cambridge, MA.

Gleason, P. (1980), "American Identity and Americanization", in S. Thernstrom (ed.), *Harvard Encyclopedia of American Ethnic Groups*, Harvard University Press, Cambridge, MA, pp. 31–58.

Gleason, P. (1982), "Immigration and American Catholic Higher Education", in B. Weiss (ed.), *American Education and the European Immigrant, 1840–1940*, University of Illinois Press, Urbana, pp. 161–75.

Glenn, E. (1986), *Issei, Nisei, War Bride: Three Generations of Japanese American Women in Domestic Service*, Temple University Press, Philadelphia, PA.

Glenn, E. (2002), *Unequal Freedom: How Race and Gender Shaped American Citizenship and Labor*, Harvard University Press, Cambridge, MA.

Glenn, S. (1990), *Daughters of the Shtetl: Life and Labor in the Immigrant Generation*, Cornell University Press, Ithaca, NY.

Glickman, L. (1993), "Inventing the 'American Standard of Living': Gender, Race, and Working Class Identity, 1880–1925", *Labor History*, vol. 34, spring–summer, pp. 221–35.

Gobel, T. (1988), "Becoming American: Ethnic Workers and the Rise of the CIO", *Labor History*, vol. 29, spring, pp. 173–98.

Golab, C. (1977a), *Immigrant Destinations*, Temple University Press, Philadelphia, PA.

Golab, C. (1977b), "The Impact of the Industrial Experience on the Immigrant Family: The Huddled Masses Reconsidered", in R. Ehrlich (ed.), *Immigrants in Industrial America, 1850–1920*, University Press of Virginia, Charlottesville, pp. 1–32.

Gómez-Quiñones, J. (1977), "On Culture", *Revista Chicano-Riqueña*, vol. 5, spring, pp. 29–47.

Gómez-Quiñones, J. (1994), *Mexican American Labor, 1790–1990*, University of New Mexico Press, Albuquerque.

González, G. (1990), *Chicano Education in the Era of Segregation*, Balch Institute Press, Philadelphia, PA.

González, G. (1994), *Labor and Community: Mexican Citrus Worker Villages in a Southern California County, 1900–1950*, University of Illinois Press, Urbana.

González, G. (1999), *Mexican Consuls and Labor Organizing: Imperial Politics in the American Southwest*, University of Texas Press, Austin.

González, G., and R. Fernandez (2003), *A Century of Chicano History: Empire, Nations, and Migration*, Routledge, New York.

González, R. (1983), "Chicanas and Mexican Immigrant Families, 1920–1940: Women's Subordination and Family Exploitation", in L. Scharf and J. Jensen (eds), *Decades of Discontent: The Women's Movement, 1920–1940*, Greenwood Press, Westport, CT, pp. 59–84.

Gordon, M. (1964), *Assimilation in American Life: The Role of Race, Religion, and National Origins*, Oxford University Press, New York.

Gordon, M. (1978), *Human Nature, Class, and Ethnicity*, Oxford University Press, New York.

Gorelick, S. (1981), *City College and the Jewish Poor: Education in New York, 1880–1924*, Rutgers University Press, New Brunswick, NJ.

Goren, A. (1970), *New York Jews and the Quest for Community: The Kehillah Experiment, 1908–1922*, Columbia University Press, New York.

Gossett, T. (1965), *Race: The History of an Idea in America*, Schocken, New York.

Gould, J. (1979), "European Intercontinental Emigration, 1815–1914: Patterns and Causes", *Journal of European Economic History*, vol. 8, winter, pp. 593–681.

Gould, J. (1980), "European Inter-Continental Emigration: The Road Home, Return Migration from the USA", *Journal of European Economic History*, vol. 9, spring, pp. 41–112.

Graham, I. (1956), *Colonists from Scotland: Emigration to North America, 1707–1783*, Cornell University Press, Ithaca, NY.

Graham, P. (1961), "Thomas Jefferson and Sally Hemings", *Journal of Negro History*, vol. 46, April, pp. 89–103.

Green, M. (1982), *The Politics of Indian Removal: Creek Government and Society in Crisis*, University of Nebraska Press, Lincoln.

Greenberg, C. (1991), *"Or Does It Explode?": Black Harlem in the Great Depression*, Oxford University Press, New York.

Greenberg, S. (1981), "Industrial Location and Ethnic Residential Patterns in an Industrializing City: Philadelphia, 1880", in T. Hershberg (ed.), *Philadelphia: Work, Space, Family, and Group Experience in the Nineteenth Century*, Oxford University Press, New York, pp. 204–32.

Greene, J. (1954), "The American Debate on the Negro's Place in Nature, 1780–1815", *Journal of the History of Ideas*, vol. 15, June, pp. 384–96.

Greene, V. (1968), *The Slavic Community on Strike: Immigrant Labor in Pennsylvania Anthracite*, University of Notre Dame Press, Notre Dame, IN.

Greene, V. (1975), *For God and Country: The Rise of Polish and Lithuanian Ethnic Consciousness in America*, State Historical Society of Wisconsin, Madison.

Greene, V. (1982), "Ethnic Confrontations with State Universities, 1860–1920", in

B. Weiss (ed.), *American Education and the European Immigrant, 1840–1940*, University of Illinois Press, Urbana, pp. 189–207.

Greer, C. (1972), *The Great School Legend: A Revisionist Interpretation of American Public Education*, Basic Books, New York.

Griffen, C. (1972), "Occupational Mobility in Nineteenth-Century America: Problems and Possibilities", *Journal of Social History*, vol. 5, spring, pp. 310–30.

Griffen, C., and S. Griffen (1977), *Natives and Newcomers: The Ordering of Opportunity in Mid-Nineteenth Century Poughkeepsie*, Harvard University Press, Cambridge, MA.

Grinde, D., and B. Johansen (1991), *Exemplar of Liberty: Native America and the Evolution of Democracy*, American Indian Studies Center, UCLA, Los Angeles.

Griswold del Castillo, R. (1979), *The Los Angeles Barrio, 1850–1890: A Social History*, University of California Press, Berkeley.

Griswold del Castillo, R. (1984), *La Familia: Chicano Families in the Urban Southwest, 1848 to the Present*, University of Notre Dame Press, Notre Dame, IN.

Griswold del Castillo, R., and R. Garcia (1995), *César Chávez: A Triumph of Spirit*, University of Oklahoma Press, Norman.

Guerin-Gonzales, C. (1994), *Mexican Workers and American Dreams: Immigration, Repatriation, and California Farm Labor, 1900–1939*, Rutgers University Press, New Brunswick, NJ.

Guglielmo, T., and E. Lewis (2003), "Changing Racial Meanings: Race and Ethnicity in the United States, 1930–1964", in R. Bayor (ed.), *Race and Ethnicity in America: A Concise History*, Columbia University Press, New York, pp. 167–92.

Gurock, J. (1979), *When Harlem Was Jewish, 1870–1930*, Columbia University Press, New York.

Gutiérrez, D. (1993), "Significant to Whom? Mexican Americans and the History of the American West", *Western Historical Quarterly*, vol. 24, November, pp. 519–39.

Gutiérrez, R. (1993), "Community, Patriarchy and Individualism: The Politics of Chicano History and the Dream of Equality", *American Quarterly*, vol. 45, March, pp. 44–72.

Gutman, H. (1968), "The Negro and the United Mine Workers of America: The Career and Letters of Richard L. Davis and Something of Their Meaning, 1890–1900", in J. Jacobson (ed.), *The Negro and the American Labor Movement*, Anchor Books, Garden City, NY, pp. 49–127.

Gutman, H. (1976a), *The Black Family in Slavery and Freedom, 1750–1925*, Pantheon Books, New York.

Gutman, H. (1976), *Work, Culture, and Society in Industrializing America: Essays in American Working-Class and Social History*, Alfred A. Knopf, New York.

Guy-Sheftall, B. (1990), *Daughters of Sorrow: Attitudes toward Black Women, 1880–1920*, Carlson Publishing, Brooklyn, NY.

Gyory, A. (1998), *Closing the Gate: Race, Politics, and the Chinese Exclusion Act*, University of North Carolina Press, Chapel Hill.

Hair, W. (1976), *Carnival of Fury: Robert Charles and the New Orleans Race Riot of 1900*, Louisiana State University Press, Baton Rouge.

Hall, C. (1935), *Negroes in the United States, 1920–32*, Government Printing Office, Washington, DC.

Hall, J. (1979), *Revolt against Chivalry: Jesse Daniel Ames and the Women's Campaign against Lynching*, Columbia University Press, New York.

Hall, P. (1906), *Immigration and Its Effects upon the United States*, H. Holt and Co., New York.

Hallberg, G. (1973), "Bellingham, Washington's Anti-Hindu Riot", *Journal of the West*, vol. 12, January, pp. 163–75.

Haller, J. (1971), *Outcasts from Evolution: Scientific Attitudes of Racial Inferiority, 1859–1900*, University of Illinois Press, Urbana.

Halley, L. (1985), *Ancient Affections: Ethnic Groups and Foreign Policy*, Praeger, New York.

Halliburton, R. (1977), *Red over Black: Black Slavery among the Cherokee Indians*, Greenwood Press, Westport, CT.

Halpern, R. (1994), "Organized Labor, Black Workers, and the Twentieth Century South: The Emerging Revision", in M. Stokes and R. Halpern (eds), *Race and Class in the American South Since 1890*, Berg, Oxford, pp. 43–76.

Hamilton, K. (1991), *Black Towns and Profit: Promotion and Development in the Trans-Appalachian West, 1877–1915*, University of Illinois Press, Urbana.

Handlin, O. (1941), *Boston's Immigrants, 1790–1865: A Study in Acculturation*, Harvard University Press, Cambridge, MA.

Handlin, O. (1951), *The Uprooted: The Epic Story of the Great Migration that Made the American People*, Little, Brown, & Co., Boston, MA.

Handlin, O. (1954), *Adventures in Freedom: Three Hundred Years of Jewish Life in America*, McGraw-Hill, New York.

Handlin, O. (1957), *Race and Nationality in American Life*, Little, Brown, & Co., Boston, MA.

Handlin, O. (1973), *The Uprooted: The Epic Story of the Great Migration that Made the American People*, Little, Brown, & Co., Boston, MA, 2nd edn.

Handlin, O. (1982), "Education and the European Immigrant, 1820–1920", in B. Weiss (ed.), *American Education and the European Immigrant, 1840–1940*, University of Illinois Press, Urbana, pp. 3–16.

Handlin, O., and M. Handlin (1950), "The Origins of the Southern Labor System", *William and Mary Quarterly*, 3rd series, vol. 7, April, pp. 199–222.

Haney-Lopez, I. (1996), *White by Law: The Legal Construction of Race*, New York University Press, New York.

Haney-López, I. (2003), *Racism on Trial: The Chicano Fight for Justice*, Harvard University Press, Cambridge, MA.

Hansen, M. (1927), "The History of American Immigration as a Field for Research", *American Historical Review*, vol. 32, April, pp. 500–18.

Hansen, M. (1940), *The Atlantic Migration 1607–1860: A History of the Continuing Settlement of the United States*, Harvard University Press, Cambridge, MA.

Hansen, M. (1952), "The Third Generation in America", *Commentary*, vol. 14, November, pp. 492–500.

Hansen, M. (1964 [1940]), *The Immigrant in American History*, Harper & Row, New York.

Hansen, M. (1990 [1937]), "The Problem of the Third Generation Immigrant", in P. Kivisto and D. Blanck (eds), *American Immigrants and Their Generations: Studies and Commentaries on the Hansen Thesis after Fifty Years*, University of Illinois Press, Urbana, pp. 191–203.

Hareven, T. (1977), "Family and Work Patterns of Immigrant Laborers in a Planned Industrial Town, 1900–1930", in R. Ehrlich (ed.), *Immigrants in Industrial America, 1850–1920*, University Press of Virginia, Charlottesville, pp. 47–66.

Harlan, L. (1972), *Booker T. Washington: The Making of a Black Leader, 1856–1901*, Oxford University Press, New York.

Harlan, L. (1983), *Booker T. Washington: The Wizard of Tuskegee, 1901–1915*, Oxford University Press, New York.

Harris, W. (1977), *Keeping the Faith: A Philip Randolph, Milton P. Webster, and the Brotherhood of Sleeping Car Porters, 1925–1937*, University of Illinois Press, Urbana.

Hartmann, E. (1948), *The Movement to Americanize the Immigrant*, Columbia University Press, New York.

Hayashi, B. (1995), *"For the Sake of Our Japanese Brethren": Assimilation, Nationalism, and Protestantism among the Japanese of Los Angeles, 1895–1942*, Stanford University Press, Stanford, CA.

Haynes, R. (1976), *A Night of Violence: The Houston Riot of 1917*, Louisiana State University Press, Baton Rouge.

Hechter, M. (1975), *Internal Colonialism: The Celtic Fringe in British Development, 1546–1966*, University of California Press, Berkeley.

Hechter, M. (1978), "Group Formation and the Cultural Division of Labor", *American Journal of Sociology*, vol. 84, September, pp. 293–318.

Hechter, M., D. Friedman, and M. Appelbaum (1982), "A Theory of Ethnic Collective Action", *International Migration Review*, vol. 16, summer, pp. 412–34.

Heinze, A. (1990), *Adapting to Abundance: Jewish Immigrants, Mass Consumption, and the Search for American Identity*, Columbia University Press, New York.

Heinze, A. (2003), "The Critical Period: Ethnic Emergence and Reaction, 1901–1929", in R. Bayor (ed.), *Race and Ethnicity in America: A Concise History*, Columbia University Press, New York, pp. 131–66.

Helmbold, L. (1987), "Beyond the Family Economy: The Impact of the Great Depression on Black and White Working Class Women", *Feminist Studies*, vol. 13, fall, pp. 629–55.

Henretta, J. (1977), "The Study of Social Mobility: Ideological Assumptions and Conceptual Bias", *Labor History*, vol. 18, spring, pp. 165–78.

Herberg, W. (1955), *Protestant-Catholic-Jew: An Essay in American Religious Sociology*, Doubleday, Garden City, NY.

Hershberg, T. (1981), "Free Blacks in Antebellum Philadelphia: A Study of Ex-Slaves, Freeborn, and Socioeconomic Decline", in T. Hershberg (ed.), *Philadelphia: Work, Space, Family, and Group Experience in the Nineteenth Century*, Oxford University Press, New York, pp. 368–91.

Hershberg, T., A. Burstein, E. Ericksen, S. Greenberg, and W. Yancey (1981), "A Tale of Three Cities: Blacks, Immigrants, and Opportunity in Philadelphia, 1850–1880, 1930, 1970", in T. Hershberg (ed.), *Philadelphia: Work, Space, Family, and Group Experience in the Nineteenth Century*, Oxford University Press, New York, pp. 461–91.

Hertzberg, H. (1971), *The Search for an American Indian Identity: Modern Pan-Indian Movements*, Syracuse University Press, Syracuse, NY.

Hicks, J. (1960), *Republican Ascendancy, 1921–1933*, Harper & Row, New York.

Higginbotham, A. (1978), *In the Matter of Color: Race and the American Legal Process – The Colonial Period*, Oxford University Press, New York.

Higginbotham, E. (1993), *Righteous Discontent: The Women's Movement in the Black Baptist Church, 1880–1920*, Harvard University Press, Cambridge, MA.

Higgs, R. (1971), "Race, Skill, and Earnings: American Immigrants in 1909", *Journal of Economic History*, vol. 31, June, pp. 420–28.

Higgs, R. (1977), *Competition and Coercion: Blacks in the American Economy, 1865–1914*, Cambridge University Press, New York.

Higgs, R. (1978), "Landless by Law: Japanese Immigrants in California Agriculture to 1941", *Journal of Economic History*, vol. 38, March, pp. 205–25.

Higham, J. (1955), *Strangers in the Land: Patterns of American Nativism, 1860–1925*, Rutgers University Press, New Brunswick, NJ.

Higham, J. (1963), *Strangers in the Land: Patterns of American Nativism, 1860–1925*, Atheneum, New York, 2nd edn.

Higham, J. (1982), "Current Trends in the Study of Ethnicity in the United States", *Journal of American Ethnic History*, vol. 2, fall, pp. 5–15.

Higham, J. (1984), *Send These to Me: Immigrants in Urban America*, Johns Hopkins University Press, Baltimore, MD, rev. edn.

Higham, J. (1993), "Multiculturalism and Universalism: A History and Critique", *American Quarterly*, vol. 45, June, pp. 195–219, 249–56.

Higham, J. (ed.) (1978), *Ethnic Leadership in America*, Johns Hopkins University Press, Baltimore, MD.

Hill, H. (1988), "Myth-Making as Labor History: Herbert Gutman and the United Mine Workers of America", *International Journal of Politics, Culture, and Society*, vol. 2, winter, pp. 132–200.

Hill, P. (1975), "Relative Skill and Income Levels of Native and Foreign Born Workers in the United States", *Explorations in Economic History*, vol. 12, January, pp. 47–60.

Hine, D. (1979), *Black Victory: The Rise and Fall of the White Primary in Texas*, KTO Press, Millwood, NY.

Hine, D. (1989), *Black Women in White: Racial Conflict and Cooperation in the Nursing Profession, 1890–1950*, Indiana University Press, Bloomington.

Hing, B. (1993), *Making and Remaking Asian America through Immigration Policy, 1850–1990*, Stanford University Press, Stanford, CA.

Hirsch, A. (1983), *Making the Second Ghetto: Race and Housing in Chicago, 1940–1960*, Cambridge University Press, Cambridge.

Hirsch, E. (1990), *Urban Revolt: Ethnic Politics in the Nineteenth-Century Chicago Labor Movement*, University of California Press, Berkeley.

Hirsch, S. (1978), *Roots of the American Working Class: The Industrialization of Crafts in Newark, 1800–1860*, University of Pennsylvania Press, Philadelphia, PA.

Hirschman, C., and M. Wong (1986), "The Extraordinary Educational Attainment of Asian Americans: A Search for Historical Evidence and Explanations", *Social Forces*, vol. 65, September, pp. 1–27.

Hodes, M. (1999), *White Women, Black Men: Illicit Sex in the Nineteenth-Century South*, Yale University Press, New Haven, CT.

Hoerder, D. (1991), "International Labor Markets and Community Building by Migrant Workers in the Atlantic Economies", in R. Vecoli and S. Sinke (eds), *A Century of European Migrations, 1830–1930*, University of Illinois Press, Urbana, pp. 78–107.

Hoerder, D. (1996), "Immigration History and Migration Studies Since *The Polish Peasant*: International Contributions", *Journal of American Ethnic History*, vol. 16, fall, pp. 26–36.

Hoerder, D. (ed.) (1983), *American Labor and Immigration History, 1877–1920s: Recent European Research*, University of Illinois Press, Urbana.

Hoerder, D. (ed.) (1985), *Labor Migration in the Atlantic Economies: The European and North American Working Classes during the Period of Industrialization*, Greenwood Press, Westport, CT.

Hoerder, D., and C. Harzig (eds) (1987), *The Immigrant Labor Press in North America, 1840s–1970s: An Annotated Bibliography*, 3 vols, Greenwood Press, Westport, CT.

Hoffman, H. (1974), *Unwanted Mexican Americans in the Great Depression: Repatriation Pressures, 1929–1939*, University of Arizona Press, Tucson.

Hofstadter, R. (1944), "U. B. Phillips and the Plantation Legend", *Journal of Negro History*, vol. 29, April, pp. 109–24.

Hofstadter, R. (1955), *The Age of Reform: From Bryan to FDR*, Alfred A. Knopf, New York.

Hofstadter, R. (1970), "Reflections on Violence in the United States", in R. Hofstadter and M. Wallace (eds), *American Violence: A Documentary History*, Alfred A. Knopf, New York, pp. 3–43.

Holli, M., and P. Jones (1977), (eds), *The Ethnic Frontier: Essays in the History of Group Survival in Chicago and the Midwest*, W. B. Eerdmans, Grand Rapids, MI.

Hooks, B. (1982), *Ain't I a Woman: Black Women and Feminism*, Pluto Press, London.

Horne, G. (1988), *Communist Front? The Civil Rights Congress, 1946–1956*, Fairleigh Dickinson University Press, Rutherford, NJ.

Horowitz, I. (1977), "Ethnic Politics and US Foreign Policy", in A. Said (ed.), *Ethnicity and US Foreign Policy*, Praeger, New York, pp. 175–80.

Horowitz, R. (1997), *"Negro and White, Unite and Fight!": A Social History of Industrial Unionism in Meatpacking, 1930–90*, University of Illinois Press, Urbana.

Hostetler, J. (1980), *Amish Society*, Johns Hopkins University Press, Baltimore, MD, 3rd edn.

Howe, I. (1976), *World of Our Fathers*, Harcourt, Brace, Jovanovich, New York.

Hoxie, F. (1984), *A Final Promise: The Campaign to Assimilate the Indians, 1880–1920*, University of Nebraska Press, Lincoln.

Hudson, C., and C. Tesser (eds) (1994), *The Forgotten Centuries: Indians and Europeans in the American South, 1521–1704*, University of Georgia Press, Athens.

Hueston, R. (1976), *The Catholic Press and Nativism, 1840–1860*, Arno Press, New York.

Hunt, G. (1960 [1940]), *The Wars of the Iroquois: A Study in Intertribal Relations*, University of Wisconsin Press, Madison.

Hutchinson, E. (1956), *Immigrants and Their Children, 1850–1950*, J. Wiley & Sons, New York.

Hutchinson, J., and A. Smith (1996), (eds), *Ethnicity*, Oxford University Press, Oxford.

Hutton, F. (1993), *The Early Black Press in America, 1827 to 1860*, Greenwood Press, Westport, CT.

Ichioka, Y. (1980), "*Amerika Nadeshiko*: Japanese Immigrant Women in the United States, 1900–1924", *Pacific Historical Review*, vol. 49, May, pp. 339–57.

Ichioka, Y. (1990), *The Issei: The World of the First Generation Japanese Immigrants, 1885–1924*, Free Press, New York.

Ignatiev, N. (1995), *How the Irish Became White*, Routledge, New York.

Isaacs, H. (1975), *Idols of the Tribe: Group Identity and Political Change*, Harper & Row, New York.

Isser, N., and L. Schwartz (1985), *The American School and The Melting Pot: Minority Self-Esteem and Public Education*, Wyndham Hall Press, Bristol, IN.

Jackson, K. (1967), *The Ku Klux Klan in the City, 1915–1930*, Ivan R. Dee, Chicago.

Jacobson, M. (1998), *Whiteness of a Different Color: European Immigrants and the Alchemy of Race*, Harvard University Press, Cambridge, MA.

Jalkanen, R. (ed.) (1972), *The Faith of the Finns: Historical Perspectives on the Finnish Lutheran Church in America*, Michigan State University Press, East Lansing.

James, T. (1985), " 'Life Begins with Freedom': The College Nisei, 1942–1945", *History of Education Quarterly*, vol. 25, spring–summer, pp. 155–74.

James, T. (1987), *Exiles Within: The Schooling of Japanese Americans, 1942–1945*, Harvard University Press, Cambridge, MA.

Janiewski, D. (1985), *Sisterhood Denied: Race, Gender and Class in a New South Community*, Temple University Press, Philadelphia, PA.

Jaynes, G. (1986), *Branches Without Roots: The Genesis of the Black Working Class in the American South, 1862–1882*, Oxford University Press, New York.

Jenkins, J. (1983), "Resource Mobilization Theory and the Study of Social Movements", *Annual Review of Sociology*, vol. 9, pp. 527–53.

Jenkins, W. (1990), *Steel Valley Klan: The Ku Klux Klan in Ohio's Mahoning Valley*, Kent State University Press, Kent, OH.

Jennings, F. (1976), *The Invasion of America: Indians, Colonialism, and the Cant of Conquest*, W. W. Norton & Co., New York.

Jennings, F. (1984), *The Ambiguous Iroquois Empire: The Covenant Chain Confederation of Indian Tribes with English Colonies from Its Beginning to the Lancaster Treaty of 1744*, W. W. Norton & Co., New York.

Jerome, H. (1926), *Migration and the Business Cycle*, National Bureau of Economic Research, New York.

Johnson, B. (2003), *Revolution in Texas: How a Forgotten Rebellion and Its Bloody Suppression Turned Mexicans into Americans*, Yale University Press, New Haven, CT.

Johnston, J. (1970), *Race Relations in Virginia and Miscegenation in the South, 1776–1860*, University of Massachusetts Press, Amherst.

Jones, J. (1985), *Labor of Love, Labor of Sorrow: Black Women, Work, and the Family from Slavery to the Present*, Basic Books, New York.

Jones, M. (1960), *American Immigration*, University of Chicago Press, Chicago.

Jordan, W. (1968), *White over Black: American Attitudes toward the Negro, 1550–1812*, University of North Carolina Press, Chapel Hill.

Josephy, A. (1961), *The Patriot Chiefs: A Chronicle of American Indian Leadership*, Viking, New York.

Josephy, A. (1971), *Red Power: The American Indians' Fight for Freedom*, American Heritage Press, New York.

Joyce, W. (1976), *Editors and Ethnicity: A History of the Irish-American Press, 1848–1883*, Arno Press, New York.

Juliani, R. (1978), "The Settlement House and the Italian Family", in B. Caroli, R. Harney, and L. Tomasi (eds), *The Italian Immigrant Woman in North America*, Multicultural History Society of Ontario, Toronto, pp. 103–23.

Kahan, A. (1978), "Economic Opportunities and Some Pilgrims' Progress: Jewish

Immigrants from East Europe in the United States, 1830–1914", *Journal of Economic History*, vol. 38, March, pp. 235–52.

Kallen, H. (1915), "Democracy versus the Melting Pot: A Study in American Nationality", *The Nation*, vol. 100, 18 and 25 February, pp. 190–4, 217–20.

Kallen, H. (1924), *Culture and Democracy in the United States*, Boni and Liveright, New York.

Kallen, H. (1956), *Cultural Pluralism and the American Idea*, University of Pennsylvania Press, Philadelphia, PA.

Kanellos, N., and H. Martell (2000), *Hispanic Periodicals in the United States, Origins to 1960: A Brief History and Comprehensive Bibliography*, Arte Público Press, Houston, TX.

Kantowicz, E. (1975), *Polish-American Politics in Chicago, 1888–1940*, University of Chicago Press, Chicago.

Karlin, J. (1948), "The Anti-Chinese Outbreaks in Seattle, 1885–1886", *Pacific Northwest Quarterly*, vol. 39, April, pp. 103–29.

Karlin, J. (1954), "The Anti-Chinese Outbreak in Tacoma, 1885", *Pacific Historical Review*, vol. 23, August, pp. 271–83.

Karni, M., and D. Ollila (1977), (eds), *For the Common Good: Finnish Immigrants and the Radical Response to Industrial America*, Työmies Society, Superior, WI.

Karp, H. (1985), *Haven and Home: A History of the Jews in America*, Schocken Books, New York.

Katz, M. (1968), *The Irony of Early School Reform: Educational Innovation in Mid-Nineteenth-Century Massachusetts*, Harvard University Press, Cambridge, MA.

Katzman, D. (1973), *Before the Ghetto: Black Detroit in the Nineteenth Century*, University of Illinois Press, Urbana.

Kazal, R. (1995), "Revisiting Assimilation: The Rise, Fall, and Reappraisal of a Concept in American Ethnic History", *American Historical Review*, vol. 100, April, pp. 437–71.

Kelley, R. (1990), *Hammer and Hoe: Alabama Communists during the Great Depression*, University of North Carolina Press, Chapel Hill.

Kelley, R. (1993), " 'We Are Not What We Seem': Rethinking Black Working-Class Opposition in the Jim Crow South", *Journal of American History*, vol. 80, June, pp. 75–112.

Kelley, R. (1994), *Race Rebels: Culture, Politics, and the Black Working Class*, Free Press, New York.

Kellogg, L. (1925), *The French Regime in Wisconsin and the Northwest*, State Historical Society of Wisconsin, Madison.

Kellogg, L. (1935), *The British Regime in Wisconsin and the Northwest*, State Historical Society of Wisconsin, Madison.

Kelly, L. (1968), *The Navajo Indians and Federal Indian Policy, 1900–1935*, University of Arizona Press, Tucson.

Kennedy, R. (1944), "Single or Triple Melting-Pot? Intermarriage Trends in New Haven, 1870–1940", *American Journal of Sociology*, vol. 49, January, pp. 331–9.

Kessler-Harris, A. (1976), "Organizing the Unorganizable: Three Jewish Women and Their Union", *Labor History*, vol. 17, winter, pp. 5–23.

Kessler-Harris, A. (1990), "Social History", in E. Foner (ed.), *The New American History*, Temple University Press, Philadelphia, PA, pp. 163–84.

Kessner, T. (1977), *The Golden Door: Italian and Jewish Immigrant Mobility in New York City, 1880–1915*, Oxford University Press, New York.

King, L. (1974), "Puertorriqueñas in the United States: The Impact of Double Discrimination", *Civil Rights Digest*, vol. 6, spring, pp. 20–7.

Kinzer, D. (1964), *An Episode in Anti-Catholicism: The American Protective Association*, University of Washington Press, Seattle.

Kirk, G., and C. Kirk (1978), "The Immigrant, Economic Opportunity and Type of Settlement in Nineteenth-Century America", *Journal of Economic History*, vol. 38, March, pp. 226–34.

Kitano, H. (1974), "Japanese Americans: The Development of a Middleman Minority", *Pacific Historical Review*, vol. 43, November, pp. 500–19.

Kitano, H. (1976), *Japanese Americans: The Evolution of a Subculture*, Prentice-Hall, Englewood Cliffs, NJ, 2nd edn.

Kitano, H., and S. Sue (1973), "The Model Minorities", *Journal of Social Issues*, vol. 29, June, pp. 1–9.

Klarman, M. (1994), "How *Brown* Changed Race Relations: The Backlash Thesis", *Journal of American History*, vol. 81, June, pp. 81–118.

Kleppner, P. (1970), *The Cross of Culture: A Social Analysis of Midwestern Politics, 1850–1900*, Free Press, New York.

Kluger, R. (1976), *Simple Justice: The History of Brown v. Board of Education and Black America's Struggle for Equality*, Alfred A. Knopf, New York.

Knobel, D. (1986), *Paddy and the Republic: Ethnicity and Nationality in Antebellum America*, Wesleyan University Press, Middletown, CT.

Knobel, D. (1996), *America for the Americans: The Nativist Movement in the United States*, Twayne, New York.

Kohn, H. (1957), *American Nationalism: An Interpretative Essay*, Macmillan, New York.

Kohn, H. (1965), *Nationalism: Its Meaning and History*, Van Nostrand Reinhold, New York, rev. edn.

Kolchin, P. (2002), "Whiteness Studies: The New History of Race in America", *Journal of American History*, vol. 89, June, pp. 154–73.

Kolko, G. (1976), *Main Currents in Modern American History*, Harper & Row, New York.

Konvitz, M. (1946), *The Alien and the Asiatic in American Law*, Cornell University Press, Ithaca, NY.

Korrol, V. (1994), *From Colonia to Community: The History of Puerto Ricans in New York City*, University of California Press, Berkeley, 2nd edn.

Kostiainen, A. (1983), "For or Against Americanization? The Case of the Finnish Immigrant Radicals", in D. Hoerder (ed.), *American Labor and Immigration History, 1877–1920s: Recent European Research*, University of Illinois Press, Urbana, pp. 259–75.

Krause, C. (1978), "Urbanization without Breakdown: Italian, Jewish, and Slavic Immigrant Women in Pittsburgh, 1900 to 1945", *Journal of Urban History*, vol. 4, May, pp. 291–306.

Kraut, A. (1982), *The Huddled Masses: The Immigrant in American Society, 1880–1921*, Harlan Davidson, Wheeling, IL.

Kraut, A. (2001), *The Huddled Masses: The Immigrant in American Society, 1880–1921*, Harlan Davidson, Wheeling, IL, 2nd edn.

Kritz, M. M., C. Keely, and S. Tomasi (eds) (1981), *Global Trends in Migration: Theory and Research in International Population Movements*, Center for Migration Studies, New York.

Kung, S. (1962), *The Chinese in American Life: Some Aspects of Their History, Status, Problems and Contributions*, University of Washington Press, Seattle.

Kupperman, K. (1980), *Settling with the Indians: The Meeting of English and Indian Cultures in America, 1580–1640*, J. M. Dent & Sons, London.

Kusmer, K. (1976), *A Ghetto Takes Shape: Black Cleveland, 1870–1930*, University of Illinois Press, Urbana.

Kusmer, K. (1986), "The Black Urban Experience in American History", in D. Hine (ed.), *The State of Afro-American History: Past, Present, and Future*, Louisiana State University Press, Baton Rouge, pp. 91–122.

Kuzniewski, A. (1980), *Faith and Fatherland: The Polish Church War in Wisconsin, 1896–1918*, Notre Dame University Press, Notre Dame, IN.

Kwong, P. (1979), *Chinatown, New York: Labor and Politics, 1930–1950*, Monthly Review Press, New York.

LaGumina, S. (1982), "American Education and the Italian Immigrant Response", in B. Weiss (ed.), *American Education and the European Immigrant, 1840–1940*, University of Illinois Press, Urbana, pp. 61–77.

Lancaster, J. (1994), *Removal Aftershock: The Seminoles' Struggle to Survive in the West, 1836–1866*, University of Tennessee Press, Knoxville.

Landry, B. (1987), *The New Black Middle Class*, University of California Press, Berkeley.

Lane, A. (1987), *Solidarity or Survival? American Labor and European Immigrants, 1830–1924*, Greenwood Press, Westport, CT.

Lane, A. (ed.) (1971), *The Debate over Slavery: Stanley Elkins and His Critics*, University of Chicago Press, Chicago.

Lannie, V. (1968), *Public Money and Parochial Education: Bishop Hughes, Governor Seward, and the New York School Controversy*, Case Western Reserve University Press, Cleveland, OH.

Laurie, C. (1990a), " 'The Chinese Must Go': The United States Army and the Anti-Chinese Riots in Washington Territory, 1885–1886", *Pacific Northwest Quarterly*, vol. 81, January, pp. 22–9.

Laurie, C. (1990b), "Civil Disorder and the Military in Rock Springs, Wyoming: The Army's Role in the 1885 Chinese Massacre", *Montana*, vol. 40, summer, pp. 44–59.

Lay, S. (1994), "Hooded Populism: New Assessments of the Ku Klux Klan of the 1920s", *Reviews in American History*, vol. 22, December, pp. 668–73.

Leach, D. (1958), *Flintlock and Tomahawk: New England in King Philip's War*, Macmillan, New York.

Lebsock, S. (1984), *The Free Women of Petersburg: Status and Culture in a Southern Town, 1784–1860*, W. W. Norton & Co., New York.

Lee, E. (2002), "The Chinese Exclusion Example: Race, Immigration, and American Gatekeeping, 1882–1924", *Journal of American Ethnic History*, vol. 21, spring, pp. 36–62.

Lee, S. (1993), "Racial Classification in the US Census, 1890–1990", *Ethnic and Racial Studies*, vol. 16, January, pp. 75–94.

Lemon, J. (1972), *The Best Poor Man's Country*, Johns Hopkins University Press, Baltimore, MD.

Leonard, K. (1992), *Making Ethnic Choices: California's Punjabi Mexican Americans*, Temple University Press, Philadelphia, PA.

Lerner, E. (1986), "American Feminism and the Jewish Question, 1890–1940", in D. Gerber (ed.), *Anti-Semitism in American History*, University of Illinois Press, Urbana, pp. 305–28.

Leuchtenburg, W. (1958), *The Perils of Prosperity, 1914–32*, University of Chicago Press, Chicago.

Leviatin, D. (1989), *Followers of the Trail: Jewish Working-Class Radicals in America*, Yale University Press, New Haven, CT.

Levine, E. (1966), *The Irish and Irish Politicians: A Study of Cultural and Social Alienation*, University of Notre Dame Press, Notre Dame, IN.

Levine, L. (1977), *Black Culture and Black Consciousness: Afro-American Folk Thought from Slavery to Freedom*, Oxford University Press, New York.

Levy, S. (1975), "Shifting Patterns of Ethnic Identification among the Hassidim", in J. Bennett (ed.), *The New Ethnicity: Perspectives from Ethnology*, West Publishing Co., St Paul, MN, pp. 25–50.

Lewis, E. (1991), *In Their Own Interests: Race, Class, and Power in Twentieth-Century Norfolk, Virginia*, University of California Press, Berkeley.

Lewis, J., and P. Onuf (eds) (1999), *Sally Hemings and Thomas Jefferson: History, Memory, and Civic Culture*, University of Virginia Press, Charlottesville.

Lewis, R. (1979), *Coal, Iron, and Slaves: Industrial Slavery in Maryland and Virginia, 1715–1865*, Greenwood Press, Westport, CT.

Lewis, R. (1987), *Black Coal Miners in America: Race, Class, and Community Conflict, 1780–1980*, University Press of Kentucky, Lexington.

Lichtman, A. (1979), *Prejudice and the Old Politics: The Presidential Election of 1928*, University of North Carolina Press, Chapel Hill.

Lieberson, S. (1963), *Ethnic Patterns in American Cities*, Free Press, Glencoe, IL.

Lieberson, S. (1980), *A Piece of the Pie: Blacks and White Immigrants since 1880*, University of California Press, Berkeley.

Light, I. (1972), *Ethnic Enterprise in America: Business and Welfare among Chinese, Japanese, and Blacks*, University of California Press, Berkeley.

Limerick, P. (1987), *The Legacy of Conquest: The Unbroken Past of the American West*, W. W. Norton & Co., New York.

Lincoln, C., and L. Mamiya (1990), *The Black Church in the African American Experience*, Duke University Press, Durham, NC.

Lind, M. (1995), *The Next American Nation: The New Nationalism and the Fourth American Republic*, Free Press, New York.

Lindsey, D. (1995), *Indians at Hampton Institute, 1877–1923*, University of Illinois Press, Urbana.

Ling, S. (1989), "The Mountain Movers: Asian American Women's Movement in Los Angeles", *Amerasia Journal*, vol. 15, no. 1, pp. 51–67.

Linkh, R. (1975), *American Catholicism and European Immigrants, 1900–1924*, Center for Migration Studies, Staten Island, NY.

Lipset, S. (1969), "Prejudice and Politics in the American Past and Present", in C. Glock and E. Siegelman (eds), *Prejudice USA*, Praeger, New York, pp. 17–69.

Liptak, D. (1989), *Immigrants and Their Church*, Macmillan, New York.

Lissak, R. (1988), *Pluralism and Progressives: Hull House and the New Immigrants*, University of Chicago Press, Chicago.

Littlefield, D. (1976), *Africans and Creeks: From the Colonial Period to the Civil War*, Greenwood Press, Westport, CT.

Littlefield, D. (1977), *Africans and Seminoles: From Removal to Emancipation*, Greenwood Press, Westport, CT.

Littlefield, D. (1978), *The Cherokee Freedmen: From Emancipation to American Citizenship*, Greenwood Press, Westport, CT.

Littlefield, D. (1980), *The Chickasaw Freedmen: A People Without a Country*, Greenwood Press, Westport, CT.

Litwack, L. (1961), *North of Slavery: The Negro in the Free States, 1790–1860*, University of Chicago Press, Chicago.

Loewen, J. (1971), *The Mississippi Chinese: Between Black and White*, Harvard University Press, Cambridge, MA.

Lomawaima, K. (1994), *They Call It Prairie Light: The Story of Chilocco Indian School*, University of Nebraska Press, Lincoln.

Lopez, D., and Y. Espiritu (1990), "Panethnicity in the United States: A Theoretical Framework", *Ethnic and Racial Studies*, vol. 13, April, pp. 198–224.

Lovejoy, P. (1982), "The Volume of the Atlantic Slave Trade: A Synthesis", *Journal of African History*, vol. 23, no. 4, pp. 473–501.

Lubin, A. (2005), *Romance and Rights: The Politics of Interracial Intimacy, 1945–1954*, University Press of Mississippi, Jackson.

Luebke, F. (1974), *Bonds of Loyalty: German-Americans and World War I*, Northern Illinois University Press, De Kalb.

Luebke, F. (1978), "The Germans", in J. Higham (ed.), *Ethnic Leadership in America*, Johns Hopkins University Press, Baltimore, MD, pp. 64–90.

Lyman, S. (1970), "Strangers in the City: The Chinese on the Urban Frontier", in C. Wollenberg (ed.), *Ethnic Conflict in California History*, Tinnon-Brown, Los Angeles, pp. 63–100.

Lyons, O., and J. Mohawk (eds) (1992), *Exiled in the Land of the Free: Democracy, Indian Nations, and the US Constitution*, Clear Light Publishers, Santa Fe, NM.

Lyu, K. (1977a), "Korean Nationalist Activities in Hawaii and the Continental United States, 1900–1945: Part I (1910–1919)", *Amerasia Journal*, vol. 4, no. 1, pp. 23–90.

Lyu, K. (1977b), "Korean Nationalist Activities in Hawaii and the Continental United States, 1900–1945: Part II (1919–1945)", *Amerasia Journal*, vol. 4, no. 2, pp. 53–100.

McAdam, D. (1982), *Political Process and the Development of Black Insurgency, 1930–1970*, University of Chicago Press, Chicago.

McClain, C. (1994), *In Search of Equality: The Chinese Struggle Against Discrimination in Nineteenth-Century America*, University of California Press, Berkeley.

McClymer, J. (1982), "The Americanization Movement and the Education of the Foreign-Born Adult, 1914–25", in B. Weiss (ed.), *American Education and the European Immigrant, 1840–1940*, University of Illinois Press, Urbana, pp. 96–116.

McDonald, F. (1958), *We the People: The Economic Origins of the Constitution*, University of Chicago Press, Chicago.

McDonnell, J. (1991), *The Dispossession of the American Indian, 1887–1934*, Indiana University Press, Bloomington.

McGouldrick, P., and M. Tannen (1977), "Did American Manufacturers Discriminate Against Immigrants Before 1914?" *Journal of Economic History*, vol. 37, September, pp. 723–46.

McKee, D. (1977), *Chinese Exclusion versus the Open Door Policy, 1900–1906: Clashes over China Policy in the Roosevelt Era*, Wayne State University Press, Detroit, MI.

MacLean, N. (1994), *Behind the Mask of Chivalry: The Making of the Second Ku Klux Klan*, Oxford University Press, New York.

McLoughlin, W. (1984), *Cherokees and Missionaries, 1789-1839*, Yale University Press, New Haven, CT.

McLoughlin, W. (1986), *Cherokee Renascence in the New Republic*, Princeton University Press, Princeton, NJ.

McLoughlin, W. (1990), *Champions of the Cherokee: Evan and John B. Jones*, Princeton University Press, Princeton, NJ.

McLoughlin, W. (1993), *After the Trail of Tears: The Cherokees' Struggle for Sovereignty, 1839-1880*, University of North Carolina Press, Chapel Hill.

McMillen, N. (1989), *Dark Journey: Black Mississippians in the Age of Jim Crow*, University of Illinois Press, Urbana.

McNickle, D. (1973), *Native American Tribalism: Indian Survivals and Renewals*, Oxford University Press, New York.

McWilliams, C. (1968 [1949]), *North From Mexico: The Spanish-Speaking People of the United States*, Greenwood Press, New York.

Mandle, J. (1992), *Not Slave, Not Free: The African American Economic Experience since the Civil War*, Duke University Press, Durham, NC.

Mann, A. (1979), *The One and the Many: Reflections on the American Identity*, University of Chicago Press, Chicago.

Manners, A. (1972), *Poor Cousins*, Coward, McCann, and Geoghegan, New York.

Mannix, D., and M. Cowley (1963), *Black Cargoes: A History of the Atlantic Slave Trade, 1518-1865*, Longmans, Green and Co., New York.

Marable, M. (1984), *Race, Reform and Rebellion: the Second Reconstruction in Black America, 1945-1982*, University Press of Mississippi, Jackson.

Márquez, B. (1993), *LULAC: Evolution of a Mexican American Political Organization*, University of Texas Press, Austin.

Martin, C. (1976), *The Angelo Herndon Case and Southern Justice*, Louisiana State University Press, Baton Rouge.

Martin, C. (1978), *Keepers of the Game: Indian–Animal Relationships and the Fur Trade*, University of California Press, Berkeley.

Martin, T. (1976), *Race First: The Ideological and Organizational Struggles of Marcus Garvey and the Universal Negro Improvement Association*, Majority Press, Dover, MA.

Martin, W. (1998), *Brown v. Board of Education*, Bedford Books, Boston, MA.

Martinelli, P. (1978), "Italian Immigrant Women in the Southwest", in B. Caroli, R. Harney, and L. Tomasi (eds), *The Italian Immigrant Woman in North America*, Multicultural History Society of Ontario, Toronto, pp. 324–36.

Matsumoto, V. (1993), *Farming the Home Place: A Japanese American Community in California, 1919-1982*, Cornell University Press, Ithaca, NY.

Matthews, F. (1977), *Quest for an American Sociology: Robert E. Park and the Chicago School*, McGill-Queen's University Press, Montreal.

Matthiessen, P. (1983), *In the Spirit of Crazy Horse*, Viking Press, New York.

Mayo, L. (1988), *The Ambivalent Image: Nineteenth-Century America's Perception of the Jew*, Fairleigh Dickinson University Press, Rutherford, NJ.

Mei, J. (1984), "Socioeconomic Developments among the Chinese in San Francisco, 1848-1906", in L. Cheng and E. Bonacich (eds), *Labor Migration Under Capitalism: Asian Workers in the United States before World War II*, University of California Press, Berkeley, pp. 370–402.

Meier, A. (1963), *Negro Thought in America, 1880–1915: Racial Ideologies in the Age of Booker T. Washington*, University of Michigan Press, Ann Arbor.

Meier, A., and E. Rudwick (1973), *CORE: A Study in the Civil Rights Movement, 1942–1968*, Oxford University Press, New York.

Meier, A., and E. Rudwick (1979), *Black Detroit and the Rise of the UAW*, Oxford University Press, New York.

Meier, M., and F. Ribera (1993), *Mexican Americans/American Mexicans: From Conquistadors to Chicanos*, Hill and Wang, New York.

Melendy, H. (1977), *Asians in America: Filipinos, Koreans, and East Indian*, Twayne, Boston, MA.

Menard, R. (1973), "From Servant to Freeholder: Status Mobility and Property Accumulation in Seventeenth-Century Maryland", *William and Mary Quarterly*, 3rd series, vol. 30, January, pp. 37–64.

Menard, R. (1991), "Migration, Ethnicity, and the Rise of an Atlantic Economy: The Re-Peopling of British America, 1600–1790", in R. Vecoli and S. Sinke (eds), *A Century of European Migrations, 1830–1930*, University of Illinois Press, Urbana, pp. 58–77.

Mencke, J. (1979), *Mulattoes and Race Mixture: American Attitudes and Images, 1865–1918*, UMI Research Press, Ann Arbor, MI.

Ment, D. (1983), "Patterns of Public School Segregation, 1900–1940: A Comparative Study of New York City, New Rochelle, and New Haven", in R. Goodenow and D. Ravitch (eds), *Schools in Cities: Consensus and Conflict in American Educational History*, Holmes & Meier, New York, pp. 67–110.

Merrell, J. (1989), *The Indians' New World: Catawbas and Their Neighbors from European Contact through the Era of Removal*, University of North Carolina Press, Chapel Hill.

Meyer, S. (1980), "Adapting the Immigrant to the Line: Americanization in the Ford Factory, 1914–1921", *Journal of Social History*, vol. 14, fall, pp. 67–82.

Mihesuah, D. (1993), *Cultivating the Rosebuds: The Education of Women at the Cherokee Female Seminary, 1851–1909*, University of Illinois Press, Urbana.

Miller, K. (1985), *Emigrants and Exiles: Ireland and the Irish Exodus to North America*, Oxford University Press, New York.

Miller, K. (1990), "Class, Culture, and Immigrant Group Identity in the United States: The Case of Irish-American Ethnicity", in V. Yans-McLaughlin (ed.), *Immigration Reconsidered: History, Sociology, and Politics*, Oxford University Press, New York, pp. 96–129.

Miller, R. (1968), "The Ku Klux Klan", in J. Braeman, R. Bremner, and D. Brody (eds), *Change and Continuity in Twentieth-Century America: The 1920s*, Ohio State University Press, Columbus, pp. 215–55.

Miller, S. (1969), *The Unwelcome Immigrant: The American Image of the Chinese, 1785–1882*, University of California Press, Berkeley.

Miller, S. (1974), *The Radical Immigrant*, Twayne, New York.

Miller, S. (ed.) (1987), *The Ethnic Press in the United States: A Historical Analysis and Handbook*, Greenwood Press, Westport, CT.

Miller, S. (ed.) (1996), *Race, Ethnicity, and Gender in Early Twentieth-Century American Socialism*, Garland, New York.

Mills, G. (1977), *The Forgotten People: Cane Rivers' Creoles of Color*, Louisiana State University Press, Baton Rouge.

Mills, K. (1994), *This Little Light of Mine: The Life of Fannie Lou Hamer*, Plume, New York.

Miner, H. (1976), *The Corporation and the Indian: Tribal Sovereignty and Industrial Civilization in Indian Territory, 1865–1907*, University of Missouri Press, Columbia.

Mink, G. (1986), *Old Labor and New Immigrants in American Political Development: Union, Party, and State, 1875–1920*, Cornell University Press, Ithaca, NY.

Model, S. (1988), "Intergenerational Mobility among Italians and Jews in 1910 New York", *Social Science History*, vol. 12, spring, pp. 31–48.

Modell, J. (1968), "The Japanese American Family: A Perspective for Future Investigations", *Pacific Historical Review*, vol. 37, February, pp. 67–81.

Modell, J. (1977), *The Economics and Politics of Racial Accommodation: The Japanese of Los Angeles, 1900–1942*, University of Illinois Press, Urbana.

Mohl, R. (1982), "Cultural Pluralism in Immigrant Education: The International Institutes of Boston, Philadelphia, and San Francisco, 1920–1940", *Journal of American Ethnic History*, vol. 1, spring, pp. 35–58.

Monroy, D. (1980), "La Costura en Los Angeles, 1933–1939: The ILGWU and the Politics of Domination", in M. Mora and A. Del Castillo (eds), *Mexican Women in the United States: Struggles Past and Present*, UCLA Chicano Studies Research Center, Los Angeles, pp. 171–8.

Monroy, D. (1990), "'They Didn't Call Them "Padre" for Nothing': Patriarchy in Hispanic California", in A. Del Castillo (ed.), *Between Borders: Essays on Mexicana/Chicana History*, Floricanto Press, Encino, CA, pp. 433–45.

Montalto, N. (1982a), *Forgotten Dream: A History of the Intercultural Education Movement, 1924–1941*, Garland, New York.

Montalto, N. (1982b), "The Intercultural Education Movement, 1924–41: The Growth of Tolerance as a Form of Intolerance", in B. Weiss (ed.), *American Education and the European Immigrant, 1840–1940*, University of Illinois Press, Urbana, pp. 142–60.

Montejano, D. (1987), *Anglos and Mexicans in the Making of Texas, 1836–1986*, University of Texas Press, Austin.

Moore, D. (1981), *At Home in America: Second Generation New York Jews*, Columbia University Press, New York.

Moore, L. (1991), *Citizen Klansmen: The Ku Klux Klan in Indiana, 1921–1928*, University of North Carolina Press, Chapel Hill.

Moore, L. (1993), "Historical Interpretations of the 1920s Klan: The Traditional View and Recent Revisions", in S. Lay (ed.), *The Invisible Empire in the West: Toward a New Historical Appraisal of the Ku Klux Klan of the 1920s*, University of Illinois Press, Urbana, pp. 17–38.

Morawska, E. (1985), *For Bread With Butter: The Life-Worlds of East Central Europeans in Johnstown, Pennsylvania, 1890–1940*, Cambridge University Press, Cambridge.

Morawska, E. (1989), "Labor Migrations of Poles in the Atlantic World Economy, 1880–1914", *Comparative Studies in Society and History*, vol. 31, April, pp. 237–72.

Morawska, E. (1990), "The Sociology and Historiography of Immigration", in V. Yans-McLaughlin (ed.), *Immigration Reconsidered: History, Sociology, and Politics*, Oxford University Press, New York, pp. 187–238.

Morawska, E. (1991), "Return Migration: Theoretical and Research Agenda", in R. Vecoli and S. Sinke (eds), *A Century of European Migrations, 1830–1930*, University of Illinois Press, Urbana, pp. 277–92.

Morawska, E. (1994), "In Defense of the Assimilation Model", *Journal of American Ethnic History*, vol. 13, winter, pp. 76–87.

Morgan, E. (1975), *American Slavery, American Freedom: The Ordeal of Colonial Virginia*, W. W. Norton & Co., New York.

Mormino, G. (1986), *Immigrants on the Hill: Italian Americans in St Louis, 1882–1982*, University of Illinois Press, Urbana.

Mormino, G., and G. Pozzetta (1987), *The Immigrant World of Ybor City: Italians and Their Latin Neighbors in Tampa, 1885–1985*, University of Illinois Press, Urbana.

Morris, A. (1984), *The Origins of the Civil Rights Movements*, Free Press, New York.

Morton, P. (ed.) (1996), *Discovering the Women in Slavery: Emancipating Perspectives on the American Past*, University of Georgia Press, Athens.

Mulroy, K. (1993), *Freedom on the Border: The Seminole Maroons in Florida, the Indian Territory, Coahuila, and Texas*, Texas Tech University Press, Lubbock.

Mumford, K. (1997), *Interzones: Black/White Sex Districts in Chicago and New York in the Early Twentieth Century*, Columbia University Press, New York.

Muñoz, C. (1989), *Youth, Identity, Power: The Chicano Movement*, Verso, London.

Murphy, J., and S. Murphy (1981), *Let My People Know: American Indian Journalism, 1828–1978*, University of Oklahoma Press, Norman.

Myrdal, G. (1944), *An American Dilemma: The Negro Problem and American Democracy*, Harper & Row, New York.

Nadel, S. (1990), *Little Germany: Ethnicity, Religion, and Class in New York City, 1845–80*, University of Illinois Press, Urbana.

Naison, M. (1983), *Communists in Harlem during the Depression*, University of Illinois Press, Urbana.

Nash, G. (1982), *Red, White and Black: The Peoples of Early America*, Prentice-Hall, Englewood Cliffs, NJ, rev. edn.

Nash, G. (1995), "The Hidden History of Mestizo America", *Journal of American History*, vol. 82, December, pp. 941–64.

Navarro, A. (2000), *La Raza Unida Party: A Chicano Challenge to the US Two-Party Dictatorship*, Temple University Press, Philadelphia, PA.

Navasky, V. (1971), *Kennedy Justice*, Atheneum, New York.

Neiman, F. (2000), "Coincidence or Causal Connection? The Relationship between Thomas Jefferson's Visits to Monticello and Sally Hemings's Conceptions", *William and Mary Quarterly*, 3rd series, vol. 57, January, pp. 198–210.

Nelli, H. (1970), *Italians in Chicago, 1880–1930: A Study in Ethnic Mobility*, Oxford University Press, New York.

Novak, M. (1973), *The Rise of the Unmeltable Ethnics: Politics and Culture in the Seventies*, Macmillan, New York.

Oestreicher, R. (1986), *Solidarity and Fragmentation: Working People and Class Consciousness in Detroit, 1875–1900*, University of Illinois Press, Urbana.

O'Grady, J. (1973), *How the Irish Became Americans*, Twayne, New York.

O'Grady, J. (ed.) (1967), *The Immigrants' Influence on Wilson's Peace Policies*, University Press of Kentucky, Lexington.

Olin, S. (1966), "European Immigrant and Oriental Alien: Acceptance and Rejection by the California Legislation of 1913", *Pacific Historical Review*, vol. 35, August, pp. 202–15.

Olneck, M., and M. Lazerson (1974), "The School Achievement of Immigrant Children, 1900–1930", *History of Education Quarterly*, vol. 14, winter, pp. 453–82.

Olson, J. (1994), *The Ethnic Dimension in American History*, St Martin's Press, New York, 2nd edn.

Olzak, S. (1992), *The Dynamics of Ethnic Competition and Conflict*, Stanford University Press, Stanford, CA.

Omi, M., and H. Winant (1986), *Racial Formation in the United States, From the 1960s to the 1980s*, Routledge, New York.

Orozco, C. (1990), "Sexism in Chicano Studies and the Community", in T. Córdova, N. Cantú, G. Cardenas, J. García, and C. Sierra (eds), *Chicana Voices: Intersections of Class, Race and Gender*, University of New Mexico Press, Albuquerque, pp. 11–18.

Orsi, R. (1985), *The Madonna of 115th Street: Faith and Community in Italian Harlem, 1880–1950*, Yale University Press, New Haven, CT.

Ortiz, A. (1990), "Puerto Ricans in the Garment Industry of New York City, 1920–1960", in R. Asher and C. Stephenson (eds), *Labor Divided: Race and Ethnicity in United States Labor Struggles, 1835–1960*, State University of New York Press, Albany, pp. 105–27.

Orton, L. (1981), *Polish Detroit and the Kolasinski Affair*, Wayne State University Press, Detroit, MI.

Osofsky, G. (1966), *Harlem: The Making of a Ghetto*, Harper & Row, New York.

Ostergren, R. (1988), *A Community Transplanted: The Trans-Atlantic Experience of a Swedish Immigrant Settlement in the Upper Middle West, 1835–1915*, University of Wisconsin Press, Madison.

Paredes, A. (1958), *With His Pistol in His Hand*, University of Texas Press, Austin.

Park, R. (1950), *Race and Culture*, Free Press, Glencoe, IL.

Parot, J. (1981), *Polish Catholics in Chicago, 1850–1920*, Northern Illinois University Press, De Kalb.

Pascoe, P. (1996), "Miscegenation Law, Court Cases, and Ideologies of 'Race' in Twentieth-Century America", *Journal of American History*, vol. 83, June, pp. 44–69.

Patterson, O. (1977), *Ethnic Chauvinism: The Reactionary Impulse*, Stein and Day, New York.

Pearce, R. (1988), *Savagism and Civilization: The Indian and the American Mind*, University of California Press, Berkeley.

Peckham, H. (1961), *Pontiac and the Indian Uprisings*, University of Chicago Press, Chicago.

Peiss, K. (1986), *Cheap Amusements: Working Women and Leisure in Turn-of-the-Century New York*, Temple University Press, Philadelphia, PA.

Perdue, T. (1979), *Slavery and the Evolution of Cherokee Society, 1540–1866*, University of Tennessee Press, Knoxville.

Perdue, T. (1998), *Cherokee Women: Gender and Culture Change, 1700-1835*, University of Nebraska Press, Lincoln.

Perdue, T. (2003), *"Mixed Blood" Indians: Racial Construction in the Early South*, University of Georgia Press, Athens.

Perlman, S. (1952), "Jewish-American Unionism: Its Birth Pangs and Contribution to the General American Labor Movement", Publication of the American Jewish Historical Society, vol. 41, June, pp. 297–337.

Perlmann, J. (1988), *Ethnic Differences: Schooling and Social Structure Among the Irish, Italians, Jews, and Blacks in an American City, 1880–1935*, Cambridge University Press, Cambridge.

Persons, S. (1987), *Ethnic Studies at Chicago, 1905–45*, University of Illinois Press, Urbana.

Peterson, J. (1988), "Women Dreaming: The Religiosity of Indian-White Marriage and the Rise of Metis Culture", in L. Schlissel, V. Ruiz, and J. Monk (eds), *Western Women: Their Land, Their Lives*, University of New Mexico Press, Albuquerque, pp. 49–68.

Peterson, W. (1980), "Concepts of Ethnicity", in S. Thernstrom (ed.), *Harvard Encyclopedia of American Ethnic Groups*, Harvard University Press, Cambridge, MA, pp. 234–5.

Phillips, C. (1997), *Freedom's Port: The African-American Community of Baltimore, 1790–1860*, University of Illinois Press, Urbana.

Phillips, K. (1999), *Alabama North: African-American Migrants, Community, and Working-Class Activism in Cleveland, 1915–45*, University of Illinois Press, Urbana.

Phillips, U. (1959 [1918]), *American Negro Slavery*, Peter Smith, Gloucester, MA.

Phillpott, T. (1978), *The Slum and the Ghetto: Neighborhood Deterioration and Middle-Class Reform, Chicago, 1880–1930*, Oxford University Press, New York.

Pickens, D. (1968), *Eugenics and the Progressives*, Vanderbilt University Press, Nashville, TN.

Pickle, L. (1996), *Contented Among Strangers: Rural German-Speaking Women and Their Families in the Nineteenth-Century Midwest*, University of Illinois Press, Urbana.

Pinkney, A. (1976), *Red, Black, and Green: Black Nationalism in the United States*, Cambridge University Press, Cambridge.

Polenberg, R. (1980), *One Nation Divisible: Class, Race, and Ethnicity in the United States since 1938*, Penguin, Harmondsworth, Middlesex.

Poll, S. (1962), *The Hasidic Community of Williamsburg*, Free Press, New York.

Pope-Hennessey, J. (1967), *Sins of the Fathers: Atlantic Slave Traders, 1441–1807*, Weidenfeld and Nicolson, London.

Porter, K. (1971), *The Negro on the Frontier*, Arno Press, New York.

Porter, K. (1996), *The Black Seminoles: History of a Freedom-Seeking People*, ed. and rev. by A. Amos and T. Senter, University Press of Florida, Gainesville.

Powell, L. (1980), *New Masters: Northern Planters during the Civil War and Reconstruction*, Yale University Press, New Haven, CT.

Prucha, F. (1962), *American Indian Policy in the Formative Years: The Indian Trade and Intercourse Acts, 1790–1834*, University of Nebraska Press, Lincoln.

Prucha, F. (1976), *American Indian Policy in Crisis: Christian Reformers and the Indian, 1865–1900*, University of Oklahoma Press, Norman.

Prucha, F. (1979), *The Churches and the Indian Schools, 1888–1912*, University of Nebraska Press, Lincoln.

Prucha, F. (1981), *Indian Policy in the United States: Historical Essays*, University of Nebraska Press, Lincoln.

Prucha, F. (1985), *The Indians in American Society: From the Revolutionary War to the Present*, University of California Press, Berkeley.

Pula, J., and E. Dziedzic (1990), *United We Stand: The Role of Polish Workers in the New York Mills Textile Strikes, 1912 and 1916*, Columbia University Press, New York.

Puzzo, D. (1964), "Racism and the Western Tradition", *Journal of the History of Ideas*, vol. 25, October–December, pp. 579–86.

Rabinowitz, H. (1978), *Race Relations in the Urban South, 1865–1890*, Oxford University Press, New York.

Rabinowitz, H. (1983), "Race, Ethnicity, and Cultural Pluralism in American History", in J. Gardner and G. Adams (eds), *Ordinary People and Everyday Life: Perspectives on the New Social History*, American Association for State and Local History, Nashville, TN, pp. 23–49.

Rachleff, P. (1984), *Black Labor in the South: Richmond, Virginia, 1865–1890*, Temple University Press, Philadelphia, PA.

Ransom, R., and R. Sutch (1977), *One Kind of Freedom: The Economic Consequences of Emancipation*, Cambridge University Press, New York.

Ravitch, D. (1978), *The Revisionists Revised: A Critique of the Radical Attack on the Schools*, Basic Books, New York.

Rawley, J. (1981), *The Transatlantic Slave Trade: A History*, W. W. Norton & Co., New York.

Rayback, J. (1959), *A History of American Labor*, Macmillan, New York.

Record, W. (1951), *The Negro and the Communist Party*, University of North Carolina Press, Chapel Hill.

Record, W. (1964), *Race and Radicalism: The NAACP and the Communist Party in Conflict*, Cornell University Press, Ithaca, NY.

Reich, S. (1996), "Soldiers of Democracy: Black Texans and the Fight for Citizenship, 1917–1921", *Journal of American History*, vol. 82, March, pp. 1478–1504.

Reimers, D. (1985), *Still the Golden Door: The Third World Comes to America*, Columbia University Press, New York.

Reimers, D. (1992), *Still the Golden Door: The Third World Comes to America*, Columbia University Press, New York, 2nd edn.

Resek, C. (ed.) (1964), *War and the Intellectuals: Collected Essays of Randolph S. Bourne, 1915–1919*, Harper & Row, New York.

Rhoads, E. (2002), " 'White Labor' vs 'Coolie Labor': The 'Chinese Question' in Pennsylvania in the 1870s", *Journal of American Ethnic History*, vol. 21, winter, pp. 3–32.

Richardson, R. (1943), *Texas: The Lone Star State*, Prentice-Hall, New York.

Richter, D. (1992), *The Ordeal of the Longhouse: The Peoples of the Iroquois League in the Era of European Colonization*, University of North Carolina Press, Chapel Hill.

Riddell, A. (1974), "Chicanas and El Movimiento", *Aztlán*, vol. 5, spring and fall, pp. 155–65.

Rieder, J. (1985), *Canarsie: The Jews and Italians of Brooklyn Against Liberalism*, Harvard University Press, Cambridge, MA.

Riggs, F. (1950), *Pressures on Congress: A Study of the Repeal of Chinese Exclusion*, King's Crown Press, New York.

Riney, S. (1999), *The Rapid City Indian School, 1898–1933*, University of Oklahoma Press, Norman.

Ringer, B. (1983), *"We the People" and Others: Duality and America's Treatment of its Racial Minorities*, Tavistock, New York.

Rischin, M. (1962), *The Promised City: New York's Jews, 1870–1914*, Harvard University Press, Cambridge, MA.

Roark, J. (1977), *Masters without Slaves: Southern Planters in the Civil War and Reconstruction*, W. W. Norton & Co., New York.

Robinson, C. (2003), *Dangerous Liaisons: Sex and Love in the Segregated South*, University of Arkansas Press, Fayetteville.

Robinson, J. (1987), *The Montgomery Bus Boycott and the Women Who Started It: The Memoir of Jo Ann Gibson Robinson*, ed. by D. Garrow, University of Tennessee Press, Knoxville.

Roediger, D. (1991), *The Wages of Whiteness: Race and the Making of the American Working Class*, Verso, London.

Roediger, D. (1994), *Towards the Abolition of Whiteness: Essays on Race, Politics, and Working Class History*, Verso, London.

Rolle, A. (1968), *The Immigrant Upraised: Italian Adventurers and Colonists in an Expanding America*, University of Oklahoma Press, Norman.

Romano, R. (2003), *Race Mixing: Black-White Marriage in Postwar America*, Harvard University Press, Cambridge, MA.

Romo, R. (1983), *East Los Angeles: History of a Barrio*, University of Texas Press, Austin.

Root, M. (1992a), "Within, Between, and Beyond Race", in M. Root, (1992b).

Root, M. (ed.) (1992b), *Racially Mixed People in America*, Sage Publications, Newbury Park, CA.

Rosales, F. (1999), *¡Pobre Raza! Violence, Justice, and Mobilization among México Lindo Immigrants, 1900–1936*, University of Texas Press, Austin.

Rosenbaum, R. (1981), *Mexicano Resistance in the Southwest: "The Sacred Right of Self-Preservation"*, University of Texas Press, Austin.

Rosenberg, D. (1988), *New Orleans Dockworkers: Race, Labor, and Unionism, 1892–1923*, State University of New York Press, Albany.

Rosenblum, G. (1973), *Immigrant Workers: Their Impact on American Labor Radicalism*, Basic Books, New York.

Rosenzweig, R. (1983), *Eight Hours for What We Will: Workers and Leisure in an Industrial City, 1870–1920*, Cambridge University Press, Cambridge.

Ross, E. (1914), *The Old World in the New*, Century, New York.

Rothman, J. (2003), *Notorious in the Neighborhood: Sex and Families across the Color Line in Virginia, 1787–1861*, University of North Carolina Press, Chapel Hill.

Ruchames, L. (1967), "The Sources of Racial Thought in Colonial America", *Journal of Negro History*, vol. 52, October, pp. 251–72.

Rudwick, E. (1964), *Race Riot at East St Louis, July 2, 1917*, Southern Illinois University Press, Carbondale.

Ruiz, V. (1987), *Cannery Workers, Cannery Lives: Mexican Women, Unionization and the California Processing Industry, 1930–1950*, University of New Mexico Press, Albuquerque.

Ruiz, V. (1990), "A Promise Fulfilled: Mexican Cannery Workers in Southern California", in A. Del Castillo (ed.), *Between Borders: Essays on Mexicana/Chicana History*, Floricanto Press, Encino, CA, pp. 281–98.

Ruiz, V. (1998), *From Out of the Shadows: Mexican Women in Twentieth-Century America*, Oxford University Press, New York.

Salinger, S. (1987), *"To Serve Well and Faithfully": Labor and Indentured Servants in Pennsylvania, 1682–1800*, Cambridge University Press, Cambridge.

Salyer, L. (1995), *Laws Harsh as Tigers: Chinese Immigrants and the Shaping of Modern Immigration Law*, University of North Carolina Press, Chapel Hill.

Salzman, J., and C. West (1997), (eds), *Struggles in the Promised Land: Toward a History of Black–Jewish Relations in the United States*, Oxford University Press, New York.

Salzman, J., A. Back, and G. Sorin (eds) (1992), *Bridges and Boundaries: African Americans and American Jews*, George Braziller/Jewish Museum, New York.

Sánchez, G. (1993), *Becoming Mexican American: Ethnicity, Culture, and Identity in Chicano Los Angeles, 1900–1945*, Oxford University Press, New York.

Sandburg, C. (1969), *The Chicago Race Riots, July 1919*, Harcourt, Brace, & World, New York.

Sanders, J. (1977), *The Education of an Urban Minority: Catholics in Chicago, 1833–1965*, Oxford University Press, New York.

Sandoz, M. (1953), *Cheyenne Autumn*, McGraw-Hill, New York.

San Miguel, G. (1987), *"Let Them All Take Heed": Mexican Americans and the Campaign for Educational Equality in Texas, 1910–1981*, University of Texas Press, Austin.

San Miguel, G. (2004), *Contested Policy: The Rise and Fall of Federal Bilingual Education in the United States, 1960–2001*, University of North Texas Press, Denton.

Saragoza, A. (1988–90), "Recent Chicano Historiography: An Interpretive Essay", *Aztlán*, vol. 19, spring, pp. 1–52.

Sarna, J. (1978), "From Immigrants to Ethnics: Toward a New Theory of 'Ethnicization'", *Ethnicity*, vol. 5, December, pp. 370–8.

Sassen-Knoob, S. (1998), *Globalization and Its Discontents: Essays on the New Mobility of People and Money*, New Press, New York.

Saveth, E. (1965 [1948]), *American Historians and European Immigrants*, Russell & Russell, New York.

Saxton, A. (1971), *The Indispensable Enemy: Labor and the Anti-Chinese Movement in California*, University of California Press, Berkeley.

Saxton, A. (1990), *The Rise and Fall of the White Republic: Class, Politics, and Mass Culture in Nineteenth-Century America*, Verso, London.

Scarpaci, J. (ed.) (1975), *The Interaction of Italians and Jews in America*, American Italian Historical Association, Staten Island, NY.

Schlesinger, A. (1992), *The Disuniting of America: Reflections on a Multicultural Society*, W. W. Norton & Co., New York.

Schouler, J. (1882), *History of the United States under the Constitution*, vol. 2, W. H. Morrison, Washington, DC.

Schwalm, L. (1997), *A Hard Fight for We: Women's Transition from Slavery to Freedom in South Carolina*, University of Illinois Press, Urbana.

Segura, D. (1990), "Chicanas and Triple Oppression in the Labor Force", in T. Córdova, N. Cantú, G. Cardenas, J. García, and C. Sierra (eds), *Chicana Voices: Intersections of Class, Race and Gender*, University of New Mexico Press, Albuquerque, pp. 47–65.

Seller, M. (1978a), "The Education of the Immigrant Woman: 1900 to 1935", *Journal of Urban History*, vol. 4, May, pp. 307–30.

Seller, M. (1978b), "Protestant Evangelism and the Italian Immigrant Woman", in B. Caroli, R. Harney, and L. Tomasi (eds), *The Italian Immigrant Woman in North America*, Multicultural History Society of Ontario, Toronto, pp. 124–37.

Seller, M. (ed.) (1981), *Immigrant Women*, Temple University Press, Philadelphia, PA.

Senechal, R. (1990), *The Sociogenesis of a Race Riot: Springfield, Illinois, in 1908*, University of Illinois Press, Urbana.

Shannon, W. (1963), *The American Irish*, Macmillan, New York.

Shapiro, H. (1988), *White Violence and Black Response: From Reconstruction to Montgomery*, University of Massachusetts Press, Amherst.

Shapiro, Y. (1971), *Leadership of the American Zionist Organization, 1897–1930*, University of Illinois Press, Urbana.

Sheehan, B. (1980), *Savagism and Civility: Indians and Englishmen in Colonial Virginia*, Cambridge University Press, Cambridge.

Shergold, P. (1976), "Relative Skill and Income Levels of Native and Foreign Born Workers: A Reexamination", *Explorations in Economic History*, vol. 13, October, pp. 451–61.

Sheridan, T. (1986), *Los Tucsonenses: The Mexican Community in Tucson, 1854–1941*, University of Arizona Press, Tucson.

Shoemaker, N. (ed.) (1995), *Negotiators of Change: Historical Perspectives on Native American Women*, Routledge, New York.

Shogan, R., and T. Craig (1964), *The Detroit Race Riot: A Study in Violence*, Chilton Books, Philadelphia, PA.

Showalter, M. (1989), "The Watsonville Anti-Filipino Riot of 1930: A Reconsideration of Fermin Tobera's Murder", *Southern California Quarterly*, vol. 71, winter, pp. 341–48.

Shugg, R. (1939), *Origins of Class Struggle in Louisiana: A Social History of White Farmers and Laborers during Slavery and After, 1840–1875*, Louisiana State University Press, Baton Rouge.

Simon, R. (1985), *Public Opinion and the Immigrant: Print Media Coverage, 1880–1980*, Lexington Books, Lexington, MA.

Slotkin, R. (1973), *Regeneration through Violence: The Mythology of the American Frontier, 1600–1860*, Wesleyan University Press, Middletown, CT.

Smedley, A. (1993), *Race in North America: Origin and Evolution of a Worldview*, Westview Press, Boulder, CO.

Smith, A. (1934), "The Transportation of Convicts to the American Colonies in the Seventeenth Century", *American Historical Review*, vol. 39, January, pp. 232–49.

Smith, A. (1947), *Colonists in Bondage: White Servitude and Convict Labor in America, 1607–1776*, University of North Carolina Press, Chapel Hill.

Smith, J. (1978), "Italian Mothers, American Daughters: Changes in Work and Family Roles", in B. Caroli, R. Harney, and L. Tomasi (eds), *The Italian Immigrant Woman in North America*, Multicultural History Society of Ontario, Toronto, pp. 206–21.

Smith, J. (1985), *Family Connections: A History of Italian and Jewish Immigrant Lives in Providence, Rhode Island, 1900–1940*, State University of New York Press, Albany.

Smith, T. (1969), "Immigrant Social Aspirations and American Education, 1880–1930", *American Quarterly*, vol. 21, autumn, pp. 523–43.

Snyder, L. (1962), *The Idea of Racialism: Its Meaning and History*, D. Van Nostrand Co., Princeton, NJ.

Soike, L. (1991), *Norwegian Americans and the Politics of Dissent, 1880–1924*, Norwegian-American Historical Association, Northfield, MN.

Sollors, W. (ed.) (1989), *The Invention of Ethnicity*, Oxford University Press, New York.

Sowell, T. (1981), *Ethnic America, A History*, Basic Books, New York.

Spear, A. (1967), *Black Chicago: The Making of a Negro Ghetto, 1890–1920*, University of Chicago Press, Chicago.

Spero, S., and A. Harris (1931), *The Black Worker: The Negro and the Labor Movement*, Columbia University Press, New York.

Spickard, P. (1989), *Mixed Blood: Intermarriage and Ethnic Identity in Twentieth-Century America*, University of Wisconsin Press, Madison.

Spickard, P. (1992), "The Illogic of American Racial Categories", in M. Root (ed.), *Racially Mixed People in America*, Sage Publications, Newbury Park, CA, pp. 12–23.

Spring, J. (1972), *Education and the Rise of the Corporate State*, Beacon Press, Boston, MA.

Stack, J. (1979), *International Conflict in an American City: Boston's Irish, Italians, and Jews, 1935–1944*, Greenwood Press, Westport, CT.

Stampp, K. (1956), *The Peculiar Institution: Slavery in the Ante-Bellum South*, Alfred A. Knopf, New York.

Stannard, D. (1992), *American Holocaust: The Conquest of the New World*, Oxford University Press, New York.

Stanton, W. (1960), *The Leopard's Spots: Scientific Attitudes toward Race in America, 1815–59*, University of Chicago Press, Chicago.

Stedman, R. (1982), *Shadows of the Indian: Stereotypes in American Culture*, University of Oklahoma Press, Norman.

Steinberg, S. (1989), *The Ethnic Myth: Race, Ethnicity, and Class in America*, Beacon Press, Boston, MA, 2nd edn.

Stephenson, G. (1926), *A History of American Immigration, 1820–1924*, Russell & Russell, New York.

Stephenson, G. (1932), *The Religious Aspects of Swedish Immigration: A Study of Immigrant Churches*, University of Minnesota Press, Minneapolis.

Stewart, K., and A. De León (1993), *Not Room Enough: Mexicans, Anglos and Socioeconomic Change in Texas, 1850–1900*, University of New Mexico Press, Albuquerque.

Stuckey, S. (1987), *Slave Culture: Nationalist Theory and the Foundations of Black America*, Oxford University Press, New York.

Suggs, H. (ed.) (1983), *The Black Press in the South, 1865–1979*, Greenwood Press, Westport, CT.

Suggs, H. (ed.) (1996), *The Black Press in the Midwest, 1865–1985*, Greenwood Press, Westport, CT.

Sugrue, T. (1996), *The Origins of the Urban Crisis: Race and Inequality in Postwar Detroit*, Princeton University Press, Princeton, NJ.

Taeuber, K., and A. Taeuber (1965), *Negroes in Cities: Residential Segregation and Neighborhood Change*, Aldine Publishing, Chicago.

Takaki, R. (1983), *Pau Hana: Plantation Life and Labor in Hawaii, 1835–1920*, University Press of Hawaii, Honolulu.

Takaki, R. (1990 [1979]), *Iron Cages: Race and Culture in 19th-Century America*, Oxford University Press, New York.

Takaki, R. (1990), *Strangers from a Different Shore: A History of Asian Americans*, Penguin Books, New York.

Takaki, R. (1993), *A Different Mirror: A History of Multicultural America*, Little, Brown, & Co., Boston, MA.

Tanaka, S. (1978), "The Toledo Incident: The Deportation of the Nikkei from an Oregon Mill Town", *Pacific Northwest Quarterly*, vol. 69, July, pp. 116–26.

Taylor, G. (1980), *The New Deal and American Indian Tribalism: The Administration of the Indian Reorganization Act, 1934–45*, University of Nebraska Press, Lincoln.

Taylor, H. (ed.) (1993), *Race and the City: Work, Community, and Protest in Cincinnati, 1820–1970*, University of Illinois Press, Urbana.

Taylor, P. (1971), *The Distant Magnet: European Emigration to the USA*, Eyre & Spottiswood, London.

Tentler, L. (1979), *Wage-Earning Women: Industrial Work and Family Life in the United States, 1910–1930*, Oxford University Press, New York.

Terborg-Penn, R. (1983), "Discontented Black Feminists: Prelude and Postscript to the Passage of the Nineteenth Amendment", in L. Scharf and J. Jensen (eds), *Decades of Discontent: The Women's Movement, 1920–1940*, Greenwood Press, Westport, CT, pp. 261–78.

Thernstrom, S. (1964), *Poverty and Progress: Social Mobility in a Nineteenth Century City*, Harvard University Press, Cambridge, MA.

Thernstrom, S. (1973), *The Other Bostonians: Poverty and Progress in the American Metropolis, 1880–1970*, Harvard University Press, Cambridge, MA.

Thistlethwaite, F. (1964), "Migration from Europe Overseas in the Nineteenth and Twentieth Centuries", in H. Moller (ed.), *Population Movements in Modern European History*, Macmillan, New York, pp. 73–92.

Thomas, B. (1973), *Migration and Economic Growth: A Study of Great Britain and the Atlantic Economy*, Cambridge University Press, Cambridge, 2nd edn.

Thomas, D. (1935), *Social and Economic Aspects of Swedish Population Movements, 1750–1933*, Macmillan, New York.

Thomas, H. (1997), *The Slave Trade: The Story of the Atlantic Slave Trade, 1440–1870*, Simon and Schuster, New York.

Thomas, R. (1992), *Life for Us Is What We Make It: Building Black Community in Detroit, 1915–1945*, Indiana University Press, Bloomington.

Thomas, W., and F. Znaniecki (1927 [1918–20]), *The Polish Peasant in Europe and America*, 2 vols, Alfred A. Knopf, New York.

Thompson, J. (ed.) (1994), *Juan Cortina and the Texas-Mexico Frontier, 1859–1877*, Texas Western Press, El Paso.

Thompson, M. (1990), *Ida B. Wells-Barnett: An Exploratory Study of an American Black Woman, 1893–1930*, Carlson Publishing, Brooklyn, NY.

Thornton, J. (1992), *Africa and Africans in the Making of the Atlantic World, 1400–1680*, Cambridge University Press, Cambridge.

Thornton, R. (1987), *American Indian Holocaust and Survival: A Population History since 1492*, University of Oklahoma Press, Norman.

Tindall, G. (1976), *The Ethnic Southerners*, Louisiana State University Press, Baton Rouge.

Toll, W. (1984), *The Making of an Ethnic Middle Class: Portland Jewry over Four Generations*, State University of New York Press, Albany.

Tolnay, S., and E. Beck (1995), *A Festival of Violence: An Analysis of Southern Lynchings, 1882–1930*, University of Illinois Press, Urbana.

Trelease, A. (1995 [1971]), *White Terror: The Ku Klux Klan Conspiracy and Southern Reconstruction*, Louisiana State University Press, Baton Rouge.

Trennert, R. (1982), "Educating Indian Girls at Nonreservation Boarding Schools, 1878–1920", *Western Historical Quarterly*, vol. 13, July, pp. 271–90.

Trennert, R. (1988), *The Phoenix Indian School: Forced Assimilation in Arizona, 1891–1935*, University of Oklahoma Press, Norman.

Trotter, J. (1985), *Black Milwaukee: The Making of an Industrial Proletariat, 1915–45*, University of Illinois Press, Urbana.

Trotter, J. (1990), *Coal, Class, and Color: Blacks in Southern West Virginia, 1915–32*, University of Illinois Press, Urbana.

Trotter, J. (1995), "African Americans in the City: The Industrial Era, 1900–1950", *Journal of Urban History*, vol. 21, May, pp. 438–57.

Trotter, J. (1998a), "African Americans, Jews, and the City: Perspectives from the Industrial Era, 1900–1950", in V. Franklin, N. Grant, H. Kletnick, and G. McNeil (eds), *African Americans and Jews in the Twentieth Century: Studies in Convergence and Conflict*, University of Missouri Press, Columbia, pp. 193–207.

Trotter, J. (1998b), *River Jordan: African-American Urban Life in the Ohio Valley*, University Press of Kentucky, Lexington.

Tsai, S. (1983), *China and the Overseas Chinese in the United States, 1868–1911*, University of Arkansas Press, Fayetteville.

Tsuchida, N. (1984), "Japanese Gardeners in Southern California, 1900–1941", in L. Cheng and E. Bonacich (eds), *Labor Migration Under Capitalism: Asian Workers in the United States before World War II*, University of California Press, Berkeley, pp. 435–69.

Tucker, R. (1991), *The Dragon and the Cross: The Rise and Fall of the Ku Klux Klan in Middle America*, Archon Books, Hamden, CT.

Turner, F. (1935), *The United States, 1830–1850: The Nation and Its Sections*, H. Holt & Co., New York.

Turner, F. (1962 [1920]), *The Frontier in American History*, Holt, Rinehart, & Winston, New York.

Tushnet, M. (1987), *The NAACP's Legal Strategy Against Segregated Education, 1925–1950*, University of North Carolina Press, Chapel Hill.

Tuttle, W. (1972), *Race Riot: Chicago in the Red Summer of 1919*, Atheneum, New York.

Ueda, R. (1994), *Postwar Immigrant America: A Social History*, Bedford Books, Boston, MA.

Urofsky, M. (1975), *American Zionism from Herzl to the Holocaust*, Doubleday, Garden City, NY.

Urofsky, M. (1978), *We are One! American Jewry and Israel*, Doubleday, Garden City, NY.

Utley, R. (1963), *The Last Days of the Sioux Nation*, Yale University Press, New Haven, CT.

Utley, R. (1984), *The Indian Frontier of the American West, 1846–1890*, University of New Mexico Press, Albuquerque.

van den Berghe, P. (1983), "Class, Race and Ethnicity in Africa", *Ethnic and Racial Studies*, vol. 6, April, pp. 221–36.

Vásquez, C. (1980), "Women in the Chicano Movement", in M. Mora and A. Del Castillo (eds), *Mexican Women in the United States: Struggles Past and Present*, UCLA Chicano Studies Research Center, Los Angeles, pp. 27–8.

Vaughan, A. (1989), "The Origins Debate: Slavery and Racism in Seventeenth-Century Virginia", *Virginia Magazine of History and Biography*, vol. 97, July, pp. 311–54.

Vaughn, L. (1991), "Cosmopolitanism, Ethnicity and American Identity: Randolph Bourne's 'Trans-National America'", *Journal of American Studies*, vol. 25, December, pp. 443–59.

Vecoli, R. (1964), "*Contadini* in Chicago: A Critique of *The Uprooted*", *Journal of American History*, vol. 51, December, pp. 404–17.

Vecoli, R. (1969), "Prelates and Peasants: Italian Immigrants and the Catholic Church", *Journal of Social History*, vol. 2, spring, pp. 217–68.

Vecoli, R. (1970), "Ethnicity: A Neglected Dimension of American History", in H. Bass (ed.), *The State of American History*, Quadrangle Books, Chicago, pp. 70–88.

Vecoli, R. (1977), "Cult and Occult in Italian-American Culture: The Persistence of a Religious Heritage", in R. Miller and T. Marzik (eds), *Immigrants and Religion in Urban America*, Temple University Press, Philadelphia, PA, pp. 25–47.

Vecoli, R. (1995), "Comment", *Journal of American Ethnic History*, vol. 14, winter, pp. 76–81.

Wade, R. (1969), "Violence in the Cities: A Historical View", in C. Daly (ed.), *Urban Violence*, University of Chicago Press, Chicago, pp. 7–26.

Wallace, A. (1970), *The Death and Rebirth of the Seneca*, Alfred A. Knopf, New York.

Wallenstein, P. (2002), *Tell the Court I Love My Wife: Race, Marriage, and Law – An American History*, Palgrave, New York.

Ward, D. (1971), *Cities and Immigrants: A Geography of Change in Nineteenth-Century America*, Oxford University Press, New York.

Warner, S., and C. Burke (1969), "Cultural Change and the Ghetto", *Journal of Contemporary History*, vol. 4, October, pp. 173–87.

Washburn, W. (1971), *Red Man's Land/White Man's Law: A Study of the Past and Present Status of the American Indian*, Charles Scribner's Sons, New York.

Waters, M. (1990), *Ethnic Options: Choosing Identities in America*, University of California Press, Berkeley.

Webb, W. (1935), *The Texas Rangers: A Century of Frontier Defense*, Houghton Mifflin, Boston, MA.

Webster, J. (1978), "Domestication and Americanization: Scandinavian Women in Seattle, 1888 to 1900", *Journal of Urban History*, vol. 4, May, pp. 275–90.

Weed, P. (1973), *The White Ethnic Movement and Ethnic Politics*, Praeger, New York.

Wefald, J. (1971), *A Voice of Protest: Norwegians in American Politics, 1890–1917*, Norwegian-American Historical Association, Northfield, MN.

Wei, W. (1993), *The Asian American Movement*, Temple University Press, Philadelphia, PA.

Weinberg, M. (1977), *A Chance to Learn: A History of Race and Education in the United States*, Cambridge University Press, Cambridge.

Weinberg, S. (1988), *The World of Our Mothers: The Lives of Jewish Immigrant Women*, University of North Carolina Press, Chapel Hill.

Weisser, M. (1985), *A Brotherhood of Memory: Jewish Landsmanshaftn in the New World*, Basic Books, New York.

Wells, R. (1975), *The Population of the British Colonies before 1776: A Survey of Census Data*, Princeton University Press, Princeton, NJ.

Whalen, C., & B. Whalen (1985), *The Longest Debate: A Legislative History of the 1964 Civil Rights Act*, Seven Locks Press, Cabin John, MD.

White, D. (1985), *Ar'n't I a Woman? Female Slaves in the Plantation South*, W. W. Norton & Co., New York.

White, R. (1978), "The Winning of the West: The Expansion of the Western Sioux in the Eighteenth and Nineteenth Centuries", *Journal of American History*, vol. 65, September, pp. 319–43.

White, R. (1983), *The Roots of Dependency: Subsistence, Environment, and Social Change among the Choctaws, Pawnees and Navajos*, University of Nebraska Press, Lincoln.

White, R. (1993), "Civil Rights Agitation: Emancipation Days in Central New York in the 1880s", *Journal of Negro History*, vol. 78, winter, pp. 16–24.

White, S. (1994), " 'It Was a Proud Day': African Americans, Festivals, and Parades in the North, 1741–1834", *Journal of American History*, vol. 81, June, pp. 13–50.

Wiggins, W. (1987), *O Freedom! Afro-American Emancipation Celebrations*, University of Tennessee Press, Knoxville.

Wikramanayake, M. (1973), *A World in Shadow: The Free Black in Antebellum South Carolina*, University of South Carolina Press, Columbia.

Wilentz, S. (1984), *Chants Democratic: New York City and the Rise of the American Working Class, 1788–1850*, Oxford University Press, New York.

Wilkins, T. (1970), *Cherokee Tragedy: The Story of the Ridge Family and the Decimation of a People*, Macmillan, New York.

Wilkinson, J. (1979), *From Brown to Bakke: The Supreme Court and School Integration, 1954–1978*, Oxford University Press, New York.

Williams, E. (1966 [1944]), *Capitalism and Slavery*, Capricorn Books, New York.

Williamson, J. (1965), *After Slavery: The Negro in South Carolina during Reconstruction, 1861–1877*, University of North Carolina Press, Chapel Hill.

Williamson, J. (1974), "Migration to the New World: Long-Term Influences and Impact", *Explorations in Economic History*, vol. 11, summer, pp. 357–91.

Williamson, J. (1980), *New People: Miscegenation and Mulattoes in the United States*, Free Press, New York.

Williamson, J. (1984), *The Crucible of Race: Black–White Relations in the American South since Emancipation*, Oxford University Press, New York.

Wilmore, G. (1972), *Black Religion and Black Radicalism*, Doubleday, Garden City, NY.

Wilson, W. (1980), *The Declining Significance of Race: Blacks and Changing American Institutions*, University of Chicago Press, Chicago, 2nd edn.

Wilson, W. (1987), *The Truly Disadvantaged: The Inner City, the Underclass, and Public Policy*, University of Chicago Press, Chicago.

Wish, H. (1937), "American Slave Insurrections Before 1861", *Journal of Negro History*, vol. 22, July, pp. 299–320.

Wish, H. (1939), "The Slave Insurrection Panic of 1856", *Journal of Southern History*, vol. 5, May, pp. 206–22.

Wittke, C. (1939), *We Who Built America: The Saga of the Immigrant*, Prentice-Hall, New York.

Wittke, C. (1956), *The Irish in America*, Louisiana State University Press, Baton Rouge.

Wittke, C. (1973 [1957]), *The German-Language Press in America*, Haskell House, New York.

Wollenberg, C. (1976), *All Deliberate Speed: Segregation and Exclusion in California Schools, 1855–1975*, University of California Press, Berkeley.

Wolters, R. (1984), *The Burden of Brown: Thirty Years of School Desegregation*, University of Tennessee Press, Knoxville.

Wood, B. (1997), *The Origins of American Slavery: Freedom and Bondage in the English Colonies*, Hill & Wang, New York.

Wood, P. (1989), "The Changing Population of the Colonial South: An Overview by Race and Region, 1685–1790", in P. Wood, G. Waselkov, and M. Hatley (eds), *Powhatan's Mantle: Indians in the Colonial Southwest*, University of Nebraska Press, Lincoln, pp. 35–103.

Woodman, L. (1950), *Cortina: Rogue of the Rio Grande*, Naylor, San Antonio, TX.

Woodson, C. (1918), "The Beginnings of the Miscegenation of the Whites and Blacks", *Journal of Negro History*, vol. 3, October, pp. 335–53.

Woodson, C. (1919), "American Negro Slavery", *Mississippi Valley Historical Review*, vol. 5, March, pp. 480–2.

Woodward, C. (1955), *The Strange Career of Jim Crow*, Oxford University Press, New York.

Wright, J. (1986), *Creeks and Seminoles: The Destruction and Regeneration of the Muscogulge People*, University of Nebraska Press, Lincoln.

Wunder, J. (1994), *"Retained by the People": A History of American Indians and the Bill of Rights*, Oxford University Press, New York.

Wyman, M. (1993), *Round-Trip to America: The Immigrants Return to Europe, 1880–1930*, Cornell University Press, Ithaca, NY.

Yang, E. (1984), "Korean Women of America: From Subordination to Partnership, 1903–1930", *Amerasia Journal*, vol. 11, fall/winter, pp. 1–28.

Yans-McLaughlin, V. (1971), "Patterns of Work and Family Organization: Buffalo's Italians", *Journal of Interdisciplinary History*, vol. 2, autumn, pp. 299–314.

Yans-McLaughlin, V. (1977), *Family and Community: Italian Immigrants in Buffalo, 1880–1930*, Cornell University Press, Ithaca, NY.

Yee, S. (1992), *Black Women Abolitionists: A Study in Activism, 1828–1860*, University of Tennessee Press, Knoxville.

Yim, S. (1984), "The Social Structure of Korean Communities in California, 1903–1920", in L. Cheng and E. Bonacich (eds), *Labor Migration Under Capitalism: Asian Workers in the United States before World War II*, University of California Press, Berkeley, pp. 515–47.

Yoo, D. (2000), *Growing Up Nisei: Race, Generation, and Culture among Japanese Americans of California, 1924–49*, University of Illinois Press, Urbana.

Young, M. (1958), "Indian Removal and Land Allotment: The Civilized Tribes and Jacksonian Justice", *American Historical Review*, vol. 64, October, pp. 31–45.

Yu, R. (1992), *To Save China, To Save Ourselves: The Chinese Hand Laundry Alliance of New York*, Temple University Press, Philadelphia, PA.

Yun, L., and R. Laremont (2001), "Chinese Coolies and African Slaves in Cuba, 1847–74", *Journal of Asian American Studies*, vol. 4, June, pp. 99–122.

Yung, J. (1995), *Unbound Feet: A Social History of Chinese Women in San Francisco*, University of California Press, Berkeley.

Zamora, E. (1993), *The World of the Mexican Worker in Texas*, Texas A&M University Press, College Station.

Zangrando, R. (1980), *The NAACP Crusade Against Lynching, 1909–1950*, Temple University Press, Philadelphia, PA.

Zunz, O. (1982a), *The Changing Face of Inequality: Urbanization, Industrial Development, and Immigrants in Detroit, 1880–1920*, University of Chicago Press, Chicago.

Zunz, O. (1982b), "Comment", *Journal of Urban History*, vol. 8, August, pp. 463–71.

Zunz, O. (1985), "American History and the Changing Meaning of Assimilation", *Journal of American Ethnic History*, vol. 4, spring, pp. 53–72.

Zunz, O. (1995), "Comment", *Journal of American Ethnic History*, vol. 14, winter, pp. 91–4.

Name Index

Subject Index